S0-BBO-437

PELICAN BOOKS

A501

PREHISTORIC CRETE

Richard Wyatt Hutchinson was born in 1894 and educated at Birkenhead School and at John's College, Cambridge. After serving in France and Belgium at the end of the First World War, he was elected Foundation Scholar and Craven Student at Athens in 1921, and later F.S.A. and F.R.A.I., and corresponding member of the German Archaeological Institute. He was Curator in Crete for the British School at Athens from 1934 until 1947, but actually served in British G.H.Q. at Cairo from 1941 to 1945 during the German occupation of the island. He was appointed lecturer in classical archaeology at Liverpool University in 1948 and at Cambridge in 1952. Since 1921 he has taken part in excavations at Mycenae, Traprain Law, in Poland and Macedonia, in Mytilene, at Nineveh, and at Colchester, besides the 'digs' he conducted in Crete. Richard Hutchinson has contributed articles to many learned journals and collaborated in *A Century of Exploration at Nineveh*.

R. W. HUTCHINSON

PREHISTORIC CRETE

PENGUIN BOOKS

Penguin Books Ltd, Harmondsworth, Middlesex, England
Penguin Books Inc., 7110 Ambassador Court, Baltimore, Maryland 21207, U.S.A.
Penguin Books Australia Ltd, Ringwood, Victoria, Australia

—

First published 1962
Reprinted 1963, 1965
Reprinted (with revisions) 1968

—

Copyright © R. W. Hutchinson, 1962

—

Made and printed in Great Britain
by Cox & Wyman Ltd,
London, Reading and Fakenham
Set in Monotype Bembo

This book is sold subject to the condition
that it shall not, by way of trade or otherwise,
be lent, re-sold, hired out, or otherwise circulated
without the publisher's prior consent in any form of
binding or cover other than that in which it is
published and without a similar condition
including this condition being imposed
on the subsequent purchaser

CONTENTS

LIST OF PLATES

Grateful acknowledgement is made to Dr Audrey Furness for Plates 1, 2; to Mrs Hilda Pendlebury for Plates 3, 4, 5, 6, 11, 12, 14a, 19 by J. D. S. Pendlebury; to Miss Natalie Lubowidsky for Plates 7, 8, 15; to Dr O. G. S. Crawford for Plates 10, 18, 21; to Mr G. Maraghiannis for Plates 9, 13, 14b, 17; to Mr E. M. Androulakis for Plates 21, 22, 23, 24, 25, 26; to the Society for the Promotion of Hellenic Studies for Plate 27; to *The Times* for Plate 16; to Mr R. E. M. McCaughan for Plates 28, 29, 30, 31, 32. I am indebted to Mr J. Chadwick for help in amendments to Chapter 3.

LIST OF TEXT FIGURES

9

LIST OF TEXT FIGURES

Grateful acknowledgement is made to Mr R. E. M. McCaughan for Figures 1, 2, 7, 10, 11, 18, 19, 20, 23, 35, 37, 38, 39, 44, 45, 46, 50, 52, 54, 55, 61, 71, and 73, and also for Figures 4, 5, 24, 25, 31, 33, 37, 65, 66, and 67 previously drawn to illustrate my article 'Prehistoric Town Planning in Crete' published in the *Town Planning Review* Vol. XXI (1950); also to Miss Honor Frost for Figures 6, 12–17, 41, 43, 49, and 64; to Mrs Hilda Pendlebury for Figure 51, reproduced from *Handbook to the Palace of Minos* (Macmillan), and for Figures 3, 21, 22, 26, 27, 30, 32, 34, 36, 53, 56, 59, and 60 reproduced from *The Archaeology of Crete* (Methuen) by J. D. S. Pendlebury; to the Consejo Superior de Investigaciones Científicas, Madrid, for Figure 8, reproduced from *Lexicon Creticum*, and Figure 9, reproduced from *Minoika* by B. Gaya Nuño; to the Society for the Promotion of Hellenic Studies for Figure 10, reproduced from *Journal of Hellenic Studies* (1953 issue) and Figures 38, 40, 42, and 63 reproduced from 1901 issue; to Macmillan & Co. Ltd, for Figure 18 from *The Palace of Minos* by A. J. Evans and Figure 70 from *How the Greeks Built Their Cities* by R. E. Wycherley; to the British School at Athens for Figure 52, reproduced from the *Annual*, 1951; to La Renaissance du Livre for Figure 61, reproduced from *La Civilisation égéenne*; to Vincent Desborough for Figure 58; to the Society of Antiquaries for Figure 62, reproduced from *Archaeologia*, 1905; to *Kretica Chronica* for Figure 68, reproduced from the 1950 issue; to Piet de Jong for Figures 47, 48, and 69; and to Mrs Corbett for Figure 72.

EDITORIAL FOREWORD

JUST over thirty years ago I travelled extensively in Crete and was shown round the island by Mr R. W. Hutchinson who was then Curator of the Villa Ariadne which Sir Arthur Evans had built next to the site of Knosos. It was fascinating to be in the company of a man who had dug with Evans, was familiar with everything that he had done and that he had found, and understood to the smallest detail the structure of the great archaeological framework which Evans had set up. From that time onwards I had it in mind to persuade Mr Hutchinson to put down on paper as much as he could of what he knew about ancient Crete, and it is fortunate that he has at last done so, for he is one of the few direct links with the great Evans who resurrected for us the ancient Minoan world.

Since this book has taken several years to write, the text was complete before the beginning of the more violent controversies on certain Minoan problems, so that on one of them, the question of the date of the Linear B tablets, Mr Hutchinson has had to comment in a brief additional note on page 90. He himself is in many ways uniquely fitted to act as a surviving personal liaison between Evans and Ventris whose genius deciphered the script after Evans's death, and to pass judgement on these additions to knowledge. The discussion in Chapter 3 on the 'Cretan Peoples, Languages, and Scripts' provides us with an important objective survey of the criticisms affecting the decipherment. These and other problems Mr Hutchinson contrives to view with an admirable freedom from personal bias. He has indeed at times inevitably criticized some of Evans's conclusions, not generally on matters of fundamental importance, although he has a well-imagined and well-reasoned reconstruction of the events which led to the catastrophe that overwhelmed Knosos; but archaeology would be a poor thing if one generation did not add depth to the achievements of another.

Arthur Evans had the acuteness to realize that a tripartite classification of the Minoan period – Early, Middle, and Late, with subdivisions of each – was comprehensive enough to cover the entire development and yet at the same time sufficiently elastic to allow for the inevitable modifications which subsequent discovery, not only at Knosos, but in other parts of the island, was bound to bring. It is at the very end of this period in the Late Minoan that his conclusions have been seriously attacked by Professor L. R. Palmer who, like others, found it difficult to account for the fact that the writings on the tablets at Knosos are, apart from a few minor details, extraordinarily similar to those found by Blegen at Pylos, and that Evans's findings imply a difference of at least two centuries between the two. Professor Denys Page in his great book on *History and the Homeric Iliad* (1959), while admitting that this was astonishing, accepted the chronological gap without further question. The fact is that many of the Linear B tablets were burnt, apparently in the holocaust of the late palace that was contemporary with them; we have no evidence for a subsequent burning and no adequate grounds for rejecting Evans's and Mackenzie's conclusions that the intact stirrup vases are later than the great conflagration.

As Mr Hutchinson has pointed out, Professor Palmer, whilst drawing attention to the difficulties, has not provided evidence to prove his case and his elaborate re-organization of the archaeological sequences does not commend itself to others who are still in agreement with the orthodox views. At the earlier end of the scale it is admitted by nearly all scholars that Evans's chronology for the Early Minoan period must be reduced, but the three sub-divisions of that period as organized by him would seem to be fully justified. It is most probable that continued work in Crete and indeed elsewhere in Greece and in the Aegean area will eventually provide solutions to all these questions.

No less exciting and indicative of the live state of Cretan archaeology, which first took sharp definition with Evans's work at the very beginning of this century, is the fact that within the last year excavations by Professor John Evans (not to be confused with Sir Arthur) in the deep Neolithic levels at Early Knosos have yielded C.14 dates which take us back to the sixth and fifth millennia B.C. and thus have rocked the top end of Mr Hutchinson's chronological table while the ink on it was still wet. Here again Arthur Evans, with a strange prescience, had himself suggested the possibility of dates even higher than those of these new findings.

30 April 1962   M. E. L. MALLOWAN

PREFACE

THIS book is intended not so much as a revision of but rather as a supplement to Pendlebury's *The Archaeology of Crete*, which dealt in more detail and so admirably with Minoan and Hellenic art in Crete, but left almost untouched the subjects of my Chapters 1, 3, 4, and 9. I have also endeavoured to summarize the results of later researches on Cretan prehistory, especially those of Dr Michael Ventris and of Dr John Chadwick in the decipherment of Linear Script B.

I am indebted to the help of various friends who are not, however, responsible for any of my statements. First and foremost I must thank Professor M. E. L. Mallowan for his trouble in reading and criticizing my original typescript, Mr R. M. E. McCaughan for his great kindness in drawing so many plans and figures, Dr J. C. Trevor who checked and revised my pages on physical anthropology, my mother who listened to much of my manuscript, and Mrs Hilda Pendlebury for permitting me to reproduce without charge many figures from her late husband's book.

I have benefited by conversations or correspondence with the late Sir John Myres, Sir Frederick Bartlett, Dr R. W. Hey, and Mr T. C. Lethbridge. I should also like to thank my cousin, Miss May Clarke, for typing numerous corrections and additions.

CHRONOLOGICAL TABLE

	CRETE	GREEK MAINLAND	EGYPT	WESTERN ASIA
6000	Aceramic Culture	Aceramic Culture		Jarmo Catal Huyuk 'Hassuna & Samarra'
5500	Early Neolithic			
5000				
4500		Sesklo Arapi	Fayum Neolithic	Tell Halaf Al Ubaid
4000	Middle Neolithic	Dhimini		Uruk V
3500				
3400		Larissa	Badari and Predynastic Cultures	Uruk IV and Early Dynastic I
3300				Uruk III
3200				Jamdat Nasr
3100	Late Neolithic			
3000		Rhakhmani	Dynasties I and II	Nineveh V
2900	Early Minoan I	Early Helladic I		
2800				
2750				
2700			Dynasty III	Kish I
2650				Lagash II
2600			Dynasty IV	
2550	Early Minoan II	Early Helladic II		Mesannipadda Ur Dynasty I
2500				
2450			Dynasty V	

17

CHRONOLOGICAL TABLE

	CRETE	GREEK MAINLAND	EGYPT	WESTERN ASIA
2400				Lugalzaggisi / Sargon of Akkad
2350				
2300	Early Minoan III		Dynasty VI	
2250		Early Helladic III		
2200			Dynasties VII, VIII & IX	Invasion by the Guti
2150				
2100				
2050	Middle Minoan IA	Early Helladic	Dynasty XI / Mentuhotep I	Gudea of Lagash
2000			Dynasty XII	Dynasty III of Ur
1950				
1900	Middle Minoan IB	Middle Helladic I		
1850	Middle Minoan IIA			Destruction of Kultepe / Troy City VI
1800		Greeks infiltrate into Greece		
1780	Middle Minoan IIB		Dynasty XIII	Shamshi-Adad I / Hammurabi of Babylon / Kassite dynasty founded
1750	Middle Minoan IIIA	Middle Helladic II		
1700			Hyksos	
1650				
1600	Middle Minoan IIIB	Middle Helladic III	Dynasty XVII at Thebes	Murshilish I sacks Aleppo and Babylon

CHRONOLOGICAL TABLE

	CRETE	GREEK MAINLAND	EGYPT	WESTERN ASIA
1550		Late Helladic I	Dynasty XVIII	
1500	Late Minoan I		Ahmose the Liberator	
1450			Thutmose I and II	
			Hatshepshut and	
			Thutmose III	Saustatar of Mitanni
1420	Late Minoan III			
1400		Late Helladic III		
		Deucalion's Flood		
1350			Akhenaten	Suppiluliumash
1300	Minos I?		Dynasty XIX	
1250	Minos II?	Theseus?	Ramesses II and Battle	
			of Kadesh	Hittite collapse
1200	Idomeneus?	Agamemnon?	Peoples of the Sea	Trojan War
1150		Orestes?	Dynasty XX	
			Setnakt	
1100		Temenos?	Dynasty XXI	Tiglath Pileser I
		Kodros	Nesubanebded	
1050	Dorians invade Crete	Dorians attack Athens		
1000				David of Israel
970				Solomon of Israel
950	Early Protogeometric			

CHRONOLOGICAL TABLE

	CRETE	GREEK MAINLAND	EGYPT	WESTERN ASIA
920			Dynasty XXII ('Libyan')	Ashurdan II
900	Middle Protogeometric		Sheshonk I	Ashur-nasirpal III
870				
850				Shalmaneser
835	Protogeometric B			
820				
800	Mature Geometric		Sheshonk III	Adadniari III
770	Late Geometric	1st Olympiad		
750		1st Greek colony sent to Sicily		Tiglath Pileser III
735		Protocorinthian vases	Shabaker and Dynasty XXIII ('the Ethiopian')	
700	Early Orientalizing			Sennacherib
680	Late orientalizing		Taharqa	Esarhaddon & Teispes
660			Esarhaddon conquers Egypt	
650	Protodedalic sculpture		Assyrians evicted	Elam destroyed
635	Late Dedalic sculpture	First coins of Aegina	Dynasty XXVI Psamtek I	
620				
612	Post-dedalic sculpture	Spartans crush Messenia		Cyrus I of Persia, Cyaxares the Mede
610		Periander at Corinth	Necho	Cyrus II of Persia
600			Naucratis founded	Nineveh destroyed

INTRODUCTION

In historical times Crete has often appeared as a wild and unruly place, a mountain nursery for rebellions, massacres, and piracy – we remember the civil wars of the classical period, the nest of pirates destroyed by Metellus Creticus and Pompey, the Saracen raiders who dug the moat from which Candia took its name, the stories of the Venetians who used the island as a bastion against the Turks, and of the countless rebellions, savagely repressed, of the freedom-loving mountaineers of Crete against Roman, Saracen, Venetian, and Turk successively, and more recently against the Germans.

In the Bronze Age, however, Crete was a very different place, the centre of the first naval power known to history, a land where the people lived in peace and plenty with unwalled cities, a people boasting a culture that we term Minoan and that may be not unfairly compared to those of its great contemporaries in Asia Minor, Syria, Mesopotamia, and Egypt, a people that must certainly have regarded as barbarians their contemporaries in Europe.

For a millennium and a half this culture which we associate with the name of the legendary King Minos continued without any real break, though local disasters such as fires and earthquakes affected individual sites, and Mycenaean Greeks began to settle in the islands about 1500 B.C.

About 1400 B.C. a great catastrophe befell the island, a catastrophe of which we have no clear record in history, but one which is marked by destroyed and abandoned cities and villages, and from which the civilization as a whole never recovered. Most of the old sites, indeed, were reoccupied, but the next four hundred years were marked by the steady decadence of the splendid Minoan civilization.

Later a new life and culture arose in Crete, but it was primarily the creation of Greek colonists who had settled there, not of the survivors of the old Minoan race. Even this revival of culture in Crete, however, did not survive the seventh century B.C., and a new decline set in which lasted all through the great days of Athens and Sparta and the period of the Macedonian Empire.

The island of Crete was prosperous certainly in a humdrum way under the Roman Empire, but its inhabitants lived in a backwater, playing no great part in the more stirring events of the time. In the classical and Hellenistic period, when Athens, Sparta, Corinth, and the other mainland states were at their height, Crete was a land of internal strife, a land which supplied its more fortunate neighbours with bowmen and slingers, the poorer-armed type of mercenaries (a sure sign that all was not well at home), and reached its final period of degradation just before the Roman occupation, when it became the headquarters of the pirates in the Mediterranean.

Greek folk-memory, however, had always preserved the recollections of a golden age, when King Minos had ruled over Crete of the hundred cities and many islands, and when his navy had swept pirates from the seas around. Folklore had told too of the great engineer, the Athenian Daedalus, who had worked for Minos and had fashioned a dancing place for the Princess Ariadne, and had even manufactured flying wings which had caused the death of his son Icarus who had flown too near the sun and had been drowned near the island which still bears his name. We hear too, of the Minotaur, the monstrous man-headed bull, the offspring of Minos's wife Pasiphae, the monster to whom were sacrificed seven youths and seven maidens of Athens every nine years until Theseus, prince of Athens, slew the beast and escaped from the labyrinth where it had lived by means of a clue given him by the Princess Ariadne.

Folk-memory and the Homeric poems had dated Theseus only one generation before the Trojan war. Why then does the *Iliad* read like a saga with a historical background, while the story of Minos reads like a fairy tale? Some allowances must doubtless be made for the personality of the story-teller and the character of his audience, but I think there are two other major reasons why the historical element in the Cretan legends is so slight. Firstly, the inhabitants of Crete during the greater part of the Bronze Age probably spoke what the Greeks term a 'barbarian', that is a non-Greek, language, whereas those of the mainland were already speaking Greek. Secondly, the destruction of the Bronze Age settlements in Crete was far more thorough and devastating than on the mainland.

Classical Greece had no archaeologists, no antiquarian princes like King Nabonidus at Babylon. If a man opened an ancient tomb it was in the hope of finding jewels or gold to melt down; if he dug an ancient palace it was as a quarry for stones which he might use in some building he was engaged in constructing or repairing. Little therefore remained visible to the classical Greeks of the more monumental objects of Minoan culture. Engraved seals and beads continued to be handed down as ornaments, amulets, or milk-charms for nursing mothers (even up to the present day, when they are called 'milk stones'), but their original history and significance had been lost.

The Minoan people who had inhabited Crete during the Bronze Age had not been exterminated, and some of them were still speaking a non-Greek language up to Hellenistic times or later. The most permanent feature of Minoan culture, however, was their religion, which deeply affected the classical religion of Crete and to a lesser degree that of Greece as a whole. The amalgamation of Minoan and Hellenic cults must have started in the middle of the second millennium B.C., but even in the time of the Roman empire there remained cults and practices which were peculiarly Cretan, and of which the non-Hellenic elements were presumably inherited from the Minoan civilization of the Bronze Age. Some deities such as Britomartis, Velchanos, and Eileithyia were actually Minoan, but even Olympic figures such as Zeus, Hera, Apollo, and Athena were apt to retain Minoan features in their ritual and in the folklore referring to them.

It has been suggested that Plato's account of Atlantis, that island with its wonderful culture, its cult of Poseidon, and the emphasis on roads and water supplies, might be a reference, derived from folklore, to the lost island culture of Crete, and even that the reference to Solon deriving his information from Egypt might refer to information about Minoan Crete preserved in Egyptian records.[1] It is clear, however, that Plato himself did not identify Atlantis with Crete, and if he used folklore referring to Minoan Crete he was quite unconscious of any connexion between them. He knew the tradition about the laws of Minos and the relationship between the Dorian customs of Sparta and Crete, and of course, like all his contemporaries, he knew how Epimenides had been summoned from Crete to purify Athens after the murder of Cylon's associates in 632 B.C.

This eclipse of Crete during the classical period has left us with

1. Seltman, C., 'Life in Ancient Crete: Atlantis', *History Today*, 1952, p. 332.

little information from the classical authors, who in general were not particularly interested in the island. A few scattered but valuable remarks are preserved in the poems of Homer and the Histories of Herodotus and Thucydides, and we have to employ these as tests of the reliability of statements by authors of Hellenistic and Roman date. The poems of Epimenides, and the works of the historians who wrote specially on Crete in the Hellenistic period, have vanished, and practically all that remains of them is preserved in the history of Diodorus Siculus, an honest but uncritical historian who compiled his work about 40 B.C. His contemporary, Strabo the geographer, far more critical and better able to make use of the sources available to him, has left us some interesting information on Cretan religion, but practically nothing on the political history. Polybius, of course, is reliable on the political history of his own time, but in his days the Cretan forces were only as pawns moved about in the great game of chess played by the Hellenistic monarchs of Egypt and Macedon.

Sound evidence on many matters is provided by inscriptions and coins, but neither kind gives much information before 500 B.C., though from that time onwards these sources become more abundant and important. The most valuable evidence we possess from them is a long though incomplete inscription preserved on the walls of a Roman theatre at Gortyn in the Mesara giving the laws of that city mainly on questions of property valid in the fifth century B.C. The inscription is beautifully cut, and is a fine example of the local and rather archaic variety of the Greek script current in Crete, and of the local Doric dialect. It is even more valuable, however, as our longest and most complete account of the laws of property in a Greek city of the classical period.

After Diodorus there is no attempt by classical historians to delve into Cretan history, although writers on religion, both pagan and Christian, occasionally quote some detail of interest. Byzantine writers are no more curious, though chroniclers like Eusebius and Malalas quote from the older authorities, and the church historians give us interesting material about the early Christian church founded by St Titus.

In A.D. 832 Crete was seized by a band of Saracen adventurers from Egypt (and ultimately from Cordova in Spain) under the leadership of Abu Ka'ab and was held for Islam till it was recaptured by Nicéphorus Phócas in A.D. 960.

The Saracens had founded the city of Candia, named after the 'Kandaiki', a moat they dug round their original settlement, but they were tough adventurers merely intent on plunder, and no Islamic university like those of Spain ever developed in Crete.[1] There is therefore practically no history of Crete during the period of the Saracen occupation, though we must note the effort made by the emperor Alexis Comnenus to replace the Saracen governing class by importing twelve noble Byzantine families known as the Archontópouloi.

In 1204 Crete was captured by the Crusaders and assigned to Boniface, Marquis of Montferrat, who sold his rights to Venice, and by 1210 a Venetian governor was appointed. The Venetians colonized the island, taxed it, exploited it, and suppressed rebellions, but they also built cities and introduced their own culture and the Latin church. Gradually the island settled down and some of the Venetian colonists, like the English colonists in Ireland, fraternized and intermarried with the Cretans, so that in 1363 many Venetians united with Cretans to rebel against the city of Venice and even went as far as to join the Orthodox church.

This union of Crete and Venice created not only a Creto-Venetian culture but also an interest in the earlier history of Crete, though the first medieval writer to display an interest in Cretan archaeology was the Florentine monk Buondelmonte, who visited the island in 1422, and whose observations were used by Cornelius in his *Creta Sacra* published in 1755. In 1596 Honorio de Belli dedicated his history of Candia, recording from personal observation many monuments and inscriptions. Of later writers Meursius in his *Creta* of 1675 and Hoeck in his *Kreta* of 1823 were both concerned with the history of the classical period derived from texts rather than from monuments.

Descriptions of the island itself and of contemporary Cretan life were given by Tournefort, Pococke, and others, but the first to combine classical scholarship with accurate topographical and sociological details was Robert Pashley in his *Travels in Crete* (1837) followed by Captain (later Admiral) T. A. B. Spratt in his *Travels and Researches in Crete* published in 1865, but embodying the results of a

1. No site even of a mosque of Saracen date has yet been discovered in Crete.

survey interrupted by the Crimean War. Spratt and Downes compiled the Admiralty Charts for Crete that were the best maps until the production of the staff maps during the Second World War. Victor Rawlin published his *Description physique de l'île de Crète* in 1869, an excellent account of the parts he had visited, but less comprehensive than the title suggests. It was not, however, till the last two decades of the nineteenth century that any serious attempt was made to excavate ancient sites in Crete, and the credit for the foundations of Cretan archaeology must chiefly be given to three men: Dr Joseph Hazzidakis, the founder of the Syllogos (the local Cretan archaeological society), Professor Federigo Halbherr, who conducted the first excavations of the Italian Mission in Crete, and Sir Arthur Evans, whose untiring efforts uncovered the Palace of Minos and revealed anew the great Minoan civilization of the Cretan Bronze Age and its neolithic predecessor.

Evans first visited Crete in 1893, attracted there by his study of the engraved seals then known as 'island gems', and the following year published the *Cretan Pictographs, and Pre-Phoenician Script*. In 1897 he acquired a permit for excavating part of the site of the Palace of Minos, then virgin ground, except for two small trial excavation pits, one sunk by Heinrich Schliemann and the other by Minos Kalokairinos. The Cretan rebellion of 1897 induced the Candia Turks to massacre some of the local Christians and rather unwisely to include in the massacre the British Vice-Consul and seventeen British sailors. Admiral Noel turned his guns on the city and gave the Pasha ten minutes to surrender. That, at least, is the local version of the story, and the name of Admiral Noel is still remembered with honour in Crete. Arthur Evans, whose liberal spirit had sympathized with this and other rebellions, was backed up by the new Cretan authorities and his title to the land was secured according to the new archaeological law proposed by Hazzidakis and Xanthoudides.

Hogarth describes the scene when he rode out with Evans, who was to start excavating his new site. 'For us then and no others in the following year Minos was waiting when we rode out from Candia. Over the very site of his buried throne a desolate donkey drooped, the only living thing in view. He was driven off and the digging of Knosos began.' On 23 March 1899 Evans, assisted by Duncan Mackenzie and by Theodore Fyfe as his architect, began those excavations which were to be continued every year until 1914 and again from 1920 until 1932. In 1901 Evans published his division of the Cretan Bronze Age into Early, Middle, and Late Minoan, and his article, 'The Mycenaean Tree and Pillar Cult'. In 1906 he published his *Essai de classification des époques de la civilisation minoenne* (a revision of his report to the Congress at Athens in 1905), a short but important article on Minoan weights and mediums of currency, and his *Prehistoric Tombs of Knosos*.

These discoveries attracted world-wide attention. The first general book to deal with them (a remarkably good one considering its early date) was H. R. Hall's *Oldest Civilization of Greece* published in 1901, followed by Miss Edith Hall's *The Decorative Art of Crete in the Bronze Age* (1907), L. P. Lagrange's *La Crète ancienne* and R. M. Burrows's *The Discoveries in Crete* (both 1908), and by Diedrich Fimmen's *Zeit und Dauer der kretisch-mykenischen Kultur*, C. M. Hawes's *Crete, the Forerunner of Greece*, and P. Kavadhias's *Proistoriki Archaeologia*, all in 1909.

In 1906 Evans had built the Villa Ariadne to serve as a permanent headquarters for his work, and in 1907 and 1908 he not only continued to excavate the Palace of Minos but also uncovered the Little Palace. In 1909 Evans published the first volume of his *Scripta Minoa* and in 1911 he was knighted for his services to archaeology.

Excavations in Crete were interrupted by the First World War but resumed in 1920, and in 1921 Evans published the first volume of his *Palace of Minos*. His devoted assistant Mackenzie was present at all the excavations until 1928, when ill-health forced him to retire, and he was succeeded as Curator at Knosos by J. D. S. Pendlebury. In 1932 Evans opened the Temple Tomb at Knosos, and in 1935 he visited Crete for the last time and published the fourth volume of his great book.

The British School of Archaeology at Athens started to excavate in Crete in the nineteenth century, when Hogarth opened the Dictaean cave at Psychro and the following year excavated a Minoan settlement at Zakros in the eastern end. In 1901 Bosanquet, who had been excavating the most important Bronze Age site in the Cyclades at Phylakopi in Melos, transferred his activities to Crete and excavated the archaic and Hellenistic site of Praisos, where he found an Eteocretan inscription (the first having been found by Halbherr).

In 1902 Bosanquet also began to excavate the Minoan city and tombs at Palaikastro on the east coast, and his work was continued by R. M. Dawkins.

In 1928 Evans presented his property in Crete to the British School at Athens, and from this date excavations at Knosos were conducted by the successive Directors – Humfry Payne, Alan Blakeway, Gerard Young, and Sinclair Hood – and by successive Curators, Pendlebury, myself, and P. de Jong. A large number of tombs of the early Iron Age were opened by Payne, Blakeway, Young, J. K. Brock, and T. J. Dunbabin.

In 1935 Pendlebury began an exhaustive examination of sites on the plain of Lasithi, a work terminated by the Second World War. During that war he made his gallant sortie against the German parachutists and was wounded, and later killed, in April 1941. Before his death, however, he had completely excavated the post-Minoan village of Karphi – a feat only equalled in Crete previously by Miss Boyd at Gournia – and also excavated a Neolithic cave site at Trapeza and other sites nearby.

In January 1940 I opened three tombs of the orientalizing period at Khaniale Tekke near Knosos, one with a rich treasure of jewellery of the seventh century B.C.

In May 1941 the Germans occupied the area round Knosos and the Villa Ariadne became the headquarters of General Ringel, who not only looted the antiquities in the house, but committed a much worse archaeological crime in destroying the Royal Tomb at Isopata to use the stones as foundations for three army huts. It should be remarked, however, that the German officers who succeeded Ringel treated the antiquities with great respect.

Halbherr had started excavating in Crete some years before Evans, but his earlier researches were concerned with remains of the classical period, including the famous inscription of the laws of Gortyn. In 1900, however, he began to excavate the palace site at Phaistos on the east end of an isolated ridge in the Mesara plain. In 1901 Professor Luigi Pernier took over the direction of the excavations. Pernier was able to complete the first volume of the final publication *Il Palazzo di Festos*, but the second volume, which he had left incomplete at his death in 1937, was completed and edited by Professor Luisa Banti in 1950. Further excavations have been made since the Second World

War by Professors Banti and Levi. Savignoni and Paribeni published their excavations of the cemeteries of Phaistos and Hagia Triada in the eleventh volume of the *Monumenti Antichi*. Only summary accounts have been published of the recent excavations at Phaistos.

The excavations of Pernier and Banti at Hagia Triada have not yet been published in full, though there are excellent preliminary reports. For the archaic and classical periods, Pernier gave an account of his excavations at Prinias in 1914, and Doro Levi of his work at Arkades in 1924. Last but not least there is the splendid corpus of Cretan classical inscriptions which Signorina M. Guarducci has been producing since 1935. The Americans were also early on the field and concentrated on the Gulf of Merabello.

During all this period a great deal of fine, if often unspectacular, work had been carried out by the Greek archaeological service under its successive officers Drs Hazzidakis, Xanthoudides, Marinatos, Theophanides, Platon, Petrou (a casualty in the Albanian war), and Alexiou.

The French School at Athens were slower to turn their attention to Crete, but in 1899–1900 P. Demargne excavated the interesting city of Lato. The French continued to be interested in this district, but of recent years they have devoted more attention to Mallia, where a splendid Minoan palace was uncovered on a site discovered and first tested by Joseph Hazzidakis.

The Germans took no part in Cretan excavations until their military occupation of Crete in 1941, but after that date they carried out a few minor excavations.

All these excavations had produced a mass of material which needed to be set in order and correlated with contemporary finds from other parts of the Levant.

A great deal of the preliminary spadework for this correlation of cultures was done by Evans himself in his great work *The Palace of Minos*, but there were many debatable points, and a battle royal developed between Evans and Wace on the vexed question of how far Mycenae might be said to be under Minoan influence or even domination during the Late Minoan I–II periods.

It is not possible here to give a bibliography of these excavations outside Crete, but readers may consult the various excavation reports by the scholars concerned.

CHAPTER I

The Islands of Crete: Geology, Geography, Climate, and Flora and Fauna

THE long mountainous island of Crete (Figs. 1 and 2) forms a natural stepping stone between Europe and Africa, and between Europe and Asia, but whereas there are many stepping stones for the latter interval, Crete is the only convenient link between Europe and Egypt. It was no accident therefore that this island became the medium for the transmission of cultural influences from the older civilizations of the Near and Middle East to barbarian Europe, and that the first civilization that we can term European was that of Crete.

In Late Miocene and Pliocene times the island seems to have been connected with Asia Minor rather than with Europe. Certain forms of land snails and wingless beetles appear on Crete and on Anticythera in forms akin to those of Asia Minor, whereas those of Cythera resemble those of the mainland of Greece, suggesting that at one time the strait dividing Cythera from Anticythera was the division between Europe and Asia. What is now the northern part of the Aegean Sea was then probably a lakeland, and as long ago as 1856 T. A. B. Spratt had noted that the Miocene deposits near Khersonnesos in Crete contained fresh-water molluscs in an abundance implying that the deposit was lacustrine, since the hills at this point would not have allowed the formation of so large a riverine deposit.

In the Pleistocene period there were evident convulsions which submerged the area now called the Aegean Sea, heaved up mountain ranges, and severed Crete from Asia Minor. Henceforward Crete was more nearly related to the mainland of Greece, and its present fauna and flora are European though retaining faint traces of their old connexions with Asia Minor and Cyrenaica. One such relic is the *agrimi*, the Cretan ibex, also found in the small Cycladic island of Antimelos; this splendid animal, though related to the ibex of Sardinia and Corsica, is more nearly akin to that of Cyprus and Asia Minor.

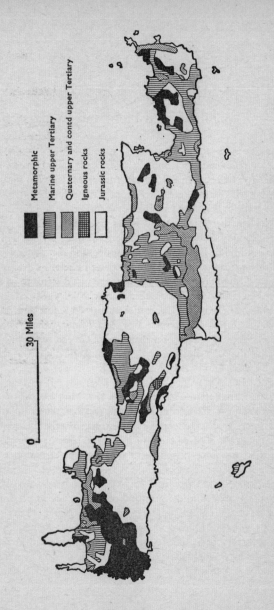

Metamorphic

Marine upper Tertiary

Quaternary and contd upper Tertiary

Igneous rocks

Jurassic rocks

30 Miles

Fig. 1. Geological map of Crete

The connexions with Europe were further strengthened by the fact that nearly all the harbours of Crete are on its north coast, and that after the first fifty miles there is a double string of islands joining Crete to the mainland of Greece. Another string of islands, Kasos, Karpathos, and Rhodes unites Crete to Asia Minor. On the south side, however, there is deep water and two hundred miles of open sea without any intervening islands between Crete and Africa.

The island has never yet been systematically examined by a geological survey though individual geologists have explored particular areas.[1]

The most recent geological map of Crete is the one based on the work of N. Liatsikos and published in the Rockefeller survey of Crete. Doubtless it corrects Captain Spratt's map in some parts, but for the general reader it is disappointing, because it is far more summary and leaves out a great deal of information contained in Spratt's work. According to Liatsikos the great limestone backbone of the island, including the promontories enclosing the bays of Kisamos, Khania, and Soudha in the west, the great ranges of the White Mountains, Ida, Lasithi, the Kophinos range in the south, and the moorlands beyond Seteia in the east are labelled as dark limestone and dolomite of the 'Tripolitza sub-zone'. Impure marly limestone, calcareous sandstone, and conglomerate mark the coastal plains of Khania and Rethymnon, all the valleys south of Herakleion between the Ida block on the west and the Pedhiadha valleys on the east, and also the quaternary alluvial plain of the Mesara on the south. In this rather mixed group Liatsikos evidently includes the white 'Kouskouras' marls, and though he marks gypsum outcrops on the Kisamos–Selinon boundary he does not mark either the historic hill of Gypsadhes, which provided the gypsum quarries for the Palace of Minos, or those in the Mesara, which furnished gypsum blocks for the palaces of Phaistos and Hagia Triada.[2]

The coastal district east of Kophinos and one or two other patches are classified by Liatsikos as limestone of the Adriatic–Ionian group.

---

1. e.g. west Crete by Ardaillon and Cayeux, *Annual of the American Geographical Society*, 1901, p. 445; and cave deposits in central Crete by Simonelli, *Rendiconti Accademia dei Lincei*, Rome, 1894, p. 236.

2. This observation is not intended as a criticism of Liatsikos, since these outcrops, though archaeologically important, are small in area.

Finally there is a solid block of country round Kandanos in the west, and smaller patches south of the Rethymnon plain and elsewhere labelled schist, phyllite, slate, quartzite, and marble.

Igneous rocks (serpentine, gabbro, syenite, and a little granite), mainly of the Jurassic and Cretaceous periods, but possibly including some of Eocene date, occur near the east end of the Asidheroto mountains and south of the Lasithi massif. Two small volcanic outcrops occur at Galatas and Xerokambos in the Khania district, and Spratt claims that the islands of Pondikonisi and Gaidharonisi are volcanic formations, though the latter is stated by a later authority to be Tertiary limestone.

In general, however, the base of the land of the island consists of metamorphic phyllites, slates, mica schists, and quartzites, and these crop out on the surface in the Kisamos and Selinon districts. Elsewhere the metamorphic rocks are usually covered by a vast mass of coarse-grained limestones of the Jurassic, Cretaceous, and Eocene periods often drained by swallow-holes rather than by streams. Caves are frequent and have so regularly provided refuges in troubled times that they added a word to the ancient lexicon, Kresphygeton, the Cretan refuge.

The lower areas were also largely covered by marine upper Tertiary rocks, especially conglomerates but including limestones, marls, chalks, and sandstones.

Quaternary and upper Tertiary deposits, though not extensive, form the most fertile areas such as the Mesara and the coastal plains of Herakleion and Rethymnon. Many details missing from the Rockefeller version of Liatsikos's map[1] may be filled in from the books and articles of earlier explorers such as that of Captain Spratt and M. Victor Raulin, summarized by Burchard.[2]

The province of Seteia was also discussed in detail in a book in German by L. Chalikiopoulos, and the same area was examined more recently by H. Lehmann, who in his brief summary of the districts he visited, states that east Crete is composed mainly of Mesozoic and old Tertiary limestone, crystalline schist and conglomerate overlaid

1. The original map, which I have not seen, may be much more informative.

2. Article 'Kreta' in the *Real-Enzyklopädie* of Paully-Wissowa-Kroll, pp. 174-9.

by late Tertiary limestone, conglomerate, and marls in the marginal troughs at Ierapetra and Seteia.

PIRACY AND THE DISTRIBUTION OF THE POPULATION

Lehmann's two plans illustrate how the Minoan settlements follow the alluvial deposits and the schist valleys and avoid the limestone. The schist not only breaks up more easily into cultivated terraces, but it also provokes intercommunication, forming natural roads along the hillside comfortable for a loaded mule, without any of the rough boulders that beset a limestone path. He also notes how the occupation zones swing away from the coastal plains to the uplands when there is increased danger from piracy. Thus Minoan sites are rarely more than a hundred metres above sea level, testifying to the power of the Minoan navy, and I think this is true of Minoan settlements elsewhere, though of course the rule only applies to villages, not to religious shrines such as peak and cave sanctuaries. In the Homeric and geometric period, however, when there was no Minoan navy and piracy was a fashionable profession, the villages spread into the higher dales and the lower slopes of the schist hills.

Piracy continued into classical times and reached a new peak of intensity in the late Hellenistic period, but after Metellus Creticus and Pompey had wiped out the Cretan pirates in the first century B.C. the island began again to enjoy peace and prosperity and the coastal plains filled up with a contented population of farmers, artisans, and traders. With the arrival of the Saracen raiders under Abu Ka'ab, however, in A.D. 825 the bad times began again, and the coastal plains hardly filled up again until the firm hand of imperial Venice had imposed peace (a peace less secure, however, than those of Minoan and Roman times).

A letter from R. C. Bosanquet to a friend alludes to more recent piracy on the coast by Palaikastro. 'Curiously enough until the Greek revolution the seas were so infested by pirates that no one dared to live on this exposed sea-board and the whole plain was uncultivated. ... A Venetian writer says it was uninhabitable on account of corsairs. ... We heard many stories of the last of the Christian corsairs, a certain Papa Boyatzes, "Father Dyer", a valiant priest who commanded a swift forty-oared galley and was the terror of the Turks.'

Admiral Spratt at an earlier date commented on the remarkable knowledge of the coastlines of Crete, Kasos, Karpathos, and Kastellorizo displayed by his ex-pirate pilot, 'the patient and gentle' Captain Manias. In the fourteenth book of the *Odyssey* the hero pretends to be a Cretan and boasts that 'nine times before the war at Troy I raided men of another race with my ships, and my house grew great and my reputation was established among the Cretans'.

EARTHQUAKES AND TIDAL WAVES

The only volcano at present active in Greece is that of the Cycladic island Thera, perhaps better known by its Italian name Santorini, but earthquakes affect many parts of Greece, and Crete averages about two severe earthquakes a century with minor tremors every year. Evidence of destruction by earthquakes was noted by Sir Arthur Evans when he excavated the Palace of Minos at Knosos, the clearest evidence being that of the House of the Fallen Blocks and the adjacent House of the Sacrificed Oxen. These two small houses had been destroyed by great blocks hurled southwards from the south-east part of the Palace, and it should be remarked that the earthquakes recurring now shake the island from north to south, the epicentre being presumably somewhere between Crete and Thera. The great fire which destroyed the Palace about 1400 B.C. was also supposed to have been the result of seismic activity, and Evans notes what he takes to be evidence of other earthquakes. This theory has been further developed by S. Marinatos and C. F. C. Schaeffer. (See page 301.)

SURFACE GEOLOGY AND TOPOGRAPHY

The surface topography of the island has been admirably treated by the late Captain J. D. S. Pendlebury in his *Archaeology of Crete* in which he summarized the previous evidence from the *Stadiasmus*[1] and from the earlier travellers, and supplemented them with his own

1. op cit., pp. 13, 24; I think, however, that the temples cited in the *Stadiasmus* were quoted mainly as prominent landmarks for navigators rather than as 'facilities for devotion'.

unrivalled knowledge of the by-paths and mountains of Crete. Individual muleteers doubtless knew their own district better, but no man knew the whole island as well as Pendlebury, and he stresses the point, which may be forgotten by armchair archaeologists and historians, that distances on a map have little meaning in considering ancient trade routes, and that what really matters is the number of foot-hours occupied by a normal man walking between one site and another.

Pendlebury's first chapter, 'The Island', should be taken as a basis for surface topography, and it has since been supplemented by some further researches during and since the Second World War by the German archaeological expedition under Friedrich Matz in western Crete, by T. J. Dunbabin in the Amari district, by N. Platon the Ephor of Antiquities, and by the survey of Crete executed for the Rockefeller Foundation under the direction of L. G. Allbaugh in 1948.

If the island is considered simply as an environment for human culture, we may divide Crete into the following types of country: (a) fertile coastal plains and valleys; (b) mountain-locked upland plains sometimes drained by a river but often drained only by natural swallow-holes (called *katavôthra* on the mainland but in Crete more often termed *chónoi*), often snow-bound in the winter and sometimes waterlogged if the swallow-holes get blocked; (c) low hills and table-land providing good pasture and even arable land; (d) forests; (e) the *madara* or bare lands on the higher mountains providing summer pasturage but snowbound in the winter; and (f) the high peaks, crags, and torrents that are unusable for pasture.

FAUNA

In the far west the schist valleys of the Kandanos and Ennea Khoria districts are better watered than the average and tolerably fertile, as are also the two coastal plains of Kisamos and Khania. In the White Mountains are the remains of the great cypress woods that still supplied material to the Venetian navy as late as the sixteenth century and which in the Keramia district still grow up to a level of 6500 feet. These parts have always been a refuge for the hunted, whether man or beast. In the time of Pliny, or at least in that of his authority, the province of Khania was the only part of Crete where deer still survived, and the wooded heights west of the Hagio Roumeli gorge are now the last refuge of the *agrimi*, the Cretan ibex which was still to be found in the Ida and Lasithi districts fifty years ago. Evans's statement, however, that they still existed on Dhia is not correct.

It will be remarked that among the recorded wild fauna of Crete not one is the ancestor of any domestic animal later found in the island; even the domestic cats of Minoan days would appear to be the offspring of Egyptian sires, not those of the native wild cat. The domestic animals of Crete must have been introduced in Neolithic times or later and are therefore more properly considered in the chapter on social organization. (See Chapter 8.)

There is no evidence on the varieties of fish available to the first settlers in Crete, but they must have included most of the Mediterranean varieties. Even now there are plenty of fish round the island, and before the Cretans began to fish with dynamite the fishing grounds must have been much more prolific; but fishing must always have been complicated by the fact that the main fishing grounds were off the south-east coast, where the off-shore water was very deep and there were no good harbours.

Game common on the island includes rock pigeons and red-legged partridges all the year round, and duck, snipe, woodcock, and quail at the migration times. Even storks have been seen in passage, but certainly the most exciting bird migration is that of the cranes, who fly in large flocks over Crete in a north-westerly direction in the spring, returning south-eastwards in October.

CLIMATE, RAINFALL, AND WATER SUPPLY

The Cretan climate varies greatly according to altitude. The plains have a pleasant, dry climate with practically all the rain falling between October and March, usually some heavy rain in October and again in February or March ('the former and the latter rains' referred to in the Bible). The temperature only occasionally falls below freezing point and snow is rare.

There is only one lake in Crete, Lake Kournas (160 acres in area), situated about eleven miles west of Rethymnon.

Allbaugh speaks of three permanent rivers, but this estimate

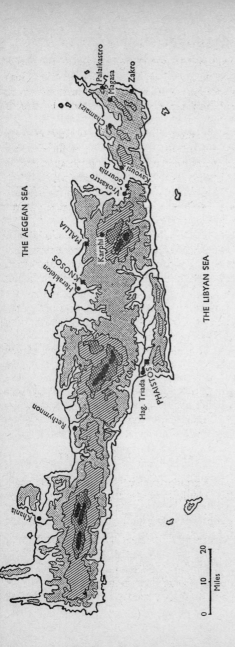

THE AEGEAN SEA

THE LIBYAN SEA

Khania
Rethymnon
Hag. Triada
PHAISTOS
Herakleion
KNOSOS
MALLIA
Karphi
Vrokastro
Gournia
Kavousi
Chamaizi
Palaikastro
Magasa
Zakro

0   10   20
Miles

Fig. 2. General map of Crete

depends on where one draws the line between a river and a stream. Pendlebury quotes five that have never been known to dry up, namely the Platanias west of Khania (the ancient Iardanos), the Gazanos west of Herakleion ('formerly the Triton'),[1] the Metropolitanos or Yeropotamos (the ancient Lethaios) and the Anapodhiari (formerly the Katarrhactes) both in the Mesara, and the Mylopotamos (the ancient Oaxes) which flows out at the east end of the Rethymnos bay. Other places which have permanently flowing streams though they may not merit the title of rivers are Amnisos, Seteia, Zakros, and Kato Viannos. Water is thus relatively scarce (though usually quite good in quality); however, of the villages sampled by the Rockefeller Survey, only one had to carry its drinking water from a neighbouring settlement.

Springs are fairly common in the mountains and in the coastal plains water is drawn from wells (in the Mallia plain at a depth of only five metres, but at Knosos some twelve to fourteen metres).

MINERAL RESOURCES

The mineral resources of Crete are indicated by two reports presented to the Rockefeller Survey. One prepared in Herakleion indicated twenty appearances of iron ore, twelve of copper, ten of gypsum, and three to six each of manganese, talc, lignite, lead, and zinc. Another report alleged that in three unworked mines near Palaiokhora, Meskla, and Kastelli Kisamou there were precious stones, gold, silver, copper,[2] tungsten, platinum, magnetite, emery, graphite, and possibly tin apatite (most of them presumably in small quantities).

The forests, which still provided abundant cypress wood for the Venetian navy in medieval times, have now largely been destroyed. Half of the forest still remaining is in the province of Khania (half is scrub and half Aleppo pine mixed with scrub). There are also, however, some small chestnut forests in this province. Rethymnon has forests of carob and oaktrees. The southern and eastern slopes of the Ida range have oaks and conifers (constituting one fifth of the

---

1. I should have thought the Giophyros Potamos was more permanent and more likely to have been the Triton; in this I agree with Pashley.

2. Evidences of a Middle Minoan copper mine were found at Chrysokamino.

whole forest area of the island). Lasithi has almonds and carobs and there is a fine wood of *prinári* (evergreen oak) above Kritsa. The extreme east of the island is almost treeless except for plantations of olives or carobs, and the grove of wild palms at Eremopolis (traditionally supposed to have sprung from the date stones thrown away by the first Arab invaders).

EDIBLE PLANTS AND CULTIVATION

Very large areas of Crete are and always have been unproductive. No statistics are available for ancient times, but Allbaugh gives the following figures for 1948: eight per cent of the total land area was under cultivated crops such as wheat, barley, beans, etc., ten per cent was vine, olive, and other fruit orchards, five per cent was fallow land, seven per cent was grazing land and meadows of a permanent or semi-permanent type, two per cent was forests, no less than forty-eight per cent were lands used for nomadic grazing, and the remaining twenty per cent consisted of entirely unproductive land, such as mountain crags, torrent beds, and the like. It is impossible to form a fair estimate of what the proportions would have been in prehistoric times, but obviously much of the present *madára* – the bare lands used for nomadic grazing – would then have been virgin forest. At a very rough guess I should imagine that the cultivated land would not have been much less than the present and the unproductive twenty per cent of crags and torrents just the same, but that at least half of the present *madára* would then have been covered by cypress and other forest trees.

Before 1939 Cretan olive trees averaged a yield of five pounds of oil per tree, as compared with an average of 3·7 pounds for Greece as a whole and 3·1 pounds for Italy and Turkey, and the crop represented a large percentage – more than a third – of the Greek crop as a whole. Pre-war crops of wheat and barley in Crete averaged 12·8 and 15 bushels per acre respectively. Grapes, largely in the form of sultanas, form the largest Cretan export abroad now, though Pashley records that in his day oil paid 8,750,000 piastres duty against only 168,000 from raisins (which presumably includes sultanas). Today a considerable proportion of the olives exported from the island is simply sent to other parts of Greece. The annual output of olives is some 25,000 tons, and according to Elliadi[1] about 10,000 tons of grapes are exported annually.

Both olives and grapes were grown in Crete during the Bronze Age. How far they were exported is a matter for speculation, but it is of interest to note that Greek tradition attributed the introduction of the cultivated olive into the Peloponnese to the Cretan Herakles, who was said to have brought it from the land of the Hyperboreans, which Pausanias interprets as Crete; and very probably he is right in this instance, since the cultivation of the olive cannot have been introduced from a country in the far north. The actual development of the cultivated olive and the preparation of its fruit were attributed to the goddess Athena herself (who according to one tradition had been born in Crete).

Visitors to Crete are often surprised to find the valleys full of vineyards and wheat planted on the flatter tops and slopes of the lower hills – such wheat being said to produce whiter flour than that of the valleys – while the slopes of the lower hills are terraced for olives. In eastern Crete and in some western districts the carob bean tree vies with and even replaces the olive in popularity, while citrus fruits are grown in the valleys behind Khania; but the last-named are unlikely to have been known in Crete in prehistoric times. The present annual crop of carob beans amounts to about 20,000 tons.

The prehistoric Cretans were well supplied with leguminous plants, having peas, chickpeas and some form of beans, but for sweetening their food they must have relied mainly on honey.

NATURAL VEGETATION

The vegetation of Crete has probably not altered much since prehistoric times, with two great exceptions: the first, the diminution of forest timber, especially cypress, owing to excessive cutting, to fires, and to the failure to protect the young shoots from goats; and the second the introduction of numerous fruits, such as apples, peaches, apricots, plums, and citrus fruits in the west, and certain vegetables

1. In 1937, however, Crete produced 32,000 tons of olive oil and 2500 tons of table olives; Tournefort states that the crop of oil in 1699 was 300,000 measures, but cautions us that whereas the Rethymnon measure weighed 10 okes that of Canea weighed only 8½.

such as potatoes (now extensively grown on the Lasithi plain). If we bear in mind these exceptions we may take Rawlin's list, as modified by Trevor Battye, as a fair indication of what existed in ancient times.

From sea-level up to 500 feet we find common lentisk, large seeded juniper, tamarisk, a willow, *agnus castus*, and oleanders. The almond and quince, both probably native to Crete, are confined to this level. Elliadi, in 1933, quotes the crop of shelled almonds as averaging 600 tons and states it was increasing every year.

From 500 to 2000 feet up we find the terebinth (a softer lentisk), a deciduous oak, myrtle, arbutus, oleander, black mulberry, and styrax. From 2000 to 3000 feet, in the lower woods, we find dog rose, plane tree, and ivy (the latter two are also found lower). From 3000 to 4000 feet, in the higher wooded areas, there is the tree *salvia cretica* peculiar to the island, with oak, maple, and cypress, and spiny shrubs are common.

Between 4000 and 6000 feet, the limit of the true forest, we have the evergreen cypress, the Cretan maple, and the low prickly form of the *prinári*, or evergreen oak. Between 6000 and 8000 feet we find the bare subalpine slopes which the Cretans call *madára*. We still find there the common juniper, Cretan barberry (never more than bush size), and in the higher regions the woods flatten to creeping forms such as the creeping barberry, creeping plum, and buckthorn. The pine, chiefly *pinus haricio* or *pinus halepensis*, occurs at all levels up to 3000 feet, but the only considerable forests are in the Aradena district in the west and on the southern slopes of the Dhikte and Effendi Kavousi ranges.

Cypresses seem confined to the limestone country. Evergreen oak and myrtle are most common among, though not restricted to, the schist district.

Trees like the Cretan oak and myrtle tend to develop into prickly shrubs on the higher slopes. The centre of the island is now largely devoted to the culture of vines and olives, but in the Khania plain citrus fruits are grown. The wild pear may be found up to 3000 feet and the black mulberry up to 2000, but the latter was introduced probably for the silk trade, and there is a tendency for each village to have about one tree. White mulberries grow up to 3000 feet.

Cedar of Lebanon and Cefalonian pine have been identified in the remains of wood in the Palace, but whether these then grew in Crete or were imported is uncertain. We do know that Thothmes III used to import cedars from the Lebanon to Egypt 'in ships of Keftiu', but whether this means in Cretan ships is open to question (see page 108). There are a few natural salt marshes on the coast, but there is no evidence yet to show whether the Minoan people attempted to exploit these. Pepper, however, seems to be a pre-Hellenic word, and the Greek word for mustard also is of foreign derivation.

The wild vegetables include the wild forms of celery, carrot, cabbage, lettuce, and asparagus (of which only the young shoots are eaten, since the rest is spiny); but the Cretans also boil for the pot many *khorta* (grasses) which are despised by householders elsewhere, including the bulbs of asphodel and grape hyacinths.

The hills of Crete are particularly rich in aromatic herbs and bushes, of which the more fragrant are thyme, the various kinds of *cystus*, and sage, marjoram, and mint.

By July most flowers have vanished from the valleys, though even then the stony river beds grow pink with oleanders and the sandy river beds mauve with *agnus castus* (which is used for making baskets), and the vineyards are a rich green, only turning brown about the time of the autumn rains. But as the valleys grow brown, the snows melt from the high mountains, the upland plains of Nidha, Omalo, Lasithi, and others yield their best pasture, and many little flowers come out on the high mountains, such as chionodoxa, a rock-cress, forget-me-nots, and an alyssum (the last found by Trevor Battye right on the summit of Mount Ida).

CHAPTER 2

The Stone Age

PALAEONTOLOGICAL EVIDENCE

WE can say nothing definite about the existence of men in Crete during the Old Stone Age. A stone scraper resembling an Aurignacian type was discovered by Pendlebury in Lasithi, but not in a Palaeolithic context. It must be admitted, however, that the average archaeologist who works in Crete would not recognize the less obvious type of Palaeolithic tool, and is not a good enough geologist to look in the right places. One or two palaeontologists, however, have examined some early cave deposits, and so far have discovered no artefacts associated with the fossils contemporary with the Old Stone Age.

In 1893 Signor Simonelli excavated some caves in the Rethymnon district and identified bones of a large elephant and of a small deer which he named *Anoglochis cretensis*. In 1904 Miss Dorothea Bate spent some months in Crete examining Spratt's cave and some twelve others near Sphinari, two others at the north end of the Phalasarna plain, one each side of the promontory dividing Khania from Kisamos, four from within the limits of the Akrotiri peninsula, and a number of caves near Rethymnon. Later in the same year, she examined cave deposits in east Crete near Milatos, on Katharo plain, and at Kharoumes, recording the bones of pigmy elephants and hippopotami, as well as those found by Simonelli, and others existing on the island, such as the *agrimi*, or Cretan ibex (*Capra aegagrus cretensis*), but no *Bos primigenius*, nor any signs of man.

It would appear that the land bridge to Asia Minor had already sunk when the first Cretans came by boat from island to island by way of Karpathos and Kasos, and then sailed along the coast of Crete, which may perhaps help to explain the curious fact that no Early Neolithic pottery has yet been found except at Knosos. The first

45

Neolithic settlers in Crete cannot have arrived later than 3000 B.C. and probably arrived earlier.

Evans had early realized and stressed the Anatolian elements in Crete, such as the stone maces and the squatting figurines which seemed to imply the cult of a great mother goddess like that of Anatolia. This evidence has been reinforced by Dr Audrey Furness, who pointed out analogies between the decoration of the earliest Neolithic pottery in Crete and that of Chalcolithic pottery from the Alaca district of Asia Minor.

It may also be remarked that the colonization of Crete in such primitive boats as were likely to be available to the Neolithic inhabitants would hardly be practicable from anywhere except the Dodecanese or the Cyclades. (See p. 91 and Fig. 12.)

M. L. Franchet in 1912 examined a small habitation site on the coast three kilometres west of Herakleion, which he claimed to be earlier than that of Knosos and which produced some microlithic obsidian tools.

THE EARLY NEOLITHIC PERIOD

Apart from Franchet's site, of which the date is a little uncertain, we are dependent for our knowledge of the Early and Middle Neolithic culture of Crete entirely on the site of the Palace of Minos at Knosos. The permanent and abundant evidence from the deep test pits is preserved in the Stratigraphic Museum at Knosos. Recently this material has been studied in detail by Dr Furness. She retains Evans's division of the pottery into three main periods entitled Early, Middle, and Late Neolithic, but subdivides the first period into Early Neolithic I and Early Neolithic II. The pottery from these deposits was quite well made, well mixed, and tempered with powdered gypsum, and sometimes with larger grit, but rather irregularly fired, perhaps in an open fire, so that the colour of the surface varies from black through grey to buff and even red, though the fabric is tough and does not crumble. There is no slip, but the surface is usually very well burnished, although sometimes uneven burnishing left red scribblings on buff or black on grey. The commonest shape was a deep store jar, which might be anything up to half a metre in diameter, with large strap handles set vertically, occasionally on the rim, but usually some way below it. The profile seems to vary from cylindrical, through inverted conical, to round forms. Shallow bowls of various sizes, conical bowls with straight, thinning rims (a Neolithic trick common all over the Near East), round bowls with inverted rims, carinated bowls with similar rims: all these occur. Raking handles of wishbone type are not uncommon, and a broad, flat, double-horned type also occurs, though it is confined to Knosos and is not common even there.

Dr Furness divides the Early Neolithic I fabrics into (a) coarse burnished ware and (b) fine burnished ware, only differing from the former in that the pot walls are thinner, the clay better mixed, and the burnish more carefully executed. The surface colour is usually black, but examples also occur of red, buff, or yellow, sometimes brilliant red or orange, and sometimes highly variegated sherds.

Dr Furness justly observes that 'as the pottery of the late Neolithic phases seems to have developed at Knosos without a break, it is to the earliest that one must look for evidence of origin or foreign connexions', and she therefore stresses the importance of a small group with plastic decoration that seems mainly confined to the Early Neolithic I levels, consisting of rows of pellets immediately under the rim (paralleled on burnished pottery of Chalcolithic date from Gullucek in the Alaca district of Asia Minor), of large knobs singly, in threes, or in rows, mostly lower down on the vase, of curved mouldings running parallel with the scalloped rims that occur on certain bowls, of dentated rims, plastic imitations of a rope, unpierced lugs, and a few unclassified oddments. In all she noted that 137 sherds in the Stratigraphic Collection at Knosos, all probably Early Neolithic I in date, had plastic decoration of this kind. Incised ornaments were more rare and when they did occur were usually in the pointillé or punctuated ribbon style (Plate 1), but also included filled triangles, chevrons, chequered stepped patterns, and fringed lines. Human and animal figurines in the same technique as the pottery also appear.

The Early Neolithic II period is marked by better mixed clay and better firing, which reduces the variations in colour, and by the disappearance of plastic ornaments, flanged handles, and certain forms of wishbone handle. Highly burnished black or red sherds are still normal, but they begin to be progressively replaced by less burnished buff or grey sherds. The shapes of the vases and handles are the same and so is the technique of the burnished ware, except that occasionally the surface was rippled by the burnishing tool, a trick that appeared for the first time now but was to become more popular later.

Incised decoration was common (Plate 2 and Fig. 3) and was applied to most of the fine pottery, except that, since it was only applied to the exterior, the very wide bowls were usually left plain, while

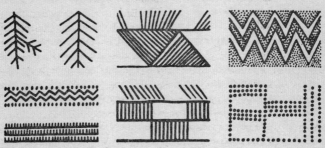

Fig. 3. Designs of Neolithic pottery

decoration was naturally more common on narrow-necked jars, where it showed to better advantage. The designs included a plaited ornament, zigzag and chevron bands, and fringed lines. It is also very common arranged vertically on strap handles. Other ornaments which occurred were hatched rectangles, chequers, and diamonds, and sometimes the zigzag band or other ornament was reserved as a pointillé background. Fragments have also been found of human and animal figures with similar decoration.

THE MIDDLE NEOLITHIC PERIOD

In the Middle Neolithic period there appeared a growing tendency to leave the coarser wares unpolished, possibly because they were now better baked and therefore the polishing was less necessary to make them impervious to water, and such polishing as did appear on the coarse vases was of the scribbled type. The large coarse bowls and jars continued to be common, though even in these there were some changes, hard to define, in the profiles of the rims. True wishbone handles were rare and the normal form was a large strap handle (not flanged). Innovations of the Middle Neolithic period were the introduction of lugs, rectangular, round, or pointed, rising from the rim, and also loop handles set on the rim. There is one example on a coarse buff vase of a horizontal lug with two vertical perforations, a form characteristic of the earliest Bronze Age in Crete, the Cyclades, Mytilene, and Troy.

The shapes and fabrics of the Middle Neolithic fine pottery did not differ very much from those of the Early Neolithic period though the vase walls were rather thinner, nor did the incised designs differ much from the Early Neolithic II ones, but ornamentation by undulating ripples executed with a heavy polishing instrument became common, always as an alternative, never as an addition to the incised decoration. Middle Neolithic sherds in general might be jet black, brown, buff, bright red, or yellow in colour, but the rippled sherds were usually coloured a moderately uniform brownish black. Ribbon handles and tubular lugs were very common. The rippled bowls often had small token handles, obviously only a skeuomorphic ornament since they sometimes appear in vertical or diagonal rows.

At Knosos the people must have lived in mudbrick houses, but a large proportion of the population doubtless lived in caves. In the transition from Early Neolithic II to Middle Neolithic deposits, axes occur in greenstone, serpentine, dioprase, jadeite, haematite, and schist, usually either of a heavy type with roughened butt to facilitate hafting, or of a smaller trapezoid type for use rather as an adze or chisel. Obsidian blades and arrowheads are found, as are cores, which show that the material was imported, presumably from Melos, and worked on the spot. Bone pins and needles and clay spools and spindle whorls testify to the existence of spinning and weaving, probably as a household industry.

THE LATE NEOLITHIC PERIOD

It is not till the very end of the Neolithic period that we begin to form any idea of what a village of that period may have looked like, and by that time the basic principle, or lack of principle, that is so characteristic of the Minoan architecture of the Bronze Age is already manifesting itself. This is the characteristic which led one scholar to borrow a term from comparative philology and to refer to Minoan architecture as 'agglutinative', because the owner or architect, after constructing one rectangular room, would add others of varying sizes and shapes to it as the need arose. The resulting plan was rather haphazard in outline, giving the impression of an organic cellular growth rather than of an architectural design. Considerable ingenuity

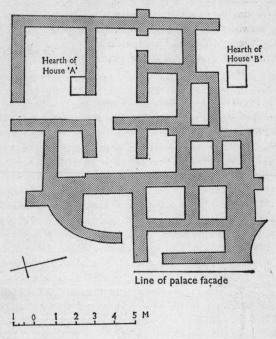

Fig. 4. Late Neolithic houses, Knosos

and architectural skill might be displayed in the design of individual parts of a building, but there was always an opportunist air about a Minoan building as a whole. The two late Neolithic houses uncovered in the central court of the Palace of Minos at Knosos (Fig. 4) already illustrate this cellular architecture. The individual rooms were rectangular and well constructed but differ in size and shape, and two rooms of house A were only accessible from the street (conceivably shops, but perhaps only outhouses or stables for donkeys). House A had one rounded corner, doubtless because the village street took a turn at this point. Both houses had fixed hearths, an amenity which went out of fashion in the Bronze Age when palaces and houses alike seem to have relied mainly for their heating on small movable braziers, though two small houses of the Middle Bronze Age at Mallia had fixed hearths and Pierre Demargne has argued that the practice was not abandoned till that time, that is, till after 2000 B.C.

Fig. 5. Late Neolithic house, Magasa

At Magasa in the very east there was a small but well-built house of the type that the Scots term 'but-and-ben', with a fairly large square room opening out of a small outer room, and also a rock shelter roughly walled in front (Fig. 5). The latter was doubtless a shepherd's hut like many still used by the upland shepherds, but the former, to judge by the number of stone

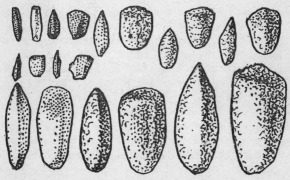

Fig. 6. Late Neolithic axes from Magasa

axes found there, may well have belonged to an artisan who made such tools and was living near his raw materials (Fig. 6).

Cave dwellings and rock shelters of the same period have been found, but are few in number and widely scattered, and were inhabited mainly, I suppose, by shepherds and hunters. One such cave at

Trapeza on the edge of the Lasithi plain was later in the Early Minoan period used as a burial pit. Another cave shelter of the Late Neolithic period was excavated at Miamou[1] in the long fertile valley connecting the Mesara plain with the bay of Lebena, and a third on the far west at Koumaro, where some of the bowls with scalloped or inverted rims recall Late Neolithic types on the mainland. Neolithic sherds have also been recorded from caves at Zakros, Sphoungaras, Skalais, and Hagia Photia in the east, at Mallia and Amnisos on the north coast, at Phaistos, Hagia Triada, and Gortyn in the Mesara, and at another cave on the island of Gavdhos. S. Alexiou excavated part of a Late Neolithic settlement at Katsaba just east of Herakleion.

In addition stone axes (mostly of local stones) have been picked up at various places, but some of these may have belonged to the Early Minoan period. The pottery of the Late Neolithic period has been discussed in detail by Dr Furness. The coarse ware consists chiefly of what she calls 'red wiped ware', and is no longer black grey in colour but usually fired an even brick-red right through, implying the use of a potter's oven. The pottery was less pervious now because of the better firing, so the burnishing of the surface was not necessary and the surface was simply rubbed with a cloth or brush leaving striations clearly visible.

The funnel-necked jars became more common, but the large bowls and stone jars were still normal, and (as in the earlier periods) there is still nothing we can identify as a cooking pot. Roasting and baking may have been done in the embers; but did the Neolithic Cretans never want to boil water or milk, or did they employ 'pot-boilers' for this purpose, as was done in more northerly parts? 'Wiped pottery' like that at Knosos has also been found in other parts of Crete, for example at Trapeza in Lasithi, where it persists as a sub-Neolithic fabric into the Early Minoan period, and constitutes the variety first identified and dubbed 'Trapeza ware' by Pendlebury. The shapes are chiefly large bowls and store jars; large strap handles are normal, but the wishbone type has vanished.

On the fine pottery of this period rippling almost died out. The fabric still resembles that of the fine pottery in the earlier periods, but the improved firing produced a chestnut brown, deep red, or wine colour beneath the surface burnish. Individual sherds may be buff

1. But S. Alexiou considers this to have been only a burial cave; see p. 138.

or light brown or have a red-flashed rim, but the genuine rainbow mottling of the early period was now rare, and the walls of the vases were usually thinner than those of the preceding periods. Spouts appear for the first time, including a bridged form which may be the ancestor of the bridged spouts so popular in the Middle Minoan period. Miniature vases continued to be common and so we find miniature token handles degenerating into incised dots and dashes with or without a small pinched knob.

At Phaistos some miniature vases of this type were discovered together with a clay figure of the squatting steatopygous type, a lump of magnetic iron, and a number of sea shells reminding us of shrines of Minoan date with figures and votive vases and shells; and we may therefore probably regard the deposit as the furniture of a small domestic shrine of the Late Neolithic period.

Incised decoration became less common on the fine ware and also less regular in form. Excised triangles appear occasionally, as in some of the earliest Bronze Age pottery of the Cyclades and the Greek mainland. There are various indications of foreign contacts, implying that the Bronze Age is near. Pierced stone maces like those of Mesopotamia appear for the first time in Crete, though they are still bored by hammering from both sides, not by the straight tubular drill employed during the Bronze Age. The most significant of the new foreign contacts is with Egypt. The late Neolithic levels at Knosos have provided an almost carinated macehead, a small limestone vase hollowed out with a tubular drill, and fragments of stone vases too small to identify but made of the variegated stones which tended to die out in Egypt at the end of the Pre-Dynastic period, all probably actual imports from Egypt.

For the excavations of 1957–60 see J. P. Evans, 'Excavations in the Neolithic settlement at Knossos', Part I (*British School Annual*, 1964), recording different techniques of building, intermural burials of children, evidence of weaving, samples of hexaploid wheat, emmer and barley, and a wealth of previously unknown pottery forms.

PLASTIC ART

The people of Crete in prehistoric times never developed monumental sculpture, but they displayed great skill in modelling and carving on a miniature scale. Even in the Early Neolithic I period we find examples of clay statuettes in the form of squatting female figures or of animals. The fragments are too scanty to identify the animals, but if we may judge by later examples they would be the ordinary animals of the farm – cows, sheep, and dogs. The human figurines of the Middle Neolithic period are still all squatting females with the development of the lumbar region and the thighs so large that Evans, followed by Weinberg, called them steatopygous, a technical description of the abnormal development to be found in certain African tribes such as the Hottentots. This impression of steatopygy is given not only by Cretan Neolithic figurines, but also by others of Neolithic date from the mainland of Greece and from Early Bronze Age tombs in the Cyclades. The racial implications of this interpretation, however, are so serious and so strange that I am inclined to follow Hogarth in believing that most of these figurines were intended simply to represent very fat women.[1] Even today the Greeks are apt to equate plumpness with health and vigour, and their ordinary word for thin means powerless. Some of these figurines were relatively naturalistic. The body was modelled with some care, with the breasts, stomach, and rump carefully distinguished, though the heads were often treated much more summarily as a mere cruciform appendage of the body.

Other examples are more schematic in form, though this is perhaps due to clumsiness of execution rather than to deliberate stylization.

Of the naturalistic group of squatting figures the most magnificent specimen, which I would assign to the beginning of the Late Neolithic period, is the splendid figure from Kato Ierapetra now in the Giamalakis collection in Herakleion. It is much larger than any other complete statuette of this period, being 14·5 cm. in height and 9 cm. broad at the base. The figure squats with the left leg crossed over the right, providing the clue to what must have been the posture intended

1. D. G. Hogarth in *Essays in Aegean Archaeology*, 1927, p. 55; R. W. Hutchinson, 'Cretan Neolithic Figurines', *Ipek*, 1938, p. 50.

to be represented on so many figurines of a rougher and more schematic kind from various parts of the Levant in prehistoric times, especially that of a large group of figurines, known as the violin-shaped idols, common in Anatolia and the Cyclades but rare in Crete (though one example in clay, incised in the fashion of the contemporary vases, was found in a Middle Neolithic deposit at Knosos). The Giamalkis Figurine in a red fabric coated with a well-burnished grey slip was far more detailed in its execution. The short arms bent at the elbows, the breasts, the long neck, and the head with its flat triangular cap or coiffure are carefully modelled, and the face, with its aquiline nose, slightly modelled mouth, incised eyes, and back hair, is far superior to that of any other figurine preserved from this period. The fingers and toes are indicated by incisions, and the incised lines on the body seem to represent creases of fat.

Many of the Neolithic figurines and fragments from Knosos were not found in any particular stratigraphic context, but one interesting group consisting of two complete figurines and fragments of two others was found in a Late Neolithic house at Knosos. It is to be remarked that among the examples surviving there are no monsters like those of Mesopotamia and Egypt, no fabulous or even wild animals, but simply the familiar inhabitants of a Cretan farm, the cow, the goat, the dog, and the dove; whether these figurines were intended to be dedications or simply toys we know not, but they were as naturalistic as the potter was able to make them.

The purpose of the female figurines is also open to question. Evans saw in them evidence of the cult of the great mother goddess of Asia Minor; Hogarth saw the figures as similar to the Ushabtis of Egypt, intended to secure the comfort of the owner in the next world. Hogarth's explanation might serve for figurines of the Cycladic type found in tombs, but Cretan Neolithic figurines are found in houses. For the excavations of 1957–60, see J. D. Evans, *Excavations in the Neolithic Settlement at Knossos, Part 1*, B.S.A., 1964, p. 100, recording different techniques of building, intra-mural burials of children, evidence of weaving, samples of hexaploid wheat, emmer, and barley, and a wealth of previously unknown pottery forms.

CHAPTER 3

The Cretan Peoples, Languages, and Scripts

SIR WILLIAM RIDGEWAY emphasized long ago the dangers of using the word Minoan as if it had a definite ethnic meaning like the word Greek, and I would like, therefore, to make it plain that if I use the terms Minoan people and language I simply mean the people who lived in Crete during the Bronze Age and the language or languages they spoke. We have evidence that at least one non-Hellenic language was spoken in Crete during the Bronze Age, but we have no right to assume that it was necessarily the only one.

Evans, in agreement with the chief linguistic scholars, stressed the number of apparently non-Hellenic places in Greece, including Crete, and in Asia Minor, ending in -ssos, -ndos, or -nda, and -nthos or -ntha, and remarked that such places had often been great cultural centres in the prehistoric period. From Asia Minor we can quote names such as Halicarnassus, Labraunda, Assos, and Perinthus, from the Cyclades Koressos and Prepesinthos, from the mainland of Greece Corinth, Tiryns (accusative case Tiryntha), Mykalessos, and from Crete itself Knosos, Tylisos, Karnassos, and Pyranthos. Platon has recently suggested that the tendency of modern Cretans to omit 'n' before 'th' may have existed in ancient times, and we may compare place names such as Marathon and Skiathos with plant names such as *marathos* and *aspalathos* or household names such as *kyathos* and *kalathos*.

Blegen and Haley discussed this group of names in an important little paper[1] and came to the conclusion that they had been brought to the mainland of Greece by the people who introduced the Early Helladic culture, the first metal users of the mainland. The natural inference is that the similar names we find in Crete were also intro-

1. J. B. Haley and C. W. Blegen, 'The Coming of the Greeks', *American Journal of Archaeology*, 1928, pp. 141–59 (the former discussing the pre-Greek place-names and the latter the prehistoric remains and other distribution).

duced early in the Bronze Age by a people with a similar language and a similar culture to that of the Early Helladic variety on the mainland and the Early Cycladic in the Cyclades. It is possible, however, that in Crete some of these names might even date back to Neolithic times, since we have reason for assuming an Anatolian element in the Cretan Neolithic civilization.

The ancient Greeks themselves were quite conscious of the fact that, from the earliest times preserved in folklore, Crete had been occupied by various nations of whom more than one had spoken a 'barbarian', that is a non-Greek, language. A celebrated passage in the ninth book of the *Odyssey* alludes to this mixture of nations: 'And one tongue is mixed with another; there are Achaeans therein, and great-hearted Eteo-Cretans, and Kydonians, and Dorians in their three tribes, and divine Pelasgians.'

The only non-Greek speaking people, the only barbarians in the Greek sense of the word, whom we can identify in Homer's passage are the Eteo-Cretans, who maintained their identity and to some extent their language up to Roman times. The Eteo-Cretan city of Praisos in the east of the island continued to be independent until about 140 B.C., when it was wiped out by a coalition of Hierapytna and Itanos.

There still survive a few fragmentary inscriptions from Praisos, and one from Dreros, written in Greek characters, but in an unfamiliar language which must be Eteo-Cretan. Most scholars regard this language as not belonging to the Indo-European group of languages; but the late Professor Conway argued strongly that it was an Indo-European language possibly related to Venetic, and Kretschmer calls it a mixed speech embodying early Anatolian elements related to Lydian in the east and to Tyrrhenian in the west. It seems likely that this Eteo-Cretan language was spoken during the Bronze Age, but was not necessarily the only language spoken in Crete in those times. The island of Karpathos, east of Crete, also possessed in classical times a survival of an earlier nation, people known as the Eteo-Karpathioi, but it would be very rash to assume that the Eteo-Cretans and Eteo-Karpathians spoke the same language.

Our doubts concerning the language spoken in the great cities of Knosos and Phaistos during the Early and Middle Bronze Age should be resolved when we can read their earlier inscriptions.

The passage in the *Odyssey* might be a later interpolation since Homer does not allude elsewhere in his poem to the Dorians, who appear to have been in western Macedonia at the time of the Trojan war. Was this an anachronism of Homer or his interpolator, or did a small band of Dorians settle in Crete even before the Trojan war? It is clear at least that the main Dorian settlement of Crete cannot have taken place before the latter part of the eleventh century B.C., and Greek traditions placed it one generation after the Dorian occupation of Sparta. What of Homer's other four nations? The Achaeans of whom Homer sings were certainly the Greek inhabitants of the Peloponnese before the coming of the Dorians. Pelasgian may be interpreted in many ways.[1] The Pelasgians of Herodotus's and Thucydides's histories were a small ethnic group in Lemnos and in two cities in Thrace speaking a 'barbarian' language. Many later writers, however, seem to use the word almost in the sense of pre-Hellenic, and even Herodotus almost uses it in this sense when he speaks of the Athenians having been formerly Pelasgians and of their becoming Hellenized later. We may therefore suppose that the Pelasgians of Crete, whoever they were, probably spoke a non-Hellenic language. The Eteo-Cretans, who claimed to be the original inhabitants, continued to speak a non-Hellenic language in eastern Crete up to Hellenistic times or later. They are usually supposed to be descendants of the Minoan people but they might possibly have been of Cretan Neolithic stock. The Kydonians were obviously the people who lived in and round the city of Kydonia and gave their name to it, but were they Greeks or barbarians? In favour of the latter theory is the fact that the people of Polyrrhenia to the south of them once spoke a barbarian tongue, and that Kydas, the legendary founder of Kydonia, was said to be the son of Minos's daughter Akakallis.

RACIAL CHARACTERISTICS OF THE CRETANS

The father of history, Herodotus of Halicarnassus, defined his conception of nationality as depending on common descent, a common

---

1. The word has been equated with 'Philistines' or with the 'peoples of the sea'; the most ingenious suggestion was that of Walter Leaf, who postulated that it might mean what Welsh meant to a Saxon, namely the neighbouring foreigners.

language, common religious beliefs, and common behaviour. His formula works well enough today, though we might add common economic interests and geographical position, and perhaps unified government. One of these factors alone will not make a nation, but no one is indispensable. England and the U.S.A. are different nations, but Switzerland is emphatically one, despite its three languages and its numerous religious sects.

Was Homer's idea of five nations in Crete true for the pre-historic period, or can we speak of a 'Minoan nation' occupying the whole or most of Crete during the Bronze Age?

Some of the factors required for qualification as a nation were present. Crete was a geographical unity, and though communications between its different valleys were difficult for wheeled traffic, they were easy enough for men and pack animals. The island could be self-supporting and function as an economic unity. We have reason also to believe that certain religious cults were common to various parts of Crete. The most important prerequisites in Herodotus's definition of 'nationality' however, are concerned with a common descent and a common language. Let us examine these in turn.

How far can we speak in Crete of common descent, the first essential according to Herodotus for the formation of a nation? The racial homogeneity of its Neolithic inhabitants must still be a matter of surmise, but it is clear that by the beginning of the Bronze Age the great bulk of the population belonged to what is usually known as the Mediterranean race.[1] The members of this are slender-boned people, of or below medium height, with dark hair and eyes and sallow complexions. Their small skulls are as a rule dolichocephalic or long-headed: that is to say the cranial index, or percentage ratio of the maximum breadth to the maximum length, falls below 75. Such a type is not uncommon round most of the Mediterranean, particularly in southern and central Italy, southern France, the Iberian peninsula, and North Africa. It also occurs in parts of Crete such as Lasithi. The majority of modern Cretans, however, are in the meso-cephalic or medium-headed category, which has cranial indices ranging from 75·0 to 79·9, while most mainland Greeks are today brachycephalic or broad-headed, with indices of or above 80. These

1. A. Sergi, *The Mediterranean Race*, 1901.

conventional limits for dolichocephaly, mesocephaly, and brachycephaly are two units higher when measurements are taken on living subjects as opposed to skulls.

Early in the Bronze Age a second racial element, the Tauric ('Armenoid'), began to enter Crete. This was taller than the Mediterranean and was brachycephalic. In Greece and the adjacent islands broad-headed people are known from Neolithic times. Early Bronze Age human remains from the Cyclades suggest varying degrees of intermixture between the Tauric, broad-headed type and Mediterranean, long-headed. Thus, while skulls from Syros were on the whole long-headed with a few broad-headed individuals, the opposite situation was found in those from Paros, Oliaros (Antiparos), and Siphnos, and mesocephaly characterized those from Naxos.

Anthropological research into the racial history of Crete has been hampered by both the scarcity and also the bad state of preservation of remains from most of the earlier periods. For example, the Neolithic burials at Magasa Skaphidia in the east, at Koumarospilio in the west, and at Miamou off the Mesara, are too fragmentary to furnish evidence of physical type, possibly having been disturbed by the nature of the funeral sacrifices as suggested by Alexiou. Since women are shorter in height and broader in the skull than men, large series of well-dated skulls and other bones to which a probable sex can be assigned are necessary for any sound conclusion. The only material approaching such requirements so far available is that from British excavations in eastern Crete in 1901, 1902, and 1903, first studied by Sir Walter Boyd Dawkins, C. S. Myers, and W. L. H. Duckworth, and later in part by A. Mosso, F. von Luschan, and J. C. Trevor, and the skeletons which Hood excavated on the Aylias hill at Knosos between 1950 and 1955, studied but not yet published by Trevor, assisted by B. G. Campbell.[1]

According to Trevor, who has recently analysed Duckworth's detailed measurements, Early Minoan I long bones from a rockshelter at Hagios Nikolaos and the Patema ossuary, sufficiently intact for the statures of their owners to be determined, probably represented twenty-four persons, fifteen males and nine females. The estimated height of the males is rather short – 162·7 cm. or 5 ft 4 ins. The Hagios Nikolaos bones previously described as being of pygmy

1. Mr Hood has kindly allowed me to refer to this unpublished evidence.

dimensions seem all to have belonged to women. An Early Neolithic I series of sixteen skulls of adults from the same two sites, together with Boyd Dawkins's skull of a woman from the Epano Zakros cave, has cranial indices of 73·5 for ten supposed males and 74·9 for seven supposed females. No certain broad skulls were included in the figures on which these averages are based, but Duckworth noted that a six-year-old child at Hagios Nikolaos with a premature closure of the sagittal suture had a cranial index of just over 80, and he also omitted the indices of two apparently broad-headed females from his Patema total for that sex because of their unreliable measurements. Early Minoan skulls found elsewhere in Crete are rare. An Early Minoan I or II brain-case from a rock-shelter at Gournia measured by Hawes, was brachycephalic with a cranial index of 81·1. Its dimensions suggest a male sex. Hawes also recorded the index of an unsexed Early Minoan II skull from the large tholos tomb at Hagia Triada as approximately 77·6. Giuseppe Sergi gave indices of 74·4 and 76·2 for two of four more skulls from the same tomb, which are now in the Anthropological Institute of the University of Rome. The third he described as either long-headed or medium-headed, and the fourth as unmeasurable but broad-headed. Trevor, who examined the Hagia Triada skulls in Rome in 1955, considers that Sergi's Early Minoan II specimens are all male.

Hawes's index for an Early Minoan III skull excavated by Xanthoudides at Koumasa is 76·2. This would seem to be the same as the specimen which Max Kiessling has previously described as dolichocephalic and for which Mosso afterwards published an indicial value of 75·8. A photograph suggests that it is likely to have belonged to a male. The average cranial index of five skulls from Xanthoudides's other Mesara tombs, probably not earlier than Early Minoan III or later than Middle Minoan II, falls as low as 72·4, without distinction of sex. Though difficult to interpret for the period as a whole, the craniological data do indicate that, while the Early Minoan period was marked by a predominance of long skulls, a broad-headed minority was also present in Crete as far back as Early Minoan II if not Early Minoan I times. One Early Minoan I Patema man had an index of 79·7, which is on the verge of our broad-skulled proportions, and that of a Hagios Nikolaos woman reached 79·0.

After the exclusion of specimens distorted by earth-pressure, the

Middle Minoan I and II skulls from the two Roussolakkos ossuaries at Palaikastro yield cranial indices of 73·1 for thirty-eight males and 74·0 for fourteen females. Three males and one female are broad-headed. The few Roussolakkos limb-bones of which Duckworth was able to measure the lengths seem to have belonged to six men and three women, the estimated stature of the men being about 166·6 cm. or 5 ft 5½ ins. This apparent increase of height since Early Minoan times is confirmed by the average Trevor has found for eighteen Middle Minoan II and III males from the Aylias hill burials at Knosos, namely 167·9 cm. or 5 ft 6 ins., a value slightly below the figure of 168·5 cm. or almost 5 ft 6½ ins. obtained by D. F. Roberts from Hawes's measurements of nearly 2000 living Cretan men during the first decade of the present century. The cranial indices of the Aylias hill Middle Minoan II and III skulls studied in 1955 are 74·0 for twenty-nine males and 76·2 for eighteen females. Five of these Knosos males and three females are broad-skulled, as is another male skull excavated by Platon at Poros, near Herakleion, and accurately dated to Middle Minoan III B, a female specimen of the same date from this site being medium-headed.

Late Minoan skulls appear to number fewer than twenty, of which about a third can be sexed. Hawes gave an average cranial index for five unsexed specimens of Late Minoan I date from Gournia as 76·5. For two of four Late Minoan II or III crania from the chambered tombs at Hagia Triada, now in Rome, Giuseppe Sergi provided indices of 73·4 and 77·2. One other he stated to be long-headed and the last doubtfully broad-headed. Trevor regards them as those of males but believes that they are too fragmentary or distorted for anything but their general form to be determined. Hawes's statement that the average index of seven Late Minoan III skulls from various sites, none long-skulled but three medium and four broad-headed, is 79·1 does not agree with that calculated from his individual indices for specimens of this data in works published by him, namely a female from the rock-shelter at Aisa Langadha near Gournia, 80·2, and six unsexed skulls, four from Sphoungaras also near Gournia, 77·0, 79·0, 80·3, and 87·6, one from Sarandari, 75·9, and one from a hillside tomb near Knosos, 80·5. With the addition to these of Trevor's value of 72·4 for a male skull, part of an almost complete skeleton excavated by Platon and Huxley at Selopoulo in the Kairatos valley in August

1957 and dated to Late Minoan III B, the Late Minoan average for both sexes combined becomes as high as 79·6.

Tables purporting to show the percentages of various skull-forms for different periods may be misleading where the series are small and have not been sexed. Of the Middle Minoan I and II males from Palaikastro, 71 per cent are long-headed, 21 per cent medium, and 8 per cent broad-headed, while of the Aylias hill Middle Minoan II and III males from Knosos 49 per cent are long-headed, 34 per cent medium, and 17 per cent broad-skulled. If the scanty Late Minoan I evidence points to a mesocephalic trend, which perhaps continued through Late Minoan II, the all but brachycephalic average of the Late Minoan III skulls suggests more than a gradual secular change, in fact the arrival of a new element in the population. Whence did this come? Hawes believed that the modern broad-headed inhabitants of western Crete could be regarded as survivors of the Dorian invaders, and both he and von Luschan agreed that the later Saracens, Venetians, and Turks were unlikely to have had much influence on already established physical types. Since four of the eight late Middle Minoan III skulls belonged to people who were brachycephals, the cultural associations of a broad-headed strain entering Crete at this time would appear to have been Achaean rather than Dorian.

It seems, therefore, even on anthropological grounds that an Anatolian element may well have existed in Crete since Neolithic times. It is true that the squatting Neolithic ladies of Crete can be paralleled by the steatopygous squatting or lying figures of prehistoric Malta, but the parallel must not be pressed too far, since Malta occupied a marginal position in the Mediterranean, partly but never completely isolated, and with cultural connexions with both the western and the eastern Mediterranean. Weinberg is surely right in saying that if we are to seek outside the Aegean for an origin of the seated figurines with legs doubled under them, we must look towards Asia Minor and Syria, and perhaps farther east to northern Mesopotamia or even Iran, and he quotes the figurines from Adalia and Amuq to support this statement.

Did these immigrants from Anatolia come via Syria or did they come down one or other of the series of valleys opening into the Gulf of Iskanderun, a route which might be expected also to bring influences from Mesopotamia? Or if the immigrants came from the Afyon

Karahisar district, did they leave Asia Minor from the Gulf of Adalia or from the coast opposite Rhodes?

This south-western district of Asia Minor is marked by a considerable number of the place names ending in -ssos, -ndos, and -nda which we have noted in Greece and believed to indicate Anatolian influences. This brings us to the second factor demanded by Herodotus in the formation of a nation, the common language.

LANGUAGES AND SCRIPTS

What evidence have we from engraved seals and inscriptions of the languages spoken in Crete during the Bronze Age before the coming of the Mycenaean Greeks?

The rare seals with pictographic designs attributed to the Early Minoan I period are abnormal and not very accurately dated. It is not until the Early Minoan II period that we begin to find engraved seals in stratified deposits at Mochlos and Sphoungaras.

The designs of these seals have an Egyptian air and suggest that they were simply monomarks, signs of ownership, and had no particular hieroglyphic significance. It was, however, from seals of this kind that the Cretans began in the third Early Minoan period to develop a native hieroglyphic script which borrowed some symbols from Egypt but was in the main an independent growth. Many seals of this period, however, still have only one design, the monomark of the owner.

In the Middle Minoan I period, however, we find numerous seals with hieroglyphic inscriptions of several symbols, usually in the form of rather long triangular prisms, or, more rarely, four-sided seals cut in a soft stone, usually steatite. Thus, of a series of forty-nine such seals from the Giamalakis collection recently published by Mme Agni Xenaki-Sakellariou, forty-three were triangular prisms and only six four-sided.

Evans enumerated ninety-one signs in this script, which he termed Hieroglyphic Script A, and distinguished from a later development of it which he termed Hieroglyphic Script B. In both scripts together he identified a hundred and thirty-five signs, of which forty-four signs were peculiar to B, forty-two signs peculiar to A, and the remainder common to both scripts.

The hieroglyphs of class A were pictures easily recognized: a man walking, a man sitting, a ship, an eye, two crossed hands, a jug, a gate, a sistrum (an Egyptian form of rattle), the head of an ox or an ass, an arrow, or a plough. Sometimes we can even recognize animals no longer existing in Crete, such as the wolf and the horned sheep. The representations of ships, though summary, are interesting since they obviously depict sea-going vessels rigged like the Egyptian and Phoenician ships with a great square sail in the centre but, unlike the Egyptian, with an asymmetric hull with high prow at an angle of about 45° but with a low projecting stern. (See Chapter 4.)

Sundwall believed that most of the Cretan hieroglyphs had been derived from Egyptian prototypes and quoted parallels in Egypt for forty-four Cretan hieroglyphs and for nine symbols of the later Linear Script A. Evans, followed by Hall, while admitting that certain symbols were derived from Egypt, considered that the majority were Cretan inventions. The A hieroglyphs were usually executed as silhouettes, though sometimes internal details were carefully rendered; but those of Script B or 'the developed hieroglyphic script', as it is often called, were executed in a more summary fashion, in outlines, already suggesting that a conventionalized linear script would develop out of the old hieroglyphs.

At Knosos the seals with hieroglyphs of class B began in the second Middle Minoan period, and appeared in the following forms: (a) prism seals with three (or more rarely four) sides; (b) round seals with convoluted upper surface; (c) flattened cylinder seals; (d) signets, usually with loop handle for suspension, a form popular among the Hittites of Asia Minor; and (e) lentoid seals. These shapes continue with minor modifications into the third Middle Minoan period, the Middle Minoan II B and III seals being distinguished by increased naturalism of design and often by exquisite cutting, when the stone was hard enough to deserve it. Even many of the steatite seals are finely cut, but the best work usually appears on agates, rock crystals, jasper, and the like.

On the clay inscriptions, however, the designs were becoming less naturalistic and more schematic, a sure sign that they were in many instances ceasing to have ideographic value and were coming to represent sounds, so that the script was developing into a syllabary.

Many of the hieroglyphs shed a light on the culture of the time. The sacred double axe which gave its name to the labyrinth at

Knosos appears also as a hieroglyph and so does the Egyptian hieroglyph for palace.

Another hieroglyph shows a plough with stilt, pole, and share beam (the latter two probably in one piece, as recommended by Hesiod), exactly the same as the one depicted on some early Roman coins of Knosos, and not differing greatly from some ploughs still in use today (Fig. 44).

The clay inscriptions may occur in the following forms: (a) stamped on clay sealings of jars; (b) on clay labels shaped like a cockle shell with a suspension hole at the top; (c) on clay bars with a square section often with a suspension hole at one end; or (d) on clay tablets of oblong form. Occasionally the script appears on other objects such as a stone vase or a double axe. The most remarkable instance is a very well-cut line of hieroglyphs of class B on a rough boulder found just outside the Palace at Mallia, conceivably a boundary stone (Fig. 7).

Fig. 7. Hieroglyphic inscription, Mallia

The Phaistos Disk

This hieroglyphic script was succeeded at Knosos about 1700, and at an earlier date at Phaistos, by a Linear Script developed from it, which we know by the name assigned to it by Evans – Linear Script A. But before we discuss the Linear Script we must mention a hieroglyphic inscription of a different kind known as 'the Phaistos disk' (Plate 14b), a roughly circular disk of clay impressed on both sides before baking with a hieroglyphic text. It was discovered in a rectangular clay compartment in a room in the north east part of the Palace at Phaistos containing some Middle Minoan III B vases and also a tablet in Linear Script A. Professor Pernier, who published it, compared the fine clay to that of Kamares pottery, and thought that the hieroglyphics, though differing from the normal Cretan forms, might still represent a stage in their development. Mackenzie, however, thought the clay was foreign and Evans considered it might have been manufactured in south-west Asia Minor, stressing the parallels between the hieroglyph of the plumed head with the representations of Philistines on Egyptian monuments, and of the hieroglyph showing a wooden house with Lycian rock-cut tombs imitating wooden structures. The repetition of certain phrases he thought might indicate a metrical refrain, perhaps a hymn to the great goddess who was worshipped alike in Crete and in Asia Minor. He thought that the inscription started at the centre. It was clearly divided into words, but there were some slanting lines of which the significance was open to question (Plate 14b and Fig. 8).

The late Professor Macalister considered that the inscription started at the circumference. He also thought that the succession of words beginning with a plumed head were names of men, and that the large proportions of personal names indicated that the disk was not a hymn, but more probably a legal document with the names of the presiding magistrates, the witnesses, and the date. He proceeded in a less convincing manner to suggest that some of these symbols might have developed into the ordinary Phoenician letters of the tenth century B.C.

Two bold but unconvincing attempts were made in 1931 to translate the disk, by Miss F. M. Stawell, who rendered it as a hymn to Rhea in Greek, and by Mr F. G. Gordon, who translated it into Basque as a hymn to the 'rain lord', whom he identified with the constellation Aquarius.

There are 241 signs in all, arranged in a spiral on the two faces of the disk, and 61 sign groups, separated at irregular intervals by vertical lines which presumably represent the ends of words. The individual symbols are for the most part easily recognizable figures or objects. There are however only forty-five different signs, not too many for a syllabary, but is it foreign or does it come from another part of Crete?

Pernier, supported by Pugliese Carratelli, counted the disk as Cretan, and the latter scholar has remarked on the resemblance of certain signs to symbols on the Arkalochori axe and the stone block from Mallia.

Myres, Pendlebury, and Bossert all followed Evans in regarding the disk as an import from Anatolia. Dow's objection, that the

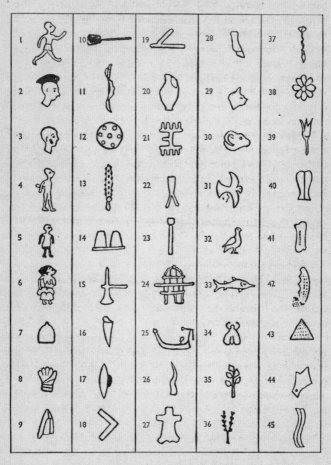

Fig. 8. Signs from the Phaistos Disk

disk was a fragile object to be exported so far, seems weak. Actually the disk is rather a solid object, much more so than the Kamares cups exported from Crete to Byblos and Ugarit, and it was probably an isolated gift or piece of plunder, not the Minoan equivalent of 'a present from Blackpool'. Different scripts of a pictographic character might have existed simultaneously in Crete. The solid argument, however, for assuming that the disk was of foreign manufacture lies in the presence of such exotic symbols as the Lycian house on piles, the lady with the very un-Minoan attire and figure, and the man with the feathered headdress.

At Phaistos an inscription in such an undeveloped syllabary was an anachronism in the seventeenth century B.C., since Levi's recent excavations have now revealed to us the surprising fact that the script we know as Linear Script A was already forming there, perhaps a couple of hundred years before the disk was placed there, and long before Script A was in use at Knosos.

The late Dr Paul Kretschmer discussed the punctuation of the Phaistos disk, and its relationship, if any, to the punctuation used in Etrusco-Venetic and late Greek inscriptions in diphthongs on the one hand, and the dots employed to modify consonants in Phoenician and other Semitic scripts on the other.

Marinatos has suggested that the late survival of hieroglyphs in Crete, such as those of the Arkalochori axe, the Mallia stone, and the Phaistos disk, might be explained by their use as a sacred script (as happened in Egypt) long after linear characters had been employed for secular purposes. This might be true of the axe and the stone in question, but the Anatolian features of the disk require more explanation. Who were the people with the feathered headdress whom Kretschmer connected with the Illyrians and with the Venetic name Fremaistina? (We may recall Conway's parallels between the Venetic and Eteo-Cretan languages.)[1] A feather headdress of this kind was worn by some of the peoples who joined the sea raid on Egypt in 1223 B.C., not only by the Philistines, but also by the Zakkarai and the Danuna. In classical times this headdress was regarded as so characteristic of the Carians of western Asia Minor that the Persians called them *Karka* (cocks),

1. P. Kretschmer, *Minos*, op. cit.; R. J. Conway, *Annual of the British School at Athens*, 1902, p. 125.

which is presumably the meaning of the word 'Carian'. Kretsch-mer also identified one of the signs on the Phaistos disk as the Carian round shield with the central handgrip which, according to Herodotus, was one of the military innovations of the Carians along with helmet crests and blazons on their shields. Herodotus also states in the same passage that the Carians, then termed Leleges, were subject to Minos, paying no tribute but providing feudal levies for his navy. Since the group of helmet and shield occurs thirteen times on the Phaistos disk, Kretschmer suggested that we have the names of thirteen soldiers, that Evans's suggestion that the disk was in a metrical form is therefore unlikely, but that it might be a Carian document. The later Carian script of the seventh and sixth centuries B.C. was partly syllabic, partly vocalized, and also had a slanting line dividing the words.

This mingling of Carian and Phoenician fashions of writing might have taken place in some Ionian colony such as Miletus, which claimed to have been founded by Cretans from Milatos before it received its Ionian settlers, and Kretschmer remarks that Priene once bore the name Kadme and claimed to have been founded by pre-Boeotian Cadmeans from Boeotia.

Linear Script A

By 1600 B.C., however, Linear Script A must have been employed by the priestly scribes at least over a large part of Crete, though older systems lingered in some parts and the mass of the population were probably illiterate. The list of sites where inscriptions in this script have been found as given by Pugliese Carratelli contained 219 inscriptions of which 186 texts and 86 scalings were found at Hagia Triada. To these must be added the Linear Script A inscriptions recently found at Phaistos. The inscription on the door jamb of the Tholos tomb 1 opened at Knosos in 1938 must be classified as Linear Script A. It should be remarked that tablets in Script A (Fig. 9) are very rare except at Hagia Triada, most of the other writing in Script A being in the form of short dedications on steatite lamps or libation tables.

The most westerly example was the inscription on a fragment of a steatite vase picked up by Pendlebury in the ruins of a Middle Minoan 111 house later excavated by Marinatos at Apodhoulou.

The Cypriot syllabary of classical times shows a number of symbols identical, or almost identical, with those of Linear B and some, such as those for ro, se, pa, na, and ti, have the same phonetic values while the Cypriot sign for tu corresponds to Linear B da and Cypriot po to Linear B po or ro.

The recent excavations of Levi at Phaistos, however, have completely upset the tidy evolution of Minoan scripts presented by Evans. In a general sense Evans's theory may still be defended as sound: probably hieroglyphic B did develop from A, and Linear A did develop from hieroglyphic B, but there was more overlapping of the systems than we dreamed of a few years ago. We can no longer say that the Cretans only employed hieroglyphic writing till the end of the Middle Minoan II period and that Linear Script A was invented in the Middle Minoan III A period.

At Phaistos Levi found clay tablets and labels with symbols in transitions to Linear Script A in the earliest deposits of rooms LI and XXVIII, suggesting that that script must have been in use there before 1850 B.C. at the latest.

The natural inference is that Linear Script A was an invention of the Palace scribes at Phaistos and was not in general use in northern Crete till a hundred, perhaps a hundred and fifty, years later. The objection to this very obvious theory, the scarcity of tablets in this script at Phaistos, is weaker than it appears to be. The presence of so many Linear Script B tablets at Knosos and Pylos is perhaps simply due to their being accidentally baked in a palace fire, and where no such conflagration took place the disintegration of such tablets was likely to be rapid.

Fig. 9. Linear A tablet

If Knosos lagged behind Phaistos in the adoption of Linear Script A it appears that Mallia lagged further and was still employing the later hieroglyphic system in Middle Minoan III A, but with numerals adopted from the Linear Script A then current at Knosos. The inhabitants of Mallia did finally adopt Linear Script A in the Middle Minoan III B period and continued to use it during the Late Minoan

II period, but betrayed some influence from Linear Script B in that they used long thin tablets instead of the almost square tablets we associate with Linear Script A elsewhere. Indeed three of the Linear Script A tablets from Mallia were found in a deposit dated to the Late Minoan III period, so that the use of this script would appear to have continued on to the fourteenth century B.C. if not later.

The existing tablets seem to consist almost entirely of business documents or accounts. Many tablets begin with a single sign group, probably denoting the principal person concerned, followed by one termed 'the transaction sign', indicating the nature of the business, and by a series of signs followed by numbers, indicating either individual commodities in a single consignment or individual contributions (whether of persons or places) to a single transaction, referred to as the subsidiaries. The whole list may be followed by a total sign group followed by a numeral.

Myres quotes some Babylonian wage tablets as a parallel, though on these the name of 'the principal' and his errand come last. It is unfortunate that our only surviving documents seem to be accounts. Marinatos is probably right in saying that Linear Script A was invented for writing in ink or paint, not on clay,[1] for which the Mesopotamian cuneiform is far more suitable. It cannot be suggested that the Cretans had not thought of cuneiform since they were in regular communication at that time with Byblos and Ras Shamra, where cuneiform writing was normal. Marinatos notes that many of the clay sealings from Crete have traces of thin threads which appear to have been the letters of the papyrus documents to which the seal had been applied, and he remarks that the same signet had been used to seal letters at Sklavokambos in central Crete, at Hagia Triada in the Mesara, and at Gournia and Zakros in the east, implying widespread correspondence between different parts of Crete. The thin threads on the sealings implied that they were affixed to letters, not to heavy packages.[2]

The two surviving inscriptions written in ink on vases Marinatos

1. Clay, of course, is a much cheaper and easier material to obtain, but the use of papyrus seems, as Marinatos suggests, to be implied by the type of the symbols and the thread marks of some of the sealings.

2. S. Marinatos, *Minos*, 1951, p. 39.

would explain as incantations against evil spirits like those on Babylonian bowls.[1]

Fifty-four of the Linear A signs were used also in the Linear B Script, and it is a reasonable though not an inevitable assumption that most of these had the same phonetic values in both scripts. C. H. Gordon has recently used Ventris's transliterations for the Script B symbols (discussed on page 79) to provide a basis for transliterating and even translating Linear Script A. Hagia Triada tablet 31 has pictograms of various vessels with names in the Linear Script A, compared by Gordon to words in the cuneiform texts from Ugarit. Thus he compares Cretan SU-PU and KA-RO-PA to Ugaritic SP and Karpan and Cretan YA-MA-NA to Ugaritic Yaman in a passage referring to a Kaphtorian (Keftiuan) (see p. 108) God of craftsmanship.

Hagia Triada tablet 88 has A-PU followed by a pictogram for MAN + KA and may represent some sort of worker. Gordon cites Ugaritic APY = baker. Similarly A-DU-SI-SI on Hagia Triada 85 he interprets as perhaps = ADON-SISI = owners of horses. Other words he compares to Hebrew and Akkadian forms. Eleven of the nineteen identifications suggested by Gordon are Semitic, four Kaphtorian, three east Mediterranean, and one KU-ZU (compared to Ugaritic KZY = groom) of doubtful derivation.

Gordon concludes: 'While these notes tend to relate the language of Linear A to Semitic it is not my intention to oversimplify a highly complex situation. The east Mediterranean was already Levantinized by Linear A times, so that the interpenetration of cultures in the area had created a considerable east Mediterranean vocabulary that crossed linguistic boundaries. Often enough words in this vocabulary cannot yet be pinned down to any specific linguistic origin.' This solution is plausible but more speculative than that of Ventris.

Linear Script B

At Knosos, but at no other site in Crete, Linear Script A was supplanted about 1450 B.C. by another, which Evans, who first discovered and identified it, christened Linear Script B.[2] This new

---

1. *British Museum Guide to the Babylonian and Assyrian Antiquities*, 1922, pp. 191-4; the examples in the British Museum are Mandäitic, but the practice seems to date back to the late Babylonian times.

2. See note on page 90.

script contained about seventy phonetic signs adopted from the Script A series and dropped another dozen of the A signs, but supplemented these by ten new phonetic signs, and by six or seven rebus signs for more syllables than one, expressed in sign groups, and by new pictorial signs for certain commodities (Fig. 10). Some fifty sign groups resemble Script A groups, but only ten are identical. The question arises: were the two scripts intended to transcribe the same language?

The signs are now always written from left to right, usually on long narrow clay tablets, sometimes termed palm-leaf tablets because of their shape. Occasionally a subsidiary group is written sign by sign between the stems of the principal signs, either to save space or perhaps to amplify or remedy an omission.

In the second volume of *Scripta Minoa* Myres suggested that 'the larger number of signs in Script B does not indicate a different language but rather a more refined distinction between sounds; it is the converse of the presumed development of the late Cypriot script from Minoan writing by elimination of similar signs for labials, gutturals, and so forth.' The total number of phonetic signs in Script B may be as high as ninety-one, but one of these is doubtful and some others may be variants of rare signs.

In *Scripta Minoa*, 1722 texts in Linear Script B were enumerated by Evans and Myres, and 1000 short ones were added by Bennett, but later joins will doubtless reduce this number. Similarly the tablets found at Pylos in 1939 were reported as 621 but later reduced by joins to 566. In 1952 another 352 tablets were reported from Pylos and thirty-eight tablets and one inscribed vase from Mycenae. Bennett reckoned that at least thirty scribes had been employed at Pylos and at least six on the Mycenaean tablets.

Up to 1950 most scholars had believed Linear Scripts A and B to have been written in the same language, a pre-Hellenic one, but after Blegen's discovery (see page 85) it became obvious that there was at least a possibility that Linear Script B was a Greek script, since it had only been found in one part of Crete, whereas it had been found at several sites on the mainland. Knosos, however, was still the site with the greatest number of tablets, and appeared to have used the script over a hundred years before the mainland.

All scholars agreed that the number of signs in Linear Script B was too few for them to be purely ideographic and too numerous to be purely alphabetic, and that it was therefore probably a largely syllabic alphabet, without precluding the idea of certain signs having ideographic values.

Various attempts were made to translate Script B texts into Greek (Miss Stawell, Persson, and Mylonas) or Basque (F. G. Gordon) or to a purely imaginary Anatolian language by Hrozny, but none of these was convincing. A more recent attempt by B. G. Nuño to relate the Cretan texts to the Hurrian language is also unconvincing.

The general statement by Myres has, however, to be reviewed in relation to the recent finds from Pylos and Mycenae, of which the latter came too late even to be referred to in *Scripta Minoa* Vol. II, and the former, though mentioned, had not been adequately studied in relation to the researches of Ventris and other scholars.[1]

The Knosian tablets were examined and classified by their discoverer Evans who refrained from any attempt at translation, but whose monumental work in *Scripta Minoa* Vol. I laid a sure foundation for future research. The second volume dealing with Linear Script B was edited and produced after his death by Sir John Myres with such loving care and loyalty to his friend that his own very considerable share in the work is largely obscured. Much independent work on Linear Script B has also been carried out by other scholars such as Sundwall, Alice Kober, Emmett Bennett, Ventris, and Chadwick, and the whole outlook with regard to this script was changed by Blegen's discovery at Pylos in Messenia of a large hoard of Script B tablets followed later by Wace's discovery of other tablets at Mycenae, and by Ventris's work on the Linear B Script.

Bennett classified the Pylos tablets as follows:

Signs used in sign groups Probably chiefly phonetic and perhaps syllabic signs, though some might be determinatives of ideograms. The sign groups presumably represent names or other words.

Ideographic signs Always associated with numbers, and so representing the things numbered or measured.

1. See the bibliography compiled by M. Ventris and J. Chadwick, *Documents in Mycenaean Greek*, p. 428.

Numerals, punctuations, and other marks The numerals had already been identified by Evans.

The repertory of the signs on the Pylos tablets is very nearly the same as that of the Script B tablets at Knosos, so that there can be no reasonable doubt that they were written in the same language.

Ventris's Solution of the Linear B Script

The first real step towards the decipherment of Linear Script B was provided by Dr Alice Kober who compared a series of triplets differing only in their final syllables and which she believed to be evidence of declension of nouns.

Ventris started his analysis of the tablets on the following assumptions: (*a*) most of the tablets were inventories, receipts, or accounts; (*b*) the commodities were listed by ideograms following names, words, and sentences written phonetically; (*c*) the commodities or persons could be recognized by their ideograms (men, women, chariots, wheels, etc.), or by their grouping (horses, cattle, etc.), or by the way they were measured; (*d*) there are eighty-eight linear signs in Script B at Knosos and many recur with little variation at Pylos and Mycenae, and also probably at Thebes[1] and other mainland sites; (*e*) the signs were from a syllabary similar in principle to that used later in Cyprus; (*f*) signs can be classified as frequent, average, or infrequent and sometimes as predominantly initial or final; (*g*) the language is identical in all inscriptions of Linear Script B and shows inflexion for two genders, three cases, and two numbers of the noun and adjective; (*h*) many words exhibit a vowel variation in the last syllable.

A comparison of individual sign groups suggested that they might be grouped into: (*a*) place-names and names of buildings or departments; (*b*) personal names of men and women; (*c*) names of trades and professions; (*d*) general words describing commodities and their circumstances. One syllabic sign attached to the second word in a pair appeared to mean 'and' and to correspond to the Greek enclitic -*te* or the Latin -*que*, and was transliterated by Ventris first as -*te* and later as -*qe*. This, preceded by another syllable, also appeared in

1. Linear B tablets have recently been found in the Greek excavations at Thebes.

pairs with different words and presumably meant 'either' and 'or' or alternatively 'neither' and 'nor'. Ventris transliterated the latter words as '*ouqe*' – '*ouqe*'.

The syllable for '*to*' had been suggested by Evans when he identified the word that meant 'total' and Cowley had suggested the symbol for '*go*' when he identified the words for 'boy' and 'girl'. There were other couplets also which varied only in their last syllable and probably represented masculine and feminine forms of the same word. The syllabic symbol for '*a*' based on its relative frequency as an initial, had been suggested by Ktistopoulos and Dr Kober.

With the aid of these few symbols, Ventris proceeded to transliterate Dr Kober's series of triplets into the names of five well-known Cretan cities: Amnisos, Knosos, Tylisos, Phaistos, Lyktos.

A-mi-ni-so   Ko-no-so   Tu-ri-so   Pa-i-to   Ru-ki-to
A-mi-ni-si-yo Ko-no-si-yo Tu-ri-si-yo Pa-i-ti-yo Ru-ki-ti-yo
A-mi-ni-si-ya Ko-no-si-ya Tu-ri-si-ya Pa-i-ti-ya Ru-ki-ti-ya

Even the words quoted above illustrated the symbols for a, ki, ko, mi, ni, no, qe, pa, ri, si, so, ti, to, tu, ya, and yo. The last two are written 'ja' and 'jo' by Ventris, but I have preferred to use 'y' as representing better the normal English pronunciation. Gradually Ventris built up a grid which enabled him to translate most of the documents he tested into an archaic form of Greek which he calls Mycenaean and which resembles in many ways the dialect of the Homeric poems (Fig. 10). The early form of Ventris's grid, prior to the decipherment of the tablets, is given in Fig. 3 of *Documents in Mycenaean Greek* by Ventris and Chadwick.

The case endings of Homeric nouns afforded clues for the identification of certain vowels (provided that the language really was Greek). Thus personal and also professional names, such as *kerameús*, a potter, were apt to end in *-eus* in the nominative singular, *-ei* in the dative singular, *-eos* for an original *ewos* in the genitive singular, and *-eis* (for an original *ewes*) in the nominative plural. Nouns with a nominative in *-os* had a genitive ending in *-oio* (for an original *osyo*).

The final syllables of personal names or those that appeared likely to be descriptions of professions thus provided Ventris with the following syllables, e, we, wo, yo, etc., and it was possible to apply cross-checks: for example, to ascertain whether the symbol used for

WO in KE-RA-ME-WO was the same as that employed in KO-WO, where there were independent reasons for the assumption of the syllabic values. The evidence was cumulative so that even Ventris, most modest and scrupulously conscientious scholar that he was, was impelled to declare 'if the tablets are written in Greek they can hardly be explained otherwise than we have proposed; but if they are not, their language is probably, in the existing circumstances, unknowable'.

Ventris and Chadwick therefore compiled an experimental grid for the syllabic values of the signs, the horizontal lines consisting of the same consonants with different vowels while the vertical lines were comprised of different consonants followed by the same vowel (Fig. 10).

The results seemed most encouraging. The values assigned produced a list of intelligible Greek trade-names and place-names corresponding to famous ancient sites in Crete. To achieve this result, however, Ventris was obliged to formulate certain rules for the operation of his grid and to make the following assumptions:

(1) The syllabary differentiated five vowels A, E, I, O, U, but was indifferent as to their length.

(2) The second component of diphthongs in U was regularly indicated.

(3) The second letter of diphthongs in I was generally omitted except before another vowel and in the initial sign 'ai'. (Where 'i' is added to endings in 'ai' or 'oi' we should probably count the syllables as 'a(h)i' or 'oi(h)i'.)

(4) Vowels following I generally are indicated by the semi-vowel glide, J,[1] those following U by W.[2]

(5) Apart from the semi-consonants J [my Y] and W the syllabary differentiates at least ten consonants D, K, M, N, P, Q, R (=L), S, T, and Z but does not indicate double consonants.

(6) There is no mark for the aspirate nor any differentiation of aspirated consonants.

(7) L, M, N, R, and S are omitted when final or when preceding another consonant.

(8) Initial S and W are apparently omitted before a consonant.

1. The German J which I have translated by Y.
2. Corresponding to the letter digamma (F), which appears in some archaic inscriptions but was gradually eliminated from the classical Greek alphabet.

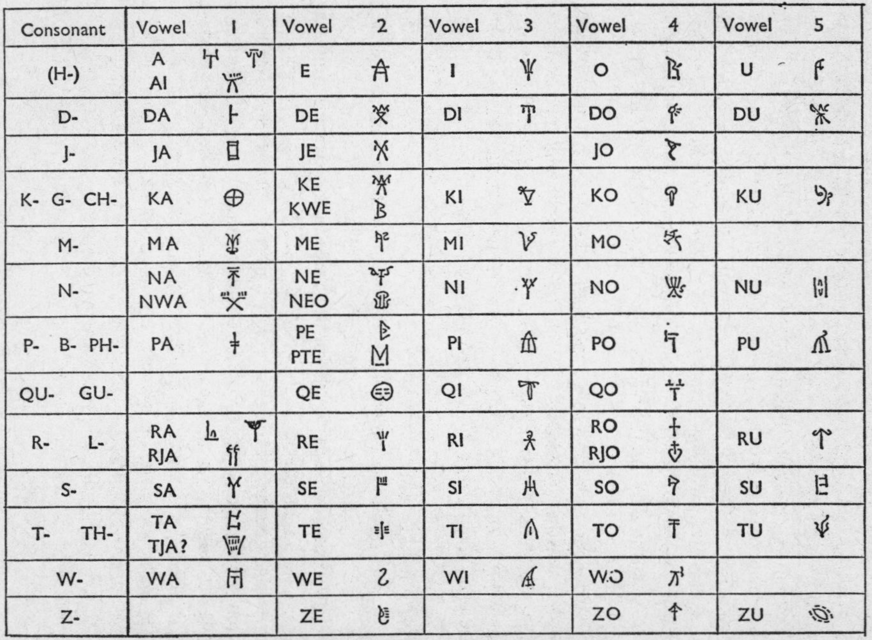

Consonant	Vowel 1	Vowel 2	Vowel 3	Vowel 4	Vowel 5
	A / AI	E	I	O	U
(H-)		E	I	O	U
D-	DA	DE	DI	DO	DU
J-	JA	JE		JO	
K- G- CH-	KA	KE / KWE	KI	KO	KU
M-	MA	ME	MI	MO	
N-	NA / NWA	NE / NEO	NI	NO	NU
P- B- PH-	PA	PE / PTE	PI	PO	PU
QU- GU-		QE	QI	QO	
R- L-	RA / RJA	RE	RI	RO / RJO	RU
S-	SA	SE	SI	SO	SU
T- TH-	TA / TJA?	TE	TI	TO	TU
W-	WA	WE	IWA	CWA	
Z-		ZE		ZO	ZU

Fig. 10. Ventris's grid for Linear B

(9) The consonant group NW is written NU-W; R before W is more often omitted.

(10) All stop consonants which directly precede another consonant are written with the vowel of the succeeding consonant. Thus KU-RU-SO for KHRYSOS.

Now several of these rules seem justified by the nature of a syllabary, and others, such as the equation of L and R, by later Greek usages, but I must confess that I am troubled by rule 7, which allows so many variants and so greatly detracts from the apparent success of Ventris's method in producing so many intelligible Greek words. Thus under Ventris's system the same three letters can be used to transliterate Tokeus and Stoicheus.

Most classical scholars have accepted Ventris's system, though Bennett has been cautious, and even Ventris himself has been far more modest in his claims than some of his supporters. The arguments for and against Ventris's system were summed up by Nicholas Platon in *Kretika Chronika*[1] as follows:

Arguments in Favour of Ventris

A. Recognition of characteristic categories of words.

(1) Place-names in appropriate contexts, including Knosos, Phaistos, Amnisos, Lyktos, and Tylisos on the Knosian tablets, and frequent mention of Pylos on the Pylian tablets.

(2) Recognition of Greek personal names such as Warnataios, Amaryntas, Antanor, Theseus, Eudamos, and names of Hellenic deities.

(3) Names of persons and professions with Greek endings.

(4) Names of materials and manufactured goods.

(5) Special and national epithets both male and female.

(6) Active, middle, and mediopassive participles.

(7) Archaic forms of words.

B. Recognition of characteristic objects.

(1) A tablet from Pylos, published by Blegen, with the words for two tripods and one tripod accompanied by the ideograms, pictures of tripods followed by the figures for two and one, and the same for

1. In a joint review of recent articles by Ventris, Chadwick, and Blegen, in *Kretika Chronika*, April 1954, p. 143.

two-handled cups; also forms apparently meaning vases with four or three lugs or without lugs accompanied by the appropriate ideograms.

(2) A tablet from Pylos referring to rowers going to Pleuron.

(3) A tablet from Pylos enumerating *de-qe-ya*, whatever they may be, and stating whether their fathers and mothers were slaves or not.

(4) A tablet from Pylos referring to coppersmiths in work or un-employed.

(5) Agricultural properties are defined according to what belonged to the people, what to the priestess, and what to the king.

(6) A Pylian text referring to a shepherd grazing sheep on the property of a certain person.

(7) A tablet enumerating payment by different classes for copper for the manufacture of weapons.

(8) A description of chariots and their parts.

(9) A string of names of Greek deities including Hera, Zeus, Hermes, and Poseidon and, best of all, a Knosian text apparently referring to a dedication of honey to Eileithyia in Amnisos.

c. Conclusions concerning the language. The language betrays the proper relationship to the Homeric dialect and to the Arcadian Cypriot dialect that one might expect of the Achaeans at this period, together with a considerable number of pre-Hellenic elements, and is still in an undeveloped state.

D. More general conclusions on the community and the state, its religious and historical inferences. The three chief estates of the realm are king, priests, and people. The professions are more developed and specialized than one might expect, certainly more so than in the Homeric poems.[1] The Achaeans have established a dynasty at Knosos from 1450 B.C. approximately, with Minoan subjects and with free intercourse with the mainland, though there is as yet no evidence for intercourse with foreign powers.

---

1. Ventris's picture of Mycenaean society recalls those of contemporary cultures in the Levant, but the simplification of this society as presented in the Homeric poems is far exceeded by the simplification of Roman life presented in the *Nibelungenlied*.

Arguments against Ventris

A. The relationship of Linear Script B to Linear Script A. Script B has fifty signs, and many combinations, in common with Script A, suggesting that the same names and words existed in both and that they had a common language. If so, and if B is in Greek, then the people in the older palaces of Phaistos and Mallia spoke Greek. (But we do not know for certain that they did not speak Greek in Middle Minoan cities.)

B. The relationships between Cretan and Cypriot scripts. The Cypro-Minoan script is usually derived from the Minoan, and from the former was derived the Cypriot syllabary of classical times. If so, however, it is strange that so few signs of the Cypriot syllabary resemble the Minoan ones with the same sound.[1]

C. Cultural difficulties of accepting Greek as the language of the tablets of Script B. If Greeks were responsible for the Late Minoan II culture how can we explain: (a) the unbroken development of Late Minoan II art from that of Late Minoan I B; (b) the appearance in it of characteristically Cretan elements especially in architecture and religion; (c) the lack of evidence of destruction in 1450, when the Achaeans are supposed to have occupied Knosos, compared with the ample proof of total destruction in 1400 B.C.; (d) the fact that so many towns and flourishing districts in Crete were abandoned in 1500, and that although the other sites continued their Late Minoan I culture till 1400, there are no signs of conflict with the Achaeans at Knosos?

D. Imperfect system of the Script. The system is more ambiguous than any other known in the great centres of civilization. Owing to the omission of so many medial consonants and *iotas* in diphthongs, small words can sometimes be read in about fifteen different ways. If final s, n, and r were regularly omitted in Linear Script B how did they come to be represented in the Cypriot script? The exchange of l or r at such an early date is peculiar.[2]

1. The sounds of the Cypriot syllabary are established by inscriptions written both in the Greek alphabet and in the syllabary; J. F. Daniel (*American Journal of Archaeology*, 1941, p. 249) derived the Cypro-Minoan signs from Linear Script A.

2. Not so peculiar; they are sometimes confused in modern Greek, and Ancient Egyptian used one sign for both sounds.

E. The basis of the arrangement of signs on the grid is unreliable. The grid is based on the arrangement of syllables with the same vowels and different consonants, or with the same consonants but different vowels; but this depends on equations which are unreliable, some of the differences being due perhaps to different words rather than to changes in number or gender.

F. The first recognition of the phonetic values of the syllables pa, ma, re, po, and ro is unreliable. Thus on the tablet Py An 42 the meaning of *dorge-ja* is not clear, and so we cannot trust the *pater*, *mater* interpretation of it, nor can we trust the '*poro = polo =* horse' of the horse tablet Knosos 895, since only two of the horse ideograms have *poro* in front of them. The determined values for syllables are sixty-five and the undetermined twenty-three; moreover the latter include mu and su. (But this is no longer true.)

G. The large number of unintelligible tablets. Platon attempted without success to read eighty tablets for which Ventris had found no satisfactory translation, and found difficulties and ambiguities in others which Ventris had translated. Sponsors of rival systems, such as Hrozny, had also failed to translate many documents.[1] Certain phrases with few syllables and no proper names fail to provide names of objects, though in these instances the possible variants are few.

H. Danger of *petito principi*. We must not enthuse over the number of names ending in *-eus* since it was assumed at first that this ending would be common,[2] nor at names like Knosos and Amnisos, and the same danger exists for 'the four-footed animal' in the 'shepherd' tables.

I. The purely hypothetical character of the list of subjects. The identification of the subjects depends on (*a*) that there is no mistake in the sound values accepted; (*b*) that the transcriptions of the words are those stated (since we have to allow for omissions and corrections); (*c*) whether the new words and strange forms are as suggested by the translator or are errors; (*d*) whether the suggested interpretation can be established by other texts.

1. The previous systems of Hrozny and others, as Platon would admit, are marred by many other defects absent from Ventris's system.
2. But this ending was not assumed from the first.

J. Anomalies of dialect. The dialect, according to Ventris's readings, has some rather strange features: words with an etymology obviously different from that recognized by scholars; late forms; some very improbable words and forms; the absence of the digamma where you might expect it and its unexpected appearance in other words; no difference between the dialects of Pylos and that of Knosos, though the inscriptions of the latter site were two centuries earlier and the site was presumably inhabited by a proletariat speaking a non-Hellenic language.

Platon ends his review with the statement that, while he thinks these objections should be given due weight, he does not wish to belittle the very real achievement of Ventris's work and the hope it gives of a satisfactory translation of the Bronze Age tablets. In a tribute to Ventris written after his death Platon later expressed his conviction that Ventris's system was sound.[1]

In general, scholars agree on the validity of Ventris's system, though the variants permitted by it leave ample room for corrections and amplifications. The most compelling argument is the agreement with the grid values of the sounds implied by the pictograms on the vase tablet (Fig. 11).

It was emphasized by Evans that Minoan documents were likely to be only accounts and business records, and were not likely to give us any literature. This limited literacy devoted to one purpose only has been defined by Dow as 'special literacy'. 'Literacy arrived tightly associated with practical bread and butter. Created for these purposes it was all too adequate for them, writing remained specialized and ossified.' He suggests, however, that this designation may have been a blessing in disguise, that it may have fostered the oral tradition of the heroic lays that led up to the Homeric poems, and have saved the Greeks from the embarrassment of the persistence into classical times of an awkward and inadequate script, such as happened in Cyprus and even in Egypt.

A sober but favourable review of Ventris's work has been given by S. E. Mann,[2] who welcomes the rediscovery of the Mycenaean

1. N. Platon, 'Michael George Francis Ventris', *Kretika Chronika*, 1956, pp. 317–20.

2. S. E. Mann, 'Mycenaean and Indo-European', *Man*, February, 1956, No. 26.

TI RI PO DE · AI KE U · KE RE SI JO · WE KE · QE TO RO WE
τρι πο δε · Αι γευς · κ ρη σι ο · Fεργες · qε το ρο Fεσ
tripod · Aigeus · of Cretan · work · fourhandled

⊙T 𝌆 QE TO
      ? ?

ME ZO E · DI PA
με ζο ε · δε πα
large · cup · 3

TI RI JO WE · DI PA
τ ρι ο Fεσ · δε πα
threehandled · cup · 3

ME WI JO · DI PA
με Fι ο · δε πα
small · cup · 1

ME WI JO · DI PA · A NO WE
με Fι ο · δε πα · aνοϝεσ
small · cup · handleless · 1

TI RI PO DE · E ME · PO DE · OWO WE
τρι πο δε · ε με · πο δε · οϝοϝε
tripod · · foot · threehandled

TI RI PO · DI PA · ME ZO E · TI RI O WE
τρι πος · δε πα · με ζο ε · τ ρι ο Fε ε
tripod · cups · large · threehandled · 2

TI RI PO · KE RE SI JO · WE KE · WE KE A PU KA U ME
τρι πος · κ ρη σι ο · Fεργες · Fεργες α πυ κα υ με
tripod · of Cretan · work · work (burnt?)

KE RE A
σκε λε α
(legs?)'

DI PA · ME WI JO · QE TO RO WE
δε πα · με Fι ο · qε το ρο Fεσ
cup · small · fourhandled · 2

DI PA · ME WI JO · QE TO RO WE
δε πα · με Fι ο · qε το ρο Fεσ
cup · small · fourhandled · 2

Fig. 11. Tripod tablet from Pylos

language in the following early characteristics: (a) the w phoneme; (b) Indo-European ā as in Doric and old Attic; (c) intervocalic yod (like the English 'y'), and (d) the labial triad (π, β, ϕ) as distinct from the labio-velar group (represented by Q).[1] The unfortunate disappearance of so many medial consonants (if the transliterations are accepted) must, he says, be due to the phonetic poverty of the 'Eteo-Cretan' language. I should prefer to say 'pre-Hellenic' myself, since the few Eteo-Cretan inscriptions preserved seem to have almost a superfluity of internal consonants. 'As to the older language,' he continued, 'the values discovered in Linear B ("Mycenaean") have been applied to the older Linear A inscriptions ("Eteo-Cretan" dated tentatively about 1500 B.C.) but the resulting jumble of words cannot be interpreted, and its links, if any, with other Mediterranean languages cannot be established. The Ibero-Caucasian theorists will no doubt study it with interest.'[2] He concludes that, despite the numerous 'pitfalls and ambiguities', 'Mycenaean will in course of time supply the answer to many of our urgent queries'; and in a later review, though criticizing the phonology, states that 'the work of Ventris and his able ally Chadwick rests on virtual certainty'.

A violent attack on the Ventris–Chadwick system has been delivered by A. J. Beattie. It is impossible to do justice here either to his arguments or the contrary arguments, but a brief summary must be given of his position.[3]

He thinks that the degree of conjecture demanded in the formation is higher than Ventris realized. The evidence for assuming the final values of the -eus -ewos declension is 'insufficient'. 'The intelligibility of the documents seems to decrease as their length increases.' ... 'There must be a limit to the number of phonemic differences that can be left. Otherwise the script will become too inexact to be of any use. So in Greek, if you do not show separately the five cardinal vowels and note the -i and -u series of diphthongs you run the gravest

1. For the suggested Mycenaean phonology see Ventris and Chadwick, *Documents in Mycenaean Greek*, p. 76 ff. (especially pp. 81, 82).

2. Compare P. K. Kretschmer, 'Die Vorgriechischen Sprach- und Volkschichten', *Glotta*, 1943, pp. 84–218, and O. J. L. Szemereny, *Classical Review*, March 1958, p. 57.

3. A. J. Beattie, 'Mr Ventris's Decipherment of the Minoan Linear B Script', *Journal of Hellenic Studies*, 1956, pp. 1–17; replied to by J. Chadwick, in 'Minoan Linear B, A Reply', *Journal of Hellenic Studies*, 1957, p. 202.

risk of being misunderstood. If you do not write u and s and i you destroy the syntax of your sentences. If you confuse r and l you obliterate the distinction between important suffixes and you obscure many roots. If in addition to all these things you omit a variety of medial consonants you create havoc. Mr Ventris's syllabic pattern is really far too simple, and we may say with confidence that it is in-sufficient for the writing and reading of Greek. It irons out the sound system of the language. On the other hand, just because it is so imprecise it enables Mr Ventris to discern Greek words in groups of syllables that look entirely un-Greek to classical scholars.'

Some of what Professor Beattie alleges against the decipherment would be admitted by Ventris and Chadwick and their followers, but is not particularly damning. The script postulated is admittedly very unsatisfactory for writing Greek, but this can be explained if we assume that Linear Script A, from which it was developed, had been devised for writing a very different language. The cuneiform script devised by the Sumerians was very unsatisfactory for writing Semitic languages (even though both had a distaste for closed syllables) until it had been amended and improved.

Beattie is, however, wrong in thinking he can refute Ventris's interpretation of TA-RA-NU as a footstool on the ground that the ideogram represents a flat pan with two handles. The gold ring from Tiryns proves clearly that such objects, whether pans or not, were certainly employed as footstools and this word represents one of the strongest individual arguments for Ventris's system.[1]

Beattie also raises objections to the reading of the tripod tablet. He notes 'the curious feature' of 'the writer's insistence on handles. . . . We should in any case suspect the validity of a list that has no one-handled or two-handled pots but knows only those with three or four handles or none at all.' This is certainly curious but does not explain away the fact that such are the pots represented in the ideograms.

He also emphasizes the only weakness in the Ventris system which really troubles me – the number of possible variants. He asserts with reference to the tripod: 'If we apply these variations to the words in

---

1. The object bears a superficial resemblance to the hot water cans also used as footstools and employed to heat railway carriages before these were furnished with central heating, though I am not suggesting ta-ra-nu was such an article.

the text we find that TI-RI-O-WE migh tbe interpreted in 5760 different ways and QE-TO-RO-WE in 92,160 ways. Even so short a word as DI-PA could mean about 300 different things.' I have not checked Beattie's figures but I think we may admit that the number of variants is uncomfortably large, and not quite so irrelevant perhaps as Professor Webster believes. The latter also complains, more justly, of Beattie's evasion of the evidence from 'the furniture tablets', his failure to recognize Ventris's symbols for sa, ke, ta, pa, yo, mu, za, and ro, and the weakness of his objections to the identifications of *Athena potnia*, *Paian*, and *Enyalios*.

Beattie's criticisms have been tested more carefully by A. P. Treweek, who, being a mathematician as well as a classical scholar, was able to assess the value of Beattie's computations of the possible ambiguities resulting from the rules of the Ventris grid. Beattie's individual statements of fact are usually correct except when based on an incorrect reading of the sign, but the inferences drawn are unjustifiable. 'Beattie's attack is in fact made from a bewildering variety of logically inconsistent positions. . . . Had he warned us of the dangers of making wrong interpretation of the words written by the syllables in the language where we are still feeling our way, that would have been a salutary warning, but his attack was misdirected against the one part of the work where the results have been established with certainty.'

It is a great tragedy that the death of Mr Ventris deprived Aegean studies of the man best qualified to answer these questions, a man whose modesty and conscientiousness never allowed his enthusiasm to lead him astray beyond reasonable assumptions.

Minoan Mathematics

The Minoan people evolved or borrowed from Egypt a mathematical notation (based on the ten fingers as are so many systems), but their mathematics does not seem to have reached a higher standard than was demanded for the keeping of accounts or the measurements made by masons and carpenters.

In the Cretan Hieroglyphic Script units were indicated by vertical or slightly curved lines, tens by dots, a hundred by a long slanting stroke, and a thousand by a lozenge. A v was used for some fraction, perhaps a quarter.

In Linear Script A the same decimal system persisted but the notation changed. Units were now always shown by straight vertical strokes. The dot for ten appears on some of the earlier tablets but was soon replaced by a horizontal line. A hundred was represented by a circle, and a thousand by a circle with four short lines projecting from the circumference. Quarters were indicated by an ^{L}.

The decimal system which we, like the Minoans, employ, is obviously inferior to the duodecimal. It is well enough for arithmetic, but breaks down badly for geometry because you cannot divide ten exactly by three or four. The ancient Sumerians realized this defect at an early date and combined both systems in a sexagesimal one. Sixty is an admirable number, being exactly divisible by 2, 3, 4, 5, 6, 10, 12, 15, 20, and 30. The Babylonians and Hittites followed suit and the Maya peoples of America were also not blind to the beauties of sixty. But the Greeks and Romans, as Dow remarks, 'copied the decimal system of the Egyptians and Minoans'; we are still paying the penalty.

The Greeks and Romans also followed the Minoans in having no symbol for zero, and the classical Greek phrase for nothing literally means 'not even one'. Bennett has shown that the Minoan symbol x was a check, not a symbol for zero. Addition and subtraction would have been easy for Minoan scribes but multiplication and division would have been as difficult for them as it was for the Romans.

Besides their ordinary decimal system of notation the Mycenaeans had systems of weights and measures based on miscellaneous ratios: $1 \times 30 \times 4 \times 12$ for weights, $1 \times 3 \times 6 \times 4$ for liquids, and $1 \times 10 \times 6 \times 4$ for solids.[1]

Bennett also remarked that while the Linear A scribes had a single set of fractional signs for all kinds of measurements wet or dry, Linear B scribes had a different set of fractional signs for each kind of measurement, each being an exact multiple of all smaller fractions; no sign for a numerical fraction had been discovered. The fundamental difference between the system of measuring quantities employed by the scribes of Linear Script A, as opposed to those of Script B, is well demonstrated by Bennett. The Script A store-keeper, after filling six unit measures of grain from a bin containing $6\frac{4}{5}$ units,

---

1. And the Minoans also, at least after the Achaean occupation of Knosos.

would fill a half measure and then test the remainder by pouring it into smaller measures until he had several full, and the corn would finally be in the form $6 + \frac{1}{2} + \frac{1}{4} + \frac{1}{20} = 6\frac{4}{5}$. The Script B store-keeper, after filling his unit measures, would test the remainder by a tenth measure and the final tally would be $6 + \frac{8}{10} = 6\frac{4}{5}$. The second system is obviously quicker and more convenient, but it is of interest that the former system of counting corresponds rather to the Egyptian method, whereas the latter corresponds to the Babylonian.

A Mesopotamian system might have been introduced to the Peloponnese from Anatolia by Pelops himself, but the system could equally well have been introduced both to Crete and to the mainland by Phoenician merchants from Ugarit or Byblos, or by Mycenaeans trading with those ports.

NOTE: Professor L. R. Palmer in his recent book *Mycenaeans and Minoans* has attacked Evans's dating of the Linear B tablets, using material derived from the excavation notebooks of the late Duncan Mackenzie. He claims that these tablets were consistently found associated with pottery of Late Minoan III B, not Late Minoan I I, date, and that the tablets should therefore be dated no earlier than the twelfth century B.C. This theory has been counter-attacked by Mr John Boardman who pointed out that Professor Palmer seemed to have supposed an otherwise unrecorded conflagration about 1150 B.C., since the Late Minoan III B pottery he quotes had not been damaged by the fire that burnt the tablets. Further, although in the 1900 excavation of the Stirrup Jar room Evans and Mackenzie had attributed tablets and vases to the same period, nevertheless after a subsequent excavation in 1901 Mackenzie reported: 'In no deposit which was recognized as belonging to this period of partial habitation at Knosos was a single inscribed tablet or sealing, broken or unbroken, ever found during the whole course of the excavation here.'

Mr Sinclair Hood has also defended Evans's dating of the tablets stressing that there is no evidence that Mackenzie ever disagreed with Evans on this point (both originally dated them Late Minoan III and both later dated them Late Minoan I I). Recent excavations by Hood have confirmed Evan's account of the Late Minoan I B period also.

CHAPTER 4

The Minoan Marine, Trade, and Communications

THE EARLIEST CRETAN BOATS

THERE is no evidence of an indigenous Neolithic culture developing out of a Palaeolithic one in Crete, and the old land barrier between the island and Asia Minor had broken down long before the opening of the Neolithic period in Crete. The first Neolithic settlers must have come by sea. We have no evidence concerning the form of boats they employed, but we may exclude the idea of floats or canoes of reeds or rushes like those of Pre-Dynastic Egypt. Presumably the first settlers came in dug-out canoes of cypress wood of the type still used till recently on Lake Prespa in Macedonia. (I travelled on one there in 1927.[1] A pointed prow and stern had been added separately, giving the appearance of a rude gondola, but the otherwise primitive effect was somewhat marred by the fact that the dug-out had been liberally repaired with petrol tins.) Just such a dug-out canoe, except for the petrol tins, seems to be illustrated by a clay model found in an Early Minoan deposit at Mochlos (Fig. 13). Such a boat would serve well for offshore fishing,[2] but for inter-island traffic something larger would be required, even though it might still be a dug-out, since cypresses grow to a great height and have straight trunks capable of being turned into long boats. The first immigrants, like the first Viking explorers, probably relied on oars and not on sails,[3] and I

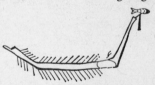

Fig. 12. Long boat from Cycladic vase

1. In A.D. 449 the general Maximinus and his suite, while on their way to meet Attila, were ferried across the Danube in dug-outs; compare L. Dindorf, *Historici Graeci Minores*, 1870–1, p. 292.

2. The two pairs of thole-pins are set as far apart as possible, presumably to leave the centre of the boat free for drawing in the net.

3. The Minoans, Mycenaeans, and Classical Greeks seem always to have used 'oars', not 'paddles', for which the Greek language appears to have no special term.

think they must have come via Rhodes, Karpathos, and Kasos, whatever may have been their original port of embarkation. Direct evidence for boats in the Early Minoan period is slight, but it would appear that besides the simple dug-out canoe of the Mochlos type, the Cretans also had a long boat with a high projecting bow and a low projection at the stern, interpreted by Evans as a fixed rudder. Such a boat is represented by a clay model of Early Minoan II date

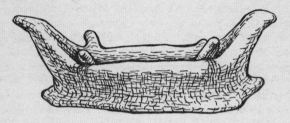

Fig. 13. Mochlos dug-out

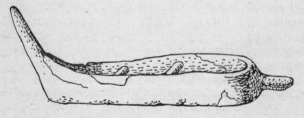

Fig. 14. Palaikastro model boat

from Palaikastro (Fig. 14). Some authorities would interpret the low projection as a ram on the prow and the high slanting projection as the stern, but Evans's interpretation is justified by the comparison with Minoan ships on Middle Minoan I seals and by Cycladic ships represented in the Early Cycladic vases known as frying-pans, where the fish at the prow shows clearly the direction in which the ship is travelling. Even in the Middle Bronze Age, when the Cretans were building ocean-going ships, this distinction between the high prow and low stern continued to distinguish them from the more symmetrical Egyptian and Phoenician ships.

The ships of the earliest dynastic period in Egypt were of the 'nuggar' type, of which Herodotus describes the construction, and which are still used on the upper Nile above the second cataract.[1] They were adequate for river work, but quite unsuitable for the open sea.

THE EARLIEST SEA-GOING SHIPS

By the time of the Third Dynasty, however, the Egyptians had already constructed a ship capable of sailing on the Mediterranean, though even as late as the Fifth Dynasty the ships of Sa-hu-re still preserve some characteristics of the old Nile 'nuggar', including the curious bifid mast, a relic of the reed-built boats which would not stand the strain of a mast stepped on the centre. Even as early as the Second Dynasty, however, we hear of a ship called the 'Byblos ship'. It is often assumed that this phrase simply means the ship employed on the Byblos run, as no doubt in fact it was. Nevertheless I think that if we consider the lack of timber suitable for ships in Egypt and its abundance on the Lebanon coast and the later shipbuilding traditions of the Phoenicians, we may perhaps go so far as to suggest that 'Byblos ship' meant the type of ship built at Byblos, without of course excluding the possibilities of Egyptians also building such ships either at Byblos or in Egypt.[2]

It is at least certain that by about 2000 B.C. we find on Minoan seals (Fig. 15) representations of large sea-going vessels which still preserve the high prow but low stern of the boats of Palaikastro and the Cyclades, but which have been transformed by the influence of ships of the Byblos type and now have a central mast with a square sail like the sea-going ships of Egypt.

Most representations of Minoan ships, however crude, display a triangle of lines each side of the mast illustrating a form of rigging

1. J. Hornell, 'The Sailing Ships in Ancient Egypt', *Antiquity*, 1943; 'nuggars' are characterized by their shallow depth, great width, and absence of ribs or any proper keel.
2. Probably the earliest ships of this type were built by Egyptians, but a local shipbuilding trade must have grown up at an early date on the coast of what was later termed Phoenicia, perhaps at the mouth of the Dog River.

which was normal during the Eighteenth Dynasty in Egypt and is described by Laird Clowes. The mast, which is a single pole, is stepped amidships, and the sail, of much greater width than that employed in the boats of the Twelfth Dynasty, has its foot extended by a heavy spreader yard. This lower yard, just as in these earlier boats, is supported by a number of lifts[1] which lead through a series of 'bees' lashed to the mast head very similar in form to the 'bees' of the eighteenth-century bowsprit. He remarks that 'each yard is formed of two spars fished together in the middle' and further that the

Fig. 15. Ships from Minoan seals

'vessel was sailed very much more by the manipulation of two braces or vangs, attached to the upper yard, than by means of the sheet which controlled the lower yard', and that the method of steering was essentially the same as that adopted by a whaleboat, where the very long oar used for steering is ordinarily rotated about the axis of its shaft by means of a short vertical handle, instead of its blade being bodily displaced from the side.

Minoan seals from the Early Minoan III periods onwards suggest that the rigging and method of sailing were the same as the Egyptian. It is true that most gem engravings only show the mast and the triangular rigging of the lifts but occasionally other details, such as the steering sweeps, the oars, the two-piece upper yard, and the lower spreader yard, are illustrated.

The Greeks later abandoned this system of the spreader yard and the triangular rigging of the 'lifts' required to sustain it. I do not know how early this improvement occurred, but the spreader yard

1. Diagonal ropes leading from the spreader yard to the mast head; the phrase 'eighteenth-century bowsprit' refers of course to the eighteenth century A.D.; there was possibly no bowsprit in the ordinary sense of that word in the eighteenth century B.C. despite the appearance of what looks like a bowsprit on some Minoan ships.

and its 'lifts' had both vanished before the middle of the sixth century B.C.

But the Minoan ships were not slavish imitations of the Egyptian, and from certain Cretan peculiarities we may infer the existence of a local shipbuilding trade, perhaps carried out at Nirou Khani, where the existence of two small dry docks suggests such a possibility.

Two idiosyncrasies which distinguish Middle Minoan ships from their contemporaries in Egypt are the very high prow rising at an angle of about sixty degrees, and the low stern with the keel projecting, a form persisting from the old long-boat type of the earliest Bronze Age both in Crete and in the Cyclades, and probably conditioned by the dug-out origin of the hull.[1]

The result of this lack of fore-and-aft sails, coupled with the fact that the regular Etesian winds, the summer winds of the eastern Mediterranean, now known as the *meltémi*, usually blow steadily from the north or north-west, probably implies that the ancient trading vessels (like the Lloyd Triestino vessels up to 1939) used to ply a circular route southwards from Crete to Egypt, up the coasts of Palestine and Syria, across to Cyprus, and back by way of the Dodecanese to whatever Cretan port they had sailed from.

We know now that fore-and-aft rigging was not unknown in the ancient world, since Professor Lionel Casson has recently published three illustrations of sprit-sails and one of a 'lateen sail' (better described as a short luff lug sail). I cannot quote any certain ancient example of a gaff sail or any reliable Minoan examples of sprit or lateen sails, but certain ancient illustrations suggest that the square sail could be pulled down at one corner and used (rather clumsily perhaps) as a lateen sail; oblong sails are employed in this way on the Malayan fishing vessels termed *perahu mayang*.[2]

Some Minoan seals depict ships with three masts joined by a lattice pattern with crescents on top giving an impression that it is a deck awning formed of matting slung on poles, as shown on Early Dynastic and Late Pre-dynastic drawings in Egypt. Marinatos, however, interpreted these as masts and sails, and Sir John Myres in a letter to me suggested that while the central line might represent a

1. Suggested to me by Mr T. C. Lethbridge.
2. H. M. Frese, 'Small Craft in the Rijks Museum van Volkerkunde, Leiden', *Mariners Mirror*, 1948, Fig. 2.

mast, the outer vertical lines might be halyards depending from the yard arm.[1] It might even be argued that these were sprit-sails. The sagging lines of the crescents seem also consistent with the suggestion of a tent-like deck cabin, but I must confess that such a cabin seems less appropriate for the Aegean Sea or the Libyan Sea than for the river of Egypt. Whatever be the true explanation, it is clear that this ship with the three masts or poles is a type quite distinct from the ordinary cargo ship with the great square sail. Small dinghies with transom sterns seem to be represented by the models from Christos (Early Minoan III–Middle Minoan I) and Hagia Triada (Late Minoan I).

SACRED BARGES

The gold ring from the Tiryns treasure (Fig. 16) illustrates yet another type of vessel, perhaps used as a sacred barge. The design appears to

Fig. 16. Ship from Tiryns ring

show the central mast with its normal rigging rising from the top of a square cabin, an impossible position since the mast would blow overboard with any wind. Either this is only a flagpole, which I think unlikely, or else we must imagine the mast as passing through the cabin down to the keel. The Tiryns boat may, of course, be a Mycenaean variant unknown in Crete, but there are other similar boats, except that they have no deck cabin as a rule, appearing on Minoan seals, usually in religious scenes. These boats resemble an old Mesopotamian type employed by the Marsh Arabs and illustrated by a silver model found in the royal graves at Ur.

DECKED MERCHANTMEN

The question how far Minoan merchant vessels were decked is open to dispute. The adoption of the watertight deck for warships was a

1. See the two right-hand seals in Fig. 15, one from an amygdaloid carnelian in the British Museum, the other from a similar seal in the Southesk Collection.

late innovation inasmuch as the Athenians had not yet adopted it for war-galleys at the time of the Persian invasions at the beginning of the fifth century B.C. Merchant ships, however, were sometimes decked during the Bronze Age, as is shown by the clay model of Late Minoan II date from Hagia Triada and by the painting on a Cypro-Mycenaean vase of a cargo ship decked from stem to stern.[1] We cannot prove that the Minoans had ships like the Cypriots, but I think it not unlikely. Pernice asserted that cargo ships of this kind relied entirely on their sails and had no oars, but the true distinction between the methods of propelling warships and merchant ships is more justly stated by Geoffrey Kirk (writing of ships in the Early Iron Age), 'Greek ships of all periods, both warships and merchant vessels, carried equipment for both forms of propulsion, although the primary motive power of the warship was undoubtedly oars and that of merchant ships sail. With favourable winds it would be foolish to row, but equally foolish not to have oars available for manoeuvring in harbour, or in case of calm, even for the most unwieldy vessel.' In other words, oars were employed like the engine of a *gasolina*, the modern fishing caique of the Greek islands fitted with a small subsidiary motor.

WARSHIPS

The earliest representation of a Greek warship is on a Protogeometric vase from Pylos, but it already foreshadows the archaic type, undecked save for small fighting platforms fore and aft – a form dictated by the necessity for manoeuvrability and the consequent need for more rowers and increased length of hull. 'The weight of a deck imposed severe strains, and it was only the lightly-built open-boat type which was found to support with safety the keel length of at least ninety feet [27 m.] necessitated by an increase to twenty-five rowers each side.'[2]

Apollodorus records a tradition that the first ship had been built by Danaus, and a scholiast more reasonably states that that king had constructed the first *pentekontor*, the first fifty-oared vessel designed

1. No. 262 from Tomb 3 at Enkomi; see E. Sjoqvist, *Swedish Cyprus Expedition* I, 1934, pl. XXXI, 3, 4.
2. Kirk.

purely as a warship. Danaus himself is a legendary character, but the nation of whom he was supposed to be the founder were the inhabitants of the plain of Adana who raided Ugarit in the fourteenth century and Egypt in the twelfth century B.C.[1] The chief port of this plain in the Late Bronze Age was Tarsus, so that even if the Biblical description for an ocean-going ship as a 'ship of Tarshish' refers to Tartessus in Spain or Tartous in Syria it is still not impossible that the story of Danaus's invention of the *pentekontor* may refer to an achievement of the shipwrights of Tarsus,[2] and most probably the Biblical Tarshish meant Tarsus.[3]

Greek traditions, however, also claimed Danaus for Argos, and our earliest representation of a Greek warship is on a twelfth-century B.C. vase from Pylos, so that we might also argue that warships of this kind were first laid down in the Peloponnese.

Both districts had ample supplies of suitable timber, and Barnett notes that the Biblical word for ship in the passages referring to Tarshish is not Semitic and might possibly be derived from the Hellenic *naus*.

Starr has vigorously attacked what he terms the 'Myth of the Minoan Thalassocracy' and makes some very good points. Even if we assign the greatest expansion of the Minoan marine to the Middle Minoan II period, we ought not to imagine that any prehistoric king of Crete (whether Minoan or Achaean) had a navy like that of fifth-century Athens, or regarded the Aegean Sea as *mare nostrum*. A Minoan warship would simply be a merchant vessel equipped with fighters. In England, writes Clowes, 'this interchangeability of the role of merchantman and man-of-war, as need arose, continued right up to the death of Queen Elizabeth'. Lionel Cohen's attempt to prove the existence of ships' rams in Minoan times was refuted by Marinatos.

The coasts of Crete were protected by the sea rather than by the fleet, and if any permanent naval force existed, which is doubtful,

1. Compare a note on Mopsos by R. D. Barnett in *Journal of Hellenic Studies*, 1953, pp. 140–3.

2. See T. C. Lethbridge, *Boats and Boatmen*, 1952, p. 117; R. Dussaud, *Topographie historique de la Syrie antique*, 1927, p. 121; and C. F. A. Schaeffer, *Ugaritica II*, 1949.

3. Barnett, 'Early Shipping in the Near East', *Antiquity*, 1958.

its function would have been rather the protection of its own merchant ships from piratical raids and the execution of piratical raids on enemy ships and ports, not coastal protection.

Starr, however, perhaps underestimates the size of Minoan ships. The fact that many representations of ships only show five or six oars may be due merely to the difficulty of representing them on a small seal stone (Fig. 15).[1] All the representations of Minoan ships are summarily executed and only illustrate the most salient features, yet one of them clearly indicates fifteen oars on one side apart from the steering sweeps, corresponding to the crew of thirty sent to Pleuron (Ventris and Chadwick, loc. cit., tablet 53). The same number of oars were used to propel Hatshepshut's ships on the expedition to Punt, and also the old ship preserved at Athens till Demosthenes's time and reputed to have been Theseus's ship.[2]

Marinatos has taken this ship as indicating the probable maximum for Minoan vessels and has estimated that it would have been about 21 metres long and about 4 to 4½ metres broad. He suggests that the large sail shown on Late Minoan ships may have implied the existence of vessels 30 metres in length but not much more. (The abnormally large barge constructed in Egypt for Hatshepshut's obelisk was 63 metres long, 21 metres broad, and had a displacement, according to Koster, of 1541·31 tons.)[3]

Some curious designs on Minoan seals of the amygdaloid form so popular in the Middle Minoan III period (but by no means confined to it) have been identified as sails with their buntline rings by Marinatos, who has suggested that these seals were the property of sailmakers.

Childe has commented on the relatively very large areas occupied by magazines and workshops in Minoan Palaces implying surplus products used for trade, and draws the conclusion: 'in other words the priest-king's economic power must to a quite high degree have depended on secondary industry and commerce as contrasted with agricultural production.'[4] Contrast Starr's remark that 'the splendour

1. Other seal stones depict seven a side, while the seal from Phaistos quoted above showed fifteen a side, apart from the two steering sweeps.

2. Plutarch, *Life of Theseus*, Chap. 23; Evans, *Palace of Minos*, Vol. II, Fig. 139.

3. Koster, A., *Studien zur Geschichte des Antikenseewegens*, 1934, pp. 1-10.

4. V. Gordon Childe, *What Happened in History* (Penguin Books, 1942), p. 173.

of its palaces rested mainly upon the work of farmers, and the Cretan artisans were fed from Cretan farms'. Cretan industries, however, must have depended very largely on imported materials. Gold, silver, tin, and lead all had to come by ship, and the island sources of copper must have been very inadequate for its needs. The luxury trades would also have imported ivory, lapis lazuli, musical instruments, and portable works of art from Egypt and Syria.

MINOAN HARBOURS

Platon has remarked how often Minoan ports were situated on small promontories affording a harbour on either side according to the direction of the wind;[1] to this category belonged not only Khersonnesos and Palaikastro, but also probably Amnisos and Mochlos before the sinking of the eastern coastline. The choice of such sites is reasonable and natural. It is less easy to conjecture why the ancient planners both in the Bronze Age and later should have displayed a preference for small islands lying a few miles off the coast; we may quote such celebrated ports as Tyre, Sidon, the Pharos, and Aradus in the Levant, and in Minoan Crete Pseira, Leuke, and perhaps Dia. (Mochlos, now an island, was perhaps a peninsula in Minoan times.)

Holland Rose offers two explanations, neither very convincing, but I have nothing better to suggest. 'Sometimes these islands or even ports on an open shore were placed under a kind of perpetual truce; or else exchange went on without the parties actually meeting. . . . It is probable,' he continues, 'that trade on these and many other islets long preceded trade on the mainland near by. . . . Note that early traffic avoided narrow inlets like the Piraeus for fear of being cut off'; and he points the moral by quoting how the Laestrygonian wreckers had trapped Odysseus's companions, whereas the hero himself, who had tied up at the entrance, escaped. Perhaps this explains why no important Minoan port developed in the splendid natural harbour of Suda Bay.[2]

1. I doubt whether the island at Amnisos was ever fully united to the mainland, but if a sandy bay had existed between it and the Kastro it would have provided some calmer water for boats beaching east of the Kastro.

2. Minoa, of which Theophanides discovered traces (Ephemeris *Archaiologiki*, 1950–1, Supp. 1–13), hardly appears to have been a port of any importance.

The numerous references to piracy in the Homeric poems[1] imply that it was a common practice in the Early Iron Age, and Thucydides's reference to the suppression by Minos of the Carian pirates obviously alludes to piracy in the Minoan period (whatever value we attach to the names 'Minos' and 'Carian').[2]

Signal flares were often lit on prominent headlands, both by coast-guards to warn traders of the presence of pirates, and by the friends on land of pirates lying in ambush off the coast.

NAVIGATION BY PIGEONS

In the dialogue termed the Kevaddha Sutta of Dighha[3] of the fifth century B.C. the Buddha states: 'Long ago ocean-going merchants were wont to plunge forth upon the sea on board a ship taking with them a shore-sighting bird. When the ship was out of sight they would set the shore-sighting bird free. And it would go to the east and to the south and to the west and to the north and to the inter-mediate points and rise aloft. If on the horizon it caught sight of land thither it would go, but if not it would come back to the ship again.' The story of Noah and the Mesopotamian *Epic of Gilgamish* show that this device must have been practised by Sumerian captains back in the third millennium B.C.[4]

It would be interesting to know whether Minoan merchant cap-tains ever employed this device, hardly necessary when they were sailing to the Cyclades, but not to be despised for longer voyages out of sight of land, since stars are not always visible, even on Mediter-ranean waters. Cosmas Indicopleustes records this practice in Ceylon as late as the sixth century A.D. but there is no mention of it in the Homeric poems. But what of the pigeon which Jason set loose to ascertain whether the Argo could pass through the clashing rocks?

1. *Odyssey* XIV 86, XVI 425, etc.
2. Thucydides I, 4; Cleidemus quoted by Plutarch (Thesrus, Chap. 19) even refers to police work executed by Jason.
3. Professor I. W. Rhys Davids, *Journal of Royal Asiatic Society*, 1899, p. 432; and compare W. H. Schoff, *The Periplus of the Erythraean Sea*, 1912, pp. 228, 229.
4. R. C. Thompson, *The Epic of Gilgamish*, 1928, 52, verses 145–55; Uta-Napishtim (the Sumerian Noah) released in succession a dove, a swallow, and a raven.

Was this a reminiscence of the bird that every good captain of a Minoan or Mycenaean ship would have taken with him on a long voyage?

ODYSSEUS'S SHIP

In the fifth book of the *Odyssey* we are given a brief but graphic description of the construction of a sea-going ship. The trees, poplar and fir, were felled with double axes, trimmed with an adze to the required shape, bored with a drill, and fastened together with pegs and what were termed *harmoniai*, a word used by Galen of the union of broken bones by the mere apposition of their surfaces, and therefore in Homer's passage presumably implying that the ship was carvel-built, not clinker-built. The other evidence agrees with this: indeed all ancient ships in the Mediterranean may have been carvel-built.

Representations of Odysseus's ship on classical vases often interpret it as a war galley, but this is obviously wrong. Homer states very explicitly that it was a broad cargo ship, and I suspect that the word *ikria* (decks), if it does not imply a fully decked ship like the one on the Mycenaean vase from Enkomi, at least implies a half-decked ship with fairly substantial decks fore and aft.

The hull was probably strengthened by the insertion of U-shaped transverse frames just below the gunwale, struts which would serve as thwarts for the rowers in long boats or small boats, or would carry the deck in the larger cargo boats; two such frames appear to be suggested on the Enkomi ship referred to on page 97.

TRADE WITH EGYPT AND PHOENICIAN COAST

Direct trade with Egypt seems to have been slight during the Early Minoan period. Egyptian influences are certainly discernible in the shapes of some of the stone vases and in the designs and occasionally in the shapes of Early Minoan seals, but many of these influences might have come indirectly from places where Egyptian culture was prominent, such as the ports of Syria and Palestine, and it should be remarked that after the appearance of Proto-Dynastic bowls in a sub-Neolithic context at Knosos, the earliest imports of Egyptian objects are the fragments of a faience bowl and the necklace of faience beads found at Mochlos in Tomb 6, of which the earliest interment dated from the Early Minoan II period. A few scarabs of the First Intermediary Period (Dynasties VII–X inclusive) found their way to Crete, and some Cretan ivory seals of the Early Minoan III period seem to have been influenced by Egyptian scarabs of that period, but most of the actual imports of Egyptian seals date from the Twelfth or Eighteenth Dynasties. Not till the Twelfth Dynasty do we find any hint of Cretan influences on Egypt, and even then the evidence is a little ambiguous.

M. Money-Coutts Seiradhaki has pointed out the analogies between the Cretan lids in steatite with the handle carved in the form of lying dogs and the lid of a vase in the Beirut Museum from Byblos with the handle in the form of a squatting bull.[1] The bull looks like a Sumerian animal, but the material, green schist, and the incised herring-bone decoration recall such east Cretan art as the *pyxis* from Maroneia. The Mochlos lid was found with an Early Minoan II burial and the other Cretan example was presumably of about that date. The Byblos vase was found by Montet below the Twelfth Dynasty temple II on that site in a foundation deposit dated about 2100 B.C. The exact date of this deposit is open to question but it was certainly contemporary with the Middle Kingdom and Schaeffer is inclined to date it slightly earlier than the deposits found later by M. Dunand. This correlation agrees well enough with the limits 2300–2100 B.C. which I have suggested for the Early Minoan II period.

If the Byblos vase could be reckoned as Cretan, it would be the earliest Minoan export that we know of to a foreign country, but it may well have been made in Byblos. One motive of Egyptian art which has sometimes been supposed to have been derived from, or at least influenced by, Minoan art is the spiral decoration which suddenly becomes popular under the Twelfth Dynasty, especially in the form of rapport designs[2] and quadruple spirals arranged in chequer

1. M. Money-Coutts, 'A Stone Bowl and Lid from Byblos', *Berytus*, 1936, p. 139.

2. Most English dictionaries do not define this phrase, which is employed by many archaeologists; I should define a rapport design as an all-over, interlocking, net-like pattern suggesting but not necessarily implying the influence of textiles.

fashion. Spiral decoration was characteristic of the Neolithic cultures of the Danube basin and of the Chalcolithic pottery of Thessaly and Thrace. Running spirals appear very early in the Bronze Age in the Cyclades and Crete may have derived its spiral decorations from those islands. It has been suggested that spiral ornaments were derived from a late Palaeolithic source or from Sumerian metal work. Egypt, however, had known simple spirals in the Pre-dynastic period and later, but was practically devoid of spiral decoration from the Fifth Dynasty period to the First Intermediate Period when we do find some scarabs with primitive spiral curls or tendrils. These, however, were comparatively scarce and gave no hint of the abundance of quadruple and interlocked C spirals which appeared under the Twelfth Dynasty and induced Matz to suggest an Aegean origin for them. The adopting of the spiral into quadruple squares or other rectangular patterns, including the meander, which is only a rectilinear version of the spiral, may have been carried out by Egyptian craftsmen familiar with rectilinear designs in textiles and matting.

The Egyptian meander patterns at least are unlikely to have been derived from north of the Balkans, but it is not impossible that Egyptian textiles might have penetrated to the Danube valley. It is a curious and perhaps not altogether insignificant fact that the spiral and meander designs, which were a thousand years later to be the symbols of the labyrinth of Minos on the classical coins of Knosos, became popular in Egypt and in Crete at the time when Amenemhat III constructed his great 'labyrinth' in the Fayoum and a Cretan prince constructed his 'labyrinth' at Knosos. I imagine indeed that the word 'labyrinth' would never have acquired its modern significance of maze but for the fact that Amenemhat's great funerary temple was more or less contemporary with the earliest palace at Knosos, and so invited comparisons between the two. The Egyptian temple was 'labyrinthine' in the modern sense but had nothing to do with the double axe, the *labrys* from which the Cretan palace derived its name; but long after the destruction of the latter building the folk-lore about the Minotaur and the maze-like building he lived in was confirmed and crystallized by the maze-like intricacies of the great temple in the Fayoum, which existed up to Roman times.

Another evidence of intercourse with Egypt is provided by the symbols obviously borrowed from the hieroglyphics of that country by the Cretans in their Hieroglyphic Script A. Here we must cut out from Sundwall's list such naturalistic representations as a man's leg or a scorpion or a ship, symbols which might arise independently in both countries, and confine examples of intercourse to such conventional designs as have a specially Egyptian character and meaning, the Ankh sign, the symbol of life, Ana, the palace sign, Byty, the bee-keeper sign, perhaps Ka, the raised hands sign for 'worker' or 'activity', and the 'adze' sign (adzes indeed might occur anywhere, but Egyptian and Minoan adzes had handles of a peculiar form). We cannot, however, quote any Cretan exports to Egypt in the Early Minoan III or Middle Minoan I periods.

MINOAN EXPORTS TO EGYPT, SYRIA, AND CYPRUS

Minoan vases were exported to various parts of the Levant. Tomb 6 A at Lapithos in Cyprus contained a Middle Minoan I A spouted jar associated with pottery of the types known as Early Cypriot II and III, and metal vases of the same Minoan period were found at Tod in Upper Egypt in chests inscribed with the name of Amenemhat II (1929–1895 B.C.). A Middle Minoan vase was found at Level II (2100–1900 B.C.) at Byblos in Syria. Beakers resembling Middle Minoan I B examples from various Cretan sites were found in Stratum II at Alisar and in Level IV A at Bogaz Koï in Asia Minor, Middle Minoan II A sherds were found in a later deposit at Byblos, and in the Middle Ugarit II period (1900–1750 B.C.) at Ras Shamra, and in Egypt at Haraga Middle Minoan II sherds were deposited at Lahun before 1700 B.C., perhaps about 1750. A Middle Minoan II B spouted vase was found at Abydos in a tomb belonging to the end of the Twelfth or beginning of the Thirteenth Dynasty.

The converse side of this picture is a Babylonian cylinder seal from Platanos of the type current in Hammurabi's reign (1792–1750 B.C., according to Dr Sidney Smith), and an amethyst scarab of late Twelfth or early Thirteenth Dynasty type from the lowest deposit of the Psychro Cave. Two other cylinders dating from the First Dynasty of Babylon are recorded from Crete, but these were not found in datable contexts. Perhaps it was at this time that the Cretans became acquainted with the use of papyrus and called it after Byblos, by the name from which was derived the modern Greek word for a book and the English word for the Bible.

Cretan traders also probably visited the city of Alalakh, capital of the little Syrian state of Mukishe, and its excavator, Sir Leonard Woolley, was at first inclined to stress Minoan influences on its architecture, frescoes, and pottery. After further excavations, however, it became evident that some of the frescoes, stone lamps, and pottery that had recalled Middle Minoan III to Late Minoan I A designs in Crete had been thrown away some time between 1350 and 1275 B.C. Indeed the most definitely Aegean pottery consisted of imported Mycenaean and Cypriot vases and was not Minoan at all, and the quasi-Minoan features in frescoes and on pottery of the so-called Nuzi ware remind us of Heurtley's description of Philistine vase motifs as 'patterns that had gone out of currency in their own country' and were perhaps due to a certain number of Minoan refugees calling or even settling there after 1450 B.C. when an Achaean dynasty was probably ruling at Knosos.

The food and raw materials exported from Minoan Crete to Egypt probably included oil, olives, wine, and perhaps dried grapes and almost certainly timber, especially cypress.

A curious export from Greek lands to Egypt was that of lichens used there for breadmaking, even to the present day when they may be purchased under the name of *sheba*. Greek lichens have been found in Middle Dynastic deposits at El Assassif, Thebes, and also elsewhere in Middle Kingdom tombs. Persson points out that the distance from the Peloponnese is not so very much greater than that from Crete, but I think that in the Middle Dynastic period the lichens would have come rather from Crete or the Dodecanese, though in the Late Dynastic period they were doubtless inported from the mainland.[1]

EGYPT AND THE KEFTIU

The Late Minoan I A period (1580–1550 B.C.) was the time when Queen Hatshepshut ruled Egypt and developed peaceful trade with her neighbours. The tomb paintings of her chief architect Senmut

1. Recently J. T. Killen has argued that the wool trade played an important, perhaps dominant part in Cretan exports (*B.S.A.*, 1964, pp. 1–16), and P. G. Kntikos in *Praktika tes Akademias Athinon* xxxv 2 (1960) p. 56 f. has suggested the activity of a Minoan export trade in opium,' see also R. S. Merrilees, *Antiquity*, 1962, p. 287 f.

depicted foreigners in Minoan costume bringing tribute to Egypt in the form of vases, fillers, and various gifts so accurately portrayed that we can confidently assign them to the Late Minoan I A period. Unfortunately so little of this painting survives that we do not know what name was assigned to these foreigners. Were they or were they not the same people mentioned in later tomb texts as coming from 'the shores of Keftiu'? (See Fig. 54.)

Even some of the supporters of the theory that Kaphtor meant Crete have suggested that the Aegean vessels brought to Egypt from the land of Keftiu were perhaps not Minoan but Late Helladic works from Mycenae or some other site on the mainland. The Late Minoan I A period (1550–1500 B.C.), parallel with the second half of the first Late Helladic period on the mainland of Greece, was the period when Minoan art exercised its strongest influence on that of the Peloponnese and southern Greece in general, so that it is often hard to say whether an individual vase was made on Crete or on the mainland. Large metal jugs with a decorative band level with, or just below the base of the handle were characteristic of the Middle Minoan III B to Late Minoan I A period at Knosos and were found in the Second Shaft Grave at Mycenae; and they were also represented on the offerings brought by Aegeans in the tomb paintings of Senmut (about 1510 B.C.) and of User-Amon.

A large palace amphora of the type found by Seager at Mochlos and by Evans in the north-east house at Knosos seems also to be represented in Senmut's tomb. The patterns below the top row of handles on this vase were interpreted by Evans as a second row of handles. Mr Alexiou's discovery of a fine Late Minoan II vase with plastic figure-of-eight shields, which also occurred on the silver 'siege rhyton' from Mycenae, suggests that these patterns should be interpreted as similar ornaments.

The so-called 'Vapheio cups' shown in the paintings of Senmut and User-Amon are Minoan rather than Helladic in that their shape is rather squat and they lack the raised horizontal rib which appears on so many of the Mycenaean examples. (See Fig. 54.)

The gold cups which gave their name to this shape from the *tholos* tomb at Vapheio near Sparta must, I think, be imports from Crete or works of a Cretan resident on the mainland, not Mycenaean work as suggested by Snijder and Miss Kantor. The rather squat shape and the free-field naturalism with no attempt at balanced groups are Minoan characteristics.

User-Amon was succeeded in the office of Grand Vizier by his nephew, Rekhmire, whose tomb was closed about 1450 B.C.; in this tomb the Foreigners are said to come from the land of Keftiu, the islands (or coasts) of the Green Sea, and the wording of the Egyptian would allow us to consider the words 'coasts of the Green Sea' as in apposition to 'Keftiu' and so explaining its meaning, but would also allow us to supply an 'and' between 'Keftiu' and 'the islands', differentiating one from the other. There is no radical difference, however, between the foreigners that would enable us to claim one group as coming from the land of Keftiu and another as coming from the islands. Wainwright emphasized that the foreigners of Rekhmire's tomb are less Minoan in their dress than those of Sehmut and the vases they bring include Syrian or Anatolian as well as Minoan forms. Indeed he would regard all the Keftiuans labelled as such as coming from Cilicia. Supporters of the theory that Keftiu meant Crete regard the progressively less Minoan appearance of its inhabitants in later tombs as due to the careless copying of earlier paintings, but the appearance of Late Minoan I B vases in Rekhmire's tomb, whereas only Late Minoan I A forms occur in Senmut's painting, implies that the former is not a mere slavish copy of the latter and this conclusion is supported by the statement of N. de G. Davies that the foreigners represented in Tombs 71, 39, and 131 at Qurna (those of Menkheperrasenb, Puimre, and Amen-user respectively) seem to have been studied afresh in each instance.

Nothing can be inferred from the order of the places mentioned in Rekhmire's inscription, since the offerings of the 'Great Chief of Keftiu and the Isles (or Coasts) of the Green Sea' are sandwiched between the offerings of Punt and those of Nubia.

The linguistic evidence is hardly conclusive. Keftiu seems to be the same country that is called Kaphtor in the Hebrew and Kaptara in the cuneiform records, and it is quite certain that this country must be either an island or a coastal district. The Philistines are said to have come from Kaphtor, and we can no longer, as Macalister did, regard them simply as Minoan refugees. Their pottery is rather a local variety developed from Mycenaean pottery of the Late Minoan III C type. The Philistine invasion of Egypt, however, was much later than any references to Keftiu in the Egyptian records, and the Pelethim of the Hebrew records were accompanied by Cherethim who might have been Cretans.

The cuneiform references to Kaptara are not much more helpful. The French excavators of the palace at Mari on the Euphrates interpreted Kaptara to mean Crete.

The Keftiuans are depicted bearing bull's head rhyta like the one found in the Little Palace at Knosos. We may even have one of these rhyta that were sent to Egypt still existing, namely the fine bull's head rhyton formerly owned, and published, by my friend Dr Charles Seltman. Its history is obscure, since it turned up in France without any proper information as to its source in the collection of a man who had acquired it from Egypt. I have handled it, and personally regard it as genuine, especially as the forgery of Minoan antiquities was not well developed at the time when it would appear to have been acquired by its former French owner, and experts have testified that the alkaline deposit on the less exposed surfaces would have taken many years to form.[1]

A few Minoan vases have also turned up in Egypt, the most celebrated being the fine jug in the Marseille Museum known as the 'Marseille Oenochoe', but our information about this and one or two other vases that I think were Minoan imports from Crete, rather than Helladic imports from Mycenae, depends on the statements of dealers from whom they were bought.

The only certain examples of a Late Minoan I B vase in pottery derived from a proper excavation in Egypt is the baggy alabastron found in Grave 137 at Sedment dated to the reign of Thutmose III. Of the twelve vases illustrated by Miss Kantor on her Plate VII and labelled 'Late Bronze I-II Aegean', I am inclined to regard vases A, C, D, and L as Minoan and the rest as Helladic vases from Mycenae or some other site on the mainland.

Miss Kantor observes that many of the Kieftiuan decorative motives seem to be Egyptian, and it would probably be a mistake to consider the repertory of these designs as a reliable reproduction of Keftiuan textile patterns; but these patterns do not occur on Egyptian kilts, nor

1. Information given me by Seltman himself; note that no published known prototype existed for a forgery of this type before 1914 and that before 1926 the vase was already in France.

are they arranged in the same way on any other Egyptian garment so far as I remember, and it may therefore at least be argued that they were intended to give the general effect of a Keftiuan kilt. I see no reason to suppose they were merely intended to fill 'gaping blanks', since the Egyptian had no *horror vacui* like the Indian artist, and was perfectly willing to leave a blank space when he thought it appropriate.

Miss Kantor's law of the 'diminishing accuracy of successive representations' may have more validity with regard to the later tombs, but I do not think it applies to Rekhmire's tomb, where the designs, as Vercoutter remarks, are characterized by their originality. Unfortunately the figures have been repainted and altered in this and in other ancient tombs. We should like to know whether the original paintings made any difference between the Keftiu and the Men of the Isles and their offerings. Why were the alterations made? Was it because the Aegeans had ceased to come to the Egyptian court, and if so when did that occur? Alexiou's alabaster vase (Fig. 50) suggests that direct relations between Egypt and the harbour town of Knosos lasted probably up to the middle of the fifteenth century B.C. We shall see that there are reasons for supposing that an Achaean dynasty may have ruled over Knosos in the Late Minoan II period from 1450 to 1400 B.C. approximately, and if this is so it would seem that the death of Rekhmire more or less coincided with a drastic reduction of direct communications between Crete and Egypt, but not necessarily their suspension. One argument which must be faced by the supporters of the theory that Keftiu is Cilicia is the absence of any reference to any name like Kaptara in the cuneiform records of the Assyrians and the Hittites, and to which they would presumably answer that it was known by another name to these nations. Eastern Cilicia was apparently part of the country known in the cuneiform records as Kissuwadna, but coastal Cilicia might have been termed Kaptara or some such name, though Gurney includes the coastal district also under the former name. Furumark quotes Kabderos, father-in-law of Mopsos, in support of the equation of Kaptara with Cilicia, but the Hittite bilingual text referring to Mopsos dates from the eighth century B.C. and does not mention Kabderos or Kaptara.

M. J. Vercoutter has recently answered the criticism that the kilts of Rekhmire's Keftiuans are un-Egyptian by claiming that the fringed division of the kilt is really central and not really different from that of the Cup-Bearer in the fresco at Knosos. Nevertheless this kilt does differ from the type with the codpiece illustrated in Crete by the steatite vases from Hagia Triada and by representations on engraved gems. The crux of the matter is whether we are to interpret this difference as a distinction between Minoan and Keftiuan kilts or as a change in Cretan fashions (conceivably introduced from Mycenae) in the second half of the fifteenth century B.C. This later type of kilt without codpiece is the form that appears at Knosos in the Late Minoan II 'Captain of the Blacks' fresco, and at Mycenae on the inlaid daggers and later on frescoes and gems.

CRETAN TRADE WITH THE CYCLADES

There is no evidence of trade between Crete and the Cyclades during the Neolithic period except the presence on Cretan Neolithic sites of knives made from what looks like Melian obsidian. In the first Early Minoan period there is ample evidence of connexions between Melos and Crete in the Pelos ware of the former and the Pyrgos fabric, but the impression I form from this is that Cycladic people were settling in Crete rather than Cretans in the Cyclades. The Pelos ware develops naturally into the Early Cycladic II pottery of Melos and other islands of the Cyclades, whereas the similar Pyrgos pottery of Crete comes to a dead stop and is replaced by pottery of completely different forms and decorations. Obviously the Minoan Cretans continued to import Melian obsidian, but I have a strong suspicion that it was coming in Cycladic, not in Minoan ships, in the Early Minoan I period.

With the development of the Middle Minoan culture and the building of the palaces early in the second millennium B.C. the position changed. The Cretans developed a merchant marine and probably a navy of their own, and they began to compete successfully with Phylakopi and other Cycladic cities, and perhaps it was because the Phylakopi merchants were being squeezed out of the Aegean Seas that they pushed into the western Mediterranean and left traces of their pioneering enterprise at Marseille and on the Balearic Isles, many centuries before the Phocaeans or even the Phoenicians had penetrated to those waters.

Before the fall of the first city of Phylakopi we already find local pottery imitating the light-on-dark wares of Early Minoan III and Middle Minoan I A type in Crete.

The second city of Phylakopi saw the importation of Minoan vases of Middle Minoan I B and Middle Minoan II A type and the imitation of them by local potters. On Kythnos there was a hoard of bronze tools of Middle Minoan types, including an axe-adze.

At the same time Phylakopi was also importing grey Minyan pottery from the Greek mainland, and if its sphere of influence was being curtailed by Minoan Crete there is still no evidence that it formed part of the Minoan empire; indeed it seems probable that Phylakopi may have owned some of the other Cyclades, since its traders dominated this area.

In the third Middle Minoan period Cretan influences became more marked at Phylakopi and it is not unlikely that Crete might even have dominated Melos and some of the other Cyclades. In the Temple Repositories at Knosos Evans found beaked jugs with curious Cycladic birds painted on them and suggested that 'these bird vases may have held some welcome offering to the priest-kings in the shape of Melian wine'. Cretan objects found in the second city of Phylakopi include bull's head rhyta. One quarter of the city was even turned into what was almost a Minoan residential quarter, with pillar crypts and splendid frescoes of Minoan type including one of flying fish in which the art of the Cretan fresco painter is seen at its best. Similar pillar crypts and frescoes occurred in the contemporary city on the island of Thera, and the islanders also made use of a linear script which looks like a variant of the Minoan Linear Script A.

Thucydides, in the first book of his history, tells us that 'Minos, the earliest of whom we hear, formed a navy and conquered what is now the Hellenic sea for the most part and the Cycladic islands, and ruled over them, becoming the first founder of many of them, driving out the Carians,[1] and establishing his own sons as rulers; and piracy, as was natural, he removed from the seas, so that more revenues might accrue to him'. Unfortunately, we are uncertain how far the tradition quoted by Thucydides refers to the Achaean King Minos mentioned by Homer and how far it reflects the glories of an earlier, pre-Hellenic Minos of the Middle Minoan period.

1. We do not know exactly why Thucydides believed there were Carians in the Cyclades, but it seems probable that by Carians he meant people akin to the Leleges, a subject population in classical Caria (see Chapter 3).

MINOAN AND MYCENAEAN TRADE WITH THE WEST

Trade with the West developed slowly, perhaps first up the Adriatic coasts, since copper daggers of a type known in the Early Minoan graves of the Mesara were found at Remedello near Brescia, at Monte Bradone near Volterra, and at Pangia in what was later to be known as Etruria; and before the end of the Early Minoan period Cretans were already importing the volcanic stone known as liparite from the Lipari islands as a substitute for, or an improvement on, Melian obsidian.

It is possible of course that some of this western trade may have been carried on not by Minoan Cretans but by Cycladic traders from Phylakopi on Melos.

Isolated vases of a kind made in Melos in the Middle Cycladic period have been found (without context) as far west as Marseille and the Balearic isles, and a stone axe of what seems to be probably Naxian emery at Calne in Wiltshire. The faience beads, however, of Levantine manufacture scattered over Europe, especially Britain, and dated by Piggott between 1550 and 1100 B.C. must be evidence of Mycenaean, not Minoan, trade with the West.

Recent excavations in the Lipari Isles uncovered some Vapheio cups of the Late Minoan I A period, which were at first hailed as Minoan imports, but these vases are not coated completely inside with glazed paint but have only a band of paint below the rim inside, and it would, therefore, appear that they must be not Cretan imports but Late Helladic I vases from Mycenae or some other mainland site.

Most of the Aegean imports to Sicily also seem to be Mycenaean. I know no certain example of a Minoan vase from that island, and though the bronze rapiers from Plemmyrion at Syracuse look like Minoan rapiers I would not like to assert that they could not have been brought on Mycenaean ships. There is, however, a very strong folklore tradition, recorded in its most complete form by Diodorus Siculus but also mentioned by Herodotus, concerning Minos's expedition to Sicily in pursuit of Daedalus, his murder there by the local King Kokalos, and his burial in a tomb of which the description by Diodorus reminds us of the temple tomb at Knosos.

We should, however, guard against the assumption that this proves that a Minoan expedition was sent to Sicily by a pre-Achaean king of Knosos, first because, as we shall see later, the Minos who is supposed to have made the expedition may have been an Achaean king of that city, and secondly because the Greeks confused the legends of a Bronze-Age architect named Daedalus with the Dedalic school of sculpture of the eighth and seventh centuries B.C.

Diodorus was using classical writers on Crete and supplementing their stories by the folklore of his native Sicily. Herodotus seems to have been using Samian sources and puts the siege of the city of Kamikos in Sicily by the Cretans, who were angered at Minos's death, in the third generation before the Trojan war, that is somewhere in the first half of the thirteenth century B.C. But what were the architectural remains attributed to this Daedalus which still existed in Diodorus's day? Pareti suggested that the Sicilian Minoa was not a Bronze Age foundation by Minoan Cretans or even Mycenaeans, but was connected with Selinus, itself a colony of Megara Hyblaea and so perhaps possessing legends originally derived from the Minoa near Megara on the Saronic Gulf (the mother city of Megara Hyblaea). This theory has been well criticized by Dunbabin, who emphasizes the resemblances between the Tomb of Minos as described by Diodorus and the Temple Tomb at Knosos which was buried and unknown to that writer.[1] Dunbabin therefore believes that the name Minoa, like other cities of that name in the Levant, does imply a connexion with Crete in prehistoric times.

Besides the rapiers of Plemmyrion we also find a form of spearhead that might have been imported from Minoan Crete in the form of a bronze spearhead with a long tapering blade, which is easier to parallel in the graves of Zafer Papoura than in Sicilian graves. Nevertheless no indisputably Minoan pottery has been found in Sicily, and rapiers of the Plemmyrion kind, though far more common in Crete, have also been found in the earlier shaft graves at Mycenae, so that even if the Sicilian examples were made in Crete, which is not certain, they may have arrived in Mycenaean ships.

The distribution areas in Sicily of these bronze weapons that can be derived from Aegean sources is almost confined to the neighbourhood of the three cities of Syracuse, Thapsus, and Acragas. These

1. 'Minos and Daidalos in Sicily', *Papers of the British School at Rome*, 1948, p. 8.

sites correspond to Thucydides's description, in the sixth book of his history, of the areas occupied by the Phoenicians. Now the Phoenicians did settle in Sicily in large numbers, but the settlements of which we have clear evidence were planted by Carthage and the western Phoenicians in the western part of Sicily, and it seems not unlikely that Thucydides was crediting to the Phoenicians the founding of trading settlements which had really been established by Mycenaean colonists in the fourteenth and thirteenth centuries B.C.

We may therefore agree with Dunbabin that the Sicilian legends of Daedalus confuse two periods, the first in the late Bronze Age when Minoan and Mycenaean adventurers came to Sicily, and the second when Rhodians and Cretans colonized Gela in 688 B.C. and their 'dedalic' sculpture was the dominant external influence. To the earlier period more probably belong the stones of the fortifications of Kamikos, the 'columbethra', the reservoirs of Daedalus, and the structures of the tomb of Minos and of the temple of Aphrodite at Eryx. The so-called *tholos* tombs of the Second Siculan period have sometimes been derived from Crete; but Levi denies this, and in fact their plan is more reminiscent of early rock cut tombs in Euboea than of anything in Crete. Occasionally we find Aegean types of skulls differing from the normal Siculan type (including two spheroid skulls from Pantalica and others from Castelluccio).

Minoan connexions with Malta and Pantelleria are harder to establish. The oriental features of the Maltese Neolithic culture and their rather general parallels in Cretan Neolithic or Early Minoan culture seem to depend rather on a common heritage from Syria or Anatolia than on a direct connexion with Minoan Crete. Perhaps the most striking individual parallel is that between the fine Cretan Neolithic squatting figurine in the Giamalakis collection and those of Neolithic sites such as Hal Saflieni in Malta. It suggests, as Hawkes remarked, that the original colonists of Malta must have arrived before the end of the Cretan Neolithic period in all probability, even though there is no suggestion that they came from Crete; J. D. Evans, however, dates the earlier Neolithic settlements in Malta late in the third millennium B.C.[1]

1. J. D. Evans, 'Prehistoric Culture Sequence in the Maltese Archipelago', *Proceedings of the Prehistoric Society*, 1953, p. 41.

LAND TRANSPORT IN CRETE

Crete has no rivers suitable for inland transport so that most materials must have been man-handled or carried on pack animals, because the mountainous character of the island left no possibility of the roads fanning out after the fashion of the desert tracks of Egypt, Syria, and Mesopotamia. There might be a choice of ways, but these ways were always narrow, and when it was a question of crossing a saddle from one valley to another there was, and still is, often no choice available. Human porters seem to have carried their loads on poles balanced on the shoulder, varying according to the weight of the burden from a short pole with two evenly balanced packages to a long pole carried by three or four men, a method employed in Egypt from the early dynasties onwards. I can recall no evidence for the use of hods or headbands to assist the porterage of loads on the back.

A clay model of Middle Minoan I date from Palaikastro (Fig. 17) illustrates the type of wagon used; it was doubtless drawn by oxen. The model presumably represents a wagon with solid wheels and no means of pivoting the front axle. This was not such a bar to progression as might be imagined, since Miss Seton Williams records seeing in Turkey in 1951 a wagon, with solid wheels revolving with the axle and with no pivot for the front axle, turning corners slowly but without undue difficulty; similar examples are illustrated by G. R. H. Wright and J. Carswell.[1]

Stockholm Museum has a copper model of a rather similar type of vehicle from north Syria, and though this particular example cannot be accurately dated we have evidence that wagons were in use in the Orontes valley in Syria about 2000 B.C., and the Cretans who were in close touch with ports such as Byblos probably imported the idea from that country.

Professor Childe suggested the following dates for the introduction of wheeled vehicles: in Mesopotamia 3000 + (B.C.); in the Indus Valley 2500 ±; on the Central Asian steppes 2500; in north Syria, on the Khabur and Upper Euphrates, 2200 ± 100; in the Orontes valley

1. V. Gordon Childe, 'The First Wagons and Carts', *Proceedings of the Prehistoric Society*, 1951, p. 177, and Wright and Carswell in *Man*, March 1956, Note 39.

Fig. 17a. Palaikastro model wagon

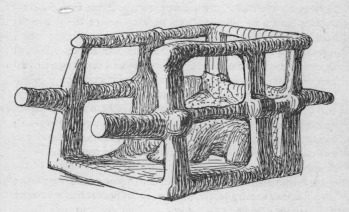

Fig. 17b. Litter from Dove Shrine, Knosos

2000 ± 100; in Crete and central Anatolia 1900 ± 100; and on the mainland of Greece 1550 ± 30.[1]

The use of the domestic ass as a pack animal may go back further in Crete, though I cannot recall any evidence for that animal on the island before Middle Minoan times or any representation of an animal

---

1. The people of Mycenae had horse-drawn chariots by this date and they may have had ox wagons as early as the Cretans.

with panniers before the Late Minoan III period.[1] Childe suggests that oxen may have been used for ploughing before they were employed for drawing carts, but I know of no Minoan evidence either for or against this suggestion.

WAR CHARIOTS

Spoked wheels appear at a very early date at Chagar Bazar, but the earliest appearance of the war chariot with spoked wheels in the Aegean would appear to be the example carved on the grave stele of the Mycenaean king buried in the Fifth Shaft Grave at Mycenae, dated about 1550 B.C. Since the earliest representation of a horse in Minoan art is on a Late Minoan II gem dated 1450–1400 showing a horse being transported on a galley, there is a distinct possibility that the war chariot and the horse were only introduced to Crete in the Late Minoan II period, perhaps by the Mycenaean dynasty which may have been ruling at Knosos at that time, though there is a seal from Avdhou in Crete showing two men in a chariot drawn by two *agrimia* attributed to the Late Minoan I period (Fig. 18).

The Minoan army certainly had no cavalry and probably no organized chariotry. The war chariot seems to have been an invention of the Sumerians, but their chariot, with its four solid wheels, and drawn by asses, must have been rather a slow, clumsy affair. The capture of Babylon by the Kassites, who had domesticated the horse, revolutionized the warfare of the Middle East. Before the middle of the second millennium B.C. a properly organized chariot arm was serving the purpose of cavalry in all the armies of the greater land powers of the Near and Middle East.

By the sixteenth century B.C. the war chariot had spread to the Greek mainland, not indeed the improved light chariot with a six-spoke wheel which we find illustrated on the later Hittite monuments and on Egyptian monuments of the Eighteenth Dynasty, but the rather slower four-spoke wheel type that appears on the earlier monuments of the Hittites, from whom the Mycenaean Greeks may

1. A figurine of Late Minoan III date from Phaistos shows a horse with two *pithoi* slung pannier-fashion, as is the practice today among the travelling potters of Thrapsanos. See D. Fimmen, *Die Kretisch-Mykenische Kultur*, 1924, p. 114, Fig. 102.

have adopted it.[1] The earliest representations of the Mycenaean chariot given on the sculptured *stelai* from the shaft graves are rather summary, and we must not therefore overstress the fact that there is only one horse and only one man in the chariot. Nevertheless it is quite possible that at Mycenae the oldest form of chariot had only one horse and that the charioteer also used the spear against his opponent.

Fig. 18. Goat chariot from Avdhou

The normal method, however, where the chariot had two horses and two men, one to drive and one to fight with spear or bow, is already illustrated by a gold ring from the Fourth Shaft Grave at Mycenae. The chariot with its four-spoke wheels and low box-like car perhaps made of basketwork is similar to those of the *stelai*, but is here drawn by two shaggy ponies.[2]

1. I do not imply that a six-spoke wheel must be faster than one with four spokes, but simply that the six-spoked form on the monument is much lighter and less clumsy than the four-spoked variety.

2. Not the fine Arabian breed illustrated on Late Minoan frescoes, vases, and gems, but something more like a modern Cretan pony; conceivably the so-called 'Celtic' variety of *Equus agilis*.

This form of war chariot was particularly favoured by the Indo-European speaking tribes and was probably a major cause of their widespread conquests and expansion. It is referred to in the *Rig Veda*, the earliest Sanscrit poems in India, in Homer's *Iliad*, and in other epic poems in Greece; it continued in use later in Cyprus, in Etruria, and among the Celts, and was still employed by the Britons when Caesar invaded Britain.

The yoke, which was appropriate for an ox-cart and which had been intended for a Sumerian war chariot, must have been rather an awkward device for a swift horse-drawn vehicle. Contenau even goes so far as to say that 'the capacity of the horse's effort is only equal to its resistance to strangulation', a superb epigram but perhaps exaggerating the difficulties. The yoke, I believe, was probably not taking the main stress of drawing the chariot, which would be taken by traces attached to the collar or breast-band, but was serving the same purpose as the shafts of a modern carriage in keeping the car in its proper position. The Homeric word *lepadna*, as Miss Lorimer observes, comprised both the collar or breast-band and the girth, which was set very far forward and attached to the collar at its top-ends just behind the base of the neck. The traces are not usually illustrated, but must surely have been attached to this dual *lepadna*, which continued to be popular throughout the classical period. This form of harness and yoke already appear clearly on the Avdhou gem (Fig. 18). The straps of the *lepadna*, which would have been of leather, broaden towards the bottom.

Some chariots of the Late Minoan II–III period illustrate another device that may have been intended to relieve the strain on the horses' necks, consisting of a long pole or thong stretching from the rim of the car to the tip of the chariot pole and attached by straps lower down to the pole.

In the Late Minoan II–III period the normal chariot was apparently what Evans termed the 'dual chariot', and is illustrated by the signs on the 'chariot tablets' of Linear Script B from Knosos, and by the fresco of the two princes in a chariot from Tiryns on the mainland. The curving projection at the back gives rather the impression of a rail, though in fact, as Miss Lorimer observes, it must be a solid affair. It may still, however, have been rounded off by a flat rail which, with the addition of the extended platform of the car, would have afforded greater facility for the warrior to mount the car while it was in motion; and this I suggest may have been the purpose of the projection at the back of the dual chariot. It would also probably allow the car to carry a third person if necessary.

It must be remarked that the horse on the ship of the Late Minoan II seal, and indeed all the horses depicted on Mycenaean frescoes or vases, is a fine animal with a small head, powerful fore and hind quarters, and small joints, recalling Shakespeare's splendid description in *Venus and Adonis*:

> Round-hoofed, short jointed, fetlocks shag and long,
> Broad breast, full eye, head small and nostril wide,
> High crest, short ears, straight legs and passing strong,
> Thin mane, thick tail, broad buttock, tender hide:
> Look what a horse should have he did not lack,
> Save a proud rider on so proad a back.

In a word, Mycenaean horses look as if they had good Arabian blood in them, and would be much superior in speed to what Ridgeway used to term 'those quarter-bred animals of the Parthenon frieze'.[1]

Did the Minoan Cretans know how to ride? The evidence from Cretan sealings would suggest that equitation was practised by goddesses rather than men,[2] since the earliest unmistakable picture of a mounted warrior in Crete is on a cremation urn from Mouliana often assigned to the tenth, but by Desborough to the ninth century B.C.[3]

Nevertheless Mycenaean Greeks both in the Peloponnese and in their colonies were riding horses in the thirteenth century B.C.[4] and the riding of asses had been known in Egypt in the days of the Middle Kingdom and of horses by the inhabitants of the Persian uplands apparently in the third millennium B.C.

The negative evidence from Crete is unreliable, and it seems probable that riding was practised in Crete certainly by the thirteenth century B.C. and perhaps considerably earlier, whether the art was learned from Mycenae or from Egypt, Palestine, or Syria.

1. A quotation from a lecture.
2. D. Levi, 'La Dea Micenea a Cavallo', *Studies Presented to D. M. Robinson*, 1951, p. 108.
3. V. Desborough, *Protogeometric Pottery* (1952), p. 269.
4. M. S. Hood, 'A Mycenaean Cavalryman', *Annual of the British School at Athens*, 1953, p. 84 ff., Figs. 47, 48; C. F. A. Schaeffer, *Ugaritica II*, 1949, p. 158, Fig. 61C.

The Minoans also employed open litters or carrying chairs. Our earliest surviving evidence for this form of transport consists of a model carrying-chair found in the Dove-Shrine deposit in the Palace of Minos (Fig. 17*b*).

The normal Minoan carrying-chair illustrated both by the Middle Minoan II model referred to and by a rather fragmentary fresco of Late Minoan I date from the Palace of Minos consisted of an open litter enclosed by a railing, attached to two carrying poles, and containing a chair for the occupant.

The Mycenaean Greeks, however, improved on this model by adding a vaulted cover[1] resembling on a smaller scale the hood of the covered wagon of the Scythian steppes, and illustrated by a clay model found in Stratum VI at Tepe Gawra (a settlement dating back to Early Dynastic[2] times on a mound now enclosed by the Assyrian walls of Khorsabad).

Pendlebury even goes so far as to say that 'the normal method of progression for the rich man was a palanquin', and he may be right, though the evidence is rather scanty for Minoan Crete.

It would be rash to assume that the Cretans ever had goat-carriages drawn by their own wild goats, despite the appearance of the chariot drawn by two *agrimia* on the Late Minoan I seal from Avdhou quoted above.

1. J. M. Cook, 'Pelino Omoioma Mykenaikou Phoreiou', *Kretika Chronika*, 1955, p. 152.
2. I refer, of course, only to the Sixth Settlement.

CHAPTER 5

Minoan Art

MINOAN art, the art of the Cretan Bronze Age, differs in spirit considerably not only from its contemporaries in the Near East, but also from its immediate predecessor, the art of Neolithic Crete.

Art for art's sake seems, I know not why, to have been a Neolithic invention and appears all over the world whenever the inhabitants reach that stage of culture, whereas late Palaeolithic art and its more recent offshoots, such as the cave paintings of eastern Spain or the relatively modern cave paintings of the Rhodesian caves, were grafted in magic. They were intended to serve the practical purpose of aiding the hunters, though doubtless the painter derived an artistic pleasure from his work.

Neolithic art on the other hand was non-representational and severely abstract in the main. If men, animals, birds, fishes, or flowers were represented at all they quickly became patterns. Features that originally had had a structural use on vases were also turned into patterns, which are termed by the archaeologist 'skeuomorphic' designs, because they had derived their *morphe* or shape from the *skeuos* or household article on which they had originally performed a practical function. Thus the stitched seams of a leather bottle, or the ribs or studs of a metal vessel may be painted as skeuomorphic patterns on pottery imitations of such vessels (Plate 1 and Fig. 3).

The 'art for art's sake' of the Neolithic potter may have been fostered by the settled agricultural life of those times, but whatever the cause was it is clear that Neolithic Cretans conformed to the general rule. The pottery of the earliest Bronze Age in Crete also continued to be adorned only with very simple patterns of a severely geometric kind such as painted vertical or diagonal lines, occasionally cross-hatched, incised dots, or semicircles – a poor and uninspired repertory, but completely devoid of any suggestions of magic.

It is evident that we cannot speak of an art common to the whole of Crete during the first Early Minoan period (2400–2300 B.C.) which was marked by the infiltration of small bands of settlers from various directions, each with its own particular style of pottery; indeed the complete fusion of these different elements of the population was scarcely complete before the beginning of the first Middle Minoan period (1950 B.C.).

Fig. 19. Minoan torsion designs

We can only surmise the origin of these bands of settlers from the artistic affinities of their arts, from those of Early Minoan II patterned ware and of Vasiliki pottery, with certain Anatolian wares; and from those of Pyrgos with those of the 'Pelos' variety in the Cyclades (Fig. 22).

The rectilinear patterns of Early Minoan III pottery were only a continuation or elaboration of those of the previous period – a zigzag line with triangles, a band of chevrons, a pattern like the triglyphs and metopes of a Doric frieze, and so on. More important than the rectilinear decoration was the introduction of curvilinear ornaments, which had scarcely ever appeared before except in the form of concentric semicircles on Early Minoan II pottery. Whole circles filled in with colour or with hatched segments or other hatched patterns also occur. Running spirals (a Cycladic pattern) appear sometimes joined by a curious leaflike scroll. This incipient interest in natural history is very slight and tentative at first, the most amusing

Fig. 20. Zakros sealings

example being a sherd on which the familiar opposed triangles or 'butterfly' pattern has been turned into a goat by adding a head with a pair of horns at the apex of one of the triangles. Perhaps this new naturalistic art may have started in the Mesara, since it is rare on the pottery but very evident on the ivory seals, which are common in the great round tombs of the Mesara. Here we find not only lively if somewhat primitive designs of men, animals, birds, scorpions, fishes, and even ships, but also meander patterns and quadruple spirals best paralleled in Egypt. A favourite animal on these seals is the lion, which still existed on the mainland of Greece and of course in Syria, but not, I think, in Crete.

SPIRAL DECORATION

The origin of spiral decoration in general does not concern us here and I think it had more than one origin; its derivation from gold or copper wire or from the spiral coils of shells or from textiles will all fit individual instances, but break down if interpreted as universal sources for spiral ornaments.

It is clear, at least, that a fashion in spirals spread over the Levant towards the end of the third millennium B.C. In Egypt the fashion is illustrated by small scrolls on scarabs of the First Intermediate Period, finally developing into four, or sometimes six, interconnected spirals outlining a roughly quadrilateral area. Similar quadruple spirals appear in Crete on the bases of seals of gold and of ivory from the Mesara, and on a stone *pyxis* from Tholos B at Platanos. The pattern is capable of developing into a spiral network of the kind fashionable in Egypt in the Eighteenth Dynasty, and in the Late Bronze Age in Crete, and on the mainland of Greece.

TORSION AS A DECORATIVE PRINCIPLE

The first real attempt to probe into the basic principles of Minoan art was made by Professor Friedrich Matz in his work on early Cretan seal stones, in which he distinguished two fundamental methods of decorating the surface of a vase, which we may translate as 'zone decoration' and 'surface decoration'. Furumark, in his works on Mycenaean pottery, prefers to employ the terms 'tectonic' and 'unity' decoration for the same two methods.

The peculiarity of Minoan surface decoration, first noted by Matz, was its partiality for 'torsion' or twisted motifs. The zone decoration in which horizontal bands of ornament play the leading part is indeed 'tectonic' in the sense that it emphasizes the structure of the vase, the greatest width, the mouth and neck, the handles, and the foot. The 'surface' or 'unity' decoration, on the other hand, treats the whole vase as a free field for a single design, or even several independent designs, without stressing any particular structural feature of the vase.

If the base of a cylindrical or round stamp seal has a frieze of animals on the circumference, or even two animals arranged in the *tête bêche* position (which is only the circular frieze reduced to its simplest form), the effect of a moving frieze can be obtained by turning the seal round, but this is not torsion. Torsion occurs when a motive which might be expected to run vertically or horizontally twists like the line of a corkscrew up and across the surface to be decorated. This can occur in purely rectilinear ornaments, but it is perhaps not surprising that it should have been particularly popular in areas where spirals were in vogue, such as the Aegean or the Danube basin. Indeed Matz in his book on Cretan seals was inclined to regard this as a European element in Minoan culture, but in his latest article on torsion he has emphasized the fact that, though torsion was certainly characteristic of large areas in Central and Eastern Europe, it was also characteristic of a wide area in the Levant including not only the Aegean, but also south-eastern Anatolia, which so strongly influenced Crete, the Cyclades, and the Greek mainland at the beginning of the Bronze Age.

Matz has contrasted the torsion style with the more widely distributed systems of the *Winkelband* or 'Zigzag Line' and the 'Meridian system', a vertical division which in one form or another occurs in most parts of the ancient world, and has come to the conclusion that the source of torsion as an aesthetic principle is to be sought not so much in Europe as in Anatolia.

Matz's account of the diffusion of torsion seems reasonable and is not incompatible with an idea of my own that the technique of decorating the surface while the vase was being turned on a mat may have contributed to its development. Indeed the technique of manufacture may have contributed something also to the zigzag band and meridian systems. Zigzag bands are common, if not inevitable, in basket work, so that the *Winkelband* might be considered as a skeuomorphic ornament derived from basketry even though the potters who developed this theme were probably quite unconscious of its origin.

Similarly meridian decoration might be derived from leather bottles with vertical seams, though it is only occasionally that we can assert such a derivation with confidence.[1]

Torsion decoration might arise naturally, I think, if a potter painted his vase while turning it on a mat or some such base. All hand-made vases, unless they are so big that the potter has to walk round them, must be turned round during the process of manufacture. When the potter's wheel was introduced the wheel would normally have been stopped before the decoration began (unless the ornament

1. For example on certain bowls and bottles of Bronze Age date in Cyprus.

was of a very simple, band-like character), and if any decoration was carried out while the wheel was still moving, this would be easy to detect. With vases turned on a mat, however, the turning would have been so slow and so easily controlled that decoration could

Fig. 21. Designs on Early Minoan I vases

easily have taken place while the vase was being turned, and this would have been apt to produce torsional effects, which later might be deliberately cultivated as an aesthetic principle. Other causes doubtless contributed to the torsional style, but I think it may be significant that the earliest motives of this nature seem to occur on hand-made or hand-turned pottery, and that they seem to be absent from Mesopotamia, Syria, and Egypt where the potter's wheel was introduced at very early dates. In the Aegean area itself torsion is particularly dominant in Crete and rarer in the Cyclades and on the mainland until it reappears under Cretan influence at the beginning of the Late Bronze Age.

MINOAN ART AND THE EIDETICS

Now it is true that we may claim the Minoan civilization as the first European civilization, as distinct from the semi-barbarous though often artistic cultures of the north, but this is no explanation of the uncanny qualities of Minoan art in the Middle and Late Minoan periods, qualities less obvious during the Early Minoan period. Minoan art is not only unlike its predecessors; it is also unlike all its successors, with the exception of arts directly influenced by it such as those of Mycenae and the Cyclades. G. A. Snijder offered an ingenious explanation of these peculiarities suggesting that they were character-istic of the artistic products of a group of people whom the psycho-logists term 'eidetics', and that these peculiarities were also to be noticed in the late Palaeolithic art of Spain and France and in related cultures of more recent times, such as the Eastern Spanish School or the Bushmen paintings of Rhodesia. This condition is very rare among European adults, and not very common among children, but is a well-attested phenomenon. Just as anybody who looks at the sun or a lighted lamp and then at a blank wall will see a little purple lamp or sun for a second or two, so an eidetic person will retain the vision of a whole picture or landscape if he transfers his gaze from it to a blank surface. This vision, which is not merely a mental picture, is termed an *eidos* and the people who are liable to such visions are termed 'eidetics'. This condition was first studied by the German scholar, E. R. Jaensch, who published his researches in 1933 in a work entitled *Die Eidetik*.

Children with eidetic vision are sometimes unable to distinguish clearly between their eidetic visions and what they see in the ordinary way. This condition is termed the phase of eidetic unity, and usually does not last long, but may persist longer with half-witted or slowly-developed children, and it is suggested by followers of Jaensch that it might be more prevalent and last longer with primitive peoples.

The Minoan ability to portray figures in rapid movement with a vividness hardly equalled before the invention of photography could be easily explained if the Minoans were eidetics, since the artist would then only have had to trace along the outline of his eidetic

Fig. 22. Designs on Early Minoan II vases

vision. This great facility is, however, accompanied by certain weaknesses. The eidetic artist is apt to concentrate on the outline and to disregard the internal bony structure which does not appear in his vision. The figures therefore sometimes tend to be slightly insubstantial, to float in air rather than to stand firmly on the ground.

Snijder's theory attracted me at first and has been supported to some extent by Pendlebury and Platon, but on a closer examination of it I doubt whether it is a satisfactory explanation of Minoan art in general.

Can the realism of Minoan frescoes be explained by assuming that the artist saw his subject as an eidetic vision? Minoan frescoes may perhaps seem fresh and natural compared to the splendid but more formal beauties of Egyptian wall-paintings, but they are not quasi-photographic representations like the bisons of Altamira in Spain. Indeed Minoan paintings abound in conventions, some obviously borrowed from Egypt, such as the procession motives, or the distinctions between the red flesh of the men and the white flesh of the women, but other conventions seem to be native Minoan. Most uneidetic of all the Cretan artist's conventions is his naturalization of the lotus flower. The photographically correct drawing of this plant on Egyptian paintings appeared too stiff to be true to the Minoan artist, who proceeded to gild the lily by painting his lotus if not 'as large as life' at least 'twice as natural'.

This idealistic tendency of the Cretan artist is well stressed by H. R. Hall in his comparison of the cat on the Hagia Triada fresco with those on Egyptian paintings of the Twelfth and Eighteenth Dynasties.

The Minoan borrowed his idea from Egypt, and his cat is in one sense a better cat than the Egyptian, in another a worse one. It gives the idea of the cat, its stealthiness and its cruelty, better than the Egyptian paintings which hardly give any such idea at all. But they are more accurate in detail; they are correct portraits of the animal taken from her in repose, and in the Eighteenth Dynasty example clumsily put into a scene meant to represent action, though all the actors with the possible exception of the butterflies, are as calm and peaceful in gesture as is the cat. Compare the Cretan cat, which is incorrectly drawn, but gives a masterly and true impression of the animal when hunting.

Hall proceeds then to contrast the purely Aegean conception of a swallow in flight on a sherd from Melos with the very dull copy of an Egyptian goose found on the same site at Phylakopi.

This difference between Minoan and Egyptian artistic practices may be observed also in the Late Bronze Age.

The octopods and dolphins of the first Late Minoan period are not correctly drawn in detail but are magnificently alive, whereas the Red Sea fish and crabs of Queen Hatshepshut's relief at Deir-el-Bahri are as accurate and lifeless as the diagrams of trilobites in a textbook of palaeontology.

Forsdyke stresses this same feature with reference to one of the gold cups from Vapheio: 'The trapped bull bellows in anger and its hind quarters are twisted the wrong way round. Such distortion is manifestly impossible, but the Minoan artist would not check at this exaggeration so long as it served to emphasize a mighty struggle and disposed a pair of legs nicely for his design.'

Surely the eidetic artist postulated by Snijder would have been more accurate and less idealistic in his draughtsmanship. The inaccuracies of eidetic art are of a different kind and consist of combining incongruous details which individually are photographically accurate.

Mrs Groenewegen-Frankfort speaks of 'the absolute mobility' and 'unhampered freedom' of Minoan figures whether human or animal and the artist's delight in moving patterns. . . . 'There is a sense of the organic even when organisms are not depicted. . . . This not only makes for a dynamic coherence of disparate motifs but gives each one of them a curious independence as if they were charged with life.'[1] She also points out how often the dominant movement in one direction is restrained by a counter-movement in a different direction such as animals in the flying gallop pose with the head turned backwards, or the falling man on the Harvester Vase from Hagia Triada.

Snijder also attempted to detect eidetic characteristics in Minoan sculpture, architecture, and even vocabulary. Minoan architecture is certainly rather queer and haphazard so that it has been rightly dubbed 'agglutinative' because rooms and wings of various shapes and sizes were added as the need arose, but I doubt if they are so very much more 'agglutinative' than the plan of the City of London, which from medieval times onwards has mainly expanded by cellular growth, nor do I see any great resemblance between a Minoan palace and a nomadic camp (to which Snijder compares it), since the latter

1. H. A. Groenewegen-Frankfort, *Arrest and Movement*, 1951, p. 191 f.

is usually laid out on a much simpler and more regular plan to meet the needs of defence against surprise attack.

It should be remarked that Snijder's best parallels between Minoan and eidetic art occur not in the Early Minoan period, as might be expected if they were primitive traits, but rather in the third Middle Minoan period, and that they might be more explicable if we supposed that a painter capable of seeing eidetic visions had played a leading role as a fresco painter and perhaps formed a school of his own, instead of trying to interpret all Minoan art in terms of eidetic visions.

MINOAN POLYCHROMY IN POTTERY AND FRESCOES

The naturalizing of geometric designs, which is barely noticeable in Early Minoan III and Middle Minoan I A pottery, becomes increasingly prominent in the Middle Minoan I B style. Purely geometric designs such as hatched triangles or spirals now not only alternate with branches, daisy chains, and triple flowers, but also intermarry with them, so that a design which starts as a hanging spiral may suddenly bloom into a cluster of berries. Among the new designs is a swastika (a very ancient motive in Mesopotamia but new to Crete). The commoner form of polychromy, especially on cups, is the alternate repetition of the same motif in white and orange on the usual black ground. The old principle of torsion is still active in the diagonal arrangement of many of the motifs, one of these torsion designs being the old Early Minoan III one, the scorpion parade, now arranged as two lobe-shaped leaves joined by a stem. Large round blobs are a favourite motif, either arranged as a frieze or forming the knots of a net pattern.

Another form of decoration, not very common in northern Crete but very popular in the Mesara, was the so-called barbotine type, consisting usually of thin strips of clay usually applied in the torsional style to jugs with beaked spouts and with no painted or only very simply painted ornaments. Another form in which the surface is worked up with a tool to form prickles like rose thorns is more characteristic of the Middle Minoan II period.

In eastern Crete pottery decorated in this Middle Minoan I B style not only began rather earlier than it did in the centre of the island (?1900 B.C. as against ?1870 B.C.) but also persisted right through the Middle Minoan II period, when the pottery that we know as Middle Minoan II A and B was in vogue at Knosos and Phaistos.

The colours employed on Middle Minoan I B vases included a modification of the old orange-yellow, a new red approximating to crimson in hue, and a brilliant white employed not only for separate ornaments but also to coat zones or panels of barbotine 'prickle' ornament between the areas adorned with polychrome ornaments (especially in the Mesara). The shapes favoured included 'fruit stands', bridge-spouted vases, beaked jugs, 'tea-cups', 'Vapheio cups',[1] and, in Knosos and along the north coast up to Gournia, chalices with strap handle and a crinkled rim obviously imitating a metallic type – one vase of this form in silver was actually found at Gournia in a grave.

These chalices are quite important from a chronological point of view since they are clearly related to, and probably contemporary with, some Hittite vases found in the fourth city at Boghaz Koi or in the city termed Alisar II in Cappadocia.

FIGURES IN THE ROUND

Very little plastic work of importance has survived from the first Middle Minoan period. The fashion of carving the handles of ivory seals in the form of an animal or a bird, so popular in the Early Minoan III period, had died out, and we have only one steatite figure, the one from the round tomb at Porti in the Mesara, that should probably be assigned to this period since the proportion and modelling of this figure show a marked advance on any of the earlier human figures.

The cheaper forms of Middle Minoan I figures, however, are well represented among the dedications at the various 'peak sanctuaries' in the form of figurine men or women, or animals, or parts of them. The earlier types of these are represented by those from the oval house at Chamaizi in eastern Crete consisting of standing male figures with the right hand raised to the chin and the left hand by the belt, to which is attached a short dagger, and of standing female

1. A truncated conical shape like that of the gold cups found at Vapheio.

figures with both hands raised to the chin, with a long, flaring skirt, and with a roll on the head that might be interpreted either as a 'Tam o'Shanter' form of cap, or as a method of hairdressing.

The later figurines from the peak sanctuaries are of the kind made familiar by the finds from Petsopha, the sanctuary above Palaikastro. Two fragments of a figure painted in the Middle Minoan II style were found in the Second City of Phylakopi on the Cycladic island of Melos.

Such figurines were obviously the cheap art of the period, but of the figures in gold, bronze, or ivory which must certainly have existed we have nothing surviving except the Porti figurine already mentioned.

We are therefore no more able to conjecture what the best work of Minoan modellers and carvers might have been at this time than we could have estimated the work of Pheidias if the Parthenon marbles had not survived and we had been dependent on reconstructing their probable forms from the cheap plaques and figurines in clay dedicated on the Athenian Acropolis.

In the Middle Minoan II B period (1830–1700 B.C.) we begin to encounter beautiful seals in hard stones engraved in a naturalistic style (cf. Fig. 34). This development is partly due to an increasing mastery over the materials by the artist, who was now using a tubular drill and a saw as well as a graver and so could cut hard stones such as agate, crystal, and emerald, and partly due to the fact that the invention of a linear script had provided an easy method of writing clay labels and so rendered the seal less important as a means of communicating a message.

Seals were now articles of luxury rather than business necessities and those who ordered them could command the services of good craftsmen. Indeed the best Middle Minoan II B seals were never surpassed in grace and finish. Prism seals with three or four sides still continue to be made, but the best engraving occurs on flattened cylinders, on lentoid or bean-shaped seals, on discoid seals with a design on both flat sides or with one side modelled to form a grip, or on signets (a form borrowed from the Hittites of Asia Minor). One design which recurs on several seals of the Middle Minoan II B and Middle Minoan III A periods was compared by Pendlebury to a Jacobean cherub, and by Evans to an Ishtar mask; I have myself wondered whether it was not a modification of the winged sun disk of Egypt turned into a grinning face by the irrepressible Minoan artist. I think that, whatever was the origin of this device, Marinatos is probably right in associating it with the faces on seals or clay sealings from Mochlos, Phaistos, and Zakros and with Greek archaic representations of Gorgon masks.

To the Middle Minoan II B period also belongs a unique amethyst scarab from the lower levels of the Psychro Cave, which by its material and modelling, should be Egyptian work of the Twelfth or at latest of the Thirteenth Dynasty but bears on its base a Minoan design consisting of two beaked jugs and some concentric circles arranged round a device usually interpreted as a rayed sun.[1]

The naturalism which was soon to blossom in the frescoes already appears on the seals in a developed form. A fine flattened cylinder in rock crystal shows a Cretan ibex bounding over its native rocks with a tree in the background, a perfect illustration of the scene so aptly described by Xan Fielding in his book *The Stronghold*:

> With no apparent means of propulsion (for its legs were invisible in motion) and with its shoulders flattened by perspective and half-concealed in dust, it came hurtling horizontally across the cliff – a disembodied head hanging on to the air by its horns.

This is certainly the finest verbal description of the pose which archaeologists term the 'flying gallop' and which the Minoan artist loved to portray (Fig. 34). Fielding's description perhaps explains why so many ancient representations of the ibex portray the head and horns too large for the body.

Of the ivory figures now in European or American museums and reported to have come from Crete it is better to follow Nilsson and not to quote them as illustrations of Minoan art, though the gold and ivory snake-goddess in Boston is usually reckoned as genuine and the Toronto figure known as 'Our Lady of the Sports', wearing the male dress for the bull ring like the ladies in the Toreador Fresco, bears a strong resemblance to the leaping figures from the Late Minoan I deposit.[2]

1. Pendlebury, *The Archaeology of Crete*, p. 119 and Fig. 19, No. 5.
2. Evans, *The Palace of Minos*, Vol. I, p. 337 and Vol. III, p. 305; but Marinatos, Mallowan, and Glotz consider the Boston statuette to be a forgery.

CHAPTER 6

The Early Minoan Period

THE Neolithic period in Crete did not end in a catastrophe; its culture developed into that of the Bronze Age under pressure from the infiltration of relatively small bands of immigrants from the south and east, where copper and bronze had long been in use. This early metal culture of Crete might be termed a Copper Age, but since the exact date when tin first became available to the Cretans is hard to define, it is best to follow Sir Arthur Evans, who christened the culture between the Neolithic and Iron Ages in Crete the Minoan culture, after Minos the legendary king of Knosos, and who divided the Minoan epoch into three periods: Early, Middle, and late Minoan with three sub-divisions each.

Professor Doro Levi has recently put forward a heretical theory, based on the absence of Early Minoan pottery at Phaistos, that there was no Early Minoan period at all, properly speaking, and that the Middle Minoan period directly followed the Late Neolithic with the intervention of only some very short-lived transitional fabrics that might be described as Early Minoan.[1] It must be admitted that at Knosos also Early Minoan pottery is very scarce, and almost non-existent in the Palace of Minos where the walls of the earliest palace usually rest on are embedded in the latest Neolithic deposits.[2]

His theory, however, does not explain the experience of extensive Early Minoan material not only in the Mesara but also especially in east Crete where such material is sometimes stratified over Neolithic or under Middle Minoan 1 deposits. The absence of Early Minoan material on the palace sites at Knosos and at Phaistos may be explained by the cutting away of such deposits caused by the terracing required for the excavation of the great Middle Minoan 1 palaces.

The Early Minoan period however, may have been shorter

1. See articles in *Illustrated London News*, 19 January 1952, 2 December 1953, 30 September 1955.

2. I have revised my dates for E. M. 1 and 11 following research by Dr Peter Warren. See chronological table.

than was supposed by Evans, whose absolute chronology was based on synchronisms with the contemporary culture of Egypt and Mesopotamia, and was dependent on the validity of what was then termed 'the shorter chronology' evolved by Dr Edouard Meyer, but which has now proved to be not short enough.

THE FIRST EARLY MINOAN PERIOD

Thus the Early Minoan I period which Evans was obliged to stretch from 3400 to 2800 B.C. is dated 2600 to 2400 by Matz, and I am inclined personally to date it 3000 to 2600 B.C.

The Early Minoan I culture is not a unity at all. I doubt if any of the more important Late Neolithic sites were abandoned. At Knosos and at Phaistos there is an absence of the new dark-on-light painted pottery found elsewhere, but this, I think, is merely because the local Neolithic pottery developed into Sub-Neolithic fabrics better baked, of finer material than that of the preceding period, and characterized by vertical burnishing, but obviously derived from the Late Neolithic types.

It is likely, too, that some of the pottery of Late Neolithic types, found by the Germans of Kumarospilio in the far west and by the Greeks at Hellenes Amariou, may belong to the Early Minoan I period. On such sites we may assume that the inhabitants were still of Cretan Neolithic stock.

The foreign influences that were already perceptible, however, in the Late Neolithic period, may now be observed to be infiltrating into the island by three main routes, from the Cyclades, from Anatolia, and from Syria.

Graves from the Early Minoan I period are scattered thinly throughout east and central Crete, at Zakros, Hagios Nikolaos, and Patema in the extreme east, at Sphoungaras on the Merabello coast, at Trapeza in Lasithi, at Miamou in the Mesara, and at Kanli Kastelli in central Crete.

Houses of the Early Minoan I period are scarce however, and it is clear that many people still lived in caves.[1] Of the thirty-three excavated sites recorded by Pendlebury sixteen were burials or bore traces of having been burials (twelve from caves or rock shelters),

---

1. Unless one believes with Levi that this period did not exist.

while only at Mochlos and at Hellenes Amariou were actual walls of stone houses recorded, though it is of interest to note that Komo, the port for ships departing for Egypt, and the little island harbour town of Mochlos on the gulf of Merabello were both founded in the Early Minoan I period.

No copper tools that can be dated as certainly Early Minoan I have yet been found, and it is not improbable that the Cretans of that period continued to use stone tools. Evans has also assigned to this period two or three stone figurines which appear to represent a transition between the Late Neolithic squatting type and a standing type, because of the abnormally wide flanks and very short legs. This characteristic, however, can hardly be quoted as evidence for an Early Minoan I date, since standing figurines were already made in Neolithic times. The use of stone instead of clay, however, may, as Pendlebury suggested, indicate an Early Minoan I date. One such figurine from central Crete is in alabaster, one from Knosos is in a marble-like stone, while a third from Gortyn is in breccia.

At Pyrgos near Nirou Khani, Xanthoudides excavated a large rock shelter which had been employed as an ossuary in Early Minoan I and later times. There was no stratification, but the Early Minoan I material, which could be identified on stylistic grounds, was abundant. Here the excavator found not only incised bottles and *pyxides* like those of Pelos, with vertically pierced suspension lugs,[1] but also beaked jugs of west Anatolian forms with simple rectilinear designs in a reddish brown lustrous paint and a grey smoked fabric with burnished decoration of which the most characteristic shape was a tall chalice, shaped like an hour glass, of a type sometimes called the Arkalochori chalices, from the site where they were first found by Hazzidakis. Evans derived these from the footed bowls of later Neolithic pottery, but now that we have more evidence from excavations in the Dodecanese and Asia Minor it appears that this ware is also in a sense Anatolian, being related to wares in the Dodecanese and Samos; but it is reasonable to assume that the people who made the incised bottles and *pyxides* characteristic of the Pyrgos cemetery near Nirou Khani, of Tholos A at Koumasa, and of the Kanli

1. A feature characteristic of the contemporary Early Cycladic vases in the Cyclades and distinguishing them from the succeeding Early Cycladic II vases with horizontally pierced lugs.

Kastelli (Fig. 23) cemetery must have come from the Cyclades where such pottery is characteristic of the very earliest deposits in Melos and Antiparos. The earliest and most primitive form of *tholos* tomb in Crete, at Krasi on the edge of the Pedhiadha district, also resembles Cycladic forms. The marble figurines found near Knosos, in the Mesara, and in eastern Crete are still clearer evidence of influence from those islands, though possibly at a later date.

Archaeologists have often been puzzled over the apparent absence of a Neolithic culture in the Cyclades, although tools which seemed to be made of Melian obsidian were discovered in early Neolithic deposits at Knosos. Saul Weinberg is probably right in explaining this by his assumption that the earliest Bronze Age culture of the Cyclades overlapped with Cretan Neolithic and with the Middle Neolithic culture of the mainland.[1]

The Early Minoan I and II pottery, characterized by jugs with high-beaked spouts and a buff surface adorned with simple linear designs in red or brown lustrous paint, found in east Crete, in the Mesara, and in the Kanli Kastelli cemetery, must have been introduced by immigrants from the south-west coast of Asia Minor.

Much of the Early Minoan I pottery from Knosos, Phaistos, and other sites, however, consists of burnished, sub-Neolithic wares but with a thinner fabric and baked much harder than the Neolithic pottery. In eastern Crete the transition to the Bronze Age was more marked, but even there we find little suspension *pyxides* in a grey sub-Neolithic fabric at Hagios Nikolaos near Palaikastro (including, however, a tall horned lid like a Trojan form) while Tomb 5 at Mochlos contained clay ladles of Neolithic type. At Knosos the sub-Neolithic vases included open bowls, handleless cups, ladles, and pedestalled bowls. A few burnished sherds, others with stripes of chalky white or crimson paint, and one or two fragments with dark-on-light designs may presumably be regarded as imports from other parts of Crete where those fabrics were more normal products.

1. See R. W. Ehrich, *Relative Chronologies in Old World Archaeology*, pp. 96 and 97; and S. Benton, 'Haghios Nikolaos near Astakos in Akarnania', *Annal of the British School at Athens*, 1947, p. 156.

THE SECOND EARLY MINOAN PERIOD

The second Early Minoan period was dated 2600–2300 B.C. by Evans, 2400–2200 B.C. by Matz, and I have myself suggested 2300–2100 B.C. as a not unlikely date, after taking into account the latest revisions in Egyptian and Babylonian chronology.

During this period the eastern peoples and the Mesara developed their Copper Age culture to a new height, though the north and west lagged behind them. Metal tools and weapons are relatively scarce but always of copper or with a very low proportion of tin, to which the Cretans probably had no direct access.

Fig. 23. Early Minoan II vases from Kanli Kastelli

Our knowledge of the pottery and of the burial customs of the Early Minoan II period has been considerably extended by the recent excavation by S. Alexiou of a burial deposit in a cave shelter at Korphi tou Vathia near Kanli Kastelli.

This deposit like others of its kind was devoid of any real stratification, not because it had apparently been robbed, but rather because of the funerary rites concerned. The question arises whether we are to interpret the Korphi tou Vathia shelter as a collection of primary burials or to treat it rather as an ossuary where burials of different dates were collected, and where it would therefore be impossible to separate individual burials and the grave goods dedicated with them. The cave shelter at least afforded a fine series of late Early Minoan I and Early Minoan II pottery comparable to that of Pyrgos. Here there were no gold jewellery or delicate vases of stone as at Mochlos, and we can therefore regard it as the grave furniture of the peasants. The confusion in the deposit might at first sight suggest that the burials had been robbed of their most expensive offerings, but the excavator is convinced that this was not the case (a conclusion supported by the fine preservation of the pottery) and he suggests that the evidence of fire and of burnt bones, human as well as animal, not only at Kanli Kastelli but at many other contemporary burial sites, such as Pyrgos, Sphoungaras, Gournia, and Kato Zakros, indicate that burnt sacrifices formed an essential part of the funeral ceremonies.

The pottery consists chiefly of two fabrics, a smoked grey ware and a ware with simple rectilinear designs in glaze paint on a buff surface. The shapes of the smoked ware include not only chalices of the Arkalochori type but also squat *pyxides*, *pyxides* with high necks intended for cylindrical lids like the Early Minoan I suspension vases from Miamou and Hagios Nikolaos, conical cups with one handle, two-handled beakers, and beaked jugs (all three west Anatolian shapes, reminding us of vases at Troy and elsewhere), ovoid jars, carinated jars with cylindrical necks (reminiscent of early Maltese shapes), cylindrical *pyxides*, conical jars with tripod feet (another west Anatolian form), and small ovoid jars with everted rims – a very comprehensive series suggesting foreign influences, especially from Anatolia. The ornaments of the vases with burnished designs that appear on Arkalochori chalices occur also on contemporary vases from the Dodecanese or Samos.

Another fabric from this site was a red ware stained in the firing, and so the forerunner of that later ware of the Early Minoan II B period known as Vasiliki ware, but having irregular, shallow grooves in the surface made by a comb. The vases in this technique were mostly beaked jugs of Anatolian forms recalling those of the painted ware found with them, and varying in form from a jug with a very high beaked spout, like that from the Hagios Onouphrios deposit, to a type where the mouth is almost horizontal with only a slight dip downwards towards the handle, like the jugs acquired by Ormerod in Pisidia, or ones found by Seager in stone at Mochlos, by Xanthoudides at Platanos, and by Bent in pottery from an Early Cycladic grave on Antiparos.

The dark-on-light painted ware of Kanli Kastelli was of the kind first identified by Evans when he assigned the jug from the Hagios

Onouphrios deposit near Phaistos to the latter part of the Early Minoan I period. Professor Banti has recently suggested that such vases belong rather to the beginning of the Middle Minoan I period, and it is true that the fabric seems to last into that period, but evidence that Evans and Pendlebury were probably right in their dating of the Hagios Onouphrios jug is afforded from Kanli Kastelli, where the shapes in this fabric included such jugs. Pendlebury's distinction between the Early Minoan I jugs with rounded bases and the Early Minoan II ones with flattened bases may not be absolutely reliable (the two forms may overlap) but it is not contradicted by Alexiou's evidence. Other shapes in this fabric included tankards not unlike Early Helladic forms on the mainland, but also paralleled in Asia Minor: squat little jugs on three short legs (a Trojan form); mugs like two-handled coffee-cups; other cups with handles set very low down; conical cups with two small lug handles; an *askos* with tubular spout; and a one-handled mug with four short legs.

The decoration consisted of vertical, horizontal, and cross-hatched lines occasionally employed in panels (Fig. 22). The maximum variety achieved consists merely of painting slanting lines on the spout, horizontal on the neck and vertical on the body of a beaked jug. This tendency to stress the structural features of the jug may have been introduced by the new settlers from their Anatolian home, since it soon dies out in Crete and is replaced by an all-over system of decoration which Matz calls 'surface decoration' and which Furumark prefers to call 'unity decoration'. Cycladic influences are naturally less noticeable at the inland site of Kastelli than they were at Pyrgos or even in the Mesara, but there was a cylindrical *pyxis* with incised decoration of Cycladic type and blades of what was presumably Melian obsidian.

Three copper daggers were found belonging to Mrs Maxwell-Hyslop's Type 16,[1] a local Minoan variety appearing first in the Early Minoan II period and developing parallel with a similar Egyptian one in the Early Minoan III period. One of these Kastelli examples had the blade formed of two thin plates welded together. One or two beads of yellow steatite were discovered in the same deposit.

1. Maxwell-Hyslop, 'Daggers and Swords in Western Asia', *Iraq*, 1946, pp. 18, 19; similar daggers have been discovered in Early Bronze Age deposits at Alisar in Anatolia, at Tarsus in Cilicia, and at Lapethos in Cyprus.

The absence from Kanli Kastelli of the mottled pottery known as Vasiliki ware confirms Pendlebury's view that the latter was an Eastern fabric typical of the Early Minoan II B period, appearing at Vasiliki before the end of Early Minoan II A, later exported to other parts of Crete, and imitated at Palaikastro, Trapeza, the Mesara, and elsewhere. By the end of the Early Minoan II period potters had begun to coat Vasiliki ware with a red slip which was mottled red

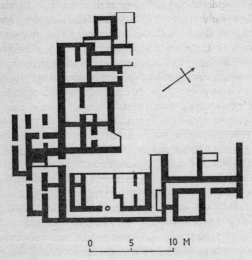

0   5   10 M

Fig. 24. Early Minoan II house at Vasiliki

and black. This mottling was at first presumably accidental and caused by baking the vases in an open fire, but later seems to have been deliberately cultivated to produce an ornamental effect.

The irregular surface of the walls at Vasiliki was covered with a red lime stucco which has a surface almost as hard as Roman cement. This cement, though convenient, was not an unmixed blessing since, like charity, it covered a multitude of sins, and encouraged a careless-ness of structure to which the Minoan mason was only too prone; but it did provide an ideal surface for internal decoration, and was one of the reasons why such a brilliant school of fresco painters developed in the Cretan palaces of later times.

The so-called 'House on the Hill' at Vasiliki not only affords the clearest example of Early Minoan II B pottery stratified over Early Minoan II A ware, but is also by far the most luxurious building of that date so far excavated in Crete. It is, indeed, a small palace and the prototype in miniature of the splendid buildings later to be erected at Knosos, Phaistos, and Mallia. It is orientated with its corners towards the cardinal points of the compass, a practice normal in Mesopotamia and the Middle East generally, but abnormal in Egypt and in the Aegean, and it is possible that this architectural orientation is due to the people who introduced Vasiliki pottery, with its Anatolian forms. Unfortunately the site is badly denuded and all that remains is the lower parts of the south-west and south-east wings of the building. It is impossible to reconstruct the original plan, but it seems not unlikely that the various wings were grouped round an open court in the centre.

The remainder of the building consists of rectangular rooms of all shapes and sizes, sometimes united internally by long passages, and illustrating that typically Minoan labyrinthine, agglutinative architecture which was to culminate in the Palace of Minos.

Simpler houses of the old 'but-and-ben' type,[1] and amplifications of these with three or more rooms, must have been common, though actually we can illustrate their forms not so much from surviving houses as from ossuaries which preserved the plans of earlier houses. A fine series of such ossuaries dating from the Early Minoan III and Middle Minoan I periods was excavated at Palaikastro by Bosanquet, and we may suspect that features of pre-existing house plans are preserved in some of the subsidiary buildings attached to the great round tombs of the Mesara. Later in the Middle Minoan I period we find small cities of the dead, a complex of small rectangular houses arranged in streets like the great Islamic 'city of the dead' at Cairo. Such cemeteries of the Middle Minoan I period exist at Mallia on the north coast and at Apesokari in the Mesara.

Similarly at Mochlos, where the earliest burials belong to the Early Minoan II period, Tomb 2 reproduces the 'but-and-ben'

1. Two-roomed houses with an outer room opening into an inner room; see p. 51 and Figure 5.

type of house we have remarked at Magasa in the late Neolithic period. Later Tombs 4, 5, and 6 were united into one complex with 4 A in the centre looking curiously like a Mycenaean *megaron*.[1]

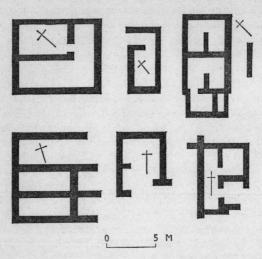

0   5 M

Fig. 25. Early Minoan II ossuaries at Palaikastro

Early Minoan Jewellery from East Crete

No jewellery has survived from the Early Minoan I period and for the two succeeding periods we depend mainly on the results of Seager's excavations at Mochlos.

Tomb I produced a small cylinder seal in silver with a large opening (sign of an early date), and some almost obliterated figures that looked more Mesopotamian than Minoan. It might perhaps have been imported from Syria, and oriental imports of this kind must have stimulated the production of ivory seals, of which only one or two were found at Mochlos, but many in the round tombs of the Mesara (see page 151). Alleged undisturbed deposits of Early Minoan II jewellery were discovered in Tombs 6 and 19 at Mochlos. In the former Seager found two long necklaces of crystal beads, and a

1. For the late Bronze Age type of house termed a *megaron* see p. 306.

still longer one of beads of stone, faience, and shell,[1] sprays of gold (olive?) leaves, a fine gold chain with seven leaf pendants, two pins with crocus flower heads, and fragments of gold armlets. The grave also contained a small silver cup. An ivory seal of the Mesara type (broken and riveted in Minoan times) bears a whorl and spiral design foreshadowing many designs popular in the Middle Minoan period, while another bears a design of two cynocephalous apes sitting back to back. A seal of the latter type was found on the town site of Mochlos in an Early Minoan III deposit, thus raising a suspicion that some of the gold jewellery from this tomb may really have dated from the Early Minoan III period, to which probably also belong the silver diadems found in Early Cycladic graves on Syros and Siphnos.

An animal mask in gold leaf, two drop pendants in silver (perhaps from ear-rings), a large disc in gold leaf, a short necklace of gold and crystal beads, two delicate chains with pendants in gold, and a miniature bronze lion also came from this tomb.

The jewellery from Tomb 19 (also dated Early Minoan II by Seager) included four gold hairpins with daisy heads (a type also found in the Chrysolakkos cemetery at Mallia), two head-bands, a gay but rather nondescript necklace of stones of different kinds, a heavy gold chain of double links, a fine chain with leaf pendants, three leaves from a spray, fragments of armlets, and three stars to be sewn on a garment, all in gold.

The jewellery from Tombs 2 and 4 would appear to be representative of the Early Minoan III period in the main. Connexions with the Cyclades are suggested by the gold diadems with punctured or impressed designs (four dogs on one and two human eyes on another) from Grave 2 and the chalcedony pigeon pendant from 4, recalling silver diadems with punctured designs from Syros and Siphnos and chalcedony pigeon pendants from the latter island, all found in graves of the Third Early Cycladic period (corresponding to Early Minoan III in Crete).

Smaller quantities of jewellery occur in other graves at Mochlos, notably in 12, 21, and 22 where, however, it is hard to distinguish between the Early Minoan burials and those of later date.

---

1. R. B. Seager, *Explorations in the Island of Mochlos*, Figs. 8–12; what I have termed faience he calls porcelain, but it is not porcelain in the English sense of that word.

The Mochlos jewellery also included flat, short tubular, flattened spherical, and pearshaped beads in rock crystal, carnelian, limestone, shell, and faience.

Gold ornaments securely dated to the third Early Minoan period are hard to find but we may probably include in this small category the gold ornaments found in the upper stratum of Tholos A at Platanos in the Mesara. The ornaments are abundant but less beautiful than those of Mochlos, and it appears that at this period the flourishing ports of the Merabello coast were setting the fashion for Crete, and that the Mesara, though prosperous enough, was more provincial and lagged behind the east in development.

Perhaps the best workmanship was displayed in a pendant shaped like a hollow cone suspended from a chain with very fine links in a very pale gold, that must certainly contain a proportion of silver, as did all the native alluvial gold of the Levant. (The term 'electrum' is only applied to such a natural alloy if it contains about thirty per cent of silver or nearly that proportion.)

The jewellery from Tholos A at Platanos also included two small heart-shaped ornaments of very thin gold leaf, one of them with a pretty border of repoussé dots. Twenty-two cylindrical beads of gold leaf were also found there, usually adorned with simple lines or grooves, often of the torsion type embossed or incised, and in two instances decorated with appliqué spirals of gold wire.

Seals and Miniature Carvings in Ivory

The second Early Minoan period saw the beginning of Minoan sculpture in ivory, and of figurines that no longer remind us of the Neolithic ones but of early Egyptian and Libyan types.

A number of Early Minoan figurines have been preserved in the round tombs of the Mesara and from the cave of Trapeza in Lasithi, but all except the most primitive examples from the 'larger tholos' at Hagia Triada belong to the Early Minoan III period, and some of the best carvings were in the form of figured handles to ivory stamp seals. This progress in modelling may have been partly stimulated by the importation from the Cyclades of the Early Cycladic figurines, of which considerable numbers would appear to have been imported into the Mesara and of which occasional examples have been found on other Cretan sites.

The ivory for the figures of Lasithi and the Mesara was probably imported from Syria rather than from Egypt, but the style of the carving is purely Minoan. Indeed some figures from Trapeza with that curious garment variously described as breeches or as a divided apron are reminiscent of certain Late Neolithic figurines from Crete rather than of anything from the Cyclades or from further east in the Levant.

During this period Crete was subjected to strong cultural influences from Anatolia and Syria, from where stamp seals of steatite and other materials were introduced, and Cretans perhaps imitated these and began for the first time to manufacture seals of their own from imported ivory and from native materials such as steatite.

Before the introduction of a written script the stamp of a well-known seal was the only guarantee that an article or package had belonged to or had been dispatched by a particular person or organization. The purpose of the seal was therefore mainly a practical one, but the necessity that the design should be easily recognizable fostered the growth of an art in gem cutting.

The principal forms current in the Middle East at an early date, the cylinder seal favoured in Mesopotamia, the stamp seal popular in Syria and the Levant in general, and the Egyptian scarab made in the form of the sacred beetle, were all of them bead seals which might be strung on a necklace or worn on the wrist like a wrist-watch. By the opening of the Early Minoan period these forms might be found anywhere in the Levant, though their popularity in individual countries remained as stated above. Another form of seal introduced into Crete in the Early Minoan III period was the signet, a form popular among the Hittites and other people of Anatolia. The Cretans might have copied any of these forms, and in later times did so, but their earliest attempts at making bead seals (if we except the rather doubtful examples assigned to the Early Minoan I period) were the Minoan modification of the cylinder seal.

Copper Working

Early Minoan copper work is represented by a few examples, well dated, from eastern Crete and by a much larger but less securely dated series from the round graves of the Mesara. Of the daggers, the most primitive type (also found in Early Minoan II graves at Mochlos) is flat and leaf-shaped with two rivet holes at the outer corners of the slightly concave base, and three of these were found in the Early Tholos A at Koumasa. A triangular type with strong midrib (perhaps to be dated Early Minoan III and represented by three silver examples, Nos. 212, 213, 214 from Tholos (at Koumasa) is of interest for its western connexions. Childe calls it a Minoan type and suggests that it inspired Chalcolithic examples at Remedello in Cisalpine Gaul and at Monte Bradoni in Etruria, but this form seems to be rather more common in Italy than in Crete.

More sophisticated and perhaps later in date is a dagger with a long slim blade, a strong midrib, and two or four rivet holes.

Copper tweezers with splayed tips have also been found in Early Minoan graves at Mochlos, at Koumasa in the Mesara, and at Kanli Kastelli in the Pedhiadha.

The Art of the Stone-cutter

Perhaps the finest artistic achievement of the Cretans in the second Early Minoan period is their astonishing skill displayed in the cutting of stone vases, and their artistic taste in exploiting the colour variations of breccia, conglomerate, or such stratified stones as calcite. They also made stone vases out of green, black, and grey steatite, limestone, schist, marble, and white calcite (all local stones) and more rarely of imported stones. Xanthoudides believed that the fragments of an obsidian rhyton from Tylisos were of Nubian rather than of Melian obsidian.[1]

These stone vases were first blocked out with a tubular drill and then finished by hard grinding with abrasives. Stone vases had been a feature of the Neolithic culture of Cyprus but the shapes there were quite different. This sudden blossoming of stone vases in Crete therefore requires some explanation and probably implies influences from Egypt; and we do occasionally encounter an Egyptian shape, though the more striking and exotic forms of the stone vases are of Anatolian origin, like those of the pottery vases.[2]

1. *Vaulted Tombs, etc.*, p. 105, discussing a core in a similar transparent obsidian from Tholos B at Platanos; this, however, was written before the Italian discovery that Giali near Cos also produced a transparent obsidian.
2. Sinclair Hood believes (perhaps rightly) that many of these vases belong to the Middle Minoan I period.

The Mesara Culture and its Tholoi

Local differences in the shapes of the stone vases from the Mesara, Lasithi, and Merabello suggest that there were several local schools of stone carvers during the Early Minoan II and III periods. Many of the stone vases from the Mesara had so small a cavity inside that they can hardly have been intended for any use except as dedications to the dead. These vases were so numerous that over three hundred were found in the walled Trench α in front of Tholos A at Platanos, but the Mesara vessels, unlike those of Mochlos, belonged mainly to the Early Minoan III and Middle Minoan I periods, and the materials employed were chiefly steatite or serpentine, much easier to cut than the hard breccias favoured by the Mochlos artists.

To the Early Minoan II period, however, we may perhaps assign the 'pepper-and-salt' trays from Tholos A and Trench α at Platanos, consisting of oblong blocks with two or more cups sunk in them, and compared by Xanthoudides to the so-called *kernoi* still used in the liturgy of the Orthodox Church.[1] These Early Minoan *kernoi*, if we may call them that, had holes for suspension and incised rectilinear decoration.

Oblong trays with two or three compartments had already occurred in pottery at Knosos as early as the Middle Neolithic period, sometimes with a flat base and sometimes furnished with four short legs, and it is therefore not impossible that a similar rite for the dedication of the first-fruits of the year may have persisted in Crete for some five thousand years. Similar vessels were also used in Predynastic Egypt, though, of course, not necessarily for the same purpose. The Platanos *kernoi* were all fashioned from a soft red ironstone. Six oval double *kernoi* were also found in the same cemetery. Most of the *kernoi* belonged, I imagine, to the Early Minoan II period, but the early character of some vases from Tholos A makes it possible that the type dates back to the Early Minoan I period.

The dark-on-light pottery forms include small beaked jugs, 'teapots', bowls with tubular spout and handle at right angles to the spout, miniature *hydriae*, two-handled bowls, cups with one or two handles, and bird-shaped *askoi* (in one instance with a ram's head)

1. S. Xanthoudides, 'Cretan Kernoi', *Annual of the British School at Athens*, 1960, pp. 9–15 and Fig. 2.

with a misleading superficial resemblance in form to Mycenaean vases of a thousand years later (Fig. 23). Some of these vases, however, belong to the Early Minoan III period and a few, especially the miniature *hydriae*, appear to have been Middle Minoan I A in date.

Most curious of all is a vase which I hesitate to describe as a votive pair of trousers, but do not know what else to call it. Xanthoudides's term for it is a cylindrical belly open at the top standing on two long tubular legs.

Village sites of this period have scarcely been examined in the Mesara, but Xanthoudides has noted the existence of one or two settlements, and remarked that probably many of the Early Minoan settlements remained undiscovered, because their ruins underlie the modern villages, the settlement corresponding to the round tomb of Marathokephalo below the village of Maroni, that of Dhrakones below Phournopharango, and that of the tombs of Christos, Koutsokera, Salami, and Hagia Eirene below Vasiliki, where Middle Minoan I sherds have been recorded.

The round tombs of the Mesara were communal graves and have sometimes been claimed as the ancestors of the beehive tombs of Mycenae, but they belong to a different category. The essential features of a Mycenaean *tholos* grave, as it is usually termed (though without classical authority of the phrase), are that it is cut in the slope of a hillside, and approached by a level or nearly level entrance passage – it is in fact a chamber tomb lined with stone masonry. The Mesara tombs, on the other hand, stand in the open plain, and most of them could never have been completely roofed with corbelled vaulting, especially with the relatively small stones employed in the existing walls. Only the smaller *tholos* at Hagia Triada and the one at Kalathiana might possibly have been roofed in this fashion. All the others must have been completed with a lighter form of roof in wood or mudbrick or something of that sort.[1] If there is any relationship between the *tholoi* of Mycenae and the round tombs of the Mesara it must have been a collateral one, since both might ultimately have been derived from the Neolithic round buildings of Khirokitia in

1. Compare Dr Johnson's account of the roofing of a Hebridean hut in *Samuel Johnson, Writer*, 1926, by S. C. Roberts, pp. 169, 170, and the account of a Macedonian hut (Pendlebury, loc. cit, p. 64, footnote 2).

Cyprus, though the positive evidence for such a descent has not yet been produced.

There exists, however, in the Cyclades a group of small primitive *tholoi* that might be claimed as intermediate between Khirokitia and Crete. These primitive *tholoi* are often free standing, but they are so small, and the stones employed in them relatively so large, that the task of covering them with a roughly corbelled vault presents no problem at all. In Crete such primitive *tholoi* are not uncommon in Lasithi, a backward district, at the very end of the Bronze Age, but that they also occur even in the Early Minoan I period probably under Cycladic influence is shown by the instance of such a tomb at

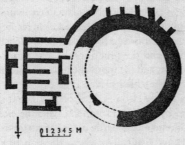

Fig. 26. Tholos A, Platanos

Krasi (in the Pedhiadha province politically, but geographically only just off the edge of the Lasithi plain), containing some silver ornaments, an ivory seal shaped like a human foot, two daggers, and some pins of bronze.

We may perhaps claim Tholos A at Koumasa, a tomb containing two Cycladic figurines and incised pottery of Early Cycladic I types (a *kernos* and *pyxides* with vertically pierced lugs), as only an improved and more elaborate form of the Cycladic primitive *tholos*.

The Mesara round tombs continued in existence till the end of the Middle Minoan I period, and in that period a small *tholos* tomb, rather primitive still but a little nearer the mainland type, was erected at Apesokari on the southern edge of the Mesara. In the late Bronze Age we shall find occasional examples of the mainland type of *tholos* tomb in Crete, but I should hesitate on the present evidence to derive either the mainland from the Cretan or the Cretan from the mainland. I should imagine rather that there were two originally independent but converging lines of development in Crete and on the mainland. If there was any direct influence from one to the other, Crete is more likely to have influenced the mainland before 1550, the mainland more likely to have influenced Crete after 1450.

The Early Minoan tombs of the Mesara have also been quoted, especially by Evans,[1] as evidences of Egyptian and Libyan influence on Crete. Sir Arthur cited as instances parallels from Hierakonpolis and Nagada for certain types of figurines in Crete, and the analogies between the forms of the round tombs of the Mesara with those of the *mapalia* or round huts which persisted in Libya up to Roman times. Professor Banti has thrown doubts on such influence from Pre-dynastic Egypt, but Pendlebury countered with the remark that it was really only the western or Libyan element in the Pre-dynastic culture that Evans claimed to have influenced the Mesara, citing not only the figurines and the round tombs, but also the type of dress, the side lock of hair, and the use of the simple bow armed with broadtipped arrows of the chisel-bladed type that the French term *petits tranchets*. Libya is only two days' sail on a caique from the Mesara, a fact emphasized by Lt-Col. Hammond when he escaped in a caique to Tobruk at the end of the Battle of Crete in 1941.

It is not unnatural that eastern Crete, through which came most of the trade from the Dodecanese, Syria, Cyprus, Palestine, and Egypt, should have led the way in the Early Minoan period.

The prosperity of Pseira and Mochlos in the Early Minoan II period was considerable. Mochlos is now an island separated from the mainland of Crete by about a hundred and fifty metres of water, but we have to allow for the subsidence of the eastern half of Crete since Minoan times. In the Early Minoan II period Mochlos was probably united to Crete by a narrow spit of land affording a good harbour on either side according to the wind. The prevailing winds are N.N.W. to W.N.W., and it would therefore be the eastern harbour that would be most employed by Minoan merchants and fishermen.

It is more difficult to account for the prominence of Pseira, which was always an island, and, as Seager remarks, 'aside from the harbour the island could have offered little to attract settlers of any sort even in Minoan days'. He points out, however, 'the excellent harborage

1. *The Palace of Minos*, Vol. II, p. 37–9.

for small craft offered by the sheltered cove. . . . It is exposed solely to
the east, and an easterly gale is a thing of rare occurrence in Cretan
waters. . . . Even in the present day the port of the ancient Minoan
town is constantly used in case of a sudden gale by the numerous
sponge fishermen who work the Cretan waters on their way to and
from the Libyan coast.' Indeed sponge-diving was probably a local
industry at Pseira in Minoan times. Perhaps the purple fisheries were
another, as they certainly were in Middle Minoan I times on the
island of Leuke off the south coast of Crete. Pseira, however, is a
barren island which can never have afforded sustenance for its population, who must have depended largely on trade and imported their
food, other than fish, from the mainland.

THE THIRD EARLY MINOAN PERIOD

The third Early Minoan period (2300–2000 B.C.) is a very short transitional period of which the most remarkable feature is the expansion
of central Cretan sites, such as Knosos and Phaistos, at the expense of
the east Cretan sites, which began to decline. Pendlebury's picture of
this period for eastern Crete is rather grim: only a few new sites; at
Vasiliki the great house on the hill is in ruins with the small huts of
squatters built against its walls; no certain habitation of Early Minoan
III date was known to him, though some of the Middle Minoan I
houses at Pseira, Mochlos, Palaikastro, Hagia Triada, and Tylisos may
well have been erected on earlier foundations, or even have been
adaptations of earlier houses. At Knosos the only structure of importance assigned to the Early Minoan III period by Evans was the great
hypogaeum near the south porch, but since there are no more Early
Minoan III sherds than Neolithic ones from this excavation, Pendlebury is probably right in assigning it to the Middle Minoan I period
to which most of its pottery belongs.

The paucity of habitations datable in the Early Minoan III period
may be due to their continued occupation in the following period,
as is indicated, perhaps, by the fact that it is much easier to point out
Early Minoan III burials.[1]

In the Mesara, communal round tombs built in the Early Minoan II

1. At Galana Kharakia, near Viannos, Platon recently opened two communal tombs of the Early Minoan period with the remains of over 300 *pithos*
burials.

period continue to have burials, and some of the great round tombs such as those of Porti, Christos, and Vorou were first erected in the Early Minoan III period. In eastern Crete burials of Early Minoan III period may be quoted from Palaikastro, from the ossuaries, and from the later tombs at Mochlos, and from rubbish dumps at Gournia. The mottled pottery and the dark-on-light ware still survive but the most characteristic pottery of the period has designs in matt white paint on a black or dark brown slip, triangles, segments of circles, and even running spirals. Partial hatching is common, and a segment of a circle may have the two corners hatched but not the centre. One two-handled mug has a St Andrew's Cross flanked by panels of vertical lines looking rather as if it had anticipated a motif of over a thousand years later.

The shapes include trough-spout tea-pots, beaked jugs, round, vertical, and conical cups with or without handles, and conical bowls. Among the straight-sided cups is the prototype of the Vapheio cup which was to become so popular in the Middle Minoan II and Late Minoan I periods.

Influence from Egypt and the Levant

The evidence from Pseira is confusing. Seager found plenty of Early Minoan III pottery and therefore inferred that this period was a long one, but he found it all in rock pockets under the houses of Late Minoan I date, and in some instances the Early Minoan III cups merged imperceptibly into those of the following period. Nevertheless, despite the shortness of the Early Minoan III period and the absence of houses datable to it, there are some important changes in Minoan art that appear to have taken place at that time. One of these was the replacement of pottery with dark-on-light patterns by vases with light-on-dark patterns, a phenomenon that seems to have taken place about the same time on the mainland of Greece. Pendlebury suggested that the Minoan Cretans disliked plain ware, and when they found that the 'mottling' of Vasiliki ware was too chancy an affair, they experimented after a very brief and unsatisfactory attempt to return to the incised and punctured patterns of Early Cycladic and Cretan Neolithic type, by covering the pots with red glaze, on which they painted simple designs in white paint.

The increasing importance of Knosos and the valleys round it was marked by some new building and perhaps by the founding of the town of Tylisos (which probably retains its Minoan name).

Foreign imports from Egypt began to come into the Mesara and the Cretan seals of this period have designs closely paralleled by those of the Egyptian seals and scarabs of the First Intermediate Period (Seventh to Tenth Dynasties).

Some of these Egyptian motifs, however, and even the ivory of which the seals were made, may have been introduced from Syria rather than directly from Egypt (since wild elephants were to be found in Syria at least as late as the fifteenth century B.C.). One saucer with a design of concentric circles in thick oily red paint discovered at Mochlos with Early Minoan III pottery was reckoned by Frankfort to be an import from Syria, and he quoted as other instances of Syrian influence the animal-shaped ivory seals found at Platanos and Kalathiana. Some ivory seals of this date have on them a parade of two, four, or more scorpions swimming round like goldfish in a bowl, and this motif develops before the end of the Early Minoan III period into the tennis racket motif of Middle Minoan I vases, a motif sometimes regarded as more Mycenaean than Minoan. The fact is that the origins of this motif, the scorpion parade and the single or double tennis racket developed from it, are purely Minoan motifs. It is only the late development of this motif, when the tennis rackets are attached to a central stem and treated as the leaves, that is Mycenaean more than Minoan. Strictly speaking this motif never resembles a tennis racket though it does rather resemble a lacrosse racket, but the Minoan examples always have the twist to one side, which preserves the twist of the scorpion's tail (Fig. 30). Other seals have a kind of swastika made up of four spirals, which became a very popular motif with many variations. Some seals have representations of the Minoan ships of the period, which we discussed in another chapter. Other seals have rectilinear meander patterns or spiral variations of them on the bases, motifs that became suddenly popular on Egyptian–Libyan seals of the Sixth Dynasty and continued on those of the First Intermediate Period (though isolated examples of spirals and meanders occurred later).

An ivory signet from Hagia Triada shows a cable design surrounding an Egyptian draught-board with three men (shaped like chess pawns) on top, while another Early Minoan III seal from Crete

Fig. 27. Designs on Early Minoan III vases

actually shows us a Cretan sitting on a high-backed chair playing draughts. There is nothing Egyptian about this seal except the draught-board, and the reverse, showing a seated figure with a two-handled vase, perhaps taking it from the oven, is purely Cretan.

The connexions between Egypt and Crete, however, should not be exaggerated, and Miss Kantor stresses certain fundamental differences, particularly the absence of the Cretan torsional or interlocked ornaments, as a basic element in Egyptian design.[1]

Quadruple spirals do appear on some Middle Kingdom scarabs, but as an all-over ceiling pattern they seem not to occur before the new Kingdom.

At Pyrgos on the north coast we find clay chests or *larnakes* with rounded corners and side handles for passing a rope through to carry them. In the Early Minoan III period and at Pachyammos on the gulf of Merabello there were not only Early Minoan *larnakes* of this type, but also burial jars like super-*pyxides* with lids into which the bodies must have been thrust with great difficulty, either by trussing tightly (as Evans suggests) or by breaking the bones.

Cycladic Influences

Early Cycladic idols in marble were imported into central Crete and imitated locally both in the Mesara and in the district round Knosos. Relations with the Cyclades are perhaps also indicated by the appearance of spirals (running spirals and a line of s spirals) on the painted pottery, and still more clearly by the appearance of small *pyxides* with incised spirals. As examples we may quote an Early Minoan III *pyxis* in stone (the variety not stated) with running spirals in relief from Tholos B at Platanos, and a fine schist *pyxis* with carinated profile, complete with lid and spirals in relief, from Maronia near Setea.[2]

Relations with the Cyclades of course had never been broken, but they are more apparent in the Early Minoan I and III periods than in Early Minoan II, when east Crete was being infiltrated by settlers from Asia Minor, and I think it would not be unfair to say that whenever the Cycladic influences are more important than those of Asia

1. It is true that torsion designs occur on one or two metal vases from the Tod treasure, but these, if not actual Minoan imports, at least display very strong Minoan influence. A. Vandier, *À propos d'un dépôt, etc.*, Syria, 1937.

2. H. Kantor, op. cit., Plate II, J and F.

Minor, then central Crete, from Knosos to Mallia on the north, is more important than the part of eastern Crete from Hagios Nikolaos to Palaikastro.

The little incised *pyxides* found in the Vat Room deposit at Knosos (earliest Middle Minoan I A), despite the resemblance of their patterns to certain Neolithic vases, should be reckoned rather as instances of Cycladic influence.[1]

In accordance with this transfer of power and influence from east to central Crete it may be noted that the quality of the stone vases at Mochlos shows a marked decline. The vases are smaller and usually of black steatite instead of the fine variegated breccias popular in the Early Minoan II period. The Lasithi plain, however, seems to have been prosperous, having direct contacts with the Mesara, perhaps through Lyttos and the Pedhiada, and so with trade connexions to Syria and Egypt.

Some of the seals were clearly influenced by Egyptian types either in forms (such as the scaraboid seals) or in decoration – for example a curious double sickle effect which Evans traced back to an Egyptian type with two reversed lions. The button seals, however, may well represent a Syrian tradition, and even when the designs are paralleled in Egypt the Cretan forms of the animal-shaped seals are sometimes nearer to the original Syrian prototype. In some of the ivory seals the handle was skilfully carved in the form of an animal – a sitting monkey (as at Trapeza in Lasithi or at Platanos in the Mesara) or an ox (Platanos).

One Platanos seal has a cynocephalus ape squatting in the ritual attitude familiar in Egyptian representations of that animal, but the incised design on the base consists of three lions contorted in a fashion which no Egyptian artist would have tolerated, but which came naturally to a Cretan artist trained in the 'torsion' school of art (see Chapter 5).

Cretan, too, is the habit of treating a cylinder seal as if it were a button seal, drilling the suspension holes through the short axis and executing the design that was to give the impression on the flat sides, thus making nonsense of the whole principle of a cylinder, which was intended to roll out the design.

---

1. Unless one follows Levi in practically eliminating the Early Minoan culture; on that supposition the patterns could well be survivals from the Neolithic repertoire.

CHAPTER 7

The Middle Minoan Period

THE URBAN REVOLUTION IN CRETE

IT rarely happens that one historical period is neatly divided from its successor by a widespread catastrophe, and in the absence of such an event the line of demarcation chosen between two successive periods will often seem arbitrary. The late Sir Arthur Quiller-Couch used to refer to the mysterious cataclysm of A.D. 1485 which (to judge by the history books) suddenly plunged Britain from the Middle Ages into modern times. The line of demarcation between Early and Middle Minoan may seem almost equally arbitrary, but just as there is a real distinction between the England of Henry VI and that of Elizabeth I, so there is a real and significant difference between the simple village communities with their large communal tombs of the Early Minoan period and the rich sophisticated culture of Middle Minoan Crete, with its cities and palaces, its marine supremacy, and its expanding trade with Egypt, Syria, and Anatolia, and with the barbarian north.

Early in the second millennium B.C., Crete was the scene of an urban revolution which developed with startling rapidity, providing not only a model for similar but later events in Greece, but also a channel through which flowed the cultural products and influences of the older civilizations of Mesopotamia, Syria, Anatolia, and Egypt into the less developed lands of Europe.

The immediate causes are obscure and doubtless bound up with local politics. We can see dimly what happened but not why it happened, and we would give much to be able to read the letters of a Minoan Margaret Paston.

The north-east coast of Crete with its island ports, which had provided the main driving force during the Early Minoan period, now sank into relative obscurity and was eclipsed by the centre of the island, where large cities with splendid palaces appeared at Knosos and Mallia in the north and at Phaistos in the Mesara. We gain the impression that a large part of the island was united under a strong central government, at least a confederacy if not an empire, which not only exploited the rich agricultural plains of the Mesara, the Pedhiadha, Herakleion, Mallia, and the Mylopotamos valley but also carried on a thriving foreign trade with Egypt and the Near East.

TOWN PLANS IN MINOAN CRETE

Architectural planning develops to heights unprecedented in Crete, but it is still the planning of individual architects for particular buildings or at most a group of buildings. There is no town planning as it was understood in the contemporary cities of Egypt.

It is true that no Middle Minoan sites have been excavated completely, like the Late Minoan settlement of Gournia or the Sub-Minoan one on Karphi, but the British excavations at Palaikastro and those of the French at Mallia afford us some idea of the central and poorer quarters of a Middle Minoan city, while the villas of Tylisos and the houses in Gypsadhes illustrate the houses of the upper classes.

The governing principle underlying the lay-out of Minoan towns and villages is well illustrated by the 'House on the Hill' of the Early Minoan II period at Vasiliki (Fig. 24), though it can hardly be termed town-planning. The big man, whoever he was, grabbed the best site and built his palace or large house there, and his relatives and dependants built houses round it. There was therefore an accidental but quite noticeable tendency for towns and villages to be centrifugal, with streets radiating out from one central building and united laterally by roughly concentric streets. This is very noticeable in the Late Minoan town of Gournia.

Defensive considerations seem to have played no part at all in the lay-out of a Minoan settlement until very late on in the Bronze Age. There are no city walls like those of the Early Bronze Age settlements in the Cyclades. I think, therefore, that the tendency of the small houses to cluster round the big house of the village was not so much due to a desire for security against robbers, pirates, or foreign raiders, but was simply because the prehistoric Cretan, like his modern counterpart, was naturally sociable and gregarious.

There are relatively few isolated farms in Crete. A smallholder may have a hut that he occupies for special purposes at some season of the year, but his home is in a village if possible. The unsociable Englishman prefers to live near his work even if he has to walk miles to visit his neighbours, his pub, or his chapel. The sociable Greek prefers to live in a crowded village among his friends and relatives and near his church and his café, even though he may have to walk miles to till his fields or trim his vines, and I think the prehistoric Cretan was like him.

Huddling in a crowded village for company, however, is one thing, but deserting the fertile coastal valleys to live in bleak upland dales is quite another matter, and I think Lehmann makes a good point when he observes that in the periods when a strong central government, such as the Minoan power, or the Roman empire, or the Duchy of Venice, kept the sea free of pirates the coastal plains were well populated, but in the bad times when piracy was rife, such as the Early Iron Age or the Homeric period or the Hellenistic period or that of the Saracen raids, people tended to abandon the coastal villages for those in the uplands.

The Middle Minoan period, however, was very prosperous, and perhaps the fleet of Knosos was already controlling the central Aegean. The question how far 'Minos' of the classical legends was a 'Minoan' king in the sense of belonging to a non-Hellenic race is of course very debatable, and I think that Ridgeway was right in calling him an Achaean,[1] but Herodotus may also have been right in admitting the possibility of an Aegean sea power before that of Minos.

THE HYPOGAEUM AT KNOSOS

A vaulted *hypogaeum* or chamber cut in the soft rock, with a spiral staircase leading into it, was dated Early Minoan III by Evans, whose section restores a passage leading to the south, the whole forming an elaborate entrance system to a hypothetical predecessor of the Palace of Minos. But there is no evidence for this underground tunnel to the south, and I can see no point in the large vault if this was an entrance system. It resembles more an underground granary, since there is no sign of cement or plaster and the rock here is too sandy and

1. W. Ridgeway, 'Minos the Destroyer, etc.', *Proceedings of the British Academy*, 1909.

porous to be suitable for a cistern. Evans dated it to the third Early Minoan period, but Pendlebury pointed out that the Early Minoan III sherds found in it were not much more numerous than the Neolithic, and was inclined to assign it to the Middle Minoan I A period.

THE FIRST PALACE OF MINOS

Early in the Middle Minoan I A period the top of the Kephala mound was levelled for the construction of the first palace, and any Early Minoan structures that might have existed were swept away so that in the central court late Neolithic buildings directly underlie the

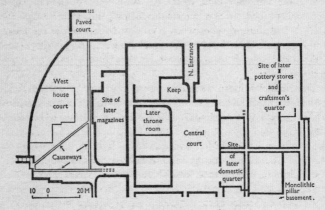

Fig. 28. Plan of earlier Palace of Minos

paving of the central court (a condition paralleled in several parts of the Palace of Phaistos).

The general plan, which in its main outlines continued to dominate the later buildings, consisted of a great, rectangular court surrounded by isolated blocks which Evans termed *insulae*.

The north entrance was flanked by two towerlike blocks. The western tower, which Evans termed the 'Great North Keep', was constructed of very massive blocks of limestone, with foundations sunk deep into the Neolithic earth, enclosing small, windowless cellars known as the 'dungeons'. Sir Arthur used to relate with glee how he had once shown a party of German tourists round his excavations when he had a workman employed at the bottom of one of the dungeons. The Germans had looked surprised and inquired why the man was down there. Sir Arthur had replied 'we had some trouble with that man, in fact he has been down there for several days', and he used to add that they had gone away much impressed with British discipline.

The rounded corners of this early keep were evidently a characteristic of the early *insulae*, since another such corner was preserved even in the latest reconstruction of the block containing the Late Minoan II throne room. Indeed repair and cleaning operations carried out by Dr Platon and myself in 1945 proved that the main scheme of the ceremonial rooms immediately west of the great court go back to the earliest days of the palace. The throne room as it stands belongs to the Late Minoan II period, but below the floor of the ante-room leading to it was an earlier floor of the type known as *mosaiko* – a sort of crazy pavement of irregular stones of different shapes and colours fitted together – that should not be later than the Middle Minoan III A period (1700–1600 B.C.). Immediately south of this the pillar shrine and the temple repositories behind it date from the Middle Minoan III B period (1600–1550 B.C.), but the east Pillar Crypt behind had an earlier floor covered with pure Middle Minoan I A material – sherds, broken lamps, and burnt bones of oxen, sheep, and pig – implying that the main plan of this area must go back to the earliest days of the first palace (Plate 7).

The west quarter of the earliest palace, however, projected farther into the west court than does the present façade, and there was originally direct access between the west and central courts. The domestic quarters on the east side of the great court consisted of a series of rooms built terrace fashion down the hill and served by what Evans called the east-west corridor, with a staircase at its west end giving access to the central court.

In the Middle Minoan I B period[1] (1900–1850 B.C.) some important building operations were conducted, of which perhaps most important was the construction of the great Stepped Portico, a splendid

---

1. It is dangerous to employ this phrase except at Knosos because the Middle Minoan I B pottery in east Crete and the Mesara may have started earlier.

covered approach to the south end of the palace from the terminus of the great south road that brought the produce from the Mesara ports and from Egypt. The Portico is so ruined that its reconstruction cannot be attempted in detail, but we can surely see how it made the right-angled turn to cross the Vlychia ravine, where the great south road split into three branches – one entering the Stepped Portico, one entering the west court by a long ramp, and a third continuing almost on the line of the modern motor road towards the harbour town of Knosos. To this period belongs also the setting back of the façade facing the west court, and it is not unlikely that there may have been some precursor of the later west porch giving indirect access to the central court at its south end.

MIDDLE MINOAN I CEMETERY AT KNOSOS

The Middle Minoan I A houses of the city have hardly been excavated, but Middle Minoan I A sherds are common everywhere. In 1935 under Sir Arthur Evans's auspices and guidance (and at his expense) I opened a rock shelter on Monasteriako Kephali, the acropolis hill west of the Minoan city. It proved to be a continuation of the rock shelter previously tapped by R. J. H. Jenkins, who found Middle Minoan III *pithos* graves there.[1] I also found remains of about three *pithos* graves of Middle Minoan III date and a considerable quantity of pottery of that period, but, underneath and separated from it by a sterile layer of fallen rock representing a collapsed roof, I found the remains of an ossuary of Middle Minoan I date with one complete skull, a number of crania, and plenty of bones. There was, however, no possibility of distinguishing between those of one skeleton and of another.

The most interesting individual find was a limestone head (published in *Journal of Hellenic Studies* Vol. LV and also by Pendlebury in his *The Archaeology of Crete*). It has a distinctly Sumerian appearance, and Frankfort compared it to Early Dynastic sculpture from Mesopotamia, that is sculpture of the middle of the third millennium. The head, however, was found in the Middle Minoan III deposit, and though its battered condition makes it quite likely that it may have

1. Unpublished; H. G. G. Payne, 'Archaeology in Greece', *Journal of Hellenic Studies*, 1934, does not mention them.

Fig. 29. Designs on Middle Minoan IA vases

been derived from the Middle Minoan I deposit, it certainly cannot be dated earlier than about 1900 B.C. on the Cretan evidence and might be later. It might of course have been an *antica* even then, acquired in the course of a raid on the Syrian coast, but the stone looks not unlike a hardened variety of the local marl known as *kouskouvas*.

The back view of this head looks very like those of the Palaikastro boys. The latter, however, if not Egyptian work, were clearly influ-

Fig. 30. Designs on Middle Minoan IB vases

enced by it, whereas the Knosos head, though not Sumerian handy-work, was influenced by oriental sculpture, perhaps from Syria (Plate 14a).[1]

THE OVAL BUILDING AT CHAMAIZI

The Middle Minoan I A building excavated by S. Xanthoudides at Chamaizi on the high ground separating the coastal plain north of Tourloti from the Seteia valley is unique, the only oval building of Minoan date. Some well-intentioned but misguided attempts have been made to interpret this structure as an intermediate form between circular and rectangular houses, an explanation which might possibly suffice for some early houses on the mainland of Greece, but will certainly not do for Chamaizi, since there are no round houses preceding it.

Mackenzie pointed out that the interior walls were all set at right angles and explained it as an ordinary house with an open court in the centre. He suggested the oval wall outside was simply dictated by the space available on the crown of the hill (Fig. 31).

Platon, who interprets it as a variety of peak sanctuary, stresses the evidence for cult worship indicated by an altar and an ash stratum, by the presence of three large idols and the head of a fourth, and by the fact that the so-called well would neither collect nor hold much water, and would be far more suitable for a *bothros* or sacred rubbish pit. The filler, the lamp, and the cylindrical vessel can all be paralleled at the Koumasa shrine.[2] For the apsidal plan Platon cites the survival into Protogeometric times of apsidal models of shrines in pottery, quoting an example in the Giamalakis collection (Fig. 68). The evidence is rather inconclusive, but Platon may be right since the Chamaizi building has no exact parallel in domestic architecture.

House A at Vasiliki also belongs to the Middle Minoan I period and is a normal example of Minoan agglutinative planning. The individual rooms are rectangular and well constructed but have been added when and where the occasion demanded, so that the overall plan appears accidental. One might say that the house had grown over

1. Professor Mallowan states that the head is certainly not Sumerian but probably an archaic work from north Syria.
2. Xanthoudides, *Vaulted Tombs of the Mesara*, p. 50 and Plate XXXIII.

the ground like an ivy plant. Most of these Middle Minoan I houses were destroyed by Middle Minoan III buildings, though at Chamaizi there was no reoccupation. Since Middle Minoan II pottery is

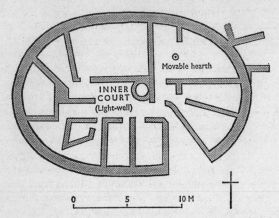

Fig. 31. Middle Minoan I house, Chamaizi

confined to so few sites it is not unnatural to attribute the destruction to the same catastrophe which caused great destruction at Knosos during that period.

THE SECOND MIDDLE MINOAN PERIOD

The second Middle Minoan period (1850–1750 B.C.) is hard to define in most parts of Crete where pottery of Middle Minoan I B and even of Middle Minoan I A type continued to be made, but at Knosos and at Phaistos the period[1] can be more accurately represented both by its pottery and by architectural reconstructions and improvements in the Palace of Minos.

The semi-independent *insulae* of the Middle Minoan I palace (Fig. 28) with the open passages between were now for the first time

1. At Phaistos, however, we must date the beginning of this period not later than 1900 B.C. (see pp. 191, 197).

linked up into a single structure. The west court was extended by destroying some early houses, levelling the whole area, and digging three great circular pits known locally as *koulouras*. Evans and Pendlebury interpret these as dug simply to receive the broken pottery from the palace rubbish dumps. It is evident, however, that the similar but smaller *koulouras* in the west court of the palace at Mallia were intended for use as cisterns or granaries, since they were lined with plaster and often have a central Neolithic pillar to support a wooden roof. The rubbish found in the Knosos *koulouras* is no evidence for their original purpose, since all granaries and cisterns, when they go out of use as such, degenerate into rubbish pits. More serious objections to identifying the Knosian *koulouras* as granaries or cisterns are that they have no plaster lining, no central pillar to carry a roof, and are very large and awkward to roof.

The level of the old north-west court was raised and a broad flight of steps led up from the south side to meet the paved causeway crossing the west court towards the west porch. The alterations to the ceremonial block of state rooms between the west and central courts are rather hard to detect, as they have been obscured by later improvements, but they apparently included the construction of the west magazines and the setting back of the façade facing the central court, and so might have contained in some form the pillar shrine facing the central court.

It is clear at least that the Vat Room and the two adjacent pillar crypts preserved the plan they had in the Middle Minoan I period.[1] The old North Keep had its dungeon basements filled in, and its remains now served only as a substructure for the west side of the new north entrance with its broad ramp running up to the central court.

West of the main north gate there was constructed a smaller and more private entrance, associated with a fine new lustral area, and with a passage that skirted the remains of the old North Keep and communicated with the north-west corner of the central court near the rounded corner of the *insula* that later contained the throne room.

---

1. Evans's excavations proved this for the Vat Room, and the material found by Platon and myself in 1945 below the Middle Minoan III paving proved the Middle Minoan I A date at the two pillar crypts (Plate 7).

Fig. 32. Designs on Middle Minoan II A vases

To the latter half of the Middle Minoan II period Evans assigned the earliest fresco with a human figure in it, that of the Saffron Gatherer, of which the fragments were found above a Middle Minoan II floor laid down over one of the 'dungeons' of the old North Keep. Snijder pointed out, however, that the stratification of the room would allow it to be assigned to a Middle Minoan III A or even Middle Minoan III B date, and in view of the advanced character of the fresco such a date is probably to be preferred.

In the north-east part of the palace some new rooms were built for the Royal Pottery Stores which contained some of the finest polychrome pottery (Middle Minoan I B and Middle Minoan II A) found on the site, and south of these a special magazine for the great knobbed *pithoi*, dated Middle Minoan II B.[1]

The most radical alteration to the palace, however, was the construction of a great new domestic quarter in a cutting of the hillside on the east side of the great central court, and although this quarter was again remodelled in the Middle Minoan III period, certain features still existing, such as the terrace walls of the cutting, the south wall in the light-well of the 'Queen's *megaron*', and the walls of the lower east-west corridor, date from the Middle Minoan II period, as does also the elaborate drainage system of this quarter.

Some idea of the general appearance of the Minoan town at this time may be gathered from the details of the town mosaic, of which fragments were found in a Middle Minoan II B stratum north of the domestic quarter.

THE THIRD MIDDLE MINOAN PERIOD

The Middle Minoan II period ended about 1700 B.C.[2] in a disaster perhaps caused, as Pendlebury remarks, by 'the first of that series of earthquakes which periodically laid the palace in ruins'. The damage was soon repaired but it is possible, however, that the Cretan marine never quite recovered its control of the Levantine seas, since, as Miss Kantor has noted, exports of Minoan pottery to Egypt and Syria

1. This date is confirmed by the similar but smaller examples found at Phaistos sealed by a floor of the later palace.

2. Conceivably the earthquake of 1730 B.C. recorded by Schaeffer, *Stratigraphie comparée*, etc., p. 6.

seem to stop after the Middle Minoan II period though they still continued to the Cyclades and the mainland of Greece.

There is no sign of internal decay, however, in Crete. At Knosos the third Middle Minoan period is that of the greatest building activity. In the palace of Minos the domestic quarter was remodelled and the east-west corridor, though still existing in a modified form, was replaced as the main line of communication in the domestic quarter by the Grand Staircase, a splendid structure rising from the Hall of the Colonnades (Plate 15) right up to at least two storeys above the level of the central court. The central space in the Hall of the Colonnades was unroofed and acted as a light-well for all the storeys of the staircase. These light-wells, so reminiscent of modern hotels or blocks of flats, are a typical feature of Minoan architecture, and were the natural solution of the problem of lighting a large number of small internal rooms.

At Knosos the light-wells are normally situated at one end of the room, but the architects of the palaces of Phaistos and Hagia Triada in the Mesara sometimes illuminated a long room on the ground floor by a light-well in the middle of the room.[1] The light-well at the bottom of the Grand Staircase, known as the Hall of the Colonnades, was bordered on the north by the lower east-west corridor which thus still preserved something of its old importance as a main line of communication in the domestic quarter.

A few steps along the corridor was a door opening into the west end of the Hall of the Double Axes, so called because the double axe recurred as a mason's mark on the stones of the light-well at its west end. This was the chief room, the throne room of the domestic quarter, and the impressions of a wooden throne with pillared canopy above may be seen in the mass of melted gypsum plaster adhering to the north wall of this hall.

Opposite the throne, in the Hall of the Double Axes, a short 'dog's leg' passage led into an elegant little room which has been christened the 'Queen's *megaron*', with light-wells on the east and south sides, a small lustral area or bathroom on the west side, and a passage leading to the Queen's private lavatory (Fig. 33).

---

1. These light-wells are distinguished by their fine ashlar masonry, whereas the interior wells (not subject to the damp) usually had rough surfaces with rubble masonry that would have been covered by painted plaster.

The lustral area or bathroom differs from the usual type in that its floor is not sunken, so that there are no steps leading down into it. Also it still contains a clay bath and, though the painted ornament of this shows that it was made long after the construction of the room, it may still reflect its original purpose. The convex fluting of the column has been restored from those of the columns in the lustral area at the Little Palace. The terminus of the south road, where it joined the Vlychia bridge, is now supported by a massive viaduct, perhaps the most imposing structure still visible at Knosos.

The entrance from the north-west was made much more impressive. The steps leading from the oblong court at the end of the Royal Road were preserved, but were flanked on the east by a platform forming a royal box where the King could receive or review deputations, and the east end of the court was blocked by another flight of steps, the whole forming a Theatral Area (Plate 8) analogous to the earlier example at Phaistos, on which it was presumably modelled. The eastern steps led up to a private entrance to the palace flanked by what Evans termed the north-west 'lustral area', leading past the old North Keep direct to the throne room. Presumably only important visitors or officials would have been allowed to enter this way, and such persons may have had first to purify themselves by some ceremony in the lustral area.[1]

Structural innovations of this period include the regular employment of light-wells to give light to inner rooms; the replacement of the *kalderim*, or cobbled floors characteristic of the Middle Minoan II rooms, by the type called *mosaiko*, consisting of irregular slabs of almond stone with the interstices filled with red or white plaster; the replacement of high-column bases in breccia by low ones in limestone; and a fondness for inserting *kaselles* or stone-lined cists in the floors of magazines. The south-west wing of the palace was disused and private residences encroached on it.

One of the most notable features at this period is the excellent sewage and drainage of the domestic quarter of the palace (Fig. 33b).

The Queen's lavatory with its traces of a wooden seat and arrangements for flushing, and the system of drains and sewers connected with it (Fig. 33a), are one of the most interesting refinements of the palace

1. If these 'lustral areas' had been only sunken bathrooms, one would have expected to find some drain for the surplus water.

The first floor of the domestic quarter clearly reproduced the plan of the ground floor, and we have sufficient evidence to infer the existence of an upper Hall of the Colonnades giving access to an upper hall of the Double Axes and beyond to an upper Queen's *megaron*. Further, the upper Hall of the Colonnades has a fresco consisting of representations of figure-of-eight shields of the regular Minoan type, representing a spiral frieze as hanging above, which

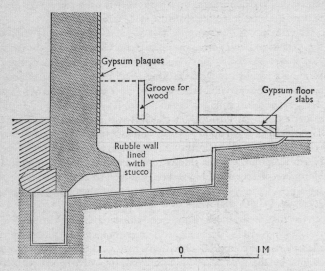

Fig. 33 a. Section of Queen's lavatory, Knosos

enabled Evans to put forward an ingenious and, I think, convincing deduction. The lower Hall of the Double Axes has a similar spiral frieze but without representations of shields, and Evans suggested that, since the most important room in the domestic quarter could hardly have been decorated merely with a narrow spiral frieze, we might infer that the actual shields were hung on the wall behind the throne, and he therefore caused replicas to be made and hung there.

The shield fresco was badly damaged but could be restored in detail from a Mycenaean reproduction of it on the mainland in the Palace of Tiryns.

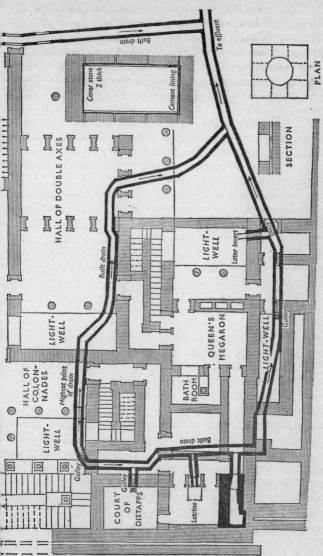

Fig. 33 b. Drainage of domestic quarter

Naturalism in Middle Minoan III Frescoes

The naturalism that became more marked in the Middle Minoan II period reached its height in Middle Minoan III times. A fine fresco in the Queen's *megaron* at Knosos depicted dolphins, at least one flying fish, and some fish resembling *melanouria* (which the French term *blades*). The flying fish was a favourite motif at this time. It appears engraved on seal stones, and modelled in faience in the temple repositories at Knosos. The second city of Phylakopi on Melos contained a splendid mural with flying fish, surely painted by a Cretan painter, and a few pieces of floral fresco discovered in the city destroyed by the great eruption on Thera indicate that Minoan fresco painters were probably active on that island also.

At Knosos painters also began to produce frescoes in low relief. Some magnificent fragments of a charging bull and an olive tree in

Fig. 34. Middle Minoan II B seals

this technique were uncovered which had fallen from the little porch overlooking the west side of the north entrance to the Palace of Minos.

The Middle Minoan III B period (1600–1550 B.C.) was characterized by the appearance at Knosos of some remarkable miniature frescoes with crowds of people represented in a very impressionistic manner (Plates 11 and 12).

A French expedition under M. André Parrot excavated at Mari on the Upper Euphrates the palace of its king Zimri-Lim (?1790–?1760 B.C.), a contemporary of Hammurabi of Babylon who finally captured Mari in 1760 B.C. (or according to some authorities a few years later). This palace contained some miniature frescoes which recall those of Knosos, and a suggestion has been made that they were influenced by Minoan frescoes, especially as the palace accounts of Mari record imports from Kaptara (usually regarded as Minoan Crete, though Wainwright and Furumark interpret it as Cilicia).

The Mari frescoes, however, appear to be over a hundred years earlier than the miniature frescoes of Knosos (which may well have been influenced by them rather than have influenced them), since if we exclude the doubtful instance of the Saffron Gatherer, which might possibly be Middle Minoan III A, there are no figured frescoes in Crete before the Middle Minoan III B period. To the Middle Minoan III period, however, we may certainly assign some fresco fragments from the lower east-west corridor at Knosos, consisting of a dado with imitation marbling (a curious anticipation of the earliest Pompeian style) with a labyrinthine pattern above it executed in dark brown on a yellow ground. It has been suggested also that Minoan frescoes were influenced by those of Level VII at Atchana (intermediate both geographically and chronologically between those of Mari and of Crete).

From the Loom-Weight Area in the Palace of Minos came some other fresco fragments of Middle Minoan III A date with two diagonals crossing at right angles, a design paralleled by a similar fresco in the great central court at Phaistos, and by a design on an engraved gem depicting a man seizing a bull by the horns.

The earliest miniature fresco is represented by some fragments found in a cist in the thirteenth magazine at Knosos (a cist which was filled in during the Middle Minoan III B period). It shows a columned building with horns of consecration on the roof, and with double axes stuck in the capitals of the columns, obviously a shrine of some sort, though not exactly corresponding to any other one I recall; it was presumably painted in the Middle Minoan III A period.

To the Middle Minoan III B period certainly belong the more famous miniature frescoes discovered in strata probably dating from before the great earthquake, fallen from an upper room in the old North Keep. The scene illustrated a typical Minoan pillar shrine, such as existed in the central court of the palace, flanked each side by a line of court ladies sitting and ostensibly watching a dance, but obviously more interested in their own conversation. The less distinguished spectators were indicated by sketching the outlines of the heads on a brownish-red background for the men and on a white ground for the women. A long tongue of white ground inserted into a red pattern makes it clear that there was no segregation of the sexes at the Minoan court (Plate 11).

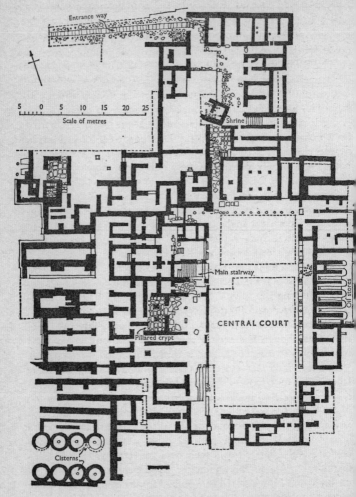

Entrance way

Scale of metres
5 0 5 10 15 20 25

Shrine

Main stairway

Oil stores

Pillared crypt

CENTRAL COURT

Cisterns

Fig. 35. Middle Minoan Palace, Mallia

Some of the spectators at this Cretan *fête champêtre* are shown standing in an olive orchard, and another fragment that may belong to the same scene shows an enthusiastic group of men waving spears, not, I think, in any hostile gesture, but rather, as Pendlebury remarks, 'like a cheering football crowd'.

From the great East Hall of the domestic quarter came some badly mutilated pieces of a magnificent fresco known as 'the Ladies in Blue', a conversation piece like the ladies in the miniature frescoes but on a heroic scale.

Frescoes with human figures, however, were almost confined to Knosos and its neighbourhood, the only other examples of Middle Minoan III date so far discovered being at Tylisos, where Hazzidakis found some fragments showing some court ladies walking from right to left, another with a design interpreted as a fan, and some small pieces of an interesting miniature fresco depicting a line of boxers like those on the steatite 'Boxer Vase' of Hagia Triada.

If it be true, as Professor Banti maintains, that Minoan painting, whether on frescoes or on vases (apart from the Knosian school), was not interested in human figures, this cannot be due to influence from the Greek mainland, which as yet had no frescoes, but might possibly be due to influence from Mari or Atchana.[1]

The Middle Minoan III period, however, also witnessed another development in frescoes that owes nothing to Mari, though it may have been influenced by Egyptian painted reliefs: namely the Minoan invention of frescoes in relief.

The Knosian Faience Industry

Even in the Early Minoan II period, faience beads had been imported into eastern Crete from Egypt, and perhaps Cretans had already learned the trick of making faience beads; but it was not till the beginning of the Middle Minoan period that we find attempts to decorate boxes with inlays of shell and faience. In the Vat Room deposit at Knosos, dating from the earliest period of the Palace of Minos, Evans found not only beads of blue and green faience but also fragments of shell and faience that had evidently been employed in an inlay as the ground work for quatrefoils of some other material.

The most remarkable inlay, however, of which we have any con-

1. L. Woolley, *A Forgotten Kingdom*, 1953, p. 76.

siderable remains consists of the fragments of the so-called Town Mosaic (Plate 6), discovered in a filling of Middle Minoan III A date near the Loom-Weight basement and themselves therefore apparently dating from the Middle Minoan II B period.

Numerous small plaques have survived illustrating the typical urban houses of the period with two or three storeys. Most of the roofs are flat, but one house has a penthouse roof to its third storey attic, and a slight outward slope on the roofs of the second floor rooms flanking the attic. Other plaques, presumably from the same mosaic, depict trees, animals, water, the prow of a ship, and some negroid figures. It has been suggested that the whole scene may have represented the siege of a town by the sea like that on the silver rhyton from Mycenae, but no actual incidents of battle have been identified.

This faience industry seems to have been confined to Knosos, and perhaps to the Palace of Minos itself, since fragments are so rarely found on other sites.[1] A lucky chance has preserved for us some important examples of this industry in the temple repositories of the palace. Two large cists sunk in the floor of a room at the back of the pillar shrine that faced the central court had been filled with a number of superfluous dedications which had evidently been removed from the shrine but had been too holy to give or throw away, and had been covered by a later floor. Among these objects was a Greek cross in grey and white marble.

The orthodox explanation of this cross is that it was not a religious symbol but might have formed a centre piece in some mosaic, though the mere fact that it was found in the temple repositories presumably indicates that it belonged to a dedication of some sort. The most striking of these offerings were two faience figurines, one of the Snake Goddess and another of a priestess or votaress (Plate 9). The goddess is a stately, rather early Victorian figure in a dress with a long spreading skirt and tight laced bodice leaving the breasts and lower arms bare. On her head is a high tiara around which coils a spotted snake whose tail intertwines with another snake which coils round her body and whose head appears at her girdle. A third snake coils over her shoulder and she holds its tail in her left hand.

1. The faience vases recently discovered at Mycenae are considered by the excavator to be probably of Syrian fabric, not Knosian or Mycenaean.

The priestess or votaress lacks the head part of the headdress, the left arm, two pieces of the hair, and parts of the skirt and apron. The flat cap with its raised medallions was found separately, and was probably crowned with a small figure of a spotted cat or leopardess which has a hole underneath corresponding to a hole in the cap.

There were also miniature models of votive robes in the same fabric adorned with designs of saffron flowers and girdles; small bowls with upright handles, and cockleshells or figure-of-eight shields moulded round the rim, and a small beaked jug with a band of running spirals in relief (copied from a metal prototype). The colours of these objects varied from white through pale green to emerald, through pale blue to turquoise, and from yellow to a chocolate brown; and the same naturalistic tendencies that appear in the contemporary frescoes and seal stones manifested themselves in the faience. Other fragments from the same deposit represented argonauts, cockleshells, and flying fish. Perhaps the finest of all the faience plaques, however, were two reliefs showing a cow suckling its calf, and another animal, usually (but I think wrongly) described as a goat, suckling its kid.

Minoan Gaming Boards

The debris from the western cist included globular, almond-shaped, and segmented beads, and pieces of inlay from a gaming board, of which we should be unable to form any conception but for the discovery of more numerous fragments of another gaming board in the so-called Corridor of the Draught Board. The latter (Plate 13) must have been a truly magnificent affair, measuring nearly a metre long and half a metre wide. The wooden base has perished, but a considerable part of the ivory framework and inlay has survived. The border had a line of faience daisies in relief with a central boss of rock crystal. The general design of the board consisted of four large rosette positions at one end, and ten smaller roundels at the other divided by parallel ribs of segmented bars.[1]

1. Gaming boards have also been found in Egypt, Cyprus, and Mesopotamia; see C. J. Gadd, *Iraq*, 1934, p. 45, and 1946, p. 66.

MALLIA

About twenty-two miles east of Herakleion along the north coast lie the ruins of another great Minoan city of which we do not know the name (though Marinatos has suggested that the ancient name may have been Tarmara)[1] and which we therefore call Mallia, after the large modern village which lies some two and a half miles west of it. The Greeks spell the name with one 'l', but most foreign authorities have followed the French excavators in spelling the name with two 'l's.

The ancient site was occupied in the Late Neolithic and throughout the Early Minoan period, but the remains from these periods were scanty. The inhabitants were perhaps backward, and continued to make pottery of Neolithic and Sub-Neolithic types during the Early Minoan I and II periods, and pottery of the Vasiliki style during the Early Minoan III period. The site was first tested by the discoverer Joseph Hazzidakis, but later the French School at Athens took over the site and excavations have taken place during a period of over thirty years under the successive directions of Renaudin, Chapouthier, Charbonneaux, Demargne, and others.

The position of this Minoan city is quite different from that of Knosos since the coastal plain is here much narrower, and Mallia was therefore itself a port.

The Palace of Mallia

The earlier palace, like the first Palace of Minos, dates from the Middle Minoan I period and is formed of a complex of rooms grouped round a central court, but seems never to have consisted of isolated blocks with open passages between like the early *insulae* at Knosos. The blocks into which the Palace of Mallia was divided should be considered rather as functional parts of a building planned as a unity from the first (Fig. 35), persisting, with some changes, into the Middle Minoan III period.

1. 'Some General Ideas on the Minoan Written Documents', *Minos*, 1951, p. 42.

Thus Block 1 consisted of the central block of the west façade, bisected by the great corridor which may have been open to the sky. The walls of this block were very thick and we may perhaps infer the existence here of a second storey. Two varieties of local stone were chiefly employed in the construction. The late Quaternary sandstone, quarried on the coast nearby, was easy to cut and was always used when good ashlar masonry was required. For inner walls, where strength was desirable but where a rough face could be covered with

Fig. 36. Designs on Middle Minoan III vases

a coat of plaster, the builders employed another local stone, much harder and less tractable, known locally as *sidheropetra* or 'ironstone', a very hard knobby limestone, half-way to a marble. In addition to these materials, interior walls of no great importance were sometimes built of mud bricks, now accidentally fired by the conflagration that destroyed the palace.

Block IV in the Mallia Palace seems to have been occupied by the palace artists and citizens, since it includes two workshops, one of an ivory carver and the other of a coppersmith. Block V was a 'keep', reminding us slightly of the early North Keep at Knosos but here constructed with huge blocks of 'ironstone', in the rough masonry often termed Cyclopean (because its most imposing example was the fortress walls of Tiryns, said to have been built by the Cyclopes).

Block VI contained some small but important rooms entered from and lighted by a loggia that was open to the central court. A small room entered from the north side of the loggia contained a hoard of ceremonial weapons, including the great bronze sword with its crystal hilt, a bronze dagger, and a battle-axe in brown schist sculptured in the form of a hunting leopard or cheetah straining at the leash. Chapouthier describes this block as 'shut in on itself' and suggests it may have been the palace centre for the 'Cult of the Hearth'.

The pottery here was still in the Middle Minoan I style, with the exception of one or two vases probably imported from Knosos, but the hieroglyphic inscriptions were of the developed type, some of the signs even betraying a tendency to develop into their counterparts in Linear Script A.

The absence of Middle Minoan II pottery at first induced Chapouthier to suggest that the hoard belonged to the Middle Minoan III period, but Evans protested that the hieroglyphic tablets found in a passage in the north-west part of the palace must be earlier, and his protest was justified by Chapouthier's later investigations in 1946 proving beyond all doubt that the hieroglyphic sealing hoard must have belonged to the earlier palace. Further Chapouthier himself stressed the relatively archaic form of the sword compared to the other swords found at Mallia. Evans had even dated the earlier Mallia sword to the transition from Early Minoan III to Middle Minoan I; Pendlebury dated it Middle Minoan I; and it cannot be later than the Middle Minoan II period to which we may, I suggest, assign the destruction of the first palace.

The battle-axe is a Cretan variant of the series of ceremonial battle-axes scattered all over Europe in the second millennium B.C. and often associated with the dispersion of the peoples speaking Indo-European languages.[1] The richest series of these axes is from south Russia, but perhaps the most famous and certainly the most splendid examples were the battle-axe of lapis lazuli and the three of a jade-like green-stone from Treasure L at Troy. The Royal Treasure at Alaca in Asia Minor has also provided us with a fine example, in silver and gold.

In the Aegean, however, such battle-axes are rare and exotic objects, and the only other example I recall from Crete is a fragment in stone in the Giamalakis collection in Herakleion.

The Mallia weapon, like the ones from the Trojan treasure, was obviously intended for ceremony, not for use in battle, since the thin blade of fragile schist would have split at the first blow, but it is an admirable example of Minoan art in the first phase of that naturalism that was to culminate, in the Middle Minoan III and Late Minoan I periods, in vase painting, in the palace frescoes, and in the miniature arts of the gem cutter, the ivory carver, and the modeller in faience.

The presence of documents in the developed form of the hieroglyphic script indicate clearly that the site continued to be occupied during the Middle Minoan II period, but the pottery in use, as on most Cretan sites except Knosos and Phaistos, continued to be painted in the style that Evans termed Middle Minoan I B.

In general the Mallia Palace suffered less from the Middle Minoan II earthquake than that of Minos, and the reconstruction carried out at the beginning of the Middle Minoan III period was therefore far less sweeping than that at Knosos; but for that very reason it is often a delicate question whether a particular wall belongs to the earlier or the later palace, and most of the walls above the later floor levels seem to have been built in the Middle Minoan III period.

Perhaps the clearest distinction between the structures of the two palaces was shown in Block III where excavations by Chapouthier

1. R. W. Hutchinson, 'Battle Axes in the Aegean', *Proceedings of the Prehistoric Society*, 1950, p. 52f. and Plate IV, No. 2; V. G. Childe, *The Aryans*, 1926; H. Hencken, 'Indo-European Languages and Archaeology', *Memoirs of the American Anthropological Association*, 1955.

revealed under the Ante-room III 9 the remains of a fine stuccoed room with benches and two magnificent rapiers of Middle Minoan III date. The magazines of Block XI and the great east-west corridor in Block I certainly belonged to the scheme of the first palace. Gallet de Santerre even gives Middle Minoan III A as the *terminus ante quem* for the earlier sword.

Little enough can be said as yet about the earlier town though a house on the coast has yielded a series of Early Minoan I–II vases and one of the town cemeteries started in the Early Minoan III period.

The town site has not been excavated in full, but the French have probed and uncovered to give us some idea of the lay-out of the second city, which was built to replace the one destroyed in the Middle Minoan II period.

The Cemetery of Mallia at Chrysolakkos

The first ossuary at Chrysolakkos was evidently used by the poor folk. The pottery, with its rather clumsy Anatolian shapes, beaked jugs, and 'tea-pots', is typical Early Minoan III, like that of eastern Crete, and is adorned both in the 'dark-on-light' and in the 'light-on-dark' styles with the latter predominating. Where mottling occurs it seems to be not later than Early Minoan III times, and before the end of that period a second ossuary was in use which continued into the Middle Minoan I period. The building of the first palace was obviously accompanied by a rapid expansion of the town, and two islets off the coast (named respectively after Christ and St Barbara) were used for cemeteries. To the same period belongs the construction of the royal burial ground of Chrysolakkos, 'the Gold Hole', a name obviously derived from the plunder taken from it by tomb robbers of later times, and comparable to the term 'treasuries' which the classical Greeks applied to the beehive tombs of the mainland. One piece of jewellery, at least, escaped this looting – the glorious gold pendant in the form of two bees (or wasps?) sampling a berry, discovered in 1945 by P. Demargne (see p. 196 and Fig. 37).[1]

South of the cemeteries, by the sea, lay a considerable town of which we do not yet know the extent, but of which the ruins always

1. R. Higgins, 'The Aegina Treasure Reconsidered', *Bulletin of Institute of Classical Studies*, 1957, p. 27.

seem to have Middle Minoan III pottery on top and Middle Minoan I below. The islet of St Barbara also had some Middle Minoan I houses, including one that had belonged to a fisherman.

Adjoining the palace on the west was an important quarter with fine houses of the Middle Minoan III period and a well-paved street with a drain at the side, but here too the houses overlay a thick deposit of Middle Minoan I sherds with the smaller, flimsier foundations characteristic of that period on this site.

South of the palace lay Quarter E, with stuccoed halls and corridors that were evidently earlier than the latest phase of the palace, since in some instances they were overlaid by its western wing.

In general the houses of the later town were built better than the earlier, with more regular plans, though often on the same sites. A Minoan house agent, if such existed, would doubtless have described them as 'furnished with all modern conveniences', paved and stuccoed corridors, reception halls, bathrooms, store-rooms, light-wells, etc.

We may take as specimens of the more luxurious residences the fine villa (excavated 1946–8) in Quarter Z east of the palace, or the house with frescoes in Quarter E south of the palace. A recent report[1] outlines the probable extent of the city.

It was at one time supposed that the Minoan city had suffered its second destruction at an earlier date than Knosos because the latest pottery seems to be a rather late variety of Late Minoan I A but the discovery of at least one fine vase of Late Minoan I B marine style in House 2 and the certainty that Late Minoan II is a local Knosian style suggest that Mallia was also perhaps destroyed about 1400 B.C. by the same catastrophe.

There was some slight reoccupation of the town site in Late Minoan III times and some sherds of that period were even found in the palace, where I believe the diagonal building to be a reoccupation shrine corresponding to that of the Double Axes at Knosos; but the chief glories of Mallia belong to the Middle Minoan period.

Chrysolakkos, the chief cemetery of the Middle Minoan I period at Mallia, seems to have become less fashionable towards the end of the Middle Minoan period, if we may judge from the fact that the

1. P. Demargne and H. G. de Santerre, 'Mallia, Maisons', *Études crétoises*, 1954.

Middle Minoan III graves are much poorer than the earlier ones, and it seems probable that we have not yet discovered the richest cemetery of the later period.

GOURNIA PALACE

To the Middle Minoan III period may be assigned the construction of the small Palace of Gournia (Figs. 43 and 57) on the Merabello coast. It is hardly more than a large villa, but is obviously aping its betters, since it has a small theatral area recalling that of Knosos, but its ashlar façade with set-backs, and the alternation of round pillars and square piers in the portico facing the court, were obviously modelled on those of Mallia. We cannot say very much about the inner rooms, which were disorganized when the building was turned into workmen's flats in the Late Minoan I A period.

There was further building activity in the latter part of the Middle Minoan III period at the eastern sites, reconstructions of houses at Pseira and Mochlos, *pithos* burials at Pachyammos and Sphoungaras, and copper smelting at Chrysokamino. Copper slag has also been found on a Middle Minoan III B dump which I tested at Knosos, on Monasteriako Kephali, but I do not know from what mine the Knosians derived that ore.[1]

At Zakros in the far east a new village was planted at a site where one would have expected to find earlier habitations, since it has one of the best streams of fresh water in the whole island. Perhaps there had been earlier settlements washed out by floods like the one of 1901 so graphically described by Hogarth.[2]

THE PALACE AT PHAISTOS

At Phaistos in the Mesara, as at Knosos, the Early Minoan strata had been cut away when the site was levelled to build the earlier palace, so that it is often difficult, despite the long and careful investigation by a distinguished series of Italian archaeologists, to determine the form of the earlier buildings. The evidence for the sequence of the various structures has been well discussed and summarized by Professor Banti,

1. H. Payne, 'Archaeology in Greece', *Journal of the Historical Society*, 1935.
2. D. G. Hogarth, *A Wandering Scholar*, p. 161ff.

her deductions reviewed and criticized by Platon, and fresh evidence has been produced by Levi's recent excavations in the south-west corner of the site.

The pottery preceding the earliest structures of the palace was of the Middle Minoan I A type comparable with that of the Vat Room deposit at Knosos.

Pendlebury dated the building of the first palace to the Middle Minoan I B period, but Professor Banti objected that she found Middle Minoan I B, Middle Minoan II A and Middle Minoan II B, and Middle Minoan III A sherds in the same deposits, which might be explained either by supposing that certain types continued much later in the Mesara, or by supposing that there was some error in Evans's chronology. She dated the destruction of the first palace about 1600 B.C. and inferred from the synchronism of these various styles of pottery that it could not have lasted more than 150–200 years, perhaps not much over 50. Her minimum estimate seems low but her maximum might well be correct. In an admirably clear statement she stresses the difference between the vases found on the floors – presumably the pottery in use just before the destruction of the first palace – and the pottery of the debris above, which includes earlier types with more varied shapes, greater use of polychrome ornament, and frequent examples of barbotine ornament. This early Middle Minoan I A pottery is easily paralleled at Knosos and in the Kamares cave, but at Phaistos was not found on the floor anywhere except in the south-west House, which Pernier always considered to have been contemporary with the first palace, but destroyed at an earlier date. This evidence should not be ignored, but it hardly seems to justify the dating of the palace by this small unimportant room which might well have been cleared down to an earlier level in the later days of the first palace.

I should prefer, therefore, to date the first palace late in the Middle Minoan I B, or at latest early in the Middle Minoan II A period, and this dating is supported by the latest excavations of Doro Levi, revealing three stages of the first palace of which we hitherto only knew the latest. In the second of these phases, Rooms XXVII and XXVIII formed a single room with a central partition, and in this deposit Levi found a glorious series of Middle Minoan II A vases apparently unmixed with other styles. The most obvious remains of the first palace are in the west court, where the façade for the later palace was set back, and the lower levels of the rooms immediately behind the earlier west façade were covered by the paving of the west court, thus preserving for us the plan of these rooms of the earlier palace. The present 'theatral area', which reminds us so much of the one at Knosos, did not exist in early Middle Minoan times in that form, since the west entrance was only a narrow unimposing doorway. Yet it was in a sense more obviously theatral than that of Knosos, seeing that the steps at the north end of the west terrace lead to nothing but a perpendicular rock face, and can only, I think, have been intended for the use of spectators watching some spectacle (dance or parade or whatever it may have been) taking place in the outer west court. The space between the theatral steps and the western entrance to the palace was partly occupied by a three-roomed shrine, of which the central room rose higher than the side ones, like that depicted on the miniature frescoes of Middle Minoan III date at Knosos or like the gold model of a shrine of the dove goddess from Shaft Grave 3 at Mycenae.

Of the three small rooms behind this façade, number two contained the bench for the cult objects normal in Minoan shrines. Below this was the earliest shrine, consisting simply of a rectangular rock-cut trench with a circular cavity in the middle. The triple shrine presumably belongs to the third phase of Levi's earliest palace and will therefore date not earlier than Middle Minoan II, probably Middle Minoan II B (that is about 1800 B.C., with a few years' margin of error). In 1953 Levi also excavated another room east of the room uncovered in an earlier campaign. The character of these two rooms, with their gypsum paving and dadoes surmounted by fresco, and the fine quality of the Middle Minoan II A pottery made it evident that these are not merely early houses but clearly a wing of the earliest palace; one room contained a stuccoed bench bearing a number of fine vases, and another two stucco consoles. Here was found a sort of dice-box in terracotta, containing what appears to be a die in the form of a small ivory disk with the numbers indicated by inlaid silver dots, as well as two possible 'chess pawns', in the form of a small lion's head and an ox's hoof, in ivory.

It would appear that those rooms marked on the earlier plans of Phaistos as pre-palatial, in the south-east and north-west parts of the

Sherds of the Early Neolithic I period

Early Neolithic I vase from Knosos

Early Minoan III vases

a Middle Minoan IB vases

b Middle Minoan IIA vases

Middle Minoan I figurines from Petsopha

Town Mosaic in faience of Middle Minoan IIB period

East Pillar Crypt, Palace of Minos

Theatral Area, Palace of Minos

Snake Goddess group in faience from temple repositories, Knosos

a Great Viaduct, Knosos

b Temple Tomb, Knosos

Miniature fresco, Palace of Minos

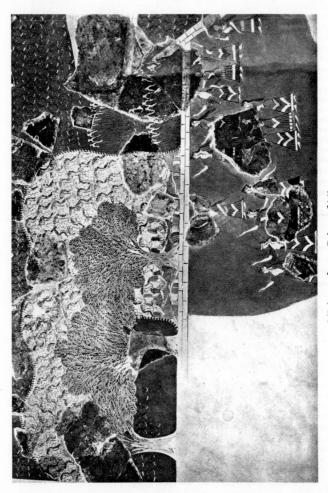

Miniature fresco, Palace of Minos

Royal gaming board

a Stone head from Monasteriako Kephali, Knosos

b The Phaistos Disk

14

Hall of the Colonnades, Knosos

Bronze statuette illustrating the Minoan bulljumping sport

a Bull Rhyton, Little Palace, Knosos

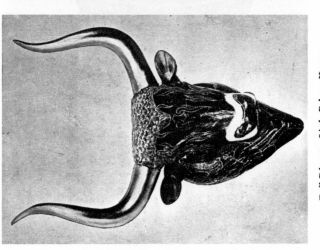

b Fresco of the Young Prince, Palace of Minos

17

Late Minoan I vase from Pachyammos

Late Minoan IA polychrome vase from Isopata

Late Minoan III sarcophagus from Hagia Triada

Cult objects from Karphi Shrine

Geometric vases, Khaniale Tekke

Geometric clay house, Khaniale Tekke

23

Jewellery from Khaniale Tekke Tholos

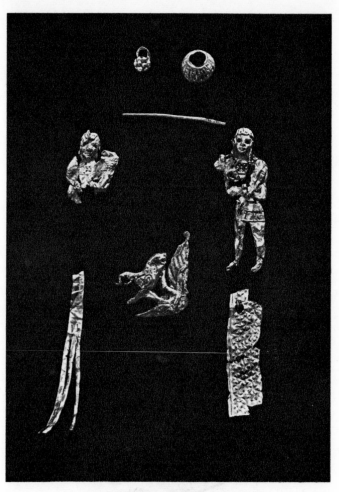

Jewellery from Khaniale Tekke Tholos

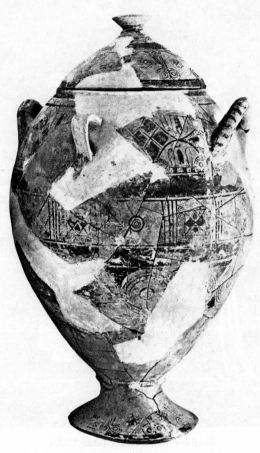

Polychrome vase from Khaniale Tekke Tholos

Hammered bronze figures from Dreros

South Propyleum and Procession Fresco, Knosos

North entrance to the Palace of Minos

Central court, Palace of Phaistos; Mount Ida in the distance

Corridor opening off Great Court, Palace of Phaistos

Magazines, later Palace of Phaistos

site, should rather be regarded as belonging to these earlier phases of the first palace revealed by Levi's recent explorations.

If the earlier palace at Phaistos was destroyed by the earthquake of the Middle Minoan II B period which, we have suggested, may have been connected with the great Levantine disaster assigned by Schaeffer to 1730 B.C., the Cretans of the Mesara seem to have recovered from it quickly.

On the ruins of the early palace was constructed a still more magnificent building. The west façade was set back seven metres and the paving of the outer west court covered the ruins of the early shrine, which was replaced not by another shrine but by a grand staircase leading to an imposing propylaea or entrance hall giving access to the central court and to the upper floor in a curiously indirect manner. The central court may also be approached through the fine 'lustral area' or 'bathroom'.

It may be remembered that the 'western approaches' to the palaces of Knosos, Mallia, and Phaistos have this in common. If the entrance is a magnificent one it is very indirect; if it is direct it is very narrow. Security may have been the object aimed at in each instance; what was feared perhaps was not so much attack by foreigners as palace intrigues and local revolutions.

The new propylaea covered over some magazines of the first palace, but the central court and the magazines to the north of it were incorporated in the later palace.

The magazines immediately north of the entrance possessed storage jars, of which one contained a quantity of grape seeds (the earliest recorded from Crete). I have suggested 1900 B.C. (rather than Levi's 2000) as a likely date for the earliest palace, but even so it is clear that Middle Minoan II A ware was plentiful at Phaistos when the current pottery in east Crete was Middle Minoan I B and when developed Middle Minoan I A was still prevalent in north central Crete.

Other substructures of the earlier palaces were uncovered by Levi under the western part of the central court. All round the palace on the slopes of the hill were houses, which the Italians are only beginning to explore, but which show that the town of Phaistos passed through the same vicissitudes as the palace.

The Italians have suggested that the enlarged west court may have been used for the toreador sports, and spectators may have watched not only from the slopes but from the windows of the palace, and because of this, the staircase joining the west court to the little court in the north-west wing was preserved and incorporated in the later palace.

Immediately south of the great propylaea system was an important series of magazines opening off both sides of a broad corridor which at its east end opened out into a two-columned hall (perhaps, it is suggested, an administrative office for the palace treasures) with a broad portico facing the central court.

The southern and most of the eastern part of the palace has been destroyed by later buildings and denudation of the site.

The north side of the great court was united to the north quarter of the palace by a broad corridor, originally perhaps open to the sky. The doorway leading to the princely apartments to the north was closed by a double door flanked by two half columns and two niches adorned with frescoes. This corridor existed in the first palace, but the floor was raised in the second palace. The store-rooms each side of the corridor form two large rectangles, indicating the measurements of the halls on the first floor, for which they had formed the substructures. North of this lay the fine hall with its central light-well (a peculiarity of Phaistos and Hagia Triada anticipating the Tuscan *atria* of Pompeii); it seems to have served as an ante-room to the splendid hall with its two annexes, the Phaistos equivalent of the Knosos Hall of the Double Axes. From this hall a dog's-leg corridor led to some private apartments with bath and lavatory, corresponding somewhat to the Queen's suite at Knosos. It is to be remarked that there is very little in the way of fresco decoration. The best rooms at Phaistos relied on the fine quality of their masonry and on a very liberal use of gypsum for doors, dadoes, and floors.

Little can be said about the Minoan town of Phaistos, but the nature of the ground makes it obvious that most of it must have lain on the southern slopes and on the plain at their foot.

The later palace, like that at Knosos, was apparently largely destroyed by the great earthquake of Middle Minoan III, perhaps more so than that of Knosos since it was not rebuilt as a palace. There was some reoccupation in the palace, but the ruling prince evidently decided that it would be better to build a new palace, and the site he chose was the western end of the same ridge on which Phaistos stands, a very beautiful position but far less defensible, perhaps showing that the Minoan fleet was still controlling the seas round Crete. (But see p. 173.)

But though the new palace, of which we do not know the ancient name and which is therefore called Hagia Triada after the little medieval chapel there, was first constructed later in the Middle Minoan III B period, it is better to consider it in the main as a building of the following period.

MIDDLE MINOAN JEWELLERY

Parallels to the Mochlos head-bands were also found in the Mesara in the form of three broad bands, and many fragments of others, often with a decoration of repoussé dots round the edge and with holes for attaching them. Twenty-one small disks (10·8 cm. in diameter) of very thin gold leaf, each with two holes for attaching it perhaps to a garment, were found in the same deposit, together with a disk with carved surface and six attachment holes, two rings of gold sheeting (possibly from the rim of a vase), three almond-shaped beads and three round ones, three finger rings of thin wire, and six rivet heads of gold.

With the exception of the pendant and of a few beads from the lower stratum, the gold seems to be pure, implying that the native silver had been removed from it.[1]

Of the gold ornaments from the Mesara, especially those from Koumasa, the majority would appear to have belonged to the Middle Minoan I period, or possibly to the Middle Minoan II, since it is hard to differentiate between the remains of these two periods except at Knosos and Phaistos. The Mesara goldsmith no longer confined his attention to decorating his work with repoussé and incised designs, but had also developed the techniques of granulation and of cloisonné work with gold wire (from Tholos B at Koumasa) in the form of a sitting toad. The same tomb also produced some gold beads (one in the form of a lilac seed capsule), and two small pierced disks of gold, which are paralleled by those on the gold bee pendant from

1. The alluvial gold of the Near East regularly contained varying percentages of silver; compare A. Lucas, 'Silver in Ancient Times', *Journal of Egyptian Archaeology*, 1928, p. 40.

Mallia and on three pendants among the so-called 'Aegina treasure' in the British Museum. R. Higgins suggests that this treasure may have been part of the gold looted from the cemetery at Chrysolakkos and from which the latter derived its name of 'the gold hole' and which he assigns very plausibly to the seventeenth century B.C. (though some scholars had tried to assign it to as late as the eighth century B.C.). The most obvious Minoan piece is the gold cup with the quadruple spirals, but the 'Master of Animals' pendant must surely

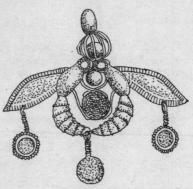

Fig. 37. Gold bee pendant, Mallia

be either Minoan or Mycenaean, and the other pendants also have Minoan parallels in some detail or another.

Fortunately the finest of all Minoan jewels was actually found in Chrysolakkos during the French excavations there. This is the splendid gold pendant in the form of two bees (or wasps?) soldered together at the heads and the tips of the abdomens (Fig. 37). The legs of gold wire held a ball decorated with granulations, and the same technique was employed on the eyes and the bevels of the abdomen. From the tips of the wings and the point where the abdomens meet hang gold disks like those of the 'Aegina treasure' pendants.

MIDDLE MINOAN CHRONOLOGY

Levi's recent excavations prove that Middle Minoan II A pottery was already in use in the earliest palace at Phaistos, and the discovery of metal vases of that style at Tod in Upper Egypt in a deposit dated to the reign of Amenemhat II (1929–1895 B.C.) indicate that that style can hardly have started later than 1900 B.C.[1]

I therefore suggest the following amendment of the Middle Minoan Chronology which I put forward in 1954.

	Knosos Early Minoan III	Northern Villages Early Minoan III	Phaistos Early Minoan III	Mesara Villages Early Minoan III	East Crete Early Minoan III
2000					
1950	M.M.IA	M.M.IA	M.M.IA	M.M.IA	M.M.IA and M.M.IB
1900	M.M.IB M.M.IIA		M.M.IB and M.M.IIA		
1830					
	M.M.IIB		M.M.IIB		
1750*					
	M.M.IIIA	M.M.IIIA	M.M.IIIA	M.M.IIIA	M.M.IIIA
1600					
	Pre-Seismic M.M.IIIB	M.M.IIIB	M.M.IIIB	M.M.IIIB	M.M.IIIB
1570					
	Post-Seismic M.M.IIIB				
1550					
	L.M.IA	L.M.IA	L.M.IA	L.M.IA	L.M.IA

* Or 1730, if the Cretan earthquake is the same as Schaeffer's one.

THE GREAT EARTHQUAKE OF 1570(?) B.C.

At Knosos the Middle Minoan III palace was badly damaged by a great earthquake, but the clearest evidence of this catastrophe comes from an area just below the south-west corner of the central court. Here two small but well-built houses have been crushed by blocks hurled southwards from the adjacent palace walls. In this, as in most Cretan earthquakes, the shocks evidently came from the north, probably from the epicentre on or near the island of Thera. One of

1. R. W. Hutchinson, 'Minoan Chronology Reviewed', *Antiquity*, 1954, p. 155.

these houses Evans termed 'The House of the Fallen Blocks', from the great palace blocks which destroyed it and which still lie there. It appears to have been the abode of a stone cutter who made stone lamps. The other house Evans termed 'The House of the Sacrificed Oxen', since it contained two pairs of horns of bulls of the great *primigenius* type and the remains of painted tripod altars.

Evans aptly quoted a line of Homer to the effect that 'the Earth-shaker delighteth in bulls' and suggested that the Minoan king had decided that this area should not be rebuilt but remain sacred to the 'earth-shaker' and had sacrificed bulls there to Poseidon the god of earthquakes, or to whatever Minoan god was the equivalent of Poseidon.[1]

The palace was quickly restored and the ruins that we still see represent for the most part this reconstruction at the end of the Middle Minoan III B period, though the north-west portico and the north-western lustral area seem not to have been rebuilt, and the cists below the Middle Minoan III floors were filled in.

1. A. J. Evans, *Palace of Minos*, II, p. 296; Pendlebury op. cit., p. 155; evidence for the epicentre of the earthquake is provided by the cracks which start at ground level on the north and travel diagonally south and upwards, exactly like the cracks made by the earthquakes of 1926 and 1935.

CHAPTER 8

Minoan Religion

PRE-HELLENIC ELEMENTS IN CRETAN RELIGION

THE inhabitants of Crete during the classical period had, like those of the mainland of Greece, inherited many beliefs and religious practices from Bronze Age times, but they were well aware that this inheritance differed from that of the ordinary Greeks. The mainland had been occupied by a Greek-speaking population since early in the second millennium B.C. By the middle of the second millennium, probably, Greeks were already settling in Crete, but only in comparatively small numbers, and these Mycenaean Greeks had already adopted many Cretan cults and religious customs. Even on the mainland we find survivals from Minoan or at least pre-Hellenic religion, but in Crete these non-Hellenic elements were much stronger and tended to survive much longer.

Herodotus in a suggestive passage of the second book of his history remarks that Hera, Hestia, Themis, the Graces, and the Nereids were among the oldest deities of Greece.[1]

In Hera and Themis we seem to have a reflection of the great mother goddess of the Minoan Cretans, and in Hestia of the Household Goddess who, according to Euhemerus, had founded Knosos.[2] In the Graces and the Nereids we may perhaps have a reflection of those rather vague groups of two or three goddesses so often represented on Minoan and Mycenaean gems, but it is often difficult to distinguish what is genuinely Minoan in the legends about them. Let us therefore concentrate on a much less important figure, but one where the Minoan element seems to have been less diluted by later tradition. I refer to Akakallis, daughter of Minos. Her name is not

1. Herodotus II, Chap. 50.
2. See F. Jacoby, *Fragmente der Griechischen Historiker*, 1923, p. 63 (a passage from Lactantius quoting Ennius's Latin translation of Euhemerus's *Sacred History*).

Hellenic and the reduplication of the first syllable certainly occurs in some Minoan names. Further it was a name for the narcissus, and plant-names, as Marinatos has stressed, are often survivals from the pre-Hellenic vocabulary. The special characteristic of Akakallis was her aptitude for arranging that her sons (usually by the god Apollo) should be suckled by animals. Such stories occur elsewhere, the best known being that of Rhea Silvia and her twins Romulus and Remus, but few girls can have displayed such a facility in this practice as Akakallis. Thus her twin children Phylakis and Philander by Apollo were reared at Tarrha by a goat, her son Kydon at Kydonia was suckled by a bitch, and her son Milatos by a wolf. (I cannot name foster-parents for her other children, but I doubt if that resourceful maiden would have suckled any herself.)

The association with Minos, the pre-Hellenic name of the daughter, and the consistency of the stories suggest that these really are derived from pre-Hellenic folklore, and also strengthen our belief, supported on independent evidence, that many features of the cult and tradition surrounding Apollo were derived from some pre-Hellenic god.[1]

The most startling heterodoxy of the Cretans in classical times was that the Zeus they worshipped had been born as a baby in Crete, had grown to manhood, and had finally been buried there. The Greeks did not so much mind the story of Zeus's birth, which was accepted by Hesiod, but the legend of his death and burial was regarded as downright blasphemy even by the Cretan Epimenides in his poem on Minos quoted by Saint Paul. The fragment preserved and brilliantly restored by Rendel Harris from a passage in a Syriac commentary has been translated as follows:

> The Cretans carved a tomb for Thee, O Holy and High,
> Liars, noxious beasts, evil bellies
> For thou didst not die, ever Thou livest and standest firm
> For in thee we live and move and have our being.

Well might orthodox Greeks be shocked at the Cretan picture of the lord of Olympus, but the question arises: why did the first Greek settlers identify their Sky-Father with a god who lived his complete

1. Perhaps the 'Master of the Animals'; see p. 207.

life and died like a man in Crete? The natural inference is that this god, whose name appears to have been Velchanos, was an important deity worshipped on the island by the Minoan Cretans.

It is therefore worth our while to examine briefly the main outlines of the story of Zeus's birth in Crete.

THE BIRTH OF ZEUS

The oldest extant version of the story of the birth of Zeus is the one presented by Hesiod in the *Theogony* written in the eighth century B.C., but the main outlines of the story go back well into the middle Bronze Age, since they appear in Hittite texts of the second millennium B.C., where we find the parts of the Greek gods, Ouranos, Kronos, and Zeus being enacted by Anu, Kumarbi, and the weather-God Teshub, deities of that element of the Hittite peoples that spoke the Hurrian language.[1]

Hesiod recounts how Kronos, the son of Heaven (Ouranos) and Earth (Gaia), mutilated his father at his mother's suggestion and became the supreme deity. Kronos, believing that he too would be destroyed by his son, used to swallow his children until Rhea his wife secreted her latest-born son Zeus and sent him to Lyktos where his grandmother, Gaia, received him and hid him in a dark cave on the wooded Aegean Mountain (the Goat's Mountain). Kronos was induced to swallow a stone wrapped in swaddling bands believing that he had swallowed his latest son also. The story is crude and primitive, and we might naturally have imagined it to be ancient, though I think few (before the discovery of the Hittite texts) would have suspected it to be an ancient Hurrian tale. The elaboration of this story and its association with Cretan place-names must be the work of Cretans, and the elaboration must have taken place in the Bronze Age, before the Dorian colonization of Crete, since it is not typical of Doric folklore elsewhere. Hesiod, of course, was a Boeotian, but he lays the scene in Crete. His 'Goat's Mountain' must almost certainly be the fine massif now called Dikte, and the cave would probably be that of Psychro. It should be remarked, however, that the name Dikte

1. Compare O. R. Gurney, *The Hittites* (Penguin Books, 1952), p. 190; note that Anu reigned for nine years in Heaven as Minos did for the same period on earth.

as applied to this mountain has only been revived by modern scholars and Hesiod himself never mentions Dikte. The Psychro cave, however, was surely one of the places where Zeus's birth was celebrated, and whatever cave Hesiod alludes to must have been situated not very far from the site of Lyktos, which is near the modern village of Xydhas.

The 'goat' of the 'Goat's Mountain' is usually identified by scholars with Amaltheia, the goat which was said to have nourished the infant Zeus. Now it is only writers of the Hellenistic period or later that refer to Amaltheia as a goat; earlier authors such as Pherekydes and Pindar call her a nymph. Nevertheless the motive of a divine child reared by an animal is a primitive one, as we have noted above with regard to the legends of Akakallis (p. 200), and classical authors very often humanized and softened down the more primitive elements in their traditional folklore. Some later author, perhaps Euhemerus, stated that Amaltheia was the daughter of the Cretan King Melisseus, who may himself be only the humanized version of the wild bees that brought honey to the infant god.

Strabo, the geographer, asserted that the birth cave of Zeus was on Mount Dikte, and Aratos confused the tradition further by saying that Zeus was reared 'in fragrant Dikton on Mount Ida'. Hellenistic traditions seem to have placed Mount Dikte east of the isthmus of Hierapetra, since Strabo, writing in the time of Augustus, denounced the absurdity of placing Dikte near Mount Ida, from which he said it was 1000 stades distant, whereas only 100 stades separated it from Cape Samonion in the far east. Bosanquet emphasized that during the classical period the cults of Dictaean Zeus were all situated in the east end of the island, and he suggested that the ruins at Palaikastro, where there was a temple dedicated to Dictaean Zeus, might represent the city of Diktaia, which Diodorus said had been founded by Zeus near his birthplace. The map of Crete drawn up in the fifteenth century A.D. by the Venetian Coronelli places Dikte near the site of the conical mountain termed Modhi and the town Dittea a little to the south-west.

Obviously we have rival stories from various districts all claiming that the birth cave of Zeus was situated on their territory. The Eteo-Cretan story represented by the traditions recorded by Strabo, Diodorus, and Coronelli and summed up by Bosanquet must have identified the birth cave with some as yet undiscovered cave near Modhi.[1]

Hesiod's story of the birth cave and the 'Goat's Mountain' must have been the canonical version in Lyktos and probably throughout the district we now term the Pedhiadha, though Marinatos has suggested that at an earlier date the cave of Zeus might have been identified with that of Arkalochori, which is nearer to Lyktos, and that the tradition might only have shifted to Psychro after the collapse of the roof of the Arkalochori cave.

A third tradition certainly associated Zeus's birth with the Idaean cave that underlies the main peak of Psiloriti and overlooks the plain of Nidha, 5000 feet above the sea. This was the cave most commonly accepted as the Birth Cave in Roman times, and dedications show that it was a sacred place before 1400 B.C. It was not, apparently, frequented in Middle Minoan times, when the Kamaras cave overlooking the Mesara may possibly have been a place where the local inhabitants celebrated the birth of Velchanos, the Minoan Zeus.

THE CURETES

Closely associated with the cult of the infant Zeus was that of the Curetes, attendants of the young Zeus.

A hymn dating in its present form from the third century A.D. but obviously derived from a much earlier prototype, invoking the young Zeus (here regarded not as an infant but as a young man) in the name of the Curetes, was discovered at Palaikastro in the country of the Eteo-Cretans on a site where there had been an earlier temple dedicated to Dictean Zeus.

According to Diodorus the nine Curetes were earth-born like the Titans, though others said they were children of the Idaean Dactyla. The Curetes were said to be 'the first to gather sheep into flocks, to domesticate the several other kinds of animals which men fatten, and to discover the making of honey. In the same manner they introduced the art of shooting with the bow and the ways of hunting animals,

---

1. R. C. Bosanquet, 'Dikte and the Temples of Dictaean Zeus', *Annual of the British School at Athens*, 1940, p. 60; the fame of Diktaia was remembered even by Ariosto, who calls it the richest of the hundred cities of Crete (*Orlando furioso*, Canto XX, verse 15).

and they showed mankind how to live and associate together in a common life, and they were the originators of concord and of a kind and orderly behaviour.'[1]

This rather sophisticated account hardly sounds like genuine folk-lore; I suspect it to be an account by Euhemerus or some such writer of the origins of the Neolithic civilization. Diodorus also records that the Curetes invented swords and helmets and the war-dance, but this is probably only an explanation of the ritual dance performed at festivals of the birth of Zeus. Later traditions refer to them as sons of Zeus, or confuse them with the Corybantes who had Rhodian associations and appear in inscriptions from Hierapytna, a city with very strong Rhodian connexions.

The legend of the dancing Curetes, however (when not confused with the Corybantes), seems to be purely Cretan.

This dance has been compared to the leaping dance performed at Rome by the Salii, the armed priests of Mars. The eastern districts of Crete, as remarked by Evans, the very districts where the Eteo-Cretans maintained themselves till a late date, are still famous for their *pedhiktos* or leaping dance.

THE DEATH OF THE CRETAN ZEUS

No legend has survived at all concerning the manner of the death of Zeus and presumably even the suspicion of it would have died out of the popular memory but for the celebration of rites by local inhabitants near the reputed site of his tomb. There is no literary reference to his death before the passage from Epimenides quoted by St Paul (but not mentioned by other Greek writers in any extant passage before Euhemerus and Callimachus).

Nilsson assumes that the Cretan Zeus was a vegetation god, born and dying each year like Osiris, but there is only one possible classical reference to the annual birth and none to the annual death, unless we are to assume that the annual spreading of carpets on the throne of Zeus in the Idaean Cave was a ceremony associated with the annual death.

Nevertheless, although these Cretan legends of Zeus seem to be saturated with pre-Hellenic myths, it is hard to identify any of them

1. Diodorus Siculus, Book v, Chap. 65.

in the representations on Minoan seal-stones. There are some seals showing a young male figure descending from Heaven who may well have been Velchanos, but there is no Bronze Age seal or other representation showing the birth of Zeus, or the Curetes dancing round him. On the contrary most Minoan gems suggest that goddesses were more important than gods to the Cretans of the Bronze Age and probably of the Neolithic period also.

Fig. 38. Gold ring (from Knosos?)

The prominence of legends referring to the young Zeus in the Iron Age is perhaps almost an accident, due to the fact that this particular Minoan deity, who may possibly have been only a deified king, happened to have been identified with the main deity of the Greek settlers.

MINOAN DEMONS

Minoan demons, which were always depicted as performing some religious rite, such as pouring libations or bringing offerings to a goddess, are consistent in type and must be carefully distinguished from the more varied and fanciful monsters devised by Minoan artists when they were aiming merely at decoration and not at any religious symbolism. They walk upright and behave like human beings, but their limbs end in paws, not hands or feet, their heads resemble those of lions or horses or asses, and their backs are covered with loose skin ending in a point like a wasp's tail. Levi has classified them as lion demons, while Evans believes they were derived from an Egyptian design showing TA-URT, the hippopotamus goddess, carrying a crocodile. Nilsson regards them as an invention of Minoan fantasy. Their origin remains obscure but their functions seem certain.

MINOAN GODDESSES

One of the most prominent figures on seals is the goddess sometimes compared to Artemis, 'Lady of the Beasts', and sometimes to Cybele, the great mother goddess of Asia Minor. There is some excuse for both parallels, but the tendency of many writers, helped by Hesychios's

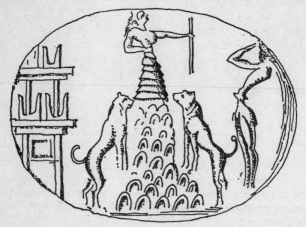

Fig. 39. Mountain Mother sealing

statement that Kybelis was a word for the double axe, has been to overstress the relationship of this deity to Anatolian religion and to the great mother goddess whom the Phrygians so appropriately addressed as 'MA'.

Nilsson has pointed out that the famous seal impressions showing the Minoan goddess standing on a mountain peak flanked by two guardian lions are relatively late; I would personally go further and regard them as Mycenaean sealings, although found at Knosos (Fig. 39). Earlier representations of the Minoan goddess depict her as a huntress like Britomartis or Artemis, rather than as the protectress 'Lady of the Beasts'.

Evans often seems to suggest that he regards most representations of goddesses on Minoan seals as personifications of the great mother goddess, but a fairer representation of his views is afforded by a quotation from a letter he wrote to Nilsson stating: 'I have always in mind the possibility that the goddess who appears in so many relations in Minoan scenes and impersonations may cover what was really regarded as separate deities with separate names equivalent to Artemis, Rhea, Athena, Aphrodite, etc. But as a provisional procedure it is convenient, in default of more definite knowledge, to treat the goddess as essentially the same great Nature Goddess under various aspects – celestial with the dove, chthonic with the snake, etc., etc.' We may recall how the Titan Prometheus in Aeschylus's play refers to 'my mother Themis and Earth, one shape with many names' (*Prometheus Vinctus*, lines 217 and 218).

THE LADY OF THE BEASTS AND THE MASTER OF THE ANIMALS

The huntress goddess figured on some Minoan seal-stones may have been called Britomartis, a name which, according to the late Latin

Fig. 40. Master of the Animals seal

author, Solinus, meant 'sweet virgin', a translation confirmed by an entry in Hesychios's Lexicon stating that '*britu*' was a Cretan word meaning 'sweet'. We need not, I think, be troubled by the fact that this goddess was worshipped as Britomartis in the east but as Dictynna in the west of the island. If Britomartis was an old Eteo-Cretan title (and it was certainly not Greek) we can understand its surviving longer in eastern Crete, where that language persisted till Roman times. In the west, however, where the country was flooded with Achaean colonists at an early date, it is natural that she might be hailed as 'The Lady of Dikte'. Worshippers had to enter her temple barefoot – possibly a Minoan custom.[1]

Parallel to the 'Lady of the Beasts' is her less prominent but well-attested male counterpart the 'Master of the Animals', a youthful figure usually depicted grasping two lions or other animals or birds by the throats. We do not know his Minoan name and it is difficult to attach a Greek name to him. The fact that the 'Lady of the Beasts' was called Artemis in archaic Greek times might suggest that we should call the 'Master of the Animals' Apollo, especially as the cult of that god was said to have been introduced from Crete to Delphi, but there is really no evidence to show that Apollo was represented as 'Master of the Animals' in archaic Greek art.[2]

THE SNAKE OR HOUSEHOLD GODDESS

Another deity very popular in Minoan times was the one known to archaeologists as the Snake Goddess, from the fact that one or more snakes are usually found coiling round the body or arms of the figures representing her (Plate 9). Her worship seems to be concentrated in small shrines in the palaces and the large houses, and she is therefore regarded by Nilsson as pre-eminently the domestic or household goddess. The snake had probably nothing to do with the snakes that appear in underworld cults in classical Greece. It was the house snake that was fed and revered as the genius, the guardian angel of the house, according to a very widespread superstition. The cult of the household snake has not entirely died out even now. In some parts of Greece peasants will sprinkle breadcrumbs round a hole in the floor regarded as the snake's door, or will pour milk into it. If the snake appears it will be hailed as 'master of the house' (*noikokýres*) or 'genius of the place' (*topákas*).[3] Similar practices are recorded from Albania, from all the Slav countries, from Lithuania, Italy, Sweden, and India (all countries characterized by their use of Indo-European languages). It is true that in classical Greece the cult of the house snake does seem sometimes to be confused, or at least associated,

1. It was certainly the normal practice among the Semites.
2. Mrs Chittenden prefers to correlate him with Hermes; see *Hesperia*, 1947, p. 187.
3. But I cannot quote any recent example from Crete.

with a cult of the dead, and we find the snake worshipped under titles such as Zeus Ktesios, Zeus Meilichios, or more commonly as the Agathos Daimon. This, however, was quite foreign to the Minoan and Mycenaean practice where the snake was not a deity but simply, in all probability, the emblem of a goddess.

A similar snake goddess seems to have been worshipped during the Bronze Age in Palestine where a *stele* was found at Tell Beit Mirsim in a deposit dated about 1600 B.C., carved with a representation of a goddess with her snake curling round her body.[1] This *stele* was practically contemporary with the faience figure of the Snake Goddess found in the temple repositories at Knosos. Unfortunately the goddess of Tell Beit Mirsim lacks both a head and a name.

The classical deity who embodied most of the spirit of the Minoan Snake Goddess was certainly Athena, not the fierce warrior goddess of Olympus as Homer represented her, but rather the maiden goddess as Pheidias saw her, the calm, benignant patron of the city, still faithful to her bird (the owl), her snake, and her pillar, all familiar elements in the cult of the Household Goddess, the Snake Goddess of Crete, by one tradition the birthplace of Athena.

Just as Athena was worshipped as Polias, the patron goddess of the city, so was her snake regarded as 'Oikouros', the household snake of the city and we can imagine the consternation of the Athenians when that snake refused its food on the occasion of the invasion by Xerxes and his Persians.[2] Nilsson has most aptly quoted a passage from Kipling's story, *The Letting in of the Jungle*: 'Who could fight against the Jungle or the Gods of the Jungle when the very village cobra had left his hole in the platform under the peepul.'[3] Sir John Forsdyke has recorded his memories of a more gallant house snake which refused to desert the Macedonian village of Kalenovo when the human inhabitants fled, and which therefore drew rations from the British unit which occupied it in the First World War. I spent a night there in 1924, but unfortunately cannot substantiate whether the snake was then still carrying out its duties.

1. W. F. Albright, *The Archaeology of Palestine* (Penguin Books, 1949), Fig. 20.
2. Herodotus, Book VIII, Chap. 41.
3. *The Second Jungle Book.*

EPIPHANIES IN THE FORMS OF BIRDS

The sacred bird was just as characteristic of the Minoan Household Goddess as it was of Athena Parthenos but it was usually a different bird in Crete. The birds associated with her in Middle Minoan deposits, such as the doves of a shrine from the Loom-Weight Basement, or from the temple repositories, or from Late Minoan shrines such as Gournia or Gaze, or Sub-Minoan shrines such as Karphi and Prinias, are often hard to identify, but when they have any characteristics at all they resemble doves rather than owls. Most of them can only be termed small birds. A bird on the double axes in the cult scene on the Hagia Triada sarcophagus is almost certainly a raven.

The miniature shrine from which the 'Dove Shrine Deposit' gained its name is particularly interesting, since it consists of a trilithon of three pillars with beam-end capitals, each surmounted by a 'dove'. It recalls somewhat the very interesting pillar-shrine of Roque-Perthuse in South France[1] (though without the human skulls and horse-head frieze of the latter). The Roque-Perthuse monument only dates from the fourth century B.C., but the Ligurians who probably erected it were a very old-established and conservative element of the population of those parts.

The epiphany of gods and goddesses in the form of birds must have been equally familiar in Mycenaean mythology. Even in classical times we have Zeus's eagle, Athena's owl, and Aphrodite's doves, but in Homer's poems such epiphanies are more numerous and varied. Athena and Apollo appropriately turn themselves into vultures to watch the battle between Hector and Ajax. Hypnos (sleep) approaches Zeus in the form of a kite. Athena on other occasions appears as a swallow or as a heron.

If then the chief gods and goddesses of the Minoan pantheon were worshipped by the Mycenaean Greeks, we should be able to identify many of them. Which, if any, of the Hellenic goddesses are we to identify with the Minoan goddess whom Evans regarded as the 'Nature Goddess' whose symbol appears to have been the double

1. Compare F. Bénoit, *L'Art primitif méditerranéen de la vallée du Rhône*, 1945, p. 14 and Plate 29.

axe and whose sacred birds appear to have been doves? The double axe might suggest that she was Cybele and the doves that she was Aphrodite. Indeed the naked Mycenaean goddess with the doves probably was Aphrodite, but our Cretan goddess of the double axe was respectably attired in full court dress.

It is at least arguable that 'the very holy one' of Crete may have been nearer to Athena than to Aphrodite, since at Corinth, a great centre of Mycenaean culture, we find the cult title 'Hellotis' (recalling the Cretan festival Hellotia dedicated to Ariadne) assigned to Athena.

ARIADNE

The first literary reference to the name Ariadne occurs in the *Iliad*, where Homer records that Daedalus prepared a fine dancing place for her in Crete.[1] Nilsson has suggested that in view of the importance of dancing in Minoan times, the said dancing place might have been prepared for the goddess Ariadne rather than for Minos's daughter, though the classical readers of the *Iliad* would certainly have interpreted the passage as referring to the princess Ariadne. Nilsson even suggested that the tales of the rapes of Ariadne, Helen, and Persephone all reflected the rape of a Minoan vegetation goddess.[2]

The name Ariadne is simply a Cretan epithet signifying 'very holy', and its modern equivalent would seem to be *Panagia*, 'The All Holy', the regular name in modern Greece for the Virgin Mary. This name, of course, is not confined to Crete, but it may not be devoid of significance that, whereas in many parts of Greece only women swear by the name of the Virgin, in Crete her name is regularly on the lips of the men also, as it might well be on an island where in Minoan times goddesses had been more important than gods,[3] and where the natives referred to their 'motherland' and not their 'fatherland'.

Some of the classical legends about Ariadne are concerned with her death. Sometimes it was said that she died in child-birth, as in the

1. *Iliad*, Book XVIII, 1.
2. *The Mycenaean Origins of Greek Mythology*, 1932, p. 170.
3. Compare Charles Seltman's reference to 'the age-old potent wish to regard Nature as Feminine and Godhead as Female'. (*Women in Antiquity*, 1956, p. 166).

story current at Amathus in Cyprus, a legend perhaps alluded to in the eleventh book of the *Odyssey*, where it is stated that Artemis (who presided over births) slew her in Dia. Plutarch, on the other hand, tells how Ariadne hanged herself on a tree when she was deserted by Theseus on Naxos. This story, and another told by Pausanias to the effect that Helen had been hanged on a tree in Rhodes on the orders of Polemo, have been quoted to prove that both Ariadne and Helen were originally goddesses connected with the Minoan tree and pillar cults.

The Greeks themselves were puzzled over these inconsistent stories and some tried to distinguish between the goddess Ariadne wife of Dionysus, celebrated by a joyous festival, and Ariadne the daughter of Minos, for whom a mourning festival was celebrated. Nilsson, however, suggests that both festivals were probably in honour of the same deity, a goddess of the spring, since it is customary to celebrate the death of a vernal deity with mourning and the resurrection of the same deity the following spring with rejoicing.

Neustadt even goes so far as to compare the dance of Ariadne with modern customs associated with the first of May, and the story of Theseus diving into the depths of the sea to receive a wreath from Amphitrite with the custom of drenching the representative of the vegetation spirit in modern country festivals. This is rather a speculative suggestion, but probably there are ancient survivals in the celebrations of the first of May. For centuries before 'Labour Day' was invented the first of May was celebrated as Lady Day. Who was the original Lady to whom it was consecrated? Not, I think, the Virgin Mary and perhaps not even the 'very holy one' of Minoan Crete.

EUROPA

Another Cretan heroine who might perhaps once have been a goddess is Europa. The orthodox legend represented her as a Phoenician princess, the sister of Kadmos and of the elder Minos, and stated that she was carried off to Crete by Zeus, who appeared to her in the form of a bull. Coins of Phaistos and Gortyn of the fifth century B.C. show a woman usually identified with Europa sitting in what appears to be a willow tree, an identification supported by the occasional presence of a bull or bull's head. But why should she be sitting in a willow tree? Vürtheim has related the names of Europa and Velchanos to *rhops* and *helike*, two Greek words meaning willow, pointing out that the willow tree was sacred to Hera on Samos. This sort of speculation is rather hazardous, but there is perhaps a slightly better case for associating Europa with tree worship than Ariadne.

TREE AND PILLAR WORSHIP

A very distinctive feature of Minoan religion and of the Mycenaean cults derived from it was the worship and veneration paid to trees and pillars, stressed by Sir Arthur Evans in his monograph *The Mycenaean Tree and Pillar Cult*. Worship of trees and sacred boughs was widespread in Europe in ancient times, and the classical work in English on primitive religions by Sir James Frazer was termed *The Golden Bough*.

It was Evans, however, who pointed the moral of the connexion between trees and *baetyls* or sacred stones, which often continued to remain sacred even when their shrines had been taken over by the followers of an iconoclastic religion such as Mohammedanism. The most famous example of such a *baetyl* still revered in modern times is the black stone at Mecca, but another example is quoted by Evans from a Mohammedan shrine at Tekekioi near Skoplje, where the sacred pillar, venerated by Christians and Mohammedans alike, was regularly anointed with olive oil, just as Jacob used to anoint his stone at Bethel. The Tekekioi pillar, which is roughly square, reminds us of the square piers in Minoan pillar crypts, and the resemblance between them is strengthened by the sunken hearthstone behind it on which candles were lit every night, reminding us of the sunken stone trough that often accompanies or surrounds the piers of pillar crypts at Knosos. On the other side of the pillar at Tekekioi there was a stone base where the votary stood to pray, finishing his prayer by embracing the stone so that his fingers touched behind it. He then visited the Tekke, the grave of the saint, with water drawn from a neighbouring spring. Over the headstone of the grave grew a thorn bush hung with rags, dedicated by pilgrims to the shrine. In 1927 I saw a similar bush decorated with rags beside a stone with a natural hole through it near Lapsista in western Macedonia, a village then

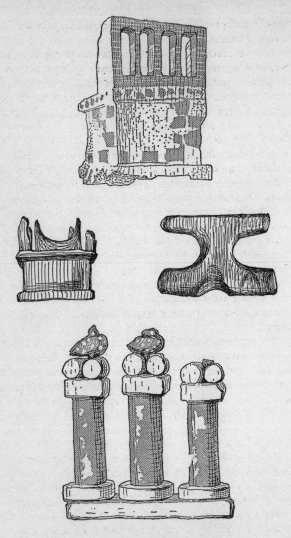

Fig. 41. Furniture of Dove Shrine

occupied by refugees from Anatolia, but before 1922 by the Greek-speaking Mohammedans known as Valláhadhes.

In both these modern instances we find the association of the *baetyl*, the sacred stone, with the sacred tree, stressed by Evans as typical of the Minoan–Mycenaean civilization. The classical cult of Athena Parthenos at Athens also shows the pillar associated with the sacred tree, the olive, and with the sacred bird, Athena's owl. The cult of Poseidon Erechtheus provides an instance of the sacred spring.[1]

We need not, indeed must not, assume that all pillars were necessarily sacred, and Nilsson points out that even the affixing of sacred symbols such as *bucrania*, or the tripod of Apollo, to a column or wall does not necessarily imply its sanctity. Clearly the pillars of pillar crypts served an obvious structural purpose in supporting the room above them, and we must not attach too much value to the fact that occasionally the double axe appears as a mason's mark on the stones of one or two of these pillars. Nevertheless I think Evans's term 'pillar crypts' is in the main justified, and their religious associations are supported by the remains of burnt offerings, pottery, lamps, and animal bones which Dr Platon and I found between the Middle Minoan I and the Middle Minoan III floors of the east Pillar Crypt of the Palace of Minos when we were carrying out repairs there in 1945.

A Mycenaean *crater* from Curium in Cyprus (No. C 391 in the British Museum) has a scene apparently showing two women adoring a pillar together with a chariot scene on one side, and on the other side what appear to be two pillar crypts, one above the other, with a couple of women adoring the pillar in each (Fig. 42).

SACRED SPRINGS

Sacred springs presided over by a goddess were characteristic of the Minoan religion and continued into classical times when the deities of the springs were worshipped as the Nereids, as Herodotus tells us; indeed traces of the cult have persisted into modern times since

1. Professor Mallowan's excavations at Chagar Bazar in Syria and at Arpachiyah produced various analogous features: goddess, figurines, birds, double-axe amulets, with the addition at Arpachiyah of *tholoi*, also in deposits of the Tell Khalaf period.

Neraïdes is still used in the sense of 'fairies'. There is a rock-cut spring-house just above the cemetery of Mavrospelaion dating from the Middle Minoan period, but it was rather bare when excavated; perhaps the best surviving example is the small shrine erected over the outflow of the spring at the caravanserai south of the Palace of Minos.

The gypsum Spring Chamber with its little niche for an image

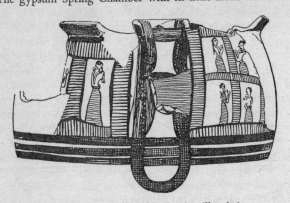

Fig. 42. Women worshipping in pillar shrine

was constructed like the rest of the caravanserai in the transitional Middle Minoan III B–Late Minoan I A period but continued as a place of worship right to the end of the Late Minoan III period, long after the caravanserai had ceased to be used for its original purpose and was lying in ruins. The date when the Spring House ceased even to be visited as a shrine is indicated by the Protogeometric rubbish choking the basin.

DOMESTIC SHRINES IN PALACES AND HOUSES

The domestic shrines of the palaces and larger houses during the Middle Minoan period seem to comprise two main forms. The simpler type, intended to serve only the needs of the family, may be seen at Knosos in the House of the Priest and the House of the Chancel Screen, and consisted of a room with a kind of chancel screen, with pillars and a central passage between the ante-chapel and the sanctuary.

The other form of domestic shrine was obviously intended to satisfy the needs of public worship for other people outside the inhabitants of the palace, and consisted of two or three rooms to which probably only the priests were admitted screened from the public by a fine façade, and a triple porch of which the centre portion rose higher than the flanks, the roof of each porch being crowned by a pair of Horns of Consecration. Such was the shrine that faced the west side of the central court at Knosos, and its appearance may be gauged from the shrine represented in the miniature frescoes (Plate 11).

This form of palace shrine was adopted by the Mycenaean Greeks of the mainland and is illustrated by the small gold models of the Dove Shrines found in the third Shaft Grave at Mycenae. The earlier shrine of the Middle Minoan II palace at Phaistos seems also to have been of this type, so far as we can judge from the extant remains.

Another and simpler type of palace shrine, however, appears before the end of the fifteenth century in the palace at Hagia Triada. This consists of an oblong room entered through a small porch from one of the narrower ends and with a ledge for the images and cult objects at the innermost end of the long room. This was to become the regular form in the very latest Minoan period, and bears such a resemblance to the Mycenaean *megaron* and to the simplest form of Greek temple that one might suspect Mycenaean influence.

In Crete only the shrines of this type at Gournia and Hagia Triada can be dated as early as Late Minoan I and some scholars would prefer to assign even these to the Late Minoan III period. Other similar shrines either date very late in the Late Minoan III period (the Shrine of the Double Axes, the one at Prinias, and, I think, the one at Mallia also), or even in the Sub-Minoan period (Karphi).

On the mainland the Mycenaean building underneath the later Hall of the Mysteries at Eleusis was also of this type, though with some special features of its own.[1] There seems to be no obvious Minoan prototype for this kind of shrine, unless we are to take the rather different domestic shrine of the south-east house at Knosos as the prototype.

1. W. B. Dinsmore, *The Architecture of Ancient Greece*, 1950, p. 24, Fig. 10.

MINOAN SHRINES AND SANCTUARIES

The places where Minoan worship was carried out differed consider-ably from those of the Greeks in that there were properly speaking no public temples, though they were not without places for public wor-ship. The holy places were peak sanctuaries, cave sanctuaries, spring houses, and domestic shrines. Certain funeral ceremonies were also carried out near tombs in small adjacent chambers, which seems to have been the practice in Early Minoan times with the great tombs of the Mesara and perhaps even with the smaller tombs of eastern Crete. The family tombs of Middle Minoan II–III and Late Minoan times either possessed a *dromos* or entrance passage or a small fore-court which could be used for the funeral rites. Spring houses had a basin from which the worshippers drew the holy water, and a niche for images and lamps, if we may judge from the very scanty evidence.[1]

Cave sanctuaries seem to have had practically no structures at all except a tenuous wall dividing the congregation from the priest and the sanctuary; rough walls of this kind were found in the cave sanctuaries of Eileithyia at Amnisos, and that of Zeus at Psychro.

PEAK SANCTUARIES

The Middle Minoan I period was marked by a new fashion in public worship, in the form of the so-called 'peak sanctuaries', which remind us of the 'high places' mentioned in the Book of Kings and inveighed against by the prophets of Jehovah. The Cretan high places, however, seem to have been ultimately converted to Christianity, and it seems likely that peaks now bearing chapels dedicated to the 'Lord Christ' or to the 'Precious Cross' once bore shrines dedicated to the Cretan Zeus. Iuktas certainly was sacred to the latter and was even regarded as his burial place, though the church on its southern summit, origin-ally monastic, is at present dedicated to the Virgin Mary.[2]

1. One Linear B tablet records the sending of olive oil to Zeus of Dicte, while another records offerings of honey to Eleuthia (=Eileithyia) at Amnisos.
2. An exception to the general practice according to which chapels erected on mountains previously sacred to Zeus were on the mainland dedicated to Elias, but on Crete to the Lord Christ.

The Minoan sanctuary on the central peak, excavated by Evans, consisted of a broad hall (8 metres wide and 5 metres deep) approached through an outer room, and flanked by two narrow passages – a plan somewhat resembling that of the more or less contemporary temple of Tell Ai in Palestine.[1]

The sanctuary continued in use till the Late Minoan I period and some of the walls may date from that period, but the sanctuary probably preserved the same plan from Middle Minoan I times onward.

The inner room had a floor of white plaster, perhaps of later date, but the same feature also occurs in the Middle Minoan I shrine on the Prophet Elias peak above Mallia, where there was a sanctuary with a similar plan, but where the inner room had a plaster bench on three sides of the interior.

These peak sanctuaries were, of course, particularly subject to denudation by natural causes, and often the only signs of their former existence are the remains of votive offerings caught in crevices of the rocks, and sometimes evidence of sacrificial fires.

This group of sanctuaries has been reviewed recently in a good article in *Kretika Chronika* by Platon,[2] who lists the following examples: (*a*) Palaikastro, (*b*) and (*c*) Zakros, (*d*) Chamaizi and (*e*) Piskokephalo Seteias in eastern Crete and (*f*) the Prophet Elias of Mallia, (*g*) Endikti, (*h*) Karphi (both in Lasithi), (*i*) Iuktas near Knosos, (*j*) Kuomasa and (*k*) Christou (both in the Mesara) in central Crete. No peak sanctuary has yet been reported from western Crete, but probably this is merely due to the fact that this area has even now been less thoroughly explored than the centre and the east of the island.

Some of the figurines from Piskokephalo described by Platon appear to be too developed in style for the Middle Minoan I period, and I should be inclined to date them Middle Minoan II or III.

One of the oddities of Piskokephalo is the series of very naturalistic representations of the rhinoceros beetle (*Oryctes nasicornis*), presumably regarded as a field pest which the worshippers hoped to render innocuous. Myres has quoted other examples of dedications of this sort. From the Iuktas sanctuary came clay models of weasels and from Palaikastro figurines of hedgehogs. The animals dedicated at

1. See M. V. Seton-Williams, *Iraq*, 1949, p. 81, Fig. 4.
2. 'To Ieron Maza', *Kretika Chronica*, 1951.

these sanctuaries, however, were not all pests, but more often domestic animals or even wild animals and birds. Platon enumerates sheep and goats, birds, pigs, dogs, hedgehogs, swallows, and ibex among the dedications. The figurines of oxen vary from twenty-five millimetres to perhaps half a metre in length, to judge from the size of a fragmentary head found at Piskokephalo.

Since Middle Minoan II pottery is practically confined to Knosos and Phaistos,[1] it is not surprising that we cannot quote examples from these sanctuaries except Iuktas, clearly datable between 1850 and 1700 B.C.; but it is likely that several of these sanctuaries continued to be frequented throughout much of the Middle Minoan period.

Marinatos was the first to stress the important clues towards determining the nature of the deities worshipped at the various sanctuaries afforded by the nature of the dedications. Thus the deity worshipped at Arkalochori was presumably a god or goddess of war, to judge by the quantity of swords and other weapons dedicated there.

The offerings at the Kamares Cave, on the other hand, were chiefly in the form of pottery. The cave which he excavated at Amnisos, however, is the only one where we can confidently name the goddess worshipped, namely Eileithyia, the patron goddess of childbirth. Here, as at Kamares, the offerings were mainly of pottery, and their paucity and poor quality suggests that Eileithyia may have been principally a goddess of the poor. We are reminded of Statius's fine description of the Altar of Pity in Athens.[2]

> Who asks is heard and night and day
> May go and seek the goddess' aid
> To ease her solitary complaints.
> Scant ritual, no sacrifice
> No incense flame ascends on high
> With tears alone her altar's wet.

Doubtless Eileithyia was also worshipped in villas and palaces but I think her cave at Amnisos was a shrine of the people.

The offerings from the peak sanctuaries, even from that of Iuktas, have given us a poor selection, but the sites were so exposed and the traces of sacrificial fires so evident that we cannot argue from the

1. The Kamares Cave is hardly an exception since it was a shrine obviously frequented by the inhabitants of Phaistos, from where it is clearly visible.

2. *Thebais* XII, 485–8.

absence of more valuable offerings which might have been burnt, looted by treasure hunters, or simply weathered away.

Sick persons also appear to have dedicated models of the limb or organ they wished to be healed. The concentration of these peak sanctuaries in eastern Crete might support the idea that the goddess worshipped was Britomartis. Platon, on the other hand, has suggested it was the great Earth Mother (interpreting Maza to mean Ma Ga, Mother Earth). There is, however, no conclusive evidence that the deities worshipped at the peak sanctuaries were inevitably goddesses, and it would not surprise me greatly if the deity worshipped had not sometimes been the 'Master of Animals' (especially if Mrs Chittenden's theory is correct that the Greek equivalent of this deity was Hermes and that his symbol was a pillar or a cairn of stones, for which the Greek word was *herma*).

MIDDLE MINOAN SHRINES OF THE HOUSEHOLD GODDESS

The palace shrines of the Household Goddess are less illuminating from one point of view, since, although they include objects of artistic value, these must represent only a small proportion, and that not necessarily a characteristic selection, of the objects originally dedicated in them. Thus both the Dove Shrine of the Middle Minoan II B period (Fig. 41) and the temple repositories of the Middle Minoan III B period were presumably concerned with the cult of the same goddess, but a comparison of the preserved dedications from them will show how little there is in common:

Dove Shrine	*Temple Repositories*
2 Pillar shrines	1 Figure of Snake Goddess
1 Altar with sacral horns	1 Figure of votaress
1 Hollow-sided altar	1 Cow suckling calf
1 Pair of sacral horns	1 Antelope suckling kid[1]
1 Beam-end capital	1 Fragment of votaress
1 Trilithon shrine with birds	2 Model robes
1 Carrying chair	Flying fish
	Painted shells
	1 Marble cross
	1 Stone table of offerings

1. Usually but wrongly described as a goat.

LATE MINOAN SHRINES OF THE
HOUSEHOLD GODDESS

A much more representative picture of the furniture of a shrine of the Household Goddess, but on a far poorer scale, is afforded by that of the Civic Shrine at Gournia, of which the furniture seems chiefly, if not entirely, to date from the Late Minoan III period. This included a clay figure of the Household Goddess, the head of a similar figure, an arm with a snake twisted round it and tightening the grasp of a hand holding a straight chisel-like object (certainly not a sword but conceivably a torch), another hand with a snake coiling round it, and the head of a snake formerly attached to something. There were also three snake tubes with multiple heads and sacral horns in relief, the fragment of a fourth, and a tripod altar of clay with the base of what was presumably a fifth tube attached to it. Other clay objects from the shrine included two birds of different sizes and a sherd from a *pithos* with a double axe in relief (Fig. 43).

Two shrines were reconstructed from the ruins of the palaces at Knosos in the very latest Minoan period.[1] Of these the 'Fetish Shrine' constructed in the ruined lustral area of the Little Palace had little except a pair of Horns of Consecration, and the four strange stalagmitic formations, one vaguely resembling a woman and another a child, which induced Evans to name it the 'Fetish Shrine'. The 'Shrine of the Double Axes' had no natural fetish stones but was better equipped otherwise. It was constructed in one of the small rooms of Middle Minoan III date near the south-east corner of the great court of the Palace of Minos. The room, though only 1½ metres square, was divided into three parts by its different floor levels. A shallow ante-room opened into the main chamber which had a floor of stamped clay containing a number of vases, including a tall plain jar, a tripod vase, a bowl with three upright handles, three other bowls, and a stirrup vase. The north end of the room was occupied by a narrow shelf containing the main objects of the cult, one bell-shaped idol that must represent

1. The diagonal building at Mallia (Fig. 35) seems to be a third example, but, if so, it had lost all its cult furniture.

the Household Goddess, two other bell-shaped figurines, one with a bird on its head, a male votary holding a bird as an offering, a female votary with incised features, the features being filled with powdered gypsum in the Neolithic fashion, two pairs of Consecration Horns in

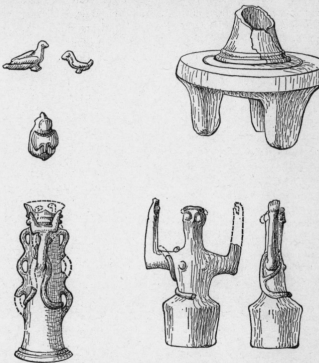

Fig. 43. Furniture of Gournia shrine

stucco with clay cores, each with a socket in the centre presumably to hold the shaft of a double axe. A small double axe in steatite, from which the shrine derives its name, was found leaning up against one of the pairs of Horns, but was too small to have been erected over it. Sometimes indeed the space between the horns is occupied by a bough and occasionally the shaft of the double axe between the horns sprouts leaves.

It will be remarked that certain features recur in these household shrines: statuettes of the goddess, double axes, snakes, and birds, but in varying proportions, the emphasis being sometimes on one element, sometimes on another. The Horns of Consecration also recur, but these are universal on Minoan shrines.

The snake tubes of Gournia have interesting parallels outside Crete, and Evans collated a convincing series of examples of clay tubes connected with the household snake cult, some with modelled snakes crawling up them, and derived them from a type of drain-pipe characteristic of the earlier palace at Knosos. The earliest examples of these snake tubes in Crete are those from the Middle Minoan I shrine at Koumasa. Some of the more interesting examples of snake tubes, however, come not from Crete at all but from Late Bronze Age sites in Cyprus and Philistia. One tube found at Kition in Cyprus shows the snake tube converted into a dove-cot, with the Dove Goddess herself looking out of a window in the fashion so characteristic of Phoenician shrines. Another tube, found in 'The House of Ashtoreth' on the Philistine site of Beth-Shan dated to the reign of Rameses II of Egypt (c. 1292–1225 B.C.),[1] shows two snakes crawling round and into the tube with two little doves perched on the handles.

The cult of the Snake Goddess may even date from Neolithic times in Crete, since figurines of birds have been found along with the female figurines of the Neolithic period.

THE DOUBLE AXE AND THE
HOUSEHOLD GODDESS

The association of the double axe with the Household Goddess is puzzling but well attested. M. Mayer, as long ago as 1892, pointed out that the double axe was the traditional weapon of Zeus of Labraunda, a name obviously connected with Labyrinthos and with *labrys*, the Lydian word for a double axe; we now know that Zeus of Labraunda was simply a Hellenized version of the old Hittite weather-god, Teshub. A. B. Cook and others have therefore argued that the double axe must be the symbol of the Thunder God, the Minoan Zeus (as the hammer was of Thor in the Scandinavian

1. Possibly six years later for both dates.

mythology). The suggestion seems very plausible at first sight, but the Minoan and Mycenaean evidence does not support it. The double axe is regularly the symbol of a goddess and in particular of the Household Goddess.[1]

It has been suggested that the double axe was simply the sacrificial weapon with which bulls were slaughtered for the sacrifices, and this is supported by the frequent appearance of double axes between the horns of bulls' heads represented on vases and gems. This seems better than the previous interpretation, but I am still puzzled why the sacrificial weapon should have been considered so appropriate for the Household Goddess. That the double axe was a sacred symbol is clear enough, and many of the existing examples such as the colossal bronze ones of Nirou Khani, the miniature gold ones of Arkalochori, and the small steatite one of the Shrine of the Double Axes would have been quite useless as tools or weapons (Fig. 46, 6).

We do, however, find a number of good, strong, work-a-day double axes in Middle and Late Minoan deposits on various sites, and very often associated with tools such as saws, double adzes, and chisels. I suspect, therefore, that the common double axe, when it was not a religious symbol, was the tool of a woodman or carpenter rather than a weapon, and possibly this might be a reason why it was considered appropriate for the Household Goddess. Professor Mallowan has suggested to me that the original idea of the root *peleku* was 'splitting', and this is supported by the modern Greek words *peléki* (cut stone) and *pelekízo* (to cut stone – used of a stone mason).

The Homeric *pelekus*, which was certainly a weapon and usually regarded as a double axe, derived its name from the Accadian word *pilaqqu*, which must surely have meant originally some other form of battle-axe, since double axes, though they occurred very early in Mesopotamia, were comparatively rare in that country.

ALTARS AND HORNS OF CONSECRATION

Various explanations, mostly very unconvincing, have been offered for the Horns of Consecration on Minoan altars and roofs of shrines.

1. Goddess figurines, birds, *tholoi*, *bucrania*, and double axes are also characteristic of the deposits of the Tell Khalaf period at Arpachiyah in Assyria. M. E. L. Mallowan, *The Excavations at Arpachiyah*, 1933, Figs. 45, 46, and 51.

They have been compared to symbols of mountains, regarded as fire-dogs, or connected with the lunate objects of Early Iron Age date from Central Europe and Italy. More often and more plausibly they are assumed to be derived from the horns of the sacred bull. Examples of the Jamdat Nasr period (3000 B.C.) have been found at Tell Brak in Syria, at Nuzu in Mesopotamia, and at Tepe Hisar in Persia, and examples of later date at Alisar and Kusura in Asia Minor.[1]

An abnormal, but I think probable, example of the Horns of Consecration was found at Mochlos in an Early Minoan I deposit. Normal examples of these horns occur on the miniature altar of the so-called Dove Shrine deposit of Middle Minoan II B date. From the Middle Minoan III period onwards such Horns of Consecration are normal on Minoan shrines and altars, or as bases for the shaft of a double axe, and they are equally common on Mycenaean shrines on the mainland – to judge by their representations in frescoes, vases, and gems. Gaerte also proposed to associate with them the small bell-shaped objects of clay of Middle Minoan I date which sometimes have two horns on top and have been classed as votive bells (Evans), votive robes (Hazzidakis), images of the goddess (Chapouthier), or ritual masks (Platon).[2]

A hieroglyphic sign resembling these curious objects occurs on some of the clay tablets from Mallia.

Minoan altars were nearly always very small, resembling incense altars or fire-altars rather than the temple altars of Greece or Rome, and no surviving Minoan altar could have been used for the sacrifice of any animal larger than a small kid. Nevertheless, representations of a trussed ox show that these animals were sacrificed, and one gem depicts an ox on a large table or altar with four low legs. Besides the altars we also have a large number of what are termed libation tables, or tables of offering, sometimes with a flat, sometimes with a low or high pedestal, but always with one or more round hollows in the upper surface. Occasionally, as on the triple-hollow table from the Dictaean Cave and on one or two from Palaikastro, they may bear short inscriptions in Linear Script A. The Middle Minoan sanctuary in the palace at Phaistos contained a rectangular clay tray em-

1. M. E. L. Mallowan, *Iraq*, 1947, Part 2, p. 184, with bibliography.

2. See p. 223 and compare N. Platon, 'Nouvelle Interprétation des idoles cloches du Minoen Moyen I' in *Mélanges Charles Picard*, 1949.

bedded in the floor with the usual central depression and with a flat rim adorned with incised spirals and figures of sheep (the latter confined to one long side and part of one short side of the tray, except for a solitary sheep at each corner). Eighteen sheep are represented, but I have no idea whether this number has any significance.

Mallia has one or two stones with a depression in the centre and a whole series of smaller depressions round the circumference of the stones. These are usually regarded as a special variety of tables of offering, though Evans suggested they were intended for some sort of game.

Tables of offering seem to appear when the *kernoi*, the multiple vases attached to a central support characteristic of Early Minoan and Early Cycladic tombs, disappear, so that it is not unlikely that they fulfilled a somewhat similar function, comparable, as Xanthoudides suggested, to that of the *kernoi* employed in the liturgy of the Orthodox Church and concerned with the offerings of first-fruits.

Triangular or leaf-shaped ladles of limestone occasionally bearing letters of Linear Script A incised on them would also seem to have been utensils in Minoan shrines. The best known example, and the one with the longest inscription, was that found at Troullos near Arkhanais.

Still more certainly associated with Minoan cults were the small tripod hearths, little round tables with broad lips and three short legs made of pottery or of plaster. Examples occurred in the Shrine of the Double Axes at Knosos, in the Gournia Shrine, and piles of five were found in the Little Palace at Nirou Khani. Examples have also been found on the mainland at Mycenae and Tiryns, and at Delos in the Cyclades. Most of the examples are Late Minoan, even Late Minoan III in date, but a possible prototype of Middle Minoan I date was found outside the round tomb at Porti in the Mesara, in the form of a round table with a slightly raised border but with no tripod legs. There is no very conclusive evidence that they were used as braziers, though a different form of brazier found in Late Minoan III tomb at Zapher Papoura (No. 32, P.T.K., Fig. 46) still held some charcoal, and the fixed hearth in the *megaron* at Mycenae was adorned with painted decoration reminiscent of that of the tripod altars of Middle Minoan III B date from the House of the Sacrificed Oxen at Knosos.

THE CULT OF THE DEAD

All peoples have some rites associated with the burial or disposal of the dead, but their views on the possibility and nature of any after-life vary extremely.

Nilsson has emphasized that the general conception of Hades in the poems of Homer as a gloomy place where the ghosts were but pale, twittering shadows[1] was contradicted by the picture of Elysium, where the more heroic spirits enjoyed a more enjoyable existence, and he suggests that the presence there of Minos's brother Rhadamanthos indicates the Cretan origin of this mythical paradise.[2]

Burial rites seem to have been very simple during the Cretan Neolithic period. The dead were not cremated but laid out in caves or rock shelters, and the funeral offerings now surviving consist only of pottery, though we must not exclude the probability that other more perishable materials such as food, clothes, and wooden implements were also offered. Similar burials in caves continued during the first Early Minoan period.

Built graves, cist graves, small rooms, and even structures like a house with two or three rooms appeared in the Early Minoan II period. Towards the end of the Early Minoan III period the grave goods became richer and included gold jewellery, beautifully cut stone vases, and engraved seal-stones; the use of *larnakes* or clay coffins appeared in the Early Minoan II period and later became common.

In eastern Crete the dead seem to have been buried separately and their bones later transferred to small family ossuaries resembling houses, with anything from one to six rooms, but resembling Neolithic rather than contemporary houses. 'The houses of the dead, in fact,' says Pendlebury, 'were the traditional houses of the living of a bygone era' (Fig. 25).

In the Mesara, however, the Early Minoan period is marked by the appearance of the so-called *tholos* tombs – large communal burial places, which Glotz regarded as tribal tombs and which certainly must have been designed to serve some larger community than a family, possibly a *génos* (clan), but hardly so large a unit as a tribe. Xanthoudides's report on the method of burial does indeed state that

1. As in the Eleventh Book of the *Odyssey*.
2. *Odyssey* IV, 560–9.

'some of them contained the bodies of many hundreds or even thousands of bodies',[1] but the individual reports of tombs hardly suggest the presence of so many burials. Xanthoudides records that although great fires had been lit in some of these tombs, he found no reliable evidence for cremation. 'In places the floor was burnt almost to terracotta, and stones were split by the heat. In the Porti *tholos* almost the whole of the thick burial stratum was blackened by the fire and smoke, and many of the skulls and bones were made quite black. Yet other scholars' examination of these remains has confirmed my view that there is no case of burning the body at burial. The fire came later, and the bones turned black from exposure to the heat and smoke at close quarters.'

What was the purpose of lighting these fires inside the *tholoi*? Frankly we do not know. It might have been to obtain light, or to fumigate the tomb from the flavour of death, or for a funeral sacrifice or feast. Yet no one of these suggested reasons would have necessitated so large a fire. Small huts of stone were often erected beside or against these round tombs, and these held vases of stone or clay of a later date than the tomb itself. A walled trench outside Tholos A at Platanos contained hundreds of small stone pots. Here we have clear evidence of a cult of the dead, implying, I think, a belief in an afterlife, even though Xanthoudides may well be right in suggesting that they were vessels kept for the descendants to pour libations rather than for the actual use of the departed. Alexiou has given us a clear and interesting account of what he believes to have been the grave rites in the Early Minoan cemetery that he excavated near Kanli Kastelli, where the whole contents of the burials had been preserved by a later fall of rock. The confusion of skeletal material observed also at Pyrgos, Sphoungaras, and Kato Zakros might have been due to later disturbances, but this could not be true at Kanli Kastelli nor in the later ossuary of Middle Minoan I date which I excavated on Monasteriako Kephali, where a similar fall of rock had prevented later interference; these last two instances might indeed be explained by the transference of bones from primary burials elsewhere to their final resting place in the ossuary, but Alexiou remarks that the Zakros burials appeared to be primary interments. He

1. *The Vaulted Tombs of the Mesara*, p. 134; his use of 'cist' as a translation for *larnax* is rather misleading.

therefore considers that the clear traces of fire and the presence of animal bones, sometimes burnt but at Krasi unburnt, should be explained by supposing that funeral sacrifices were performed inside the tomb and that these caused much of the confusion of the skeletal material; and he would regard the traces of fire and animal bones recorded by Taramelli at Miamou as evidence of similar rites rather than as traces of a previous occupation of the cave shelter as a dwelling place.

The use of the round communal tombs continued in the Mesara till the end of the Middle Minoan I period or later, but the normal method of burying in the Middle Minoan period seems to have been to crush the bones into large *pithoi*, usually specially made and painted for this purpose, though sometimes ordinary domestic store-jars were utilized for the purpose.

The *pithos* was then inverted and either simply buried in the soil, as at Pachyammos and at Sphoungaras in eastern Crete; in a small walled enclosure, as in one instance at Porti; or in chamber tombs cut in the soft rock, as was the practice at Knosos in the Middle Minoan II and III periods. The evidence for Middle Minoan I burials at Knosos is rather scanty, but some burials at least were made in *larnakes* and the bones later transferred to cave shelters used as ossuaries. An unpublished but quite certain example of a cremation in a *pithos* of Middle Minoan III date was discovered by Sinclair Hood in his excavations at Knosos in 1955.

Burials in *larnakes* continued during the Middle Minoan period but the *pithos* burials which in some parts, particularly in eastern Crete, continued throughout the Late Minoan I period were common during the Middle Minoan period from 1800 to 1550 B.C.

In the Late Minoan period chamber tombs used as family graves were the normal practice throughout Crete, but they varied greatly in type from the Mycenaean kind with a long narrow *dromos* (an entrance passage cut horizontally into the slope of a hill) opening out into a round, oval, or square chamber cut out of the *kouskouras* (the local white marl) with a vaulted roof, to large, built chamber tombs cut in more level ground, with steeply sloping *dromoi* leading through a passage or outer chamber into a rectangular chamber, all except the outer *dromos* being lined with fine ashlar masonry. To the latter group may be assigned the Temple Tomb at Knosos and the Royal Tomb at Isopata.

Wooden coffins or biers were presumably sometimes employed, though the first certain remains of a coffin in this material were found in 1952 in a Late Minoan II chamber tomb at Katsaba excavated by Alexiou. Similar tombs continued to be dug throughout the Minoan period, but the Late Minoan III period was characterized by the extensive use of clay coffins or *larnakes* painted in the style of the period, sometimes in the form of rectangular chests on four short legs with a pitched roof, perhaps reproducing, I suggest, the dowry chest which up to modern times has been one of the most important articles of furniture in a Cretan home.

The burial rite was until a late period almost invariably inhumation. Apart from the Middle Minoan example quoted on the preceding page, the only clear evidence for Minoan cremation seems to be the graves excavated by H. van Effenterre in the cemetery of Olous.[1]

THE MYCENAEAN RELIGION IN CRETE

Ventris's readings of the Linear Script B texts have provided us with a list of Mycenaean deities who were, if we accept his readings, worshipped in Crete in the Late Minoan II period, including Zeus, Hera, Demeter, Athena (with the title *potnia* = lady), Poseidon, and Dionysus. Enyalios appears (not Ares), as indeed one might expect, since scholars have always argued that the worship of the latter was imported from Thrace. It is strange to find Dionysus, who was also supposed to have been a later importation from Thrace, but his absence from Olympus only implies that his cult was not popular in Ionia before 700 B.C., not that it had not reached Crete or the mainland. Apollo appears only under his cult title Paian, I believe (but negative statements on the evidence from these texts are more dangerous even than positive ones!). Ventris also records priestesses of 'The Winds'.[2] We should not be surprised to find the winds as gods when we reflect that the cult of the Kassite god Buriash probably must have been established before 1200 B.C. in Attica, where, as Boreas, he became so acclimatized as to be reported in Athenian folklore as carrying off the maiden Oreithyia,[3] the daughter of Erechtheus and mother of Kalais and Zetes who sailed with Jason on the Argo.

1. *Études crétoises*, 1948, Chap. 2, 'La Nécropole d'Olonte'.
2. M. Ventris and J. Chadwick, *Documents in Mycenaean Greek*, p. 387.
3. The maiden's name has a good Mycenaean ring to it.

CHAPTER 9

The Social and Economic Life, Industries, and Agriculture

'ON the organization of the social group, the remains from pre-historic times leave the field free for the imagination and do not furnish us with any information. It is not impossible, however, to imagine the vague outlines of what might have been the evolution of the Aegean societies.' So said M. Glotz in 1921, and, though we know more than we did then, speculation and imagination still play an uncomfortably large role in any attempt to reconstruct Minoan society.

Already in the Neolithic period, however, we can perceive the development of village communities of peasant farmers, while at Knosos the community must have been several hundred strong at least, almost developing at the end of the Neolithic period into a small market town. We may imagine that the average lowlander tilled the soil, his own or another's, and that the highlanders would be mostly hunters or shepherds driving their flocks from the lowland to the highland pastures and down again according to the season.

It is much less difficult to reconstruct the economic life of the times than the social and political. Was there a king, an oligarchy, or a primitive democracy? Was there a tribal organization? Was the society patriarchal or matriarchal? Was Crete split into small city states or were there larger units?

It has been suggested that the large round tombs of the Mesara, which, according to their excavator Xanthoudides, had contained hundreds of successive burials, were tribal tombs and implied a vigorous tribal life extending from early in the Early Minoan period to the end of Middle Minoan I or II, and that the tendency to abandon these and construct smaller tombs coincided with a political change when the tribal units weakened and were merged in the dynasties of the priest-kings who built the palaces of Knosos, Phaistos, and Mallia.[1]

On the mainland, if we can trust the account given by Homer some centuries later than the events recorded in the *Iliad*, the tribal system was more broken down in Greece at the time of the Trojan war than it was in Scotland in A.D. 1745. The account in the *Iliad* was coloured by the conditions of Homer's own time, but in general his account of the 'Heroic Age' rings true. The late Professor Chadwick was the first to define clearly the social characteristics of an age of migrations and unrest, but the old Greek poet Hesiod had dimly apprehended these peculiarities when he inserted his 'Heroic Age' between his Ages of Bronze and Iron.

Heroic periods parallel to that of Greece had existed, as Chadwick pointed out, in various parts of the world and at various times, but were always marked by certain common features, including the establishment of new dynasties, often claiming descent from a god because the founder was not related to the previous royal family and often, like Sargon of Akkad, with no claim to power save through their own military prowess (though the latter's name actually means 'the true King'). Such heroic ages were those of the Aryan migration into India in the second millennium B.C., the Viking settlement of Iceland in the ninth century A.D., recorded by Ari Frodi, and the Maori settlement of New Zealand.

Race movements of this type are marked not only by epic poetry celebrating the heroes after the nation has settled in its new home, but also by a great break in the traditions of the families that played major parts in the migration. Very often these families, who could not trace their genealogies beyond the great event, claimed to have been descended from gods. Herodotus has recorded with admirable humour how the Egyptian priests in Thebes had shown him round their temples and had told him of a previous visit paid by the historian Hecataeus of Miletus. They told him how Hecataeus had boasted of his family, which 'went back to a god' in the sixteenth generation before, and of how they had shown him the statues of their priests, three hundred and forty-five successive generations of noblemen, the fathers

1. Halbherr estimated 200 burials for the larger *tholos* at Hagia Triada. The social unit served by such a tomb would presumably correspond not to a tribe but to something like a clan (the Greek *génos*).

succeeded by their sons, yet none of them had been gods or even demi-gods, nor had any god ruled in Egypt since Horus, the son of Osiris. And Herodotus states that the priests repeated this story to him 'though I told them no family history of mine'.[1]

Herodotus, of course, was poking fun at the insularity and snob-bishness of Hecataeus, but an important historical conclusion may be drawn from the story. Sixteen generations before Hecataeus there was probably a major crisis in Greek history, a period of upheaval and migration, whereas Egypt had not suffered such a 'Heroic Age' since the days of the Hyksos kings.

Chadwick's principle that breaks in the genealogies, when the family 'went back to a god', as Herodotus says, implied a break in the folk memory and therefore a period of unrest was ingeniously applied by Myres to the traditional pedigrees of the heroic families of Greece. He found three major breaks in folk-tradition when families went back to a divine ancestor, and these were 1400, 1260, and 1100 B.C. The earliest of these, 1400, corresponds with the catastrophe that overwhelmed Minoan Crete, the latest corresponds to the Dorian invasion of the Peloponnese and the final extinction of the Mycenaean power. The 1260 crisis is less obvious at first sight. It was a couple of generations before the Trojan war, but, since dates from gene-alogies must not be taken too literally, it may be a reflection of the Phrygian infiltration of Asia Minor, the consequent collapse of the great Hittite Empire, and the establishment of the dynasty of Pelops in Greece.[2] Myres's 1400 agrees with 1410, the date given for the elder Minos on the Parian Marble Chronicle. Myres's three crises, however, are based on the pedigrees of Greek families and therefore do not help us much for the history of Minoan Crete before 1450, the approximate date of the first Mycenaean settlers in Crete.

The great migration of the Indo-European speaking group of peoples which had such an effect on India, Mesopotamia, Asia Minor, and eastern Europe seems scarcely to have affected Crete at all, which was then about to enjoy its most peaceful and prosperous years.

1. Herodotus, Book II, Chap. 143.
2. The final collapse of the Hittite Empire, of course, did not happen till after 1200 B.C., but Hittite weakness and Phrygian pressure must have begun two or three generations earlier – one Mita caused trouble to Arnuwandas IV.

PATRILINEAR AND MATRILINEAR SUCCESSION

Archaeology can tell us much about the economic conditions of Minoan times and something about the religion, but it is more difficult to imagine the social and political structure. How much of this survived the Achaean and Dorian settlements? What customs are so peculiarly Cretan that we can assume them to have survived in a changed form from Minoan times?

We have already discussed the religious survivals, which are certain and many, but did anything survive of the social and political structure? It is sometimes assumed that Minoan society was, if not matriarchal, at least matrilinear, but the evidence for this is slight and has been overstressed, especially by those scholars who connected Minoan culture with the Carians of Asia Minor, where matrilinear succession persisted into the fourth century B.C.[1]

The neighbouring country of Lycia affords the only certain example in the Aegean of a country where children were regularly named after their mothers, not their fathers. Herodotus regards this as unique though he describes their customs as partly Cretan, partly Carian, so that it is evident that if matrilinear succession ever existed in Crete it had died out before the time of Herodotus.[2]

Matrilinear succession would therefore seem to have been the rule at an early date for certain coastal districts of Asia Minor that received Cretan settlers during the Late Bronze Age, but this does not necessarily prove that such succession was normal in Minoan Crete. It should be noted, however, that by the laws of Gortyn the son of a free mother and a slave father was a free citizen, and Aristotle tells us that the older peoples in Crete continued to obey the laws of Minos.[3] The Achaean heroes of the *Iliad* and the *Odyssey* all traced their descent through their fathers, with the possible exceptions of the two Epeian heroes, Eurytus and Cteatus, who are dubbed 'Moliones' by Nestor after their mother Molione.

Nevertheless even if matrilinear succession had prevailed in Minoan

1. See W. Ridgeway, *The Early Age of Greece*, 1901–31, Vol. II, p. 76.
2. Herodotus VI, Chapter 37.
3. R. E. Willetts, *Aristocratic Society in Ancient Crete*, 1954, p. 34, and Aristotle, *Politics*, 1271 B.

Crete[1] the king must still have exercised great power not only as leader of the armed forces but also as viceroy of the gods, and in particular of the Cretan Zeus from whom he claimed descent, and was thus the chief executive officer in every department of the state, civil, military, and religious. Many centuries after the abolition of kings as civil magistrates or generals in the field, cities such as Athens and Rome continued to appoint kings as priests to perform those rites which only kings could perform, and Professor Thomson[2] has suggested that these would include the regulation of the calendar, and has reminded us that, of the early philosophers, Thales claimed to have been descended from the Theban royal clan of the Kadmeioi, and Herakleitos from Kodros, the last true king of Athens through the royal family of Ephesus.

THE EIGHT-YEAR CYCLE

Weniger has argued that the Olympian calendar was originally based on an eight-year cycle with two periods, as were perhaps also the Delphic festivals termed the Septerium, Herois, and Charita, and perhaps even the Pythian Games with their biennial cycle.[3]

Athenian folklore about Minos introduces the same period of eight years, and although these stories are post-Minoan and the prince they refer to was almost certainly an Achaean prince, yet they were old enough to be familiar to the author of the *Iliad*. According to the orthodox legend as told by Philochorus, the Athenians had to send seven youths and seven maidens as prey for the Minotaur every eight years (or every nine years as the Greeks would say), in payment for the death of Minos's son Androgeos. Every eight years Minos went up into the mountain to converse with his father Zeus (and this tradition was known also to Homer). This custom of Minos has been compared to the practice known in many parts of the world of putting the king to death after he had reigned a certain number of years. There is no clear evidence in Greece of kings being put to death at the

1. A very doubtful assumption.
2. G. Thomson, 'The Greek Calendar', *Journal of Hellenic Studies*, 1943, pp. 52–65.
3. L. Weniger, 'Das Hochfest des Zeus in Olympia', *Klio*, 1912; it should be remembered that the ancient Greeks counted inclusively, and therefore their nine-year cycle is what we should call an eight-year one.

end of a certain period, but there is evidence that their spiritual powers needed in some places to be renewed at the end of eight years by a fresh consecration of communion with the deity. At Sparta every eighth year the Ephors had to watch the sky on a clear moonless night for appropriate signs, and if they saw a meteor they decided that the king had sinned against the gods, and he was forthwith suspended from his duties until he had been reinstated by the oracle at Delphi or by the one at Olympia. This eight-year period represents a correlation of the lunar and solar years, being the shortest period when the longest day of the year can be made to coincide with a full moon.

Solon introduced this cycle to Athens when he intercalated three months to reconcile the current lunar year with the solar one, but the system was much older in Crete, and not long before Solon's reform the Athenians had summoned the Cretan seer Epimenides to purify the city after the murder in 621 of Cylon's conspirators.

VILLAGE ECONOMY

It is easier to reconstruct the life of a village than that of the court. The economy of a Neolithic village in Crete may to some extent be reconstructed from that of some of the poorer villages of today, after making allowances for differences in tools.

Most families would probably have had a piece of land from which they produced a little wheat or barley, some olives, almonds, or grapes perhaps. For vegetables they would probably have gathered what the modern Greek calls 'grasses', but it must be remembered that these included the wild varieties of lettuce, celery, asparagus, and carrots, which all grow wild in Crete and which have pre-Hellenic names, as have also the olive and the vine.

The village industries would include those of the potter, the carpenter, and the mason, though at a pinch most countrymen would have been able to construct a house for themselves. The place of the smith would have been taken by the man who chipped and ground stone tools.

Spinning and weaving, of course, would have been done in the house by the women of the family, a fashion that has not even yet entirely died out. There was no silk or cotton, but there was plenty of wool and probably flax, and the shape of certain clay sarcophagi of late Minoan date, obviously imitating wooden chests, suggest that the maiden of that day (and perhaps the Neolithic maiden also) treasured a family dowry chest in which she had stored the garments laid by for her wedding.

FOOD SUPPLIES

How far can we assert that the average Neolithic Cretan was a farmer, or was still a pastoralist or even a hunter? No direct evidence, I think, has yet been found of the production of grain in Neolithic times in Crete, though from the mainland we have evidence of wheat, barley, and millet being grown in the Neolithic period. It is very probable, however, that the Neolithic Cretans were growing some form of grain, since true millstones have been discovered in Late Neolithic contexts at Miamou in the Mesara and at Magasa in the east (the latter example being an upper millstone fitting into a hollow of the saddle quern below). Of course all prehistoric mills were of the saddle-quern, never of the rotary, type.

It is likely enough, however, that in the Early Neolithic period there may have been more shepherds and hunters than farmers.

Hunting and trapping must have played a larger role than in modern times, but perhaps less than one might expect. There is an odd suggestion that to the Minoan Cretans hunting was a sport rather than a trade. Seal-stones do indeed show men shooting at ibexes, boars, and bears, but the scenes showing men attacking lions, if not purely fictitious, must refer to lions kept specially for royal sports, as they certainly were at a later date in Assyria. Herdsmen and shepherds must have lived a life not very different from those of today, and we must imagine the shepherds driving their sheep up into the little enclosed mountain plains in the summer and down to the lowland pastures near the villages of the foothills in the winter.

A good account of the domestic animals is provided by K. F. Vickery in his excellent monograph *Food in Early Greece*. Even in Neolithic times the Cretan was hunting hares, rabbits, and stags (varieties not stated), as shown by evidence from Late Neolithic deposits at Miamou. Roe deer (? the *Anoglochis cretensis*) is reported from a Late Neolithic level at Phaistos.

From Early Minoan I deposits we hear of domestic sheep, goats, and swine, and for the first time of dogs (variety not stated)[1]; hares (*Lepus cretensis*) and hedgehogs (*Erinaceus nesiotes*) are also reported from this period.

At Tylisos the Middle Minoan levels produced a long-horned ox resembling *Bos primigenius*, *Bos brachyceros*, and a large variant of *Bos domesticus*; agrimi or Cretan ibex (*Capra aegagrus creticus*), domestic goats (*Capra hircus*), wild boars (*Sus scrofa ferus*), and domestic swine (*Sus domesticus indicus*).

Hunting and fishing must have contributed greatly to the family larder, and some of this work was probably carried out by professionals who devoted their whole life to hunting the abundant ibex,[2] wild boar, three kinds of deer, and perhaps wild oxen, as well as shooting the pigeon, partridge, pheasant, quail, and other birds, or trapping the skin animals such as martens, badgers, and wild cats, or fishing the offshore waters of the island; these, in the days before they had been spoiled by dynamiting, must have yielded in much greater supply than today all the modern varieties of fish, including tunny, red or grey mullet, sea bass, sea bream, lobster, braize, crab, sole, mackerel, parrot wrasse, sargue, sea perch, sprats, octopus, and cuttle fish. Of freshwater fish there would not be much except crabs and eels.

Shellfish were also eaten by Neolithic Cretans, and shells of mussels, sea-crab, lobster, limpet, oyster, and whelk were found in Neolithic deposits, as well as *Murex trunculus*, the last presumably exploited not as much as food but for its purple dye; both kinds of murex are indeed edible but *Murex brandaris* is said to be the better food, and I have found shells of both on a Middle Minoan III dump at Knosos.

The Late Minoan I levels at Tylisos added red deer (*Cervus elephas*), Swiss lake-dwelling sheep (*Ovis aries palustris*), horse (*Cavallus*), and the Cretan hunting hound (*Canis creticus*). Late Minoan III strata on the same site produced also remains of a domestic goat (*Capra hircus*) and a domestic ass (*Equus asinus*). Keller recorded thirty-two jaws of sheep or goat from Tylisos and seventeen of domestic swine.

1. But the dog's lower jaw from the Krasi tomb implies an animal of medium size.
2. At Tylisos *agrimi* bones abounded in all the levels.

The last-named were relatively more numerous, but cattle less numerous, than at the present day.[1]

The domestic fowl was not introduced into Crete in the Bronze Age, despite Glotz's suggestion to the contrary, but the Bronze Age Cretans may have possessed the *Chenalopex*, the small domestic goose of Egypt illustrated occasionally on Minoan seals.

We have evidence from Neolithic deposits of the existence at Knosos of short-horned cattle, swine, and goats, at Phaistos of short-horned cattle and of horned sheep of the Cypriote type, at Miamou of cattle, sheep, goats, hares, and rabbits, and at Magasa of sheep or goats.

A dog's head in pottery of Neolithic date at Knosos resembled that of a Saluki hound (like the dog buried about 3000 B.C. at Sakkara in the tomb of Queen Her-neit, and the dogs depicted on the Mycenaean fresco of a boar hunt at Tiryns in the Peloponnese).

Domestic animals were reared by Cretan farmers in the Neolithic period. Sheep and domestic goats are recorded from Late Neolithic sites, from Knosos and its harbour town, from Phaistos and Miamou in the Mesara, and from Magasa.

The sheep include not only *Ovis palustris* (the Swiss lake-dwelling variety) but also *Ovis orientalis* (the horned type still found in Cyprus). Pigs, apparently *Sus indicus*, are recorded from Phaistos, and from Knosos and its harbour town, and so are cattle, both the Cretan short-horns (*Bos creticus*) and a long-horned variety which is more of a puzzle. Cretan art of the Middle and Late Bronze Age is addicted to portraying toreador sports with a long-horned bull resembling the *Bos primigenius* of central and northern Europe. Hazzidakis found horns of bulls of this type both in Middle and in Late Minoan deposits at Tylisos; in some instances the horns had been cut, obviously to render them less dangerous (probably for the ring).

Keller considered that the short-horns might well have been introduced by sea, but that the great *Bos primigenius* would have been too difficult to transport in the relatively small ships available. Feige on the other hand considered that the Cretan long-horns were a local domestic breed (perhaps akin to the *Bos primigenius*).

No fishing tackle seems to have survived from Neolithic times,

1. J. Hazzidakis, *Tylissos à l'époque minoenne*, 1921, p. 76.

but we possess a two-pointed fishing spear of Early Minoan date from Hagios Onouphrios, and a lead sinker with a notch at each end, part of a large barbed fish-hook, and three complete barbed fish-hooks of bronze, measuring 9·5, 7·2, and 2·6 cm. in length respectively, from the Late Minoan 1 village of Gournia (Fig. 46, 1, 2, and 5). Fish-traps were also employed.[1]

AGRICULTURE

The basic tools for agriculture in the Near East are the pick, the mattock, and the zimbeli or two-handled basket, with the addition of the plough for grain crops. The spade is not a Levantine tool even today; it exists as an exotic foreigner used for special purposes, but the man who goes to plant vines or olives or vegetables will only use a pick to loosen the soil, and a mattock to scrape it into the basket with which he dumps it where required.

The plough, as illustrated by sign 27 of the Minoan Hieroglyphic Script, was probably entirely of wood, since no metal fittings seem yet to have been identified on Minoan sites (Fig. 44). Probably it was of the *autógyes* (all-in-one-piece) form recommended by Hesiod with beam and share made from one block, but with the stilt added separately. That the form shown in the Hieroglyphic Script is a fair representation of the Minoan form is indicated by the fact that a similar plough was used in Crete in Roman times and persists even today. Hesiod recommended that the

Fig. 44.
Minoan plough

share of a plough (if not *autógyes*) should be made of oak, the beam of holm oak, and the stilt of laurel or poplar (*Works and Days*, v, 435–6).

In the Neolithic period grain was probably cut by a wooden sickle with obsidian teeth, but in Late Minoan times a bronze sickle was used of the type described by Professor Childe as 'tangential' since the line of the handle forms a tangent to the curve of the blade.

---

1. An interesting example of uncertain date but possibly Early Minoan was found near the modern village of Mochlos in 1955 by the British School expedition conducted by Mr John Leatham; probably a number of the methods described in Oppian's *Halieutica* were also employed (*Halieutica*, III, pp. 72–91). Mr Sinclair Hood, however, regards these as Roman fish tanks.

It was usually hafted by a tang fastened with one or two rivets, though miniature examples of Mycenaean date from a tomb at Enkomi in Cyprus had a socket for the handle. Such Minoan sickles were thus distinguished from the Egyptian ones where the blade was either bent forward towards the handle to form an angled sickle, or bent back to form a balanced sickle. Three of the Gournia sickles, however, belonged to Childe's 'looped' variety and must therefore have been either angled or balanced sickles.[1]

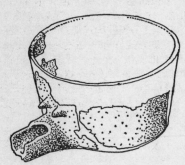

Fig. 45. Olive-oil separator

The cultivation of the olive was attributed by Greek tradition to the goddess Athena, and though Athenian patriotism might claim that this implied the olive was first cultivated in Attica, Cretans would certainly have claimed that this proved the olive was first cultivated in their island[2] and could appeal to the Peloponnesian legend which stated that the cultivation of that fruit had been introduced to Olympia by the Cretan Herakles.[3]

Middle Minoan deposits have yielded olive presses and olive separators. The oil was doubtless prepared in a manner still employed in the island. The fruit was first beaten off the tree with sticks and then winnowed from the leaves with a winnowing fork. The fruit was then drenched in hot water, crushed in a simple press, and placed in settling vats. When the oil had risen to the surface, the water was drawn off through a plugged spout at the bottom of the vat. Settling vats of this kind have been found at Mallia (from the Middle Minoan III period), and at Gournia and Vathypetro near Arkhanais (both of the Late Minoan I period).

1. V. G. Childe, 'The Balanced Sickle', *Aspects of Archaeology in Britain and Beyond*, 1951, p. 39 f.

2. For the tradition that Athena was born in Crete see p. 209.

3. The Idaean Dactyl of that name, not to be confused with his more famous namesake.

It seems not improbable that the drenching of the olives was carried out in great bronze cauldrons like the ones found at Tylisos (still notable for its fine olive orchards) unless indeed these were used for boiling the must, a normal process in the preparation of wine after the treading of the grapes.

Bees would certainly have been kept for honey. Sign 86 of the Hieroglyphic Script B is a bee, and perhaps a still better representation is the splendid gold pendant of Middle Minoan I date from the Chrysolakkos cemetery at Mallia (Fig. 37).[1] Perhaps the Minoan Cretans also made *petmez* out of their grapes. Whether they supplemented honey by planting carob bean trees is more uncertain. Sign 96 of the Hieroglyphic Script looks like a carob bean pod, but may simply be a copy of the corresponding Egyptian sign. The carob tree is native to the Mediterranean, but seems to be mainly associated with the southern shores of that sea. There are plenty of carob trees in Crete today in the parts from Mallia eastwards, which suggests that they have been introduced from Syria or Palestine,[2] and the European variants of the name from Spain to Greece are but thinly disguised varieties of the Semitic name.

Almond seeds have been found in Neolithic levels at Knosos, and in a Late Minoan I deposit at Hagia Triada, but there is no evidence to show whether the Cretans ever crushed them for oil; the wild almond trees are not uncommon in the neighbourhood of Knosos.

Date palms were not native to Crete, but they are represented in Middle Minoan art, and I have seen impressions of their leaves in the volcanic dust on Thera at a level which appeared to belong to the Early Bronze Age and was at least anterior to 1500 B.C.

Remains of figs have been found in a Late Minoan I deposit at Hagia Triada, and the so-called wild fig tree is not only common on the island but has a pre-Hellenic name. The quince (the Kydonian fruit) was supposed to be indigenous in the island. Pears, grapes, and olives, if not actually indigenous, must at least have been introduced at an early date and all occur in a wild form. Apples, too, were intro-

---

1. Unless these insects are wasps as suggested by one scholar. One of the Knosian tablets as translated by Ventris records a dedication of honey to the goddess Eileithyia.

2. But there are also large plantations of carob trees in the Rethymnon district.

duced, probably before the end of the Bronze Age, but I have never seen a crab-apple tree on the island. Other fruits such as cherries and plums had probably not yet been introduced to the island from Persia.

Wheat, lentils, and oil occur in Middle Minoan I deposits at Mallia, and their absence or scarcity from earlier deposits is probably accidental, since wheat is attested in Neolithic deposits at Olynthos in Macedonia.

Wine was certainly made from grapes from the Late Minoan I period onwards and perhaps much earlier.[1] Evans suggested that beer may have been made from Early Minoan times onwards, but Vickery has remarked that the 'tea-pot' vases of that period are rather small for beer. They would have been quite suitable, however, for *phaskó-milo* or other herbal teas of that kind.

In Egypt at least we know that wine was made from grapes in Early Dynastic times, and on the mainland of Greece the Middle Helladic people, who are not likely to have learned their wine-making from the north, also drank wine, so that we may assume that Cretans were making wine early in the Middle Minoan period and probably before that time.

The words for wine in Greek, Latin, and in the west Semitic dialects all seem to have been borrowed independently from a common source, probably some language current in the Mediterranean in prehistoric times and not improbably a language spoken in Minoan Crete. When we reach the Middle Minoan III period, evidence for garden vegetables becomes more abundant and from Knosos we have evidence of broad beans, 'Egyptian beans',[2] garden peas, lentils, as well as wheat and barley.

Crete abounds in edible herbs, and the pre-Hellenic names of mint, calamint, sesame, silphium, and wormwood suggest that these were all known to and used by the Minoan Cretans. Sesame alone bears an Akkadian name borrowed from Mesopotamia.

Kitchens seem not to have been very elaborate, and fixed hearths

1. The recent find of grape-seeds in a stone jar of the earliest period of the palace at Phaistos probably implies that grapes were dried as raisins then. D. Levi, *Illustrated London News*, 29 September 1956.

2. Evans does not state the name of the carbonized beans which his workmen recognized as a variety still imported from Egypt.

which were normal in Cretan Neolithic houses fade out in the Middle Minoan I period, from which we can quote only two examples at Mallia and none at all at Knosos.

There are no bread ovens like those of Troy and Thermi, though the Cretans may possibly have baked unleavened bread of the Arab type in the embers, and a strange clay oven found at Mallia in a house of the Late Minoan I period evidently represents an attempt to brighten the home life by some more exotic method of baking the food.

Most of the cooking, however, was carried out on portable braziers, which were common enough in Minoan houses and palaces.

EXPORTS AND TRADE

The large numbers of oil jars in the palaces of Knosos, Mallia, and Phaistos emphasize the interest taken by the royal princes in the olive trade. It is unlikely, I think, that the pressing of olives was a government monopoly, though it is possible that the export of oil and olives may have been mainly in royal hands, and it is extremely probable that a tithe or some similar agricultural tax was paid in olives and exported to Egypt either salted or in the form of oil.

Grain may also have been accepted as taxes, but there would have been no real surplus of this except the local surplus in the Mesara, and this would doubtless have been distributed to less fortunate parts of the island.

INDUSTRIES

The industrial life of Crete has changed far more than the agricultural, and this is not merely due to the mechanization of modern times. It is true that the island now can profit from all manner of industrial tools and methods unknown to ancient Crete, but most of such products are imported and the island is no longer the industrial centre it used to be in Minoan or even in Neolithic times.

The development of large cities such as Knosos, Phaistos, and Mallia created a demand for luxury industries which no longer exists in modern Crete and scarcely existed there during the classical period. Besides the ordinary craftsmen, such as the coppersmiths, masons, carpenters, potters, and the unskilled labour employed by them, and the food producers, such as the farmers, herdsmen, shepherds, hunters, and fishermen, or distributing agents, such as the merchants, boatmen, carters, and muleteers, we also find a number of purely luxury craftsmen, such as the gem cutter, the fresco painter, the ivory carver, the goldsmith and silversmith, the faience manufacturer, and the maker of stone vases, who handled not only soft stones but also much harder materials such as crystal and basalt. The close association of these luxury trades with the palaces of the kings and nobles is reflected in the stories of Daedalus and Minos, and is exemplified by the lapidary's workshop in the Royal domestic quarter of the Palace of Minos, by a workshop for casting bronze tools and implements and a supplementary one for making the stone moulds in the Mallia Palace, and by the great bronze founder's oven at Phaistos situated only a few yards from the central court of the palace.

A theocratic state, such as the Kingdom of Minos appears to have been, must have employed a large number of men and women as priests and priestesses, scribes, and acolytes or attendants of some sort or another in the service of the state cults of the Earth Mother, the Cretan Zeus, and other deities. It is impossible even to guess at the number, but the proportion of religious to secular officials must have been analogous to that in Egypt, and their power and influence no less than those of the Egyptian priests.

It is also difficult to assess how far the princely villas round the Palace of Minos were the residences of royal princes, hereditary nobles, high secular officials, priests, or a combination of any of these.

For a picture of an industrial centre occupied with the necessities rather than with the luxuries of life we must turn to Gournia, that pleasant little seaside town on the Gulf of Mirabello.

In the Middle Minoan III period there had been, indeed, a small palace or large villa on the crown of the hill, but by the Late Minoan I A period this had fallen into disrepair and been cut up into small tenements. From 1550 to 1450 or perhaps 1400 B.C. Gournia may be regarded as the Minoan equivalent of a small town in the potteries district of Staffordshire. No less than five of our scanty supply of Minoan potters' wheels were found in this little settlement.

One building had evidently belonged to a carpenter and produced a splendid saw, various chisels, an awl, a drill, and some other tools, while another had been a bronze foundry and contained moulds for casting double axes, chisels, etc.

METALLURGY

One of the more intriguing problems of Minoan industry is the sources from which the island derived its metals, since the native supplies were not rich. The scanty silver they possessed may have come from the Cyclades and the tin from Crisa (which would explain the early Cretan connexions with the Delphi district).[1] The Minoan upper classes seem to have possessed a fair quantity of gold, but they had no good local supply and must, I think, have imported Nubian gold through their trade with Egypt.[2] It has often been suggested that the copper ores of Crete were worked in Minoan times but the positive evidence for such working is slight.

At Sklavopoula on the west coast two small outcrops of malachite were tested in classical times possibly as early as the fifth century B.C. The quartz veins north and east of Kandanos have been worked more extensively, but apparently not before the time of the Roman occupation of the period, and other quartz veins were worked at Kambanou at a later date. The earliest mention of a Cretan goldmine is by Idrisi, the Arab writer of the twelfth century A.D., who refers to the existence of a goldmine at Rabdh el Djohn (the Arabic name for the Khania district).

The only copper ore deposits that we can confidently assert to have been exploited by Minoan miners are those of Chrysokamino.[3]

A copper axe was found in one of the Late Neolithic houses at Knosos but this was probably imported. Copper objects are still very

1. A. Lucas ('Silver in Ancient Times', *Journal of Egyptian Archaeology*, 1928, p. 319) notes that we have no evidence of silver being produced in Greece before the seventeenth century, but the relatively large proportion of silver objects in the early Cyclades graves suggests that the Siphnian mines may have been tapped before 2000 B.C. See O. Davies, *Journal of Hellenic Studies*, 1924, p. 89; C. F. C. Hawkes, *The Prehistoric Foundations*, 1940, p. 291.

2. The very name Nubia means El Dorado, the Land of Gold.

3. A. Mosso, *The Origins of Mediterranean Civilization*, p. 219; compare also the analyses quoted by T. Burton Brown in *Excavations in Azerbaijan*, 1948, pp. 192-7.

uncommon in the Early Minoan I period but quite common in the following period.

Minoan Weapons before 1700 B.C.

The earliest form of copper dagger from the round tombs of the Mesara is often miscalled triangular, but actually has a blade like a laurel leaf cut so that the top has a concave or more rarely two concave curves. Two rivet holes show how each blade was attached to its handle. The Early Minoan III deposits of the Mesara tombs contained more daggers of this type but associated with other blades that really do deserve to be called triangular, having a strongly marked midrib and a tang with one or two rivet holes for hafting, a form with

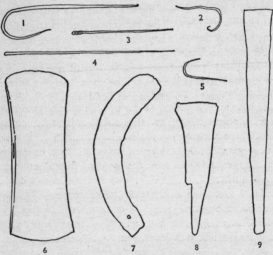

Fig. 46. Minoan bronzes, Palaikastro
(1, 2, and 5 fish-hooks, 3 and 4 needles, 6 double axe, 7 sickle,
8 axe-adze, 9 chisel)

widespread connexions, since examples of it occur in Copper Age contexts in Sardinia, in Sicily, and in Italy; three daggers of this form in silver were found in Tholos B at Koumasa.

The strange double-pointed blade from Hagios Onouphrios may probably be regarded not as a dagger but as a fish harpoon. The independence of the Cretan armourer at this period is emphasized by the absence of Early Minoan II shapes in Mrs Maxwell-Hyslop's typology for western Asia.[1] The third Early Minoan period was marked by improvements in the copper dagger, but there is still no evidence of actual bronze, doubtless because the Cretans at that time had no easy access to tin, which was then still scarce enough to be reckoned as a precious metal, as is shown by the torque of that material found in an Early Bronze Age deposit at Thermi on the island of Lesbos. The ordinary daggers resemble Mrs Maxwell-Hyslop's Type 16 and have a rounded base with three rivet holes. Some slim daggers with strong midrib and rounded base from the Mesara already foreshadow the rapiers of the Middle Minoan III–Late Minoan I period, though they themselves cannot be later than the Middle Minoan I period and may well begin in Early Minoan III times. These daggers are of bronze and terminate in a small tang for attachment to the handle, though Palaikastro has only the old tangless variety at this period and Mochlos only one dagger of the new type.

The Cretans had also evolved a long sword at least before the end of the Middle Minoan II period, though it was perhaps still rather a rarity since our only surviving example is the splendid ceremonial sword with its crystal pommel found in an intermediate deposit in the Palace at Mallia, and that would not have been a very suitable weapon for actual warfare. Possibly, however, we may assume the existence of work-a-day cut-and-thrust swords also. The stratification suggests that this sword is earlier than Middle Minoan III, and so does the absence of a tang, but a date after 1800 is not impossible.

Another rather broad dagger form with no marked midrib, but relying for strength on its thick blade, and with three rivet holes in its slightly curved base is usually dated Middle Minoan I–III. The best-known example is the one from Lasithi, incised with a design showing a man with a hunting spear awaiting the charge of a wild boar. This particular dagger probably dates from Middle Minoan III, and I doubt if any dagger of this form is earlier than Middle Minoan II because the shape does not occur among the daggers from the Mesara round tombs which are rich in daggers. This would imply that the depot of bronze implements from the oval house at Chamaizi was still occupied in the Middle Minoan II period; indeed this shape

1. *Iraq*, 1946, pp. 18, 19.

lasts from Middle Minoan II to the Late Minoan I period. This type of dagger does not occur in Mrs Maxwell-Hyslop's West Asiatic series but was imitated in Celtic circles as far west as Britain, where similar forms occur in the Early Bronze Age (?1800–1300 B.C.) associated with double axes in stone. The Lasithi dagger is asymmetrical and might even be interpreted as a halberd. Associated with daggers of this type in Middle Minoan III hoards we find work-a-day double axes, double adzes, axe-adzes, single shaft-hole axes, and fine-toothed saws, including one magnificent example over 1·6 m. long.

The bronze figurines of the Middle Minoan period may more properly be considered under the heading of fine arts rather than industry, and depended more on the skill of the modeller than of the bronze caster. The industrial art of the coppersmith is better displayed in the manufacture of bronze vases and cauldrons.

Minoan Weapons after 1700 B.C.

The defence of the island in Middle Minoan times was probably entrusted to the fleet, since not only do the cities and villages lack defensive walls but the tombs usually contain no weapons save girdle daggers, the side-arms that were part of every Minoan gentleman's normal attire. With the Middle Minoan III period, however, we find that long rapiers with pronounced midribs, rounded shoulders, and a short tang for insertion into the hilt became comparatively common, and a splendid series of those of Late Minoan I date were found by Hazzidakis in the cave at Arkalochori, a sanctuary doubtless sacred to some warlike deity, possibly the goddess who is seen striding along brandishing a long sword on a flat-cylinder of Late Minoan I A date from Knosos.

Another fine sword of this type was found in the Middle Minoan III burial in Tomb 2 and a shorter example in Tomb 20 at Mochlos. The latter tomb also contained three spearheads with split sockets formed by folding a flat plate round the shaft, and binding it with a cast ring at the lower end.

The double axes from Arkalochori, including miniature examples in gold and silver, were mostly of a kind that would be useless in warfare, and confirm Dr Marija Gimbutas's theory either that the double axe was a sacred emblem of the goddess, as suggested by Evans and as it obviously very often was, or that when it was cast in a practical form it was not intended as a weapon, but was a tool of a wood-man or a carpenter or even a butcher. It may have been also used to kill the sacred bull, but I suspect it was primarily a woodman's axe (Fig. 46, 6).[1]

The Arkalochori types of rapier and spear were quickly adopted on the mainland by the princes of the Shaft Grave dynasty at Mycenae.

Two splendid rapiers of this type with gold-plated hilts from the later palace at Mallia must be dated not later than Middle Minoan III A, but the same type of sword persisted both on Crete and on the mainland into the fourteenth century B.C.[2]

This style of rapier was improved by some swordsmiths in Knosos or Mycenae by converting the short handle tang (its great weakness) into a flat plate long enough to hold three or more rivet holes and flanged at the sides to grip the inlaid handle of wood or ivory. Further, the hand was protected by a horned guard over which the handle flanges were extended.

Swords of this type persisted into the fourteenth century both in Crete and on the mainland, and recently a representation of such a weapon has been identified incised on one of the stones of Stonehenge.[3]

Cut-and-thrust swords, except the great sword from Mallia, are not proved to have been used in Crete before the twelfth century B.C.[4]

BOWS AND SLINGS

Crete was renowned for its bowmen and slingers even in classical times and presumably they would have been still more prominent in prehistoric times before the development of body armour. No metal slingstones, like the leaden examples of classical times, have been discovered in purely Minoan strata, and we must assume that the Cretan slingers of the Bronze Age, like David, simply selected

1. 'Battle Axe or Cult Axe', *Man*, April 1953; I had suggested this view three years previously in my 'Battle-axes in the Aegean' (*Proceedings of the Prehistoric Society*, 1950, p. 58).

2. F. Chapouthier, 'Deux Épées d'apparat', *Études crétoises*, 1946; and for the date, H. G. de Santerre, *Kretika Chronika*, 1949, p. 377.

3. Compare R. J. C. Atkinson, *Proceedings of the Prehistoric Society*, 1952, p. 65, Plate 21, and O. G. S. Crawford, *Antiquity*, 1954, p. 25, Plate 1.

4. H. W. Catling, 'Bronze Cut-and-Thrust Swords in the Eastern Mediterranean', *Proceedings of the Prehistoric Society*, 1956, p. 102.

suitable pebbles from the beaches and river beds. Seager, indeed, at Pseira found three small rooms filled with beach pebbles which his workmen identified as slingstones. This 'primitive arsenal' perhaps belonged to the Middle Minoan period, since it was overlaid by a house of the Late Minoan I period. Clay sling bullets like those of Hassuna do not seem yet to have been identified.[1]

Archery was practised early in the Bronze Age, and from Early Minoan II to Middle Minoan I times the Cretans seem to have used a simple bow of Libyan type with chisel-pointed arrowheads, not of flint presumably, as in Egypt and Mesopotamia, but of obsidian.[2] (Evans, *Huxley Memorial Lecture*, 1925, p. 22.)

Pointed bronze arrowheads with a tang for hafting in a reed shaft appear before the end of the Middle Minoan period.

The 'composite' bow strengthened with keratin from *agrimi* horns appears to have been introduced into the island from the east not later than the Late Minoan I period but never superseded the simple bow which remained common in Crete.

In the Late Minoan II armoury deposit at Knosos Evans found two boxloads of bronze arrowheads associated with tablets in Linear Script B, some with the sign of an arrow, and others with that of an *agrimi* horn, an indispensable material for the manufacture of composite bows.[3] Since this deposit, however, dates from the period when we have inferred the existence of an Achaean dynasty at Knosos it might only be evidence of the employment of composite bows by the Mycenaean Greeks.

In general the composite bow seems to have been a northern weapon. The classical Greeks associated it with the Scythians and it persisted till modern times among the Turks, but the earliest example

1. V. G. Childe, 'The Significance of the Sling, etc.', *Studies Presented to D. M. Robinson*, I.

2. The seal illustrated by Evans may not be genuine, but the Mallia hieroglyphs also illustrate a bow and an arrow with chisel point, possibly however copied from an Egyptian hieroglyphic, Mallia sign 14 (Chapouthier, 'Écritures minoennes', *Études crétoises*, 1943, p. 65 and Fig. 25); but the chisel point is far more obvious on the Cretan hieroglyph than on the Egyptian, so that the evidence on the whole supports the existence in Crete of such arrowheads.

3. Compare H. L. Lorimer, *Homer and the Monuments*, 1950, p. 289, Fig. 37. The essential characteristic of the 'composite' (as distinct from the compound bow) is that it is bound with sinews on the outside of the curve and with keratin or true horn on the inside to increase its strength and flexibility.

of its use is by the Mesolithic inhabitants of Denmark. The Cretan and Mycenaean Greeks may have learned the use of this weapon from the Anatolian states of Hatti or Mitanni. Homer describes such a bow, but rather as if it was an exotic novelty, and the self-bow or the compound bow (of two pieces of wood) continued to be the normal form in Crete well into the classical period.

The flat bronze arrowheads of Mycenae, and the Cretan ones resembling them, are no improvement on arrowheads manufactured over a thousand years earlier in Persia. In the Late Minoan III period hollow-based arrowheads of Mycenaean type do appear in graves of Zapher Papoura and at Phaistos, while the Hunter's Grave in the former cemetery has some barbed arrowheads with a hollow-based tang that look like a compromise between the Minoan and Mycenaean forms.[1]

DEFENSIVE ARMOUR

The defensive armour of the Late Minoan period included a full length body shield with a figure-of-eight outline, probably implying a wooden frame covered with leather several folds deep. A semi-cylindrical shield with a curved top reminding us of Homer's description of the shield of Telamonian Ajax as 'like a tower' was fashionable on the Greek mainland but seems only to appear in Crete in the Late Minoan III period, presumably introduced by Mycenaean Greeks.

The small round parrying shield does not appear in the warfare of the Near East much before 1400 B.C. (though a different kind of parrying shield was known and used in Egypt at a much earlier date). By 1350 B.C. however, Ugarit smiths were making the slashing swords which this later type of shield was intended to parry, and the Hittites were using round shields of this form against the Egyptians at the battle of Kadesh in 1280 B.C.

There is no evidence that Minoan Cretans ever wore armoured corselets or greaves, except a large piece of bronze plating from a Phaistos tomb identified as part of a *mitra* or body-belt and fragments that might have belonged to another.[2] From Mycenaean graves we can only quote one solitary instance of a metal greave from a tomb at Enkomi in Cyprus (despite the numerous references by Homer in

1. Evans, 'Prehistoric Tombs of Knossos', *Archaeologia*, 1905, Fig. 28.
2. But the Achaeans did; compare the bronze corselet and illustrations on Linear B tablets; note also bronze greaves from Patras.

the *Iliad* to 'the well-greaved Achaeans', which may refer to leather leggings like those shown on the warrior vase from Mycenae).[1]

The Cretans, however, had several forms of helmet during the Bronze Age. The simplest form seems to have consisted of a cap made from a single sheet of metal and is illustrated by a Middle Minoan III sealing from Zakros depicting a conical helmet with earguards, a long, narrow appendage presumably representing a chinstrap, and a short upright spike on the peak, probably for the attachment of a plume.

A second type of helmet is the built-up type best illustrated by a representation of it on a polychrome vase from the Tomb of the Double Axes at Isopata, showing a close-fitting cap consisting of horizontal bands (presumably of leather) with a knob on top, earguards, and an extension at the back to protect the neck. The best known variety of the built-up helmet, however, has the horizontal bands strengthened with horizontal rows of split tusks of the wild boar, arranged so that the curves of each row face in the opposite direction to those of the rows immediately above and below it. On the whole boars-tusk helmets seem more characteristic of the Greek mainland than of Minoan Crete. Plates for such helmets have been found on six grave sites in the Peloponnese, on three in Attica, and on one in Boeotia. At Menidhi and in one tomb at Mycenae sufficient were found to allow of the restoration of such a helmet. Representations of boars-tusk helmets appear on ivories from Sparta and Menidhi, on fragments of a faience vase from the third Shaft Grave, on the silver rhyton from the fourth Shaft Grave at Mycenae, and on a gem from the Vapheio tomb, showing a helmet adorned with two *agrimi* horns (or metal imitations of them). Against this series Crete can only set a few boars-tusk plates from a Late Minoan III tomb at Knosos, the design of a boars-tusk helmet on an ivory fragment from Knosos, and the representations of four helmets with *agrimi* horns on a Late Minoan I sealing from Hagia Triada, on a polychrome vase from Tomb 5 at Isopata, on a bronze double axe in the Giamalakis collection, and on a vase from Katsaba.[2] Repre-

1. Diodorus makes it plain that 'greaves' were not necessarily of metal, since Celtiberian greaves were made of hair (*The Library of History*, Book V, Chap. 33).

2. See A. Xenaki-Sakellariou, *Bulletin de Correspondance Héllenique*, 1953, pp. 46–58 and S. Alexiou, 'The Boars Tusk Helmet', *Antiquity*, 1954, p. 211.

sentations in fresco also occur at Mycenae (one of them on a tripod hearth) and perhaps at Tiryns. The bronze helmet with cheekpieces made from one piece of metal found by Persson at Dendra is without parallel on the mainland, and is compared by Miss Lorimer to some on the Boxer Rhyton from Hagia Triada, but it would be rash to claim this helmet as Minoan without further evidence. Fortunately one Minoan helmet in bronze has recently been found in the Warrior Graves at Knosos by Hood and de Jong. It is a conical helmet of thin bronze plate with cast knob for plume and cheekpieces (or earguards) riveted on (Fig. 47). It is the more important, not merely because it is our only surviving Minoan helmet, but also because this form of helmet seems to be the prototype of the group of so-called 'bell helmets' scattered across Hungary up into north Germany, and sometimes called the 'Beitsch' type from the site where an example (now in the British Museum) was found in a bog, associated with a dagger (or halberd) and a couple of ingot 'torcs' dated to about 1400 B.C.[1]

Fig. 47. Late Minoan II helmet, Ayios Ioannis

From Middle Minoan III times onwards Minoan warriors also carried spearheads with split sockets bound at the ends by rings of the same metal. The socket was cast flat and then hammered round the shaft and fastened by a ring, a much simpler though less elegant and durable method than casting the whole spearhead, socket and all, in a bivalve mould.

In the Late Minoan II period, the type of weapons current at Knosos is well illustrated by three found in the Warrior Graves by Hood and de Jong at Ayios Ioannis. The swords were rapiers with horned or cruciform guards and flanged tangs to hold the inlaid handle of bone, wood, or other material, which was attached by rivets. Three of these spearheads still have split sockets fastened with a ring, but now completely cast in a mould except the ring which was

1. Compare H. Hencken, 'Beitsch and Knosos', *Proceedings of the Prehistorical Society*, 1952, p. 36.

added later (Fig. 48). One spearhead is a heavy type with a leaf-shaped blade and a tang, a type well known and distributed over the Aegean in the Middle Bronze Age, but in the Late Bronze Age rare, perhaps completely confined to Crete. Hood compares it to medieval boar spears. A second, a beautiful weapon with a long ogival blade, is also a rare type probably confined to Crete (where there is one example from Gournia and another in the Giamalakis collection). The two small spearheads with leaf-shaped blades probably belonged

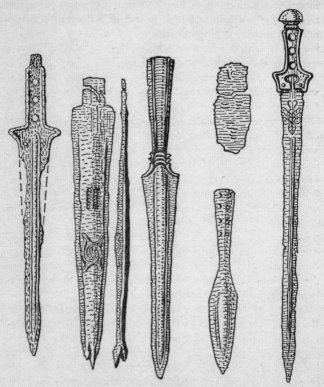

Fig. 48. Late Minoan II swords and spears, Ayios Ioannis and the Hospital site

to javelins or throwing spears. The normal equipment of the warriors buried seems to have been a short sword with cruciform hilt, or alternatively a tangless dagger and a spear.

THE SOCIAL STRUCTURE

The architecture of the Minoan cities reveals something of the social structure. The Palace of Minos is surrounded by a number of minor palaces aping the amenities of the great one. Thus the Little Palace, the Royal Villa, the South House, and the South-East House all have lustral areas, the Royal Villa has a special throne room, and the South-East House a domestic shrine. Most of these houses were appendages of the Palace of Minos, and were presumably occupied by important officials, whether priestly or secular, some perhaps members of the royal family.

The Little Palace and the Unexplored Mansion to the west of it stand apart both literally and figuratively, and must surely have been the residences of persons important in their own right, such as the Crown Prince or the Queen Mother.

The palaces at Phaistos and Mallia had apparently no such minor palaces in their vicinity, and this fact might be used to argue that Knosos controlled the central part of the island, at least during the Middle Minoan III and Late Minoan I periods.

There are no visible traces in Crete of that primitive democracy which Jacobsen claims to have perceived among the city states of southern Mesopotamia at an early date,[1] but on the other hand there is no suggestion of a ghetto system or of rigid distinctions, and the little houses of the poor nestle up against the walls of the palaces and rich villas. We cannot even guess at the political rights of the various elements of the population (whether male or female), but there seems to have been much greater social freedom between the sexes than in most ancient societies. Women went unveiled in *décolleté* dresses and mixed freely with the men at the public festivals. They danced in public before the men and even took part in the dangerous toreador sport, dressing in the male costume for the purpose.

Minoan Crete would appear, therefore, to have been governed by

1. H. Frankfort, Mrs H. Frankfort, J. A. Wilson, and T. Jacobsen, *Before Philosophy* (Penguin Books, 1949), p. 141.

a paternal theocracy, not unlike that of Egypt, and to have consisted of states where the proletariat probably had few or no political rights and was heavily taxed, but otherwise not unduly oppressed, where there was probably a rather top-heavy upper class of princes, nobles, and priests, and a very small middle class, but no very rigid caste system. There must also, I think, have been a fair number of slaves, but not, surely, a majority of the population, since we have no examples of the large workmen's suburbs that we find in Egypt, nor of the *latifundia* of Imperial Rome, those large plantations founded on huge gangs of slave labour.

In the Late Minoan II period we are conscious of the difference between Knosos and its immediate surroundings including Tylisos and Amnisos, which appear to be Mycenaeanized and were very probably ruled by a Greek prince, and the other parts, which may have still had Minoan princes perhaps paying tribute to Knosos.

MYCENAEAN SOCIETY IN CRETE

Ventris's decipherment of the Linear Script B texts has offered to those who accept his transliterations the possibility of reconstructing the outlines of the social structure in Mycenaean Greece and in such parts of Crete as had Mycenaean settlers at a date some five hundred years before the poems of Homer were in all probability written. Professor L. R. Palmer has accepted this challenge and has defined the chief members of the Mycenaean society in the following terms:

(1) The *anax* or 'overlord' elected from a single royal family

(2) The *lawagetás* or war leader chosen for a war or campaign

(3) The *teléstai* or feudal barons who gave war service in return for land[1]

(4) The *hieréwes* or priests

(5) The *damiówergoi* or workers including both free peasants and artisans

(6) The *doúloi* or slaves

Palmer is able to quote parallels from other early societies speaking Indo-European languages, such as the Hittites, the Indo-Iranians, and the Germans; but the bards who are so prominent in Homeric and

1. Paralleled at Olympia in the Peloponnese in the sixth century B.C. (though presumably in a different sense) in the meeting between Elis and Heraea.

in early Celtic society are lacking, unless they are included among the priestly class.

Let us, however, compare his analysis with the picture of the archaic Dorian society in Crete as drawn in a recent book by R. F. Willetts,[1] who bases his conclusions mainly on a study of the laws of Gortyn as they existed between 700 and 400 B.C. The laws in question were drawn up in a Dorian city several hundred years after the close of the Bronze Age, but many features, such as the tribal organization depicted, must have survived from prehistoric times, and have not been exclusively Dorian. At Gortyn (and in most other Cretan cities of that period so far as we know) there was the *startagetás* in place of the army leader of the *lawagetás* type,[2] but no kings or barons. The city was governed by magistrates called *kósmoi*, assisted by others termed *títai*, by a council, and by an assembly. These discrepancies do not matter much and could be explained as a normal development from a Homeric kingdom to a city oligarchy. But these Dorian cities also had a tribal system consisting of *phýlai* (tribes), *phratríai* (septs), and *géne* (clans), which had existed in non-Dorian Athens before Solon reorganized his constitution and which must have been common in Mycenaean times (I omit features which seem to be exclusively Dorian). I shall not, therefore, feel quite happy about Professor Palmer's reconstruction of Mycenaean society until he finds some reference to this tribal system, which should have been far more active and obvious in the thirteenth century B.C. than it was in the days of Homer.

The differences between the art of Knosos and the rest of Crete between 1450 and 1400 B.C. may be assessed fairly, but the differences in the social and economic life are much harder to gauge, especially as the Mycenaean people of the Late Minoan I period had absorbed so much of Minoan culture and religion. Nilsson has remarked, 'I must emphasize again that the Mycenaean Greeks were a mixed people who to a great extent took over Minoan culture and religion.' This is surely true and underlines the difficulties of deciding what is Minoan and what is Hellenic. Some gods, objects, and practices we

1. *Aristocratic Society in Ancient Crete*, 1955.
2. The military leader of the clan gathering or *startos*, which is only another form for *stratos*, the normal Greek word. For an army, the *phratria* was the equivalent more or less of the Roman *curia*, and the Saxon hundred.

may identify confidently as definitely Minoan or definitely Hellenic, but there remain a large number of marginal instances which we cannot classify so confidently.

MUSIC AND DANCING

It is certain that music, associated with dancing, played a large part in the life of Minoan Crete, and that it was closely bound up with religious ceremonies and festivals, though we must not assume that there was no secular music. Even in modern Crete we find, quite apart from the official music of the Orthodox liturgy, certain tunes associated with particular occasions and festivals. Thus the carol singers sing one particular air on Christmas Eve and another in honour of St Basil on New Year's Eve, while a third traditional song is sung to the bride at weddings. The folk dances too, the *khaniotikós* of the west, the *pendozáleis* of the centre, and the *pedikhtós* of the east have each their own appropriate airs, less limited in number but still not very numerous.

Minoan Music

Classical folklore credited the Cretans with having introduced several forms of musical performance to the mainland. Thus the *nome*, the solo hymn to Apollo accompanied by the singer on the lyre, was said to have been first performed at Delphi by Chrysothemis the Cretan, the *paean*, or choral hymn to Apollo, was also derived from Crete, and the *hyporchema*, the choral song and dance executed at Delos, was termed Cretan by Simonides, its invention attributed to the Curetes, and its introduction to Thaletas of Gortyn, who introduced Cretan rhythms to Sparta.

It seems likely, then, that some of the old Minoan music was not entirely lost; but what was its character? Mosso records that from the lowest levels at Phaistos, that is from the Late Neolithic period, came a bone horn similar to some still used by peasants of the neighbourhood and two bone tubes of unequal length, which he suggested might have been part of a *syrinx* or 'Pan's pipe'.[1] One of the Minoan seals depicts a woman blowing a conch horn, but the music that can be achieved by this means is rather limited, and they were perhaps

1. But surely these might be a set of double pipes of unequal length, like the pair illustrated on the Hagia Triada sarcophagus.

employed for summoning the people to attend festivals or other gatherings. Galpin notes the wide distribution of such conch horns, but seems to be unaware of the Minoan examples.

Triangular harps of the kind which the Greeks termed *trigonon* were known in the Cyclades during the Early Bronze Age[1] and an instrument like the classical lyre with seven strings would appear to have been well known in Crete from Middle Minoan I times since it appears as a symbol in the Hieroglyphic Script.[2] Sometimes the symbol is shown with only four strings. This is perhaps only a convenient simplification, not necessarily an attempt to depict a tetrachord instrument, though it may be noted that the four strings of the primitive Kafir harp of Persia are tuned to a tetrachord.[3] One example of the Middle Minoan symbol shows an instrument with eight strings, presumably implying a heptatonic scale.

The Late Minoan III painted sarcophagus from Hagia Triada depicts a seven-stringed lyre of classical type with a tortoise-shell sounding board, perhaps tuned to a double tetrachord with the central note belonging to both tetrachords. The double pipe, which appears on this sarcophagus, had also been known in the Cyclades in the Early Bronze Age,[4] but we must remember that the sarcophagus belongs to the period when Mycenaean influences were very strong in Crete, and that the bronze figurine of Late Minoan I date in Leyden cannot be quoted as a piper since his hands are broken off at the crucial point. The Geometric *phorminx*, however, had only four or five strings, and this fact has been used to support the idea that the Greeks, like the Celts, had a pentatonic scale without semitones, but the evidence seems unconvincing.[5] Both seven-stringed lyre and double pipe seem to disappear after the Bronze Age, only to

---

1. It is a variety of the Mesopotamian upright harp termed a *zakkal*; compare F. W. Galpin, *The Music of the Sumerians*, Chap. 3.; H. F. Lutz, 'A Larsa Plaque'; and T. Alvad, 'The Kafir Harp' *Man*, 1954, No. 233.

2. Galpin, op. cit.; but the Minoan instrument is Egyptian rather than Sumerian in shape.

3. T. Alvad, op. cit.; the five strings of certain Greek lyres do not prove a pentatonic scale; thus Alvad speaking of a five-stringed harp from Kafiristan thinks it was probably tuned as a diatonic tetrachord. It seems less probable that the instrument should be tuned pentatonically.

4. U. Kochler, in *Athenische Mittelungen*, 1884, pp. 156–62.

5. R. P. Winnington Ingram, *Classical Quarterly*, 1956, p. 169.

be reintroduced in the seventh century B.C., but here again the negative evidence should not be pressed, and the four-stringed *phorminx* could possibly have been tuned to a tetrachord like the Kafir harp. The seven-note scale seems to have been indigenous to Western Asia and perhaps to have spread westwards with the Indo-European peoples, but it never crushed the pentatonic scale in the Celtic areas, while in China we even hear of an earlier heptatonic scale being changed to a pentatonic by royal decree.[1]

For percussion instruments the Minoan Cretans possessed cymbals and the Egyptian rattle called a *sistrum*, but I can quote no evidence for the existence of a drum.

Minoan Dancing

A widespread tradition credited the Cretans with the invention of dancing, a tradition ridiculous in itself but reflecting the great role played by dancing in Cretan life from Minoan times up to the present day.

Fig. 49. Late Minoan dancers, Palaikastro

It has been suggested that we may have illustrations of the classical Cretan dance termed the *hyporchema* in the group of dancers in bronze from Olympia and the pottery group of dancers with a lyre player in their centre of Late Minoan I date from Palaikastro (Fig. 49).

1. F. W. Galpin, op. cit., p. 139; S. Piggott, *Prehistoric India*, 1950, p. 270.

If this suggestion has any foundation in fact we may have a descendant of the *hyporchema* in the *pendozáleis*, the only modern folk-dance in Crete where the performers grasp each other's shoulders in the manner of the groups from Palaikastro and Olympia. The musician still stands in the centre, and his instrument is still called the *lyra*, though it looks more like a three-stringed lute than any ancient type of lyre illustrated in classical art.

We have no evidence as to whether the Minoan Cretans affected airs in five or seven time, such as occur in later Greek music. I suspect, however, that most village dances of Minoan or of classical Crete were in four time, which would suit the simpler metres based on trochees, iambics, dactyls, spondees, or anapaest rhythms, and that they no more resembled the complicated rhythms of the choral dances of Pindar and Bacchylides than English folk-dances resemble those of the Royal Ballet.

Modern Cretan folk dances may be divided into two groups, which nearly but not exactly coincide in their distribution with the eastern and western divisions of the Cretan dialect. From the Malevizi eastwards the local dances are the *maleviziotikos*, the *herakliotikos*, and the *pedhiktós*.

West of Malevizi and including the Ida range other local dances, such as the *pendozáleis* and the *khaniotikós*, are based on an entirely different principle, and I suspect that the *geranos* or 'crane dance', which Theseus was said to have seen the Cretan maidens dancing, and himself to have introduced to Delos, may have been a dance of this kind.

The twice-yearly migration of the cranes is a very noticeable event at Knosos, and the cranes really do perform a dance resembling a *khaniotikós*, graphically described by Miss Rawlings in her novel *The Yearling*:

> The Cranes were dancing a cotillon as surely as it was danced at Volusia. Two stood apart, erect and white, making a strange noise that was part cry and part singing. The rhythm was irregular like the dance. The other birds were in a circle. In the heart of the circle several moved counterclockwise.[1] The outer circle shuffled around and around. The group in the centre attained a slow frenzy.

1. The two musicians still operate in the course of a *khaniotikós*, but the dancers move clockwise.

In the eighteenth book of the *Iliad* Homer describes a dance 'such as Daedalus made for Ariadne in broad Knosos' with the youths and maidens hand in hand dancing in a circle (for that is what must be implied by the comparison to a potter's wheel) and then again dancing in two ranks facing each other.

There exists a curious parallel to Homer's Cretan dances in a place where I should least have expected it, at Chichicastenango in the Quiche district of Guatemala. The 'Bull Dance', as described by Aldous Huxley, is danced about Christmastime, though the people start preparations for it in the previous Lent. The story, which is told in verse, refers to a bailiff who entrusted the care of his master's bulls to some herdsmen, but Huxley did not follow the details of the plot. The dance had two figures like those described by Homer but in the opposite order. First, two lines of dancers alternately advance on each other and retreat. Huxley compares this movement to that of 'Here we come gathering nuts in May', and east Cretan dances would produce a similar effect if danced in two lines facing each other instead of in a circle.

In the second Guatemalan movement, compared by Huxley to the 'Grand Chain' of the Lancers, the two groups of dancers circle round the whole area in groups of two who circle round each other. Since Huxley informs us that practically all the local music and folklore of that district is of Spanish, not of Maya origin, I suppose this dance of the bulls should ultimately be derived from some old Spanish dance. Moreover, the *toritos* wear bull masks which must make them look very like Minotaurs. Is it conceivable that this was an old Mediterranean dance known to Homer and danced in Minoan Crete?[1] The evidence is far too slight to support such a theory, but scholars have sometimes tried to derive the toreador sports of Spain and southern France from that of Minoan Crete.

MINOAN SPORTS

The most popular sports in Minoan times seem to have been boxing and the bull ring. The representations of boxers (usually in pairs, but also shown in procession) in relief on steatite vases or in miniature

1. Was it perchance something like the *karpaia*, the 'cattle-lifting' dance of the Aenianians and Magnesians. Compare the account given by Athenaeus in *Deipnosopishtae*, I, 15.

frescoes indicate them with leather boxing gloves of the classical cestus type, so that we can assert that the traditions of Greek and Roman boxing go right back to the Bronze Age. Representations of boxers on Mycenaean and Geometric vases and the accounts of boxing in the Homeric poems suggest that this sport never died out.[1]

The sport of the bull ring was obviously the more exciting and more dangerous, and naturally was therefore represented more often in art. The bull was not pursued on horses and overthrown, as in the rodeo sports popular in Thessaly in classical times, nor was it apparently slain by an armed matador, as in the modern Spanish bull ring. The main object of the Minoan sport seems to have been to stand in front of a charging bull, catch him by the horns, and vault over on to his back (Plate 16). Girls as well as youths indulged in this practice, but for this purpose they wore male attire. We are reminded of the old Athenian folk tales about Theseus and Minos and of the seven youths and seven maidens who were sent from Athens to be the prey of the Minotaur. We also have representations of the netting of bulls (the most famous being those of the gold cups found at Vapheio near Sparta). There is no indication that this is part of the toreador sports, but Seltman has pointed out the parallel between this scene and the one described by Plato in his account of Atlantis which, he has suggested, might contain folk memories of Minoan Crete. The relevant passage from the dialogue called the *Critias* states how 'wild bulls were turned loose in the precinct of Poseidon. The ten kings, left all alone, prayed to the God to make them capture the beast which he desired, and then set forth, unarmed, with only staves and nets. The bull which they secured they dragged to the block of brass and cut the bull's throat over the block, according as the law commanded.'

The question whether Plato's Atlantis was Minoan Crete is, of course, highly speculative and debatable, but both the netting and the sacrifice of bulls occurred in Crete in the Bronze Age, and the latter, at least, must have been a religious ritual.

Even the bulljumping and the boxing have been considered to have been religious rituals, but this is not substantiated by evidence and pending further investigation it is better to regard them as usually

---

1. The chronological gap between Hagia Triada and archaic Greece is bridged by occasional representations of boxers on Late Mycenaean and Geometric vases.

secular sports, though doubtless practised on days of religious festivals.

We have no evidence for any ball games like that played by Nausicaa and her maidens in the *Odyssey*.

For indoor games we have the evidence of dice and the royal gaming board, but no clear idea of the sedentary games in which the Cretans of that period indulged. Of the gaming boards found elsewhere in ancient Egypt, Cyprus, Elam, Assyria, and Sumer perhaps the closest parallels to the Minoan board are the splendid inlaid examples from the Royal Cemetery at Ur, but the number and arrangement of the holes are different, and I would hesitate to assume that the Sumerian game was played in the Palace of Minos.[1]

1. Compare C. L. Woolley, *Ur Excavations*, 1934, pp. 274–9, Plates 95–8; E. D. van Buren, in *Iraq*, 1937, pp. 11–16; C. J. Gadd, in *Iraq*, 1934, pp. 45–50.

CHAPTER 10

The Decline of Knosos and the Growth of the Power of Mycenae

THE Late Minoan period in Crete opens brilliantly with no obvious signs of the decay of Cretan power that was to set in later, despite the great loss of life and the extensive material damage that must have been caused by the great earthquake which rocked the island in the second quarter of the sixteenth century B.C.

At Knosos there had been widespread damage to the Palace of Minos, but this had already been repaired before the end of the Middle Minoan period, so that Evans was able on this site to classify his deposits as pre-seismic or post-seismic Middle Minoan III B according to whether they had preceded or succeeded the great earthquake.

The Late Minoan I A period (1550–1500 B.C.) was marked at Knosos by various reconstruction works, including the final form of the entrance systems on the west and south sides of the Palace of Minos. The Late Minoan I B period (1500–1450) was not marked by any major architectural work, and the succeeding period Late Minoan II (1450–1400) had no building in the palace except the reconstruction of the throne room block. There were, however, a number of minor repairs executed in the Palace of Minos, including a number of new frescoes, on which we remark a tendency to imitate in stucco the veining of marble dadoes, a curious anticipation of a trick characteristic of the earliest wall paintings at Pompeii in the so-called 'encrusted style'. The best-preserved fresco of the Late Minoan II period is that of the guardian griffins in the throne room (paralleled at a later date by a similar fresco at Pylos) with its interesting attempt at shading.

The trade balance with Egypt and the Levant had swung now from Knosos to Mycenae, but Egyptian vessels of value still reached Crete, as is proved by Alexiou's discovery of stone vases in a Late Minoan II

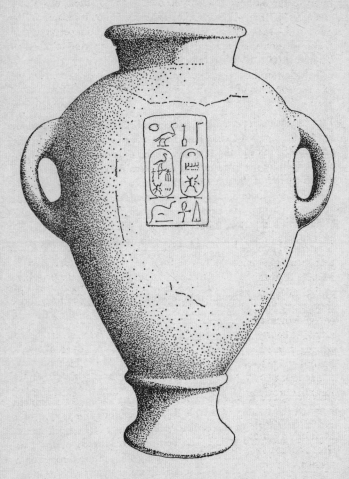

Fig. 50. Alabaster vase from Katsaba

tomb of the harbour town of Knosos.[1] One of these was a fine 'alabaster' jar (Fig. 50) bearing an incised inscription translated as 'the good god – Men-kheper-re – son of the sun – Thutmose perfect in transformation endowed with eternal life' and referring to the great Thutmose III.

The most striking and significant difference, however, between the late Minoan I B and the Late Minoan II A deposits at Knosos is the replacement in the latter of Linear Script A by Linear Script B in the palace records discussed in Chapter 3, which certainly implies that Knosos and perhaps much of central Crete was then under an Achaean dynasty, whether this was achieved by conquest, by a dynastic marriage, or by the *coup d'état* of a Mycenaean general serving over a Minoan army.

MYCENAEAN INFLUENCE ON CRETE

Even before Ventris's revelations of the mainland characteristics of Linear Script B, various scholars, such as Karo, Praschniker, and Snijder, had pointed out the presence in Late Minoan II art of features that seemed to imply influence from Mycenaean Greece, and K. Müller in particular had stressed some non-Minoan characteristics in the 'palace' amphorae from the *tholos* tomb at Kakovatos in Elis. Even when the motives were Minoan, the Mycenaean artist was apt to stylize them and turn floral elements into abstract patterns. Minoan artists, of course, had also stylized floral patterns from an early date, but the whole-hearted tectonic treatment of the palace amphorae at Knosos was different and might be due to Achaean influences.

Yet even a Greek occupation of Knosos in 1450 B.C. does not quite solve the problems of the Knosian frescoes. Human figures, formed patterns, linear borders, and frieze decoration had all appeared at Knosos, Amnisos, and other sites in the north of Crete during the Late Minoan I A period. It would not help our inquiry to push back the Greek occupation before 1550 because there were no frescoes on the mainland before 1400 B.C. The natural inference is that these features, like the relief frescoes, were a local growth of the Knosian school (perhaps influenced from abroad but certainly not from Mycenae).

1. Vases of alabaster and other stones have of course been found in other tombs, such as the Royal Tomb, the Temple Tomb, and the adjacent L.M.II tomb, but these could have been heirlooms, whereas Alexion's vase was not.

THE TRANSITIONAL PERIOD AT KNOSOS

The only *kouloura* hitherto still open in the west court was now covered with paving, and the only earlier building still left standing near the palace on this side was the north-west Treasury. The west porch in its present form, with its reception room and porter's lodge, was constructed at this time, and the Corridor of the Procession widened, but the South Propylaeum, which gave access from the same corridor to the state apartments on the first floor, was narrowed.

The palace façade on the west side of the central court was advanced, and the court itself paved with limestone slabs (though only a small proportion of these still remain *in situ*). The shrine and the staircase between it and the throne room block were reconstructed. The north-west entrance with its lustral area had never been rebuilt after the Middle Minoan III earthquake, nor had the great stepped portico on the south side, but it is clear that the old Middle Minoan I bridgehead over the Vychia ravine was still in use, because it was during the transitional Middle Minoan III B–Late Minoan I A period that the charming little caravanserai was constructed for the accommodation of travellers from the Mesara and from the south in general, implying that the bridge was still in use though the Stepped Portico it had previously served was in ruins.

The reception rooms consisted of a small pavilion approached from the palace side by a short flight of steps with a single column in the position termed *in antis* – that is half-way between the *antae*, or corner-posts, of the sidewalls. This room was adorned with a frieze of red-legged partridges and hoopoes.

Adjoining the pavilion with the partridge fresco there was another small room with a footpath fed by a conduit from a spring on Gypsadhes Hill and with its overflow filling a drinking trough for the animals that had accompanied the travellers. A few yards to the west lies a little spring house lined with gypsum slabs, and with a small niche at the back, intended perhaps to hold a lamp or a figure of the guardian deity of the spring; and indeed this spring seems to have continued as a 'Holywell' long after the abandonment of the caravanserai and even of the palace.

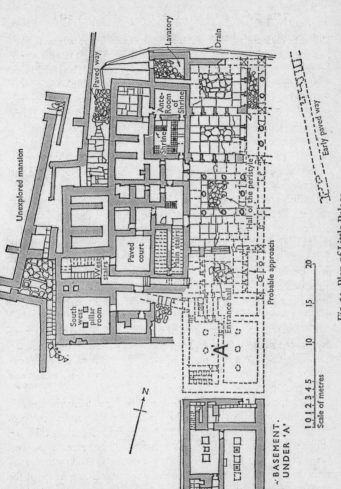

Fig. 51. Plan of Little Palace

N

Unexplored mansion

Paved way

Lavatory

Drain

Ante-Room of Shrine

Shrine

Hall of the peristyle

South west pillar room

West stairs

Paved court

Main stairs

Entrance hall

'A'

Probable approach

Early paved way

BASEMENT. UNDER 'A'

1 0 1 2 3 4 5   10   15   20
Scale of metres

The Little Palace

To the same transitional Middle Minoan III B–Late Minoan I A stage may be assigned the construction of the Little Palace, and probably also of the so-called 'Unexplored Mansion', a still larger building immediately west of the former, but unexcavated except for its east façade. Both buildings are remarkable for the fine ashlar masonry of their exterior walls facing each other on opposite sides of a narrow but well-paved road running parallel with the main arterial north-south road, and both were built into the slope, so that, like the Palace of Minos, they had more storeys on their east than on the west sides.[1]

The main entrance to the Little Palace from the east passes through a fine columned propylaea, from which short flights of steps give access northwards into a peristyle court reminding us of a Hellenistic or Roman villa, though the eastern half of it has perished. Off the north-west corner of the court lies a small room with a stone drain in it, obviously a bathroom.[2] South of this there was originally a lustral area, restored as a shrine in the latest reoccupation period, and mud brick packed in between the wooden columns of the Late Minoan I A lustral area, thus preserving the impression in the burnt clay of the convex fluting of the now vanished pillars. From the south-west corner of the peristyle a noble gypsum staircase, of which two flights are still preserved, led to an upper storey which has now vanished. South of this a narrow service stairway led down to the pillar basements at the south end of the palace.

The Little Palace, like all other important buildings at Knosos, had been badly looted, but one of its treasures was preserved for us by having been thrown into a well, a glorious bull's head rhyton or filler carved in black steatite and originally fitted with gilded horns. One of the original eyes, with a pupil of rock crystal set in a rim of red jasper, is still preserved and the vivid effect of the bloodshot eyes of a bull must be seen to be believed (Plate 17a).

The South House

Of the houses more directly associated with the Palace of Minos

1. A very common practice in Crete both in Late Minoan and in modern times (as noted by Seager; see page 286).
2. The opening is too small for a sewer.

the most splendid was the South House rising to a height of at least four storeys on the southern slopes of the Kephala. It seems more dependent on the palace than the Little Palace or the Royal Villa and may, I imagine, have belonged to some important official. It is at least significant that the occupant of this house, constructed in the transitional Middle Minoan III B–Late Minoan I A period, was allowed to encroach on the line of the old Stepped Portico.

Another entrance perhaps existed at the south-east corner of the building, leading into the light-well of the main hall of the house (a miniature version of the Hall of the Double Axes in the Palace of Minos, but with a small lustral area opening off its north-west corner). West of this hall on the same floor there lay a pillar crypt of which the religious associations were clearly emphasized, since on one side of the central gypsum pier stood a conical base of the same material of the kind reserved for the sacred double axe, while on the other side stood a more enigmatic gypsum base with three round holes in it. Below the ground-floor rooms there were cellars. These were also constructed as pillar crypts, but there is no obvious sign that they were employed for any religious purpose, though they were well constructed with a lavish use of gypsum for walls and stairs. The door into one of these rooms could be locked from inside or from outside by inserting a bronze pin into the wooden bolt. The wooden bolt has perished, but the bronze pin was found still in position in its diagonal slot.

The House of the Frescoes

Such were the mansions of princes and nobles, but to realize the astonishing degree of luxury and refinement attained by people of more moderate means we have only to examine the House of the Frescoes, lying between the west court of the Palace of Minos and the Royal Road uniting the theatral area to the Little Palace.

A small projecting wing on the north side contained an entrance lobby and an office for a doorkeeper (like the French, the Minoan Cretans seem to have been rather addicted to employing *concierges*). The lobby gave access to two corridors on the east side, and on the west to a long narrow room opening into a large room where the fresco fragments were found neatly stacked in layers, apparently in preparation for a replacement which never took place. The quality of the frescoes is as good as that of any in the palace, and their combination of extreme naturalism in the treatment of the fauna against a highly stylized background of flora and rocks is typical of Late Minoan I A frescoes, and may be remarked also on the wall paintings of the caravanserai and of the villa at Amnisos. But, although the technique is Minoan, the subjects have an exotic, half-Egyptian flavour (compare the papyrus and the blue monkey).

Late Minoan Innovations at Knosos

The domestic quarter of the Palace of Minos, east of the central court, seems to have remained without any major reconstructions, presumably because it had been cut into the side of the Neolithic tell, and had therefore suffered less damage from the great earthquake. Even in these parts of the palace, however, a considerable amount of redecoration took place, especially in the form of new frescoes. Relief frescoes die out in this period, but include one magnificent specimen, the 'Priest-King' relief in the porch connecting the Corridor of the Procession with the central court, and a ceiling pattern of rosettes and spirals on a blue ground from the same area where the Miniature Frescoes of the previous period were found. It is probable, too, that the splendid fragment of relief fresco at Pseira showing two court ladies (originally restored as one court lady) may have belonged to this period.

To this period may belong the so-called 'medallion' *pithoi* of the Palace of Minos. Evans dated those Middle Minoan III but admitted that the examples in the domestic quarter continued in use right up to the time of the destruction of the palace in 1400 B.C. Pendlebury remarks that on grounds of style these *pithoi*, or at least the examples with moulded grass ornaments, should belong to the Late Minoan I A period, and his dating is supported by the fact that the medallion *pithos* in the room behind the central pillar shrine west of the central court rests on an earlier pavement and has the later pavement built round its base.

Amnisos

Another fine villa with frescoes was erected early in the Late Minoan I A period at Amnisos, traditionally the naval headquarters of King Minos. It should be noted that Minoan ideas of what constituted a suitable site for a harbour varied considerably from our own. They did not, of course, despise a natural, land-locked harbour like Soudha Bay, but they were less fussy and were quite content with a site that had a promontory jutting out, flanked on each side by a beach, so that boats could be beached on one side or the other according to the wind, and Platon has pointed out that most Minoan harbours possess such a promontory. Amnisos, however, hardly possesses even this convenience since the rock projects very little, and even that hardy sailor Odysseus commented on the poorness of its harbour. Why then should Minos have chosen it as his naval head-quarters? The rocky eminence that lies between the modern aero-drome and the shallow bay of Amnisos may have cut some of the force of the prevailing north-west winds but only if they were more west than north, and Marinatos is probably justified in assuming that the coastline has sunk here since Minoan times (as it certainly has at Nirou Khani only a few miles farther east) and that a sandspit had probably connected the Kastro rock to the small island lying off shore, thus providing the necessary facilities for beaching ships. The 'Naval Officer in Charge' at Amnisos appears to have done himself well. His villa lies on the east side of the isolated hill known as Palaeochora, protected by it from the prevailing north-west winds, and consisted of a two-storey building with some very good ashlar masonry in the more important parts. At the north-west corner there was a typical Minoan hall, repeated in duplicate on the first floor, and served by two corridors and a flight of stone steps. The chief reception room was on the first floor, with two pillars in the centre and with fine floral frescoes adorning at least three of the four walls.

LATE MINOAN FRESCOES

The so-called House of the Frescoes between the Palace of Minos and the Royal Armoury contained the remains of fine murals neatly stacked as if they had been intended to be replaced on the walls after some reconstruction. One scene represents a gay picture of wild flowers and rocks with two blue monkeys. Some of the flora is defin-itely Cretan, including the earliest naturalistic representation of a yellow rose (*Rosa foetida*, or the Austrian briar), but the blue monkeys and the papyrus plant are exotic features probably copied from

Egyptian murals (though Platon has suggested that the scene represents a royal park rather than one taken from the wild life of Crete).

So-called rosettes occur much earlier in Mesopotamian and Egyptian art, but these might represent some other flower, and Meillet has argued that both 'rose' and 'lily' were old Aegean words, not necessarily of Minoan origin, but at least current in the Levant at a very early date.[1] Among the plants native to Crete on this and on the Amnisos frescoes were lilies, irises, vetches, and myrtle.

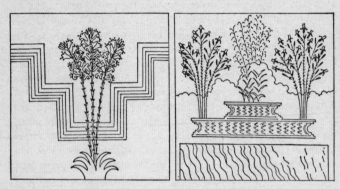

Fig. 52. Late Minoan I frescoes, Amnisos

Rather more formal than the Monkey Fresco, and perhaps to be assigned rather to the Late Minoan I A period, is the attractive frieze of red-legged partridges and hoopoes adorning the entrance hall of the Caravanserai. The fauna and flora of this painting were all native to Crete, and the multi-coloured balls that look like Easter eggs were probably intended to represent river pebbles of Cretan breccia.

To the same period (Late Minoan I A) belongs the room with garden scenes at Amnisos, a different scene for each of three walls in a room, depicting lilies on one wall, irises on another, and on the third other plants not growing wild as in the Monkey Fresco, but formally planted out in stone vases like the crocuses of the Saffron Gatherer.

From Hagia Triada in the Mesara comes what is, perhaps, the finest of all the Minoan naturalistic frescoes. The scene shows two cats stalking a pheasant and the hindquarters of a roebuck leaping over

1. A. Meillet, *Aperçu d'une histoire de la langue grecque*, 1930, p. 65

rocks in what appears to be the natural scenery of a Cretan dell. There is certainly no suggestion of a park here, except the odd fact that the cats are not Cretan wild cats but domesticated Egyptian ones.

To the Late Minoan I A period may also be assigned two Knosian frescoes that were imitated much later on the mainland in the Mycenaean palace at Tiryns. Indeed the great mural painting from the Upper Hall of the Colonnades, representing a row of 'figure of eight' oxhide shields, could never have been restored but for the better preservation of a miniature copy of it at Tiryns.

The other fresco which provided a model for one at Tiryns was the Toreador painting which originally probably adorned the walls of some room or loggia above the so-called 'School Room'. The technique of this highly difficult and dangerous sport is clearly defined in this painting which shows a girl, dressed like a boy, standing in front of a charging bull which she grasps firmly by the horns, preparing to vault over the animal. A youth has just succeeded in vaulting over the animal while another girl stands ready to catch him when he alights. One might almost adopt the old army phrase and describe the scene as 'bull-vaulting by numbers'.

In this painting we may notice certain characteristics which mark the decline of the splendid naturalistic frescoes of the Middle Minoan III B–Late Minoan I phase and herald the grandiose but rather blatant art characteristic of the Late Minoan I B period at Knosos. Human figures, hitherto mainly confined to the miniature frescoes, become more prominent. The charging bull, though spirited enough, is greatly inferior to the splendid animal in the relief fresco of the North Porch. Another characteristic of this new type of fresco, which seems confined to Knosos, is the multiplication of subsidiary friezes (sometimes imitating coloured stones) of a quasi-architectural kind. These traits may also be seen in the later Mycenaean paintings of the mainland, but we must beware of attributing the Knosian examples to Greek or Mycenaean influence on Knosos, since on the latter site they appear about a hundred years earlier than they do on Mycenae or at Tiryns.[1]

Other frescoes of this period (1550–1500 B.C.) at Knosos include a

1. We may, however, infer that the Mycenaean art of Mycenae and Tiryns was influenced by the school of Knosos, not by those of Mallia or the Mesara.

gay little piece from the Queen's *megaron*, perhaps depicting a girl dancer whirling round in a quick dance with her curls flying out. It must be admitted, however, that the analogy of similar representations of hair flying upwards on seals seems usually confined to small figures of deities descending from heaven on their worshippers. I have never seen it suggested that this figure represents a goddess making her epiphany, but that is what the analogy from the gems and sarcophagi would suggest. Another fresco fragment from a small room opening off a continuation of the Corridor of the Procession shows part of a procession, with men carrying a palanquin on which a figure in white robes is seated on a camp-stool.

LATE MINOAN I A POTTERY

The pottery of the Late Minoan I A period (1550–1500 B.C.) was distinguished by its superior baking, and Pendlebury remarks on 'the clink' that is heard when a Late Minoan I A sherd is dropped on a hard surface. In the far east of the island, at Zakros and Palaikastro, the transition to this style was gradual. We find there the same leaf and scroll patterns executed both in the light-on-dark and in the dark-on-light techniques, and not infrequently the same vase will have superimposed bands of ornament in alternative styles. One vase from Palaikastro, a pear-shaped jar with basket-like handle formed of the horns of an ibex of which the head projects in front, reminds us of the bull's head projecting from one of the vases depicted in Rekhmire's tomb.

Cups shaped like tea-cups were also quite common and adorned usually with sprays of leaves, and there were also a number of 'flower-pots', flaring conical or pear-shaped jars with a hole in the bottom of each. There were jugs of various shapes, some rather squat with bridged spouts, others taller and pear-shaped with plain or with beaked spouts. Rhyta, or fillers, were popular, varying from the old 'peg-top' form which had appeared in the Middle Minoan period, to an elegant ovoid variety, or a long conical type which appeared in Crete at the beginning of the Late Minoan I A period in steatite and was copied in clay, especially in eastern Crete and later on the mainland (where there is at least one example of the sixteenth century from Prosymna in the Argolis). (C. Blegen, *Prosymna 2*, p. 168.)

The conical rhyton was the most common form in the hands of the Keftiuans and the People of the Sea represented on the Egyptian tomb paintings. Some fragments of handsome rhyta of this shape in hard stones such as Spartan basalt were found at Mycenae (associated

Fig. 53. Late Minoan I A vase designs

with Late Helladic III pottery) and just such a filler was borne by the celebrated Cup-Bearer in the Late Minoan I B fresco at Knosos.

We also find some handsome ovoid jars with multiple handles, forerunners of the palace amphorae of the Palace of Minos in the Late Minoan II period (though the latter were made to suit Achaean tastes, perhaps even by Achaean potters). One of the finest was a splendid vase found at Pachyammos (Plate 18).

Baggy alabastra of a type common in Egypt during the Twelfth Dynasty were imported into Crete and imitated in pottery with wavy bands of paint imitating the veined calcite of their Egyptian prototypes. Most curious of all the Late Minoan I A vases were some polychrome libation vessels found at Isopata in the form of high, slim buckets with double looped handles and with the body of the vase treated like a fresco, since it was coated with a lime plaster before

Fig. 54. Minoans in Tomb of Senmut

the polychrome designs were applied (Plate 19). The most interesting and best preserved examples of these vases were those from Tomb 5 at Isopata, one with a design of a boars-tusk helmet of the type more familiar on the mainland but also known in Crete, the other with a design of a figure-of-eight shield. The more numerous examples from Hagia Triada only retained faint traces of their original decoration, but the painted sarcophagus from a tomb near that site (though later in date) illustrated the purpose of these vases. They were for libations in front of the sacred double axes at other Minoan shrines.

CARVED STEATITE VASES

From the Palace of Hagia Triada come one complete and two fragmentary vases in steatite with designs in low relief; fragments of similar vases have been found at Knosos, one representing a procession of youths carrying bowls, another an archer disembarking from a boat, and a third a building on a hill (perhaps a peak sanctuary, as Platon suggests). The complete vase from Hagia Triada is a conical cup with the design of a young prince (perhaps the 'Minos' of that day, as Forsdyke has suggested) giving orders to an officer of the guard with his men behind him. One of the fragmentary vessels is a conical rhyton with parallel zones of sporting scenes in low relief, three of boxing and one of the toreador sport.[1] The second fragment from Hagia Triada, the shoulder of an egg-shaped rhyton, depicts a harvest festival, a marching crowd of peasants carrying what look like pitchforks, shouting, laughing, and singing, with one man giving the time by a *sistrum* (the Egyptian rattle) and led by a priest in a quilted cloak.[2] The Harvesters' Vase is the most lively and vigorous relief that we possess until late in the classical period. To the same period I would assign the celebrated gold cups found in the *tholos* tomb at Vapheio near Sparta, though the pottery found with them belongs to the Late Helladic II or Late Minoan I B period. The two cups have repoussé designs, one showing the netting of wild bulls and the other the decoying of them by a tame cow, and were both obviously the work of the same artist. They are supposed by most authorities to be imports from Crete, I think rightly, first because of the highly naturalistic style of the relief; secondly because the decoration is of the free field type with no attempt to divide it into zones; and thirdly because this rather squat form of Vapheio cup is a typically Middle Minoan form and unlike the Helladic forms.

Fig.55.
Late Minoan I B vase

The Late Minoan I B period (1500–1450 B.C.) corresponds to the

1. Compare Hutchinson, *Town Planning Review*, October 1950, Fig. 10.
2. Illustrated everywhere, but compare especially F. Matz, *Kreta Mykene Truja*, Plate 67.

first half of the Late Helladic II period on the mainland and is characterized by pottery with designs of fishes, seaweed, etc. at Knosos and Gournia, Palaikastro and Zakros, but it would be a mistake to assume that it everywhere succeeded the floral and spiral designs of Late Minoan I A (Fig. 55). This marine style was never very common and was probably a local style either of Knosos or of some eastern site, since we do not find it at Mallia, and only rare examples of it at Phaistos, though the best fresco in this style is the fine floor with a marine design under the Late Minoan III floor of the shrine at Hagia Triada.

Collared rhytons in this style occur at Palaikastro and Zakros, and a vase of this shape (which does not occur in the Late Minoan I A period) is shown along with Vapheio cups and conical rhyta being brought as tribute to Pharaoh by the islanders represented on the tomb of User-Amon, vizier to Thutmose III in the earlier part of his reign.

The neck of a faience rhyton of this shape was even found at Ashur, the capital of Assyria, and a complete example except for the mouth and neck at Mycenae. A few Late Minoan I B vases were exported to Egypt and of these we may quote the fine *oenochoe* (jug) in the Marseille Museum acquired in Egypt, a tall alabastron with imitation marbling from a tomb in Sedment, a bridge-spouted jug in New York, purchased in Egypt in 1860, and a squat alabastron from Armant in the British Museum, acquired in 1890. The last is sometimes reckoned as a Helladic vase on the ground that the shape is a mainland one, but the shape is more common in Crete than is often realized, and the decoration is very close in style to the jug in New York (though not, I think, painted by the same man).

The majority of the Aegean vases found in Egypt at this time, however, seem to have been imported from the mainland of Greece, and we may consider the fifteenth century B.C. as the period when Mycenaean traders began to supplant Cretans in the ports of Egypt and the Levant.

Finest of all the Late Minoan I B vases is the stirrup jar (so-called because the false neck with a handle on each side bears a vague resemblance to a stirrup) from Gournia, with a terrifying fiercely alive octopus writhing all over the body of the vase.

Many of the floral motives of the Late Minoan I A vases continue, but usually in a modified or stylized form. Ivy leaves develop two or three stalks, the realistic palm tree of Middle Minoan III times develops into a kind of flower, in which form it became very popular in the succeeding period on Late Minoan II and Late Helladic II vases. Favourite neck ornaments were foliate bands, garlands of pendant crocus blooms, and a double band of reserved rosettes. A favourite pattern on the lip, especially on the large vases, was the one originally described by Evans as 'the notched plume' but later rechristened by him 'the adder mark' because he considered it was derived from the markings of an adder's skin. The marine ornaments, which are particularly rich on the rhyta of eastern Crete, comprise octopods, whorl shells, nautilus, starfish, and a rock formation looking rather like coral (but certainly nothing of the sort).

LATE MINOAN FRESCOES AT KNOSOS

At Knosos, where Late Minoan I B pottery occurs but is not very plentiful compared to that of Late Minoan I A, the main indications of change are to be seen in the palace frescoes.

The most important fresco of this period is that adorning the walls of the Corridor of the Procession, where a string of figures was shown bringing offerings to the king in a manner recalling that of contemporary paintings on Egyptian tombs and temples. Only the lowest parts of the figures are preserved, but they include both men and women, some of them doubtless bringing vases of metal or of stone, like the Cup-Bearer from the South Propylaeum, others carrying musical instruments, culminating in the double row of figures in the South Propylaeum and the splendid figure of the Cup-Bearer himself – the only surviving example of the head and upper half of a figure from the procession, though several legs and quite a number of feet have survived.

If the Cup-Bearer with his fine aquiline features, long curly hair, rather light brown eyes, powerful shoulders, trim muscular limbs, and very slim waist is to be taken as representative, even in an idealized form, of Sergi's 'Mediterranean Man', we must admit that the type is an attractive one, and I think that in the main Sergi was right. It is at least beyond dispute that men with similar features and figures may still be found in Crete at the present day, especially in the mountain districts.

Late Minoan II frescoes tend to imitate in stucco the veining of marble plaques in dadoes, a curious anticipation of the Pompeian 'encrusted style'.

At Knosos the reconstruction of the throne room and the heraldic fresco of the Griffins may be credited to the Achaean dynasty and so may the 'Captain of the Blacks', showing a Minoan (or Mycenaean?) officer leading off some Nubian troops at a smart double, found near the earlier House of the Frescoes.[1] On style alone I should have assigned the 'Campstool Fresco' and 'La Parisienne' to this period, though Evans and Pendlebury assign them both on stratigraphical grounds to the Late Minoan I B period. At Knosos no more relief frescoes were designed, but there was a considerable amount of painting in the flat, of which the most important was the mural from the throne room.

NIROU KHANI

In the bay immediately east from that of Amnisos lay a small Minoan port and a very interesting little palace associated with it. The Palace of Nirou Khani, as it is called,[2] was built at the beginning of the late Minoan I A period and was excavated by Xanthoudides and published in 1922. We gain the curious impression that the port and palace together formed the Headquarters for the Propagation of the Minoan Gospel to the infidels in other parts of the Levant, since the palace was stocked with cult objects, four large bronze double axes, forty tripod altars, and other ritual objects, stone lamps, vases, etc., far beyond the needs of a much larger palace and presumably intended for export (perhaps to the land of Keftiu). On the south side of the east court was found the remains of a large pair of Horns of Consecration and pieces of a fresco with sacral knots.

The palace is small but very well built and designed. The main hall, with its inlaid doors dividing into two parts like the Hall of the Double Axes at Knosos, opens on to the east court and forms the centre of the living quarter. The ground floor of the north side is

---

1. Pendlebury, op. cit., p. 200. The artists however were probably Cretans, since no fresco of this date is known on the mainland.

2. By all archaeologists, though the local inhabitants often call it 'Koukini tu Khani'.

given over to domestic store-rooms with corn bins and *pithoi* for wine and oil. The south wing has most of the missionary stores, altars, lamps, etc. The whole building must have had at least one more storey since there are staircases in both the north and south wings.

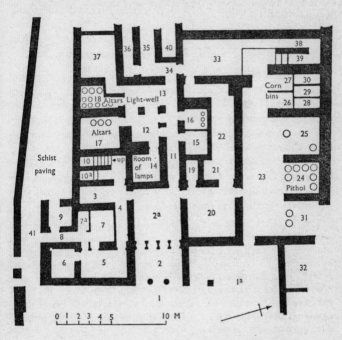

Fig. 56. Plan of Late Minoan I palace, Nirou Khani

The sinking of the coastline since Minoan times has resulted in the flooding of some of the port installations, but we can still see two rock cut basins, a long mole, and traces of some other buildings (warehouses, perhaps).

At Mallia the palace and the town both continued to be occupied, but their importance seems to have diminished greatly, and this area may now have been under the control of Knosos. Perhaps the gulfs of

Merabello and eastern Crete were also under the same control, but if so they seem to have benefited by it, and the towns of these areas may well have found the remote control exercised by Knosos less irksome than the more direct control probably exercised by Mallia in the Middle Minoan period. Ports such as Pseira and Mochlos would doubtless have benefited from the suppression of piracy by the Knosian fleet.

PSEIRA

The first Late Minoan period was the heyday of the island port of Pseira which had indeed been occupied in Early Minoan II times but flourished particularly between 1550 and 1450 B.C.[1] The little houses, clustered along the top and sides of a rocky point, with steps at intervals descending to the harbour, remind one of many an island harbour of the type called '*skála*' (= staircase) at the present day.

The Late Minoan I houses, like those of Gournia, were built of large, roughly-squared blocks of the local grey limestone, with slabs of schist (also found on the island) used for floors. Seager remarks that the houses were built in terrace-fashion.

Thus a single house would contain a number of floors yet never stand more than two storeys high at any one point. Such houses are well shown in the siege scene on the silver vase fragment from Mycenae; in fact they can be found today in Cretan hill villages which closely resemble in construction their predecessors of Minoan times. In some cases where the outer walls are built of unusually heavy stones, the superstructure may have been higher, but the general type was a large house climbing the hillside with not more than one floor of living-rooms over the basements of each tier.[2]

No palace was discovered here but there are some comfortable houses, such as those termed Houses A and B, both larger than anything at Gournia except the small palace on that site.

One house overlay a more ancient building of which the three rooms were filled with beach pebbles, which the workmen identified

1. Or 1400 B.C.; see page 290.
2. R. B. Seager, 'Excavations at Pseira' *Anthropological Publications of Pennsylvania University*, 1912, p. 13. This form of house is still very common in Crete, especially in the villages of the foothills.

as sling-stones. This earlier building, not exactly dated by the excavator but presumably belonging to the Middle Minoan rather than the Late Minoan I period, may have served as a primitive arsenal.

One small but well-constructed house even possessed a fine relief fresco, the only example found outside Knosos, and a sure indication that the relationship between the capital and the island must have been close and friendly. The existing fragments, which had fallen from an upper storey, show that the subject illustrated was two ladies or goddesses (originally thought to be only one) in richly embroidered court dresses, reminiscent of the Middle Minoan III B 'Ladies in Blue Fresco' at Knosos.[1]

GOURNIA

Our most complete picture, however, of the lives of the ordinary citizens of the Late Minoan I A period is afforded by the ruins of the little industrial town of Gournia on the Gulf of Merabello, and we owe this picture to the splendid perseverance of Miss Harriet Boyd (later Mrs Boyd Hawes), who uncovered practically the whole settlement, a feat never attempted previously and but rarely since. All honour is due to her hard and unspectacular work on this site, without which our account of Minoan culture would be a very one-sided and misleading story of palaces and villas. The town of Gournia lies on a small knoll a few hundred metres from the coast, and it seems to have been scantily occupied ever since the first Early Minoan period (Fig. 57). The first serious building on the site, however, occurred late in the third Middle Minoan period when a small palace or large villa was erected on the crown of the hill in obvious imitation of the great palaces of Knosos and Mallia. Like Knosos it boasted a theatral area on a very small scale, but there was no gypsum here, so the masonry of rubble with an ashlar facing of sandstone was rather modelled on that of Mallia, with the same small setbacks of the façade and with the same alternation of square piers and round pillars of the portico facing its central court.

The internal arrangements of this small palace are rather obscure and cannot be restored with any confidence, since the building would appear to have been destroyed by the Middle Minoan III earth-

1. R. B. Seager, op. cit., Plate v; parts of two figures wrongly united as one.

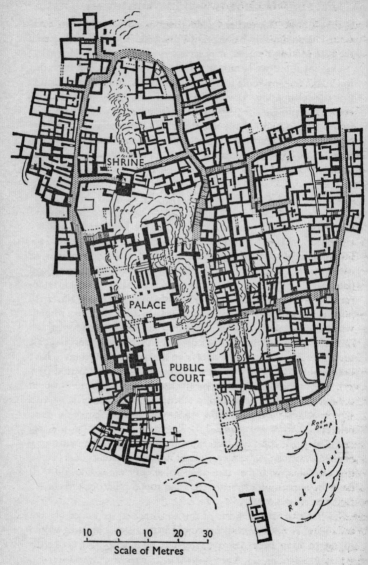

SHRINE

PALACE

PUBLIC
COURT

Rock Dump

Rock Contours

| 10 | 0 | 10 | 20 | 30 |

Scale of Metres

Fig. 57. Plan of Gournia

quake, and had been turned into workmen's flats in the Late Minoan I A period (presumably by the independent actions of refugee squatters rather than by any order of the local Housing Committee). A regular industrial settlement grew up round this nucleus, with streets radiating out from the centre and with lateral communications provided by two curving streets of the German *Ringstrasse* type (Fig. 57).

The artisans' houses are small and tightly packed together, and the surviving rooms seem to be chiefly store-room basements. The living-rooms must have been mainly on the first floor, often reached by stairs rising straight from the street (a practice for which I could quote modern parallels in Crete). Gournia, of course, was only a little market town, what would now be termed a *komópolis*, with small local industries catering for the agricultural and fishing hamlets in the neighbourhood, but the evidence for them is very complete. We possess no less than five clay disks from the tops of potters' wheels, a carpenter's workshop with a number of bronze tools including a fine saw, a fragment of a cross-cut saw, double axes, large and small chisels, an auger, the point for a drill, a coppersmith's forge, and an oil factory for pressing olives. Just below the crown of the hill at the end of a small cul-de-sac leading out of the inner *Ringstrasse* lay the remains of a small civic shrine, the humble precursor of many a temple to Athena Polias, and the first of its kind to survive to our times, since earlier shrines had always been attached to a palace or a villa if they were in a town, though peak and cave sanctuaries of a public character had existed in the country. The furniture of the shrine still surviving seems to belong chiefly, if not entirely, to the Late Minoan III period, but it seems probable that there was a shrine on this spot in the Late Minoan I period.

HAGIA TRIADA

In the Mesara the damaged palace at Phaistos was reoccupied, but was replaced as the official residence of the reigning prince by a new and smaller palace erected at the west end of the same ridge, a site known to us as Hagia Triada.

This palace seems to have been built just after the great earthquake in what Evans termed the post-seismic Middle Minoan III B period and probably lasted till 1400 B.C.

Certain local peculiarities mark off the architecture of these Mesara palaces from those of northern Crete, notably a partiality for gypsum dadoes rather than for fresco decoration and a habit of locating light-wells in the middle of the longer halls rather than at one end.

Nevertheless Hagia Triada has produced two splendid frescoes in the Late Minoan I naturalistic style (see p. 276), the more famous of the two being the Cat Fresco described above. The other fresco was a marine design with octopi and fishes adorning, not a wall, but the floor of the little shrine which used to be assigned to the Late Minoan III period, to which its second floor level certainly belongs, but which must, I think, have been first erected in the Late Minoan I period. The position of this shrine is very interesting since it is accessible both from the palace and from the town and we seem here to have the transition from the purely palatial shrines of Knosos, Phaistos, and Mallia to the civic shrine that we noticed at Gournia.

It was originally supposed that the absence of Late Minoan II pottery on this site implied that the palace had been abandoned before 1450 B.C. but now that we know that late Minoan II pottery in Crete is practically confined to Knosos, it seems more natural to suppose that the Hagia Triada palace was destroyed in 1400 B.C., though it is clear that the town site was soon reoccupied.

The pottery is chiefly of the Late Minoan I A type, and the few examples of Late Minoan I B vases found in this area were probably imported from some other part of the island.

To the Late Minoan I A period I would attribute the construction of a beehive tomb excavated by Miss Vronwy Fisher, Mr V. Desborough, and myself on the Kephala ridge about half-way between the Zapher Papoura cemetery and that of Isopata (Fig. 58). The tomb had been badly looted in Minoan times and employed as an ossuary in the Late Minoan III C period, but there were a few remains from the earlier burials, while the sherds found in or behind the walls were all Middle Minoan, except two sherds that were probably Late Minoan I A.

The tomb resembles in some respects Wace's first group of *tholoi* at Mycenae, but the side-chambers in the fore-hall and the fact that the tomb is not cut into a slope are Cretan features and recall the Royal Tomb at Isopata, which seems to date from the end of the Late Minoan I A period.

THE SECOND LATE MINOAN PERIOD

The second Late Minoan period (1450–1400 B.C.) is a chronological division which, however, has no cultural significance except in the neighbourhood of Knosos, where it was characterized by the art that we term Late Minoan II. Elsewhere pottery of Late Minoan I B

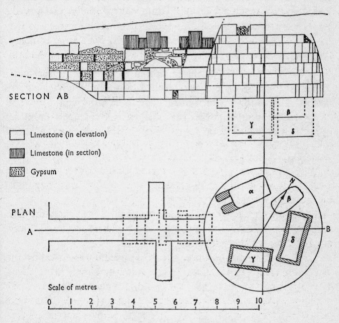

SECTION AB

☐ Limestone (in elevation)

▦ Limestone (in section)

▨ Gypsum

PLAN

Scale of metres

0 1 2 3 4 5 6 7 8 9 10

Fig. 58. Tholos tomb on Kephala

style, or in some places of Late Minoan I A style, persists without much change, though occasionally some eastern site such as Palaikastro or Gournia may reveal the fact that the deposit belongs to the second half of the fifteenth century B.C. by the presence of a Late Minoan II vase imported from Knosos or by Late Minoan II motifs on a local vase. It is evident, however, that an Achaean dynasty was now ruling at Knosos.

At Knosos the only major construction in the Palace of Minos during the Late Minoan II period was the reconstruction of the throne room block, and even this was less radical than has been supposed, since the *mosaiko* pavement of Middle Minoan III A type recently revealed under the present floor of the ante-room indicates that the plan has been little altered since that date, and I suspect that some sort of throne room existed here even in the Middle Minoan I period (see p. 165). The Temple Tomb was repaired and re-used.

ROYAL TOMB AT ISOPATA

The Royal Tomb at Isopata consists of a large rectangular burial chamber (7·90 m. by 6·07 m.), walled by splendid ashlar masonry sometimes bearing masons' marks, approached through a fore-hall (6·75 m. by 1·58 m.) with two shallow side-chambers or niches roofed by corbelled vaults terminating in flat lintel blocks. Much of the corbelled vaulting of the fore-hall had also persisted up to 1941 (when the whole tomb was destroyed by General Ringel). The roofing of the main chamber is a more doubtful problem. Evans and Fyfe restored a keel vault rising nearly eight metres high which would have implied the existence of a burial mound. This is not impossible, but the analogy of some smaller tombs with similar plans and structure of the fourteenth century B.C., excavated by Schaeffer at Ras Shamra in Syria – a site in close commercial relationship with Crete – suggests the possibility that Isopata might have possessed a corbelled barrel vault.[1] Another parallel to the Ras Shamra tombs is the curious door or window in the back wall, apparently backed by virgin soil. I understand, however, that this communicated probably with the Minoan ground surface by a narrow shaft, through which possibly offerings or libations may have been poured. It would be not unnatural to suppose influences from Ras Shamra, where this form of tomb is more common, but the Isopata example seems to be about a hundred years earlier than any of its parallels at Ugarit. The long earth *dromos*, or entrance passage, cut in the earth resembles those of Mycenaean tombs, except that the Isopata tomb follows the Minoan practice of

1. C. F. A. Schaeffer, *Ugaritica*, 1939, p. 32 f. and Plates XVI and XVII; and 'Fouilles de Minet el Beida et de Ras Shamra', *Syria*, 1929, p. 29.

being sited on the crest, not on the slope, of the hill so that the *dromos* has to slope steeply down instead of running level into the slope as on the mainland.

The tomb had contained one or more royal burials of the second Late Minoan period, from which were preserved some fine vases in Egyptian alabaster and also painted vases of clay in the Late Minoan II style. The jewellery and richer objects that it must once have contained had been looted long ago, but one small stirrup cup in the

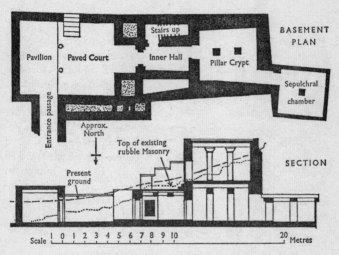

Fig. 59. Plan and section of Temple Tomb, Knosos

Middle-East style of the Late Minoan III period (see page 310) showed that the tomb continued to be used till the end of the Bronze Age. The Late Minoan II B period was illustrated by the latest burial in the Temple Tomb, which till recently constituted the only evidence for the smaller vases of this period. The Late Minoan II A period is now illuminated also by the Five Warrior Graves from the Hospital Site at Knosos and by a rich tomb at Katsaba, and the very latest period before the destruction of the palace (which I prefer to regard as still Late Minoan II B, though it corresponds to Furumark's Late Minoan

Fig. 60. Late Minoan II vase patterns

III A I) is illustrated by Alexiou's tomb from Katsaba, with the alabaster vase of Thutmose III, and by another chamber tomb which I opened near the Temple Tomb.

LATE MINOAN SEALS

The seal-stones of the Late Minoan I A period begin to exhibit a slight decline from the best work of the Middle Minoan II B or Middle Minoan III periods, but there are still plenty of fine stones.

The commonest shape is the lentoid. The amygdaloid, or almond-shape, grows longer and acquires grooves on the back side. Flattened cylinders no longer occur, but there are some examples of true cylinders. A representative group of clay sealings of this period was found at Knosos in the south-west basement; the designs include one of a youth holding two mastiffs on leash, others of dogs with collar, and a curious scene showing a young Minotaur sitting on a camp-stool with an attendant pointing to a kneeling ram.

Late Minoan II seals are still finely cut, but characterized by increasing stylization.

Naturalistic motives had, of course, often been stylized by Minoan artists from a very early period, but the whole-hearted tectonic treatment practised on the 'Palace Style' vases and gems of that period was very different from anything in the Late Minoan I period, and might well be due to Mycenaean influences.

Jerzy Pilecki, in his discussion of heraldic devices in Mycenaean art, has also stressed this tectonic treatment practised by the Mycenaean artist in his engraving of seal stones.

He divided the antithetic groups of Mycenaean art in general, and of seal-stones in particular, into three types. The first of these was the triangular, pedimental, or architectural group which characterizes so many Mycenaean gems, and not a few found in Crete also; it has no obvious prototype in Aegean art before the Mycenaean period but is an old oriental type, possibly borrowed from the Hittites. The finest monumental example of this type in the Aegean is, of course, the famous relief over the lintel of the Lion Gate at Mycenae.

Pilecki's second type is the rectangular, or frieze type which, he suggests, might be considered as a repetition of monumental motifs derived from compositions over lintels, or excerpts adapted from interior friezes. The lintel suggestion is not convincing, but there are plenty of prototypes for Pilecki's second group both in Minoan and in Mycenaean friezes.

Pilecki's third group is the 'miniaturist', where the old Minoan miniature reacts on the Mycenaean heraldic type, sometimes bending and squeezing the design to fit the circular field of the gem, sometimes adding extra motifs either as significant emblems or as landscape features.

Pilecki then proposes a curious theory that the supporting figures of an antithetical group were not merely guardians, but representations of the deity with whom they had an ideological identity, and supports it by those strange designs where the bodies of two lions or other beasts unite in the centre in a single head or mask, and quotes the double-headed eagle of the Hittites as a similar example. Here it is hard to follow him, since his theory seems to depend on representations of very ambiguous meaning, though there may well sometimes have been a confusion of ideas between a deity and his or her sacred animal, especially when there was a possibility that the deity might appear in that form.

Pilecki, however, is probably right in stressing the civic significance of so many heraldic groups in Mesopotamia, and the double-headed

Fig. 61. Sealing with warrior frieze

eagle appeared as the city arms of Lagash long before the Hittites adopted it. It would not then be surprising if the Lion Gate group at Mycenae represented the civic arms of that city, or the family arms of its ruling family, as suggested by Persson.

The engraved gems of the Late Minoan II period in Crete and of the Late Helladic II period on the mainland are marked by an increased use of the wheel and the bow-drill, and therefore, though spirited enough, rather more slap-dash in execution than the beautiful engravings of the Late Minoan I period. We witness the beginning of what Wason terms 'the drill style', which was to spread far and wide in the Early Iron Age.[1]

Many of the seal-stones of the Late Minoan II period were still cut in the old free-field, naturalistic style, though some of these may have been cut in the Late Minoan I period. But others appear more Mycenaean than Minoan, with their tendency towards heraldic and pyramidal groups and their fondness for an exergual line, as if the design had been an excerpt from an architectural frieze. These

1. C. R. Wason, 'The Drill Style in Ancient Gems', *Liverpool Annals*, 1936, pp. 51–6.

Mycenaean characteristics are displayed to the full on the famous Mountain Mother sealings from Knosos, showing the goddess on her sacred mountain guarded by two lions, with her temple behind her and with a male votary saluting her in front (Fig. 39).[1]

What should be our test whether a gem is Minoan or Mycenaean? Hood refers to 'the element of torque or feeling for the round which is habitual in all Minoan engraving', but I think it is a pity to generalize and so weaken the force of Matz's torsion principle, which surely demands not only a feeling for the round but a definite twist, often a spiral twist. Where torsion occurs the work probably is Minoan, but Mycenaean works may and do have a feeling for the round. In addition to torsion, I would suggest that Minoan engravers disliked symmetrical, pyramidal, and heraldic devices, which appealed to the Mycenaean artist. Unfortunately many gems and some of the gold rings, such as the so-called Ring of Nestor, the Thisbe Treasure, and the so-called Ring of Minos, are seriously suspected of being forgeries. Hagen Biesantz has recently tried to answer Nilsson's complaint that 'there seem to be no indications of a technical kind which allow a sure decision' by formulating some rules for the detection of forged gems and rings claimed to be Minoan or Mycenaean work.

The forgeries, he suggests, will betray themselves by one or more of the following faults:

(1) the occurrence of antiquarian details not substantiated elsewhere (not damning by itself as Biesantz admits)

(2) representation of a subject belonging to another artistic circle

(3) the mixing of two different styles which are not part of a regular development

(4) the association of several examples on grounds of style by one hand, when one of these works is known to be a forgery

(5) the occurrence of more modern technique (in perspective for example) than was normal on seals of similar style

(6) appearance of the correct picture in the impression, whereas the Minoans and Mycenaeans produced the correct picture on the original so that the impressions from originals show such anomalies as left-handed swordsmen

(7) outraging of the unity of 'time and place' in the composition.

1. Mesopotamian influences are more evident in Mycenaean than in Minoan art, and the Mountain Mother may ultimately be derived from Ninharsag.

This scheme provides some useful tests, though I do not feel quite happy about Biesantz's seventh criterion. The Ring of Nestor, with its four unrelated or at least not closely connected scenes, certainly does look very odd and must be suspected on other grounds also. It is true also that Minoan and Mycenaean seal-stones in general do depict one isolated scene or incident, but there are gems, especially from Crete, which look rather like excerpts from a frieze and which very possibly reproduce motives from the frescoes of palaces and villas. I refer of course not to objects bought from dealers, like the cylinder from Hagia Pelagia, but to the certainly genuine examples found in excavations such as the gold ring from the Agora at Athens, or the seal impressions with marching warriors from Knosos (Fig. 61).

On the whole Biezant's criteria are useful and save us from rejecting all gems and rings not found in archaeological excavations – a counsel of despair which would deprive us of most of our material so far as gems and rings are concerned. Of the seals from Warrior Grave 3 at Ayios Ioannis, the fine lentoid seal 21 and the prism lentoid 22 seem to be good native Minoan work, but No. 20 might be Mycenaean, and the cylinder 23 might be Syro-Phoenician work from somewhere like Ugarit or Byblos.[1]

The cylindrical bead seal from the Royal Tomb at Isopata and the two lentoids from the Tomb of the Mace-Bearer are typical Minoan work, and I think the same is true of the fine gold ring found there because of its asymmetrical arrangement, a question of some importance since so few gold rings have been found in Crete in archaeological excavations and doubts have been raised concerning the genuine character of those bought from peasants or dealers. The Isopata ring shows four women indulging in an orgiastic dance in a field of lilies, and the goddess herself has deigned to visit her worshippers in the form of a small figure descending from the sky with her locks flying upwards, as do the locks of all Minoan deities making their epiphanies from the heavens.

Seals found in tombs, of course, are quite often earlier than the other objects associated with them. Thus the lentoid carnelian from the Late Minoan III A Tomb 99 at Zapher Papoura cannot itself be much later than the Late Minoan I B period, and the splendid gem

1. M. S. F. Hood and P. De Jong, *Annual of the British School at Athens*, 1952, p. 275 and Fig. 16.

found by Bosanquet in a very late *tholos* tomb at Praisos cannot be later than the Late Minoan I A period.

It seems likely that the other Minoan cities continued during the second Late Minoan period to subsist in a comfortable but provincial obscurity, deprived of any external power they may once have possessed, and rapidly losing even their commercial power to Mycenae and Pylos and the new Achaean colony at Knosos.

If we exclude the abnormal site of Knosos, it is easier to find examples of Late Minoan II vases in the far east at Palaikastro and at Zakros than at sites farther west, and there is more evidence of building and prosperity, yet there is no evidence there of an Achaean settlement. Perhaps the Eteo-Cretans from Seteia eastwards were 'Quislings', glad possibly to escape from the heavy hand of Minoan Mallia, and therefore perhaps not unwilling to establish friendly relations with the new Achaean power at Knosos. There is not much evidence on this point, but there is at least a faint suggestion that the east end of the island was relatively prosperous and on friendly terms with Knosos.

The Greek seismologist Professor Anghelos Galanopoulos thinks that the story of Atlantis was founded on a misconception of the information given by Egyptian priests to Solon and transmitted by Plato. According to this story the submerged land contained ten kingdoms of equal size (3,000 by 2,000 stadia or 345 by 230 miles in area). Thus the area of Atlantis would have been about 800,000 square miles. Galanopoulos thinks that Solon may have confused the Egyptian hieroglyph for 100 with the one for 1,000, and that when he says Atlantis sank beneath the waves 9,000 years before his time (if Solon did make this error), it would give a period of 900 years between that catastrophe and the date of Solon's trip to Egypt which would agree well enough with the probable date for the eruption that destroyed the late bronze age settlements on Thera. The reduced estimate of 80,000 square miles would also agree well enough with those of Crete and Thera together.[1]

1. *The Sunday Times* of 21 August 1966; see also Ninkovich, D. and Heeze, B. C. 'Santorini Tephra', *Colston Research Papers*, 1965, p. 413f.

CHAPTER II

The Decadence of Minoan Crete: The Mycenaean Empire

MINOAN power terminated in a sudden and widespread but rather mysterious disaster. At Knosos Evans found abundant evidences of the destruction of the Palace of Minos by fire, and of its systematic looting, but very few human bones. If its inhabitants were not carried off wholesale into captivity, they must have had time to escape. Moreover the Minoan culture did not vanish overnight like the Minoan empire. After an interval refugees of the same race and religion apparently, and indeed with the same culture but on a much lower standard, began to squat and even build shrines in the ruins of the palaces and villas of the princes and nobles. It is possible that the upper classes were nearly wiped out by the great disaster, but it is clear that a large number of the common people must have survived.

A lucky chance enabled Evans to date this disaster with considerable accuracy. Painted pottery of the type found in the reoccupation period at Knosos was found in Egypt in the city of Akhetaten at Tell-el-Amarna founded by the heretic Pharaoh Akh-en-aten and abandoned after his death. Such pottery must therefore be dated between 1375 and 1350 B.C., and even though we now know that this pottery is a Mycenaean not Late Minoan fabric, this does not affect the chronology, since the same Mycenaean pottery is found at Knosos in strata immediately on top of the debris from the great fire.

But what was the cause of this catastrophe, which was not confined to Knosos but seems to have been experienced all over the island? The same destruction (followed, accompanied, or preceded by looting) seems to have affected Phaistos and Hagia Triada in the Mesara, Tylisos, Amnisos, Nirou Khani, Mallia, Pseira, Gournia, and Mochlos in the north, and in the east, though perhaps to a lesser degree, Palaikastro and Zakros.

What was the cause of so widespread a disaster? Was it caused by foreign invasion, by internal revolutions, or by natural causes such as earthquakes and floods (which curiously often cause fires as well)? It is clear that Mycenae benefited by the collapse of Crete, but this does not prove that the mainland Greeks were the primary cause of it.

Sir Arthur Evans, after considering the possibility that the great Cretan catastrophe at the end of the Late Minoan II period might have been caused by an invasion from the mainland, had rejected this idea in favour of the theory that the disaster was due to a terrible earthquake or series of quakes, and to the floods and fires that so often follow in their train. The most celebrated flood legend in Greece, that of the Thessalian Deucalion (not to be confused with the Cretan hero of that name), was traditionally supposed to have taken place about 1330 B.C. There were flood stories also on some other islands, such as Rhodes and Samothrace. If we could follow the suggestion made by Frost, and supported by Marinatos and Seltman, that Plato's story of Atlantis, that civilized island overwhelmed by a marine flood, was a garbled account of the destruction of Minoan Crete preserved in Egyptian records, then indeed we might have a folk memory of the catastrophe of 1400 B.C., but this interpretation at present lacks confirmatory evidence.[1]

Marinatos has supported the theory of the destruction of the Minoan empire by natural causes, but in a new form. He would associate the abandonment of Amnisos, and of other sites on or near the north coast of Crete after the Late Minoan I period, with the great eruption that blew up a large part of the Cycladic island of Thera and submerged a large area, leaving three islands, Thera, Therasia, and Aspronisi, as the only portions of what had been known as *Kalliste*, the 'fairest' of the Cycladic Isles. A large part of the present Thera is now buried in volcanic ash and pumice to a depth of thirty metres, and one of the strangest sights I have ever seen is the fields of flourishing vines and tomato plants growing out of lumps of pumice stone with apparently no other soil to support them.

Theophanes, the Byzantine historian, in describing the much smaller eruption on the same island in A.D. 726, tells how the pumice reached the shores of Asia Minor and Macedonia, and to this day it

---

1. K. T. Frost, 'The Critics and Minoan Crete', *Journal of Hellenic Studies*, 1939, p. 189; S. Marinatos, 'Perí toú thrýlou tis Atlantidos', *Kretika Chronika*, 1950, p. 195; C. Seltman, 'Life in Ancient Crete', *History Today*, 1952, p. 332.

is easy to pick up small lumps of pumice anywhere along the north coast of Crete.

Marinatos, arguing from the size of the prehistoric crater (eighty-three square kilometres in extent and six hundred metres deep), maintains that the great eruption which he assigns to about 1500 B.C. must have exceeded that of Krakatoa in A.D. 1883, and must therefore have been accompanied by an even greater series of tidal waves and earthquakes affecting all the neighbouring islands, including Crete. I should prefer to have dated this eruption of Thera about 1400 B.C. (though there may of course have been two serious outbreaks of the volcano) since the absence of Late Minoan II pottery except at Knosos can now be explained on other grounds. Otherwise I favour the theory of Marinatos, who points out that the Krakatoa eruption, with its much smaller crater of only 22·8 kilometres, caused tidal waves twenty-seven metres high, devastated the coasts of Java and Sumatra, and was responsible for the loss of 36,000 lives. Now Thera is only one hundred kilometres north of Crete, but at one point the sea reaches a depth of over 1800 metres, so that the tidal waves of the Cycladic earthquake should have been considerably higher and more frequent than those of Krakatoa.

A Cycladic settlement on Thera, with pottery imitating Late Minoan I types, was overwhelmed and buried in the debris from this earthquake, and it is not unnatural to suppose that the island and coastal settlements on the north of Crete, such as the harbour town of Knosos, Amnisos, Nirou Khani, Mallia, and Gournia, were destroyed at the same time or shortly afterwards by the tidal waves and earthquakes.

Marinatos had supposed that Knosos had escaped serious destruction by reason of its greater height and distance from the sea, but I think the palace may have been destroyed by earthquake and fire at that time, even though it may have escaped the tidal waves.[1]

The absence of the Late Minoan II culture (1450–1400 B.C.) from sites other than Knosos, except for an occasional import, can now be better explained by the presence of an Achaean dynasty at Knosos, rather than by assuming that Knosos persisted later than the other

---

1. Marinatos may be right, as it appears that the main eruption took place about 1500 B.C. since L.M. I A pottery was found both above and below the ashes.

Cretan cities. The late Sir William Ridgeway always maintained stoutly that the Minos of the legend of Theseus and the Minotaur must have been an Achaean king, and his theory, till recently rather unpopular, has now been magnificently vindicated by Ventris's reading of the Linear Script B tablets as documents in 'Achaean' Greek, using the term Achaean not in the limited sense in which it was applied in classical times but in the wider sense in which it is used by Homer in the *Iliad*.

Among other causes which may have contributed to the abandonment of Cretan sites was the failure of Minos's naval expedition to Sicily. This story was already known to Herodotus, probably from his Samian sources, who would be familiar with the west Cretan version of the legend as told in Kydonia. Kleidemos again knew of it in the fourth century, but his attempt to conflate it with the tradition that Daedalus was born in Athens makes his story unconvincing.[1] Diodorus Siculus, who completed his history in the reign of Augustus, gives a coherent and reasonable account, which would appear to be derived partly from fifth-century sources like Herodotus, partly from Cretan historians of the Hellenistic period, and partly from the folklore of his native island of Sicily. How strong those Sicilian traditions were in the second decade of the fifth century B.C. is proved by the action of Theron, the tyrant of Akragas, who discovered what he claimed to be the bones of Minos, and sent them back to Crete to be reburied there. Herodotus, in the seventh book of his history, gives an account of this western expedition of Minos in pursuit of his runaway engineer, Daedalus, but does not mention the name of the Sicilian king, Kokalos. Herodotus, presumably drawing on his Samian–Cretan sources, gives some interesting details, such as the five years' unsuccessful siege of the city of Kamikos by the Cretans after the death of Minos, and the very interesting local detail that all the peoples of Crete had taken part in this expedition except the citizens of Polichne and Praisos. The most interesting item provided by Diodorus, obviously derived from the Sicilian legends, is his description of Minos's burial place as 'a tomb of two storeys, in the part which was underground they placed the bones, and in that which lay open to gaze they made a

---

1. For the confusion between a legendary artist named Daedalus of Bronze Age date and the alleged founder of the Dedalic School of sculpture see. p. 340; and for Samians in Crete see p. 350.

shrine of Aphrodite', a description which reminded Evans of the form of the Temple Tomb at Knosos, a royal tomb that the classical Cretans never saw, since it was buried for some three thousand years. The resemblance between the tomb and Diodorus's description may be a coincidence, but it is easier to explain it by supposing there had been a genuine tradition of such a tomb underlying the Sicilian folklore.

The fire that destroyed Minoan halls would have had less effect if the central pillars had not been of wood, and this accounts for the good preservation of most of the pillar crypts with central piers of ashlar stonework. The account of Samson's destruction of the Philistine palace at Gaza becomes less fantastic and more credible if we imagine him as pulling together two central Mycenaean wooden columns probably affected by dry rot.[1]

Ruined adobe houses tend to retain their walls. The material – clay – unlike stones, is not worth the trouble of carting away to be used elsewhere for other constructions. If the inhabitant of a destroyed adobe house should return and desire to build another on the same spot he simply levels the walls and builds his new house at a slightly higher level. This is the explanation why mounds consisting of the accumulation of prehistoric villages of mudbrick houses are so much higher as a rule than sites of the classical and historic periods, where building materials were re-used and the levels of the new buildings did not differ much from that of their predecessors. I think, therefore, that the great diasaster approximately dated 1400 B.C. may probably have been due to natural causes, such as earthquakes followed by fires and in the coastal cities tidal waves, without excluding the possibility that it may have been aggravated by human actions, such as raids and revolutions following the collapse of the Sicilian expedition. In the nineteenth century A.D., when Ireland was struggling for Home Rule, it used to be stated that 'England's misfortune was Ireland's opportunity', and we may perhaps claim that in the fifteenth and fourteenth centuries B.C. Knosos's misfortune was Mycenae's opportunity.

During the fourteenth century B.C. Achaean settlers seem to have colonized most of the more fertile parts of the island, and enslaved

---

1. Professor Mallowan, however, points out that the Mesopotamian records reveal many evidences of such destruction; probably palaces and temples were easier to fire than cottages, because there would be more timber and more air space.

many of the native population. The more virile elements of the native Cretans fled to the hills and founded new villages, such as Axos in the Mylopotamos district, Prinias on the watershed between the northern plains and the Mesara, Karphi in Lasithi, and Vrokastro and Effendi Kavousi in the Merabello district. At Hagia Triada a Mycenaean palace was built over Late Minoan I ruins.

EFFECTS ON MINOAN TRADE

Even in the sixteenth century, trade with the western Mediterranean seems to have been in Mycenaean rather than in Cretan hands, while in the fifteenth century Mycenae managed also to capture most of the trade with Egypt, Cyprus, and the Levant in general.

In Crete, however, the Minoan culture persisted in a weakened and decadent form. There are few imports of Egyptian alabaster vases, little jewellery or engraved gems in comparison with the previous period, and no painted frescoes, with the one curious and abnormal exception, the painted sarcophagus of Hagia Triada. Fresco painters and all the best gem cutters seem to have emigrated to the mainland, where there were richer patrons and a better market for their work. The pottery immediately succeeding the catastrophe in Crete, which in Furumark's classification is Late Minoan III A 2, I would term simply Late Minoan III A, preferring to regard the short-lived style which he terms Late Minoan III A I as simply the last pottery of the Late Minoan II B period. This is merely a matter of convenience, so that we may keep Evans's correlation of the great disaster with the end of the second Late Minoan period. The contemporary Late Helladic III A I style of the mainland is a well-balanced if rather dull style, with ornaments, derived mainly from the Late Helladic I repertoire, usually confined to the shoulder and with only horizontal girding bands decorating the belly and foot of the vase.

REVIVAL OF MINOAN SHRINES

Of the larger settlements in the lowlands perhaps the only examples we can quote as surviving without great change through the fourteenth century are Palaikastro and Zakros in the far east. There was more continuity, however, in the religious than in the civic life of the Minoan towns, and shrines of the reoccupation period can be quoted from most of the great Minoan centres. At Knosos two small rooms in the south-east part of the ruined Palace of Minos were reconstructed and converted into a shrine of the Household Goddess, dubbed by Evans the Shrine of the Double Axes. Here were preserved all the essential features of a Minoan shrine, but in the cheapest form. (See p. 222.) We gain the impression on the whole that the reoccupation of the lowlands of Crete by Minoan refugees was rather a gradual process, and that the first movement came from the priests. The worship at the old shrines revived before the civil life did, but by the thirteenth century B.C. civil life was also beginning to recover. At Mallia the structure that the French excavators cautiously describe as 'the diagonal building' (Fig. 25) should also, I think, be regarded as a shrine of the reoccupation period, though no sacred utensils or vases from it seem to have survived. These small shrines recall the simplest form of the '*megaron* house' and look forward to the simplest form of the classical temples, the so-called *templum in antis*, which is simply a long narrow room entered through a porch with two columns between the *antae*, or side-posts, though the Late Minoan examples usually have either only one column or else none at all between the *antae*. But if the architectural form of these shrines has been affected by northern models, the ledge at the back and the figurines and other furniture, when preserved, remain solidly Minoan, to remind us that the deity and the ritual are Cretan.

The furniture of these Late Minoan III shrines is a travesty of those that had existed in the Minoan palaces.[1] The figurines of the goddesses are of pottery, or occasionally of bronze, but not of ivory or faience, though small faience beads of ladies or goddesses in flounced skirts are found. There are few stone vases, except at Palaikastro, which seems to have escaped the worst of the disaster; pedestal lamps in stone still occur there, but the pedestals are shorter than formerly and have a moulded band half-way up. Steatite bowls of the 'bird's nest' and 'blossom' type still continue at Palaikastro, but many, perhaps most, of these may probably have been family heirlooms made in Middle Minoan times and still in use. Occasionally stone vases are found on other sites also.

1. See Plate 21 and Fig. 43. The date of the town shrine at Gournia might be Late Minoan III or Late Minoan I, but its furniture is unquestionably Late Minoan III.

In general the Eteo-Cretan country east of Seteia seems to have escaped from the worst effects of the floods, and earthquakes, and so to have been better able to hold out against Achaean colonists. Thus Zakros has one of the best-constructed and most comfortable houses of the period and recently Dr N. Platon has uncovered a splendid palace there.

POTTERY OF THE REOCCUPATION PERIOD

The Late Minoan III A pottery of this reoccupation period starts with stirrup jars, deep bowls, cups, jugs, and *larnakes* adorned with degenerate versions of Late Minoan II 'Palace Style' motifs, and combines them in a loose, rather tasteless fashion developing into a 'close style' in which the main object of the painter seems to be a *horror vacui*, a terror of leaving any part of the vase undecorated (Fig. 62), in great contrast to the rather industrialized, but very competent, decoration of the contemporary Late Helladic III A vases introduced by the Achaean colonists, who usually confined their main ornaments to the neck and shoulder, and only painted well-spaced girding bands on the body and foot of the vase.

Mainland influences are discernible, however, also in the Late Minoan III pottery, especially in the increasing popularity of certain shapes such as the squat alabastron, the 'pilgrim bottle', the *kylix* (a champagne cup), and the small pear-shaped amphora with three handles, all forms occurring in Crete at an earlier date, but hitherto much more popular on the mainland.

During this period we may observe the gradual adoption of the Minoan-Mycenaean style based on the Late Minoan II of Knosos by other Cretan areas which had been wont to use and manufacture pottery of Late Minoan I A and Late Minoan I B types during the second half of the fifteenth century. Furumark has discerned two main groups in this Late Minoan III A pottery, one basing its decoration on the old 'free-field unity' system native to Minoan Crete, and the other on the banded-zone system introduced by the Achaean immigrants. At first the whole vase was covered by horizontal zones of ornament with no special regard to the tectonic divisions of the vase, but this was soon replaced by a more balanced system whereby the main decoration was confined to the broadest part of the vase, where the handles and spouts were placed. Later still this tectonic arrangement was further emphasized by subdivisions into vertical panels, or by breaking up the intervals between the handles and spouts into triangular quadrants. The vertical panel division is particularly characteristic of many of the larger vases of the Late Minoan III A style. Western Crete, where the Minoan population, though well distributed, had always been relatively sparse, naturally succumbed more easily to the Achaean infiltration.[1] The first extensive Mycenaean settlement in the west of which we have archaeological evidence would appear to be that at Atsipadhais, where the tombs are filled with Late Helladic III A and B pottery and contain a number of Mycenaean 'dollies', the clay figurines so typical of Late Helladic III B mainland sites and easily distinguishable from Cretan figurines.

Another cemetery of chamber tombs in the west, outside Khania, contained both Late Minoan III A and Late Helladic III A vases, and the same mixture occurred in the Zapher Papoura cemetery excavated by Evans near Knosos. Typical Late Minoan III A pottery was also found in chamber tombs at Kalyvia in the Mesara, in *larnax* burials at Gournia, Hierapetra, Seteia and other sites in eastern Crete, and in the 'Bathroom' in block C at Palaikastro.

The Late Minoan III A *kylices* differ from their mainland contemporaries in having hollow pedestals.[2] The 'Vapheio cup' has died out and been replaced by 'tea-cups' and by small cups with straight sides and a handle perched on the flaring rim. Bridge-spouted saucers with a handle at one side, or opposite the spout, or without any handle at all, are quite common.

The circular *pyxis* reappears as a Cretan vase-shape, and for the first time we encounter domed covers for lamps as in Rhodes.

In the luxury arts of the Late Minoan III A period it is often hard to distinguish between Minoan and Mycenaean work, but the best patrons were the Achaean princes and the best Cretan workman had probably emigrated to the mainland. Frescoes appear on various sites on the mainland, but no frescoes have survived in Crete except the unique and very interesting painting adorning a sarcophagus in a Late Minoan III chamber tomb at Hagia Triada (Plate 20). No other

1. M. R. Popham points out that the refugee settlements on the hills only began in the thirteenth century. Dorian infiltration must be later.

2. Two-handled goblets with characteristic decoration and fabric are found in Late Helladic II deposits on the mainland and occasionally at Knosos, but not elsewhere in Crete.

sarcophagus is decorated in this fashion, but we are entering on a period when pottery ones with designs painted on the clay were to become normal, and Nilsson has suggested that this was the grave of a Mycenaean chief and that the local Minoan painter employed to decorate the sarcophagus had used the technique and the motifs which he would have employed to decorate a Minoan shrine.

A few engraved gems have been found associated with Late Minoan III A pottery (for example Tomb 99 at Zapher Papoura), but most seals assigned to this period are dated purely on grounds of style. They include some haematite cylinder seals with a mixture of Minoan and oriental subjects, reflecting influences from Syria or Cyprus. A tomb at Aptsa, dated 1400–1350, contained a prism seal that looks about 500 years older than the objects associated with it.[1]

The Late Minoan III B style of pottery[2] (1300–1200 B.C.) is rather more uniform than its predecessor. The absorption by the Achaean power of those areas of Crete where the Late Minoan I style had reigned resulted in the development of a pottery style in which were mingled late Mycenaean elements along with motifs derived from the older traditions of the Late Minoan I A and Late Minoan I B styles and others derived from the Knosian Palace Style of the Late Minoan II period. The general effect is rather dull, and neither the ornaments nor the paint are the equal of the contemporary Mycenaean pottery imported from the Peloponnese.

GEMS

Gem engraving still continued, as is illustrated by the remains from the lapidary's workshop at Knosos. The shapes are normally lentoid, the material steatite, and the designs include not only such old favourites as the cow suckling its calf and the lion springing on a bull, but also representations of dogs attacking goats, sheep, or oxen. A seal from Arkhanes illustrates the motif of a well-known Mycenae dagger, namely the hunting cat attacking wild duck.

A certain amount of jewellery also occurs in Late Minoan III B

1. S. Xanthoudides, 'Ek Kretes', *Ephemeris Archaiologiki*, 1904, p. 1 and Fig. 4.
2. Furumark calls this Late Minoan III B 1 and his Late Minoan III B 2 corresponds to my Late Minoan III C.

chambers. Thus Tomb 7 at Zapher Papoura had a gold-plated bronze ring with the design of a sphinx, and a necklace of beads with the double argonaut design, which appears also on beads from a tomb near Phaistos. Further jewellery was found in Tombs 66 and 99 at Zapher Papoura, in Tombs 3 and 6 at Isopata, and in the Mavrospilaion cemetery.

THE MIDDLE-EAST STYLE

By 1200 B.C., or perhaps a little earlier, we are conscious of a new form of pottery decoration, a last dying flicker of the old Minoan spirit, in what Pendlebury terms the 'Middle-East Style'. It certainly was absent from western Crete, which seems to have been almost completely Hellenized and where the best pottery is all Mycenaean, but the new style was current in central Crete, both at Knosos and in the Mesara, and was exported in some quantities to Rhodes, while isolated examples have been found at Kalymnos, in Attica, Asini, and Delphi and even as far west as Scoglio del Tonno near Taranto.[1]

Not many vases of this style from Crete have been published, and the examples from Karphi were often so affected by weathering that it was impossible to illustrate their designs, but the published examples from Crete include a small stirrup jar from the Royal Tomb at Isopata, a tankard from the Psychro Cave,[2] and some sherds from Hagia Triada.[3]

The characteristics of this style as defined by Pendlebury are 'the use of thick solid elements in the decoration usually fringed and combined with a

Fig. 62. Late Minoan III C vase ('Middle-East style')

forest of fine lines and closely hatched subordinate figures. The

1. W. Taylour, *Mycenaean Pottery in Italy*, 1958, pp. 108, 131 considers most of these to be Rhodian, as some may well be, but not, I think, all of them.

2. D. G. Hogarth, 'The Dictaean Cave', *Annual of the British School at Athens*, 1900, p. 103.

3. M. Borda, *Arte Creteo-Miceneo del Museo Pigorini di Roma*, 1946, Plates XXXVII, XXXVIII.

octopus motive is a favourite one and though clearly distinguishable it has become divorced from all reality and is treated as a pure pattern.' The most imposing vases adorned in this style are some large stirrup jars from Rhodes, and it is of course quite possible that these were local Rhodian imitations. The Cretan origin of the style, however, may be inferred from the fact that vases in this style from other districts are always stirrup jars, and only in Crete do we find different shapes, such as deep bowls and bridge-spouted tankards, in this same style. Elsewhere, both in the west and in the east, we find simply a gradual decay of the Late Minoan III and Late Helladic III styles.

A SYRO-PHOENICIAN CULT IN CRETE

The trade routes with Egypt and the East, however, were still open, and the Achaean merchants were quite ready to exploit them.

To the Late Minoan III period in general belongs a series of metal statuettes representing the Syrian god Reshef, usually in bronze but occasionally in some other material such as silver. They have been found in various parts of the Levant and must have been made, neither in Crete nor in the Peloponnese, but in some Phoenician or Syrian factory.

Recently an example of such a bronze figure with round shield and sickle-bladed sword, of the type which the Egyptians called a *khepesh* (and which some archaeologists wrongly dub a *harpe*) was found by the French excavators at Delos. H. G. de Santerre and J. Tréheux, in publishing this figurine, give a list of similar statuettes, which they do not claim to be complete, but which seems much fuller than any other.

Fig. 63. Reshef figure from Sybrita

This list of de Santerre and Tréheux emphasizes the overwhelming evidence in favour of a Phoenician or south Syrian factory for these works, but they were popular imports into Greece and Crete in the Late Minoan III period, as may be seen by the following supplement to this list of thirty-eight figurines:

39, 40	bronze statuettes in Athens from Mycenae and Tiryns
41	figurine from Sybrita, Crete, in the Ashmolean Museum, Oxford
42	silver figurine in the Ashmolean from Nezero in Thessaly
43	bronze figurine from Thermon
44	bronze figurine found at Schernen in east Prussia
45, 46	two statuettes found at Olympia
47, 48	four geometric statuettes from Delphi
49	the 'Karapanos' statuette from Dodona

His title in the Karatepe inscription, 'Reshef of the Birds', suggests a comparison with the Minoan 'Master of the Animals' and with figures such as the gold figurine from 'the Aegina treasure'.

This deity was the young 'Baal' of Phoenicia and could be hailed as Teshub, Hadad, Mot, or Seth according to the nationality of his worshippers. It is possible of course that the Mycenaeans and the Cretans of Late Minoan times may have equated him with Apollo, or the Minoan 'Master of the Animals'.

THE FOLK-MIGRATIONS OF THE
TWELFTH CENTURY B.C.

The twilight of the Minoan and Mycenaean cultures is illuminated by some references to the peoples of the Aegean in the contemporary records of the Hittites and the Egyptians. In the third year of the reign of Mursil, Great King of the Hatti (about 1331 B.C.), the official records refer to a country called Ahhiyawa, associated with the name of a city called Millawanda. Many scholars believe that the country in question was an Achaean state, either in the Peloponnese or in one of the Aegean islands such as Cyprus, and that Millawanda was Miletus, which claimed to be a colony of Milatos in Crete. Some years later, perhaps still in the reign of Mursil II or perhaps in that of his successor Muwatallis (1306-1282 B.C.), often referred to as

Mutallu, a letter was written by the Great King of Hatti concerning Tawagalawas, son of Antarawas, a vassal of the King of Ahhiyawa, based on Millawanda. This letter has received rather more publicity than it deserved because the Swiss scholar Forrer identified these princes with Eteokles, son of Andreus, legendary kings of Orchomenos. Most scholars, however, now reject both this identification and also Forrer's attempt to identify a certain Attarissyas, King of Ahhiyawa and a contemporary of the Hittite king Tudhalias IV (1250–1220 B.C.), with Atreus, the father of Agamemnon. The dates fit, but neither the form of the words nor the places associated with these names seem suitable. G. L. Huxley compared Attarissyas to Teiresias, and Sayce even preferred to identify Attarissyas with Perseus. Tudhalias may be the same name as the Greek Tantalus, but it does not follow that we can identify the father of Pelops with any particular Tudhalias, or Achilles's opponent Telephus with any particular Hittite prince named Telepinush.

The one inference that we can draw from these Hittite records with some degree of probability is the existence, somewhere in the Levant, of an important Achaean power during the thirteenth century B.C., and this is confirmed by the archaeological evidence. How many such states there were is more debatable, but that of Mycenae was certainly the most important, and those of Pylos, Orchomenos, and Thebes also of considerable standing.

The Hittite empire collapsed about 1190 B.C. and we therefore hear no more about Achaeans in the records from Boghaz Koi. Here, however, the Egyptian records help us with some references to the extraordinary ferment that was brewing in the international affairs of the Near East at this time, a ferment that began with the destruction of Hatti and the racial movement of the Phrygians from Macedonia into Asia Minor, and culminated in the attacks of the sea raids and the land raids on Egypt. Priam's campaign against the Amazons on the Sangarius River and Agamemnon's capture of Troy are all part of the same story, but so many pieces of the jig-saw puzzle are missing that we cannot form a coherent picture of the whole. The first invasion of the northerners broke against the shores of Egypt even before the collapse of Hatti when, in 1221 B.C., the Egyptian Pharaoh had to repel a Libyan fleet that attacked the Delta supported by a motley group of allies whose names suggested that they came from Asia Minor. The only national contingent we can identify with absolute certainty is that of the Lycians, though the Tursha are perhaps to be identified with the Tyrsenoi, the Asiatic nation which colonized Etruria.[1] The Shakalsha have been identified with the people of Sagalassos and the Shardana with Sardians or Sardinians. In favour of the last-named identification is the fact that the Shardana wore helmets with two horns and carried very long swords and small round shields like the figures found in the Nuraghe cemeteries of Sardinia (though the Nuraghic culture is not supposed to begin before 1000 B.C.) Some of the Shardana, whoever they were, remained in Egypt and were incorporated as mercenaries in the Egyptian army.[2] Some of the raiders used cut-and-thrust swords with narrow tang of a type that became popular in Europe.[3]

The most interesting to us, however, of the Libyan allies are the Akwasha, who are identified by most historians with the Achaeans and the people of Ahhiyawa in the earlier Hittite records. The very same year (1221) Meneptah had had to contend with revolts in Palestine in the cities of Gaza and Askalon, later celebrated as strongholds of the Philistines. Indeed the Philistines may have already been

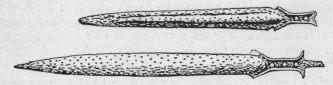

Fig. 64. Swords from Mouliana

infiltrating into this coastland since, under the name Pulasati, they appear as one nation among the motley horde of northerners that overran Syria and Palestine and attacked Egypt from the north-east in 1190 B.C.[4] Of the previous raiders from the west only the Shakalsha

1. But when and how many? For the theory that the Etruscan nation grew up in Italy, see M. Pallottino, *The Etruscans* (Penguin Books, 1955), Chapter 2.

2. See also R. Dussaud, *La Lydie et ses voisins*, 1930, p. 37.

3. C. F. A. Schaeffer, 'A Bronze Sword from Ugarit', *Antiquity*, 1955, p. 226.

4. For J. L. Myres's suggestion that Pulusati = Pelasgians, see *Who Were The Greeks?*, 1930, p. 143.

appear again, and the Akwasha are not mentioned. Of the new names the identifications for Thekel and Weshesh are very uncertain, but fresh evidence has appeared in support of the theory that the people termed Denyen in the Egyptian records were those that Homer calls Danaoi, a term he used as a rather loose equivalent of Achaeans. The recent decipherment of a Phoenician text at Karatepe in Cilicia suggests that these Denyen were the inhabitants of the plain of Adana, a district which still recalls their name and which was traditionally colonized by Mopsos of Argos, shortly after the fall of Troy.[1] The same people also appear as Danuna in the Assyrian records. The curious stories of Danaus and his brother Aegyptus, to which we owe the Greek and modern European names for Egypt (which its inhabitants have always termed Musri), must go back to the traditions of the land raid of the northern peoples on Egypt. The old Bronze Age powers of the Aegean had disappeared or were in a state of collapse. Hatti, Knosos, Troy, and even Mycenae became heaps of ruins, but the successors of these powers had lived long enough in contact with the Bronze Age civilization of these cities to have absorbed much of their culture, and the new states that emerged from the ruins, Phrygia, the late Hittite states such as Carchemish, and the small city states that arose in Greece, though simpler than their predecessors, preserved much of their cultural heritage.

Wace and Albright, for different reasons, would date the transition from the Sub-Mycenaean to the Protogeometric Period not later than 1000 B.C. Desborough's 970 B.C. depended on the date formerly assigned to stratum IV at Tall Abu Hawam in Palestine, now dated fifty years earlier by Van Beek (see Wace and Albright in *The Aegean and the Near East*, edited by S. Weinberg, pp. 134 and 163 respectively). The period between the Dorian invasion and Homer remains very obscure. Whatever we may think of the validity of Ventris's system, there seems little doubt that Greek was spoken in Crete in 1500 B.C. and that the percentage of Greek speakers rapidly increased. Why then was the native script abandoned, and was there a period of complete illiteracy at the end of the Bronze Age before the introduction of the Phoenician alphabet which, with the addition of a few letters,

---

1. R. D. Barnett, J. Leveen, and C. Moss, 'A Phoenician Inscription from Eastern Cilicia', *Iraq*, 1948, p. 56; see also G. L. Huxley, 'Mycenaean Decline and the Homeric Catalogue of Ships', *University of London Bulletin*, 1956, p. 19

was to become the official Greek alphabet and the ancestor of all the modern alphabets of Europe? The date and the method of this transmission is still a matter of dispute, but a recent survey of the evidence by Margot Falkine has suggested a date between 900 and 863 for the transmission, which she thinks may have come via Rhodes.[1] Signorina Guarducci, however, has suggested that Crete may rather have been the medium. By 750 B.C. the modified Phoenician script was in use in Athens, Thebes, Corinth, Thera, and Melos as well as Crete and Rhodes.

It would appear that the *Iliad* and the *Odyssey* must have been composed during the eighth century. 'Homer, then,' says Sir Maurice Bowra, 'stands at a point where an ancient poetical tradition has just been touched by the new art of writing and to this we may owe some of his subtlety and aptness. But it is to the purely oral art behind this that we must turn when we wish to examine his relation with the past.'[2] This statement needs to be qualified. The art of writing was not 'new' in the eighth century B.C., but, even if it had not died out, it seems that the number of writers must have diminished and that oral transmission played an important role in epic poetry.

'Heroic poetry', Finley remarks, 'is always oral poetry; it is composed orally, often by bards who are illiterate, and it is recited in a chant to a listening audience. Formally it is at once distinguishable by the constant repetition of phrases, lines, and whole groups of lines.'

The procedure of the composition of an epic lay by an illiterate poet who dictates it to a literate scribe is illustrated by the Cretan poem *The Song of Daskaloyannis*, composed in A.D. 1796 by an illiterate cheesemaker and taken down in writing by a literate shepherd.[3]

1. M. Falkine, *Frühgeschichte und Sprachwissenschaft*, 1948.
2. *Homer and his Forerunners*, 1955, p. 14.
3. See V. Laourdas, *Tó Tragoudhi toú Dhaskaloyánni*, I, 991–8.

CHAPTER 12

The Dorian Colonization, Oriental Influences, and the Growth of the City States

THE DORIAN INFILTRATION INTO CRETE

THE classical traditions concerning the entry into the Peloponnese of the people who spoke a Dorian dialect associated this event with 'the return of the Herakleidai', Herakles's three sons, Temenos, Aristodemos, and Kresphontes, who founded kingdoms, presumably with Dorian support, in Argos, Sparta, and Messenia respectively; and one generation later a certain Tektamos, son of Doros, with a mixed band of Dorians, Achaeans, and Pelasgians was stated to have founded the first Dorian dynasty in Crete.

These traditions must not be taken too seriously, since they have certainly been corrupted, sometimes unintentionally, and sometimes deliberately doctored by later genealogists seeking to bolster up the claims of Hellenistic kings to heroic pedigrees.

Herodotus, however, writing in the fifth century B.C., gives another less detailed account of the Dorian infiltration, which may not be far from the truth in its general outlines. 'In the time of King Deukalion[1] the Dorians lived in Phthiotis, in the time of Doros the son of Hellen they occupied the land under Ossa and Olympus which was called Histiaiotis. From Histiaiotis they were expelled by Kadmeians and dwelt in Pindos, being called Macedonians. Thence they moved to Dryopis (the later Doris) and from Dryopis they came to the Peloponnese and were called Dorians.'[2] Herodotus at least offers us an intelligible and not incredible account of a north Greek tribal group not so much 'moving down the spine of Pindus' (in Wade Gery's phrase), but rather across the mountain

1. Traditionally the late fourteenth century B.C. Thucydides, I, 12; Herodotus, I, 56.
2. See N. G. L. Hammond, 'Epirus and the Dorian Invasion', *Annual of the British School at Athens*, 1932, pp. 131–79.

masses shutting in the west sides of Thessaly and the Spercheius district, raiding the fertile lowlands of Boeotia, being repelled by the princely cities of Orchomenos and Thebes, and finally settling on the north side of the Gulf of Corinth in the district later known as Doris.[1]

Moreover Herodotus's account can be reconciled with the legends of the Herakleidai. The first Dorian settlements on the Peloponnese may well have been started by exiled Achaean princes trying to regain lost kingdoms or to usurp those of other princes. We might also be inclined to trust the tradition that the first Dorian settlement in Crete was planted one generation after the foundation of the three Dorian kingdoms in the Peloponnese, but for two awkward passages in Homer suggesting the possibility of early Dorian settlements in Crete and in the Dodecanese before 'the return of the Herakleidai'. The significance of these passages, which admit of more than one interpretation, must now be briefly considered.[2]

The first of these consists of some famous lines from the Odyssey Book XIX, 175 ff.) describing Crete and its inhabitants. 'In it are countless people and ninety cities. One tongue is mingled with another. In it are Achaeans, and great-hearted Eteo-Cretans, and Kydonians, and Dorians, in their three tribes, and divine Pelasgians.'

These lines might seem appropriate to the time when Homer wrote (? the eighth century B.C.), but look strange as a description of Crete before the Trojan war. Does Homer's description refer to Crete of the ninth and eighth centuries B.C., or were there really Dorians in Crete in 1200 B.C. or earlier? Strabo, in citing the passage from the Odyssey, also quotes a note on it by the historian Staphylos,[3] who stated that the Dorians were in the east, the Eteo-Cretans with their city of Praisos in the south, while the remainder (the Achaeans and Pelasgians), who were the strongest, held the plains. Now in classical times, and perhaps even in Homer's day, the Dorians controlled

---

1. For the passes traversed see N. G. L. Hammond, 'Epirus and the Dorian Invasion', op. cit., Fig. 7.

2. According to Ventris's and Chadwick's readings of the Mycenaean texts we must allow for the possibility of early settlers coming by sea from the Adriatic side, as Hammond also stresses (loc. cit.) on archaeological and topographical grounds.

3. Staphylos's date is rather uncertain; he has been dated as late as 300 B.C. and must at least be later than the foundation of Naucratis, but he was presumably quoting an earlier tradition.

the Mesara and most of the coastal plains except that of Kydonia. If, therefore, there was ever a time like that described by Staphylos, when the Achaeans and Pelasgians held the rich plains and when the Dorians were confined to the extreme east beyond Seteia and Praisos, such a state of affairs could only have existed at the beginning of the Iron Age before the Argive colonization of Knosos, when we might suppose the existence of small Doric communities in the east, planted probably by colonists from the Dodecanese. Such settlements, however, must have been relatively small and unimportant compared with the Dorian colonies planted later by Argives and Lakonians in the plains of Rethymnon, Herakleion, the Pedhiadha, and the Mesara districts. Even when the Dorians did arrive in Crete they adopted for the most part the local place names, and there are practically none that we can call certainly Doric in origin. Hierapytna, which embodies a north Greek word for rock, might possibly be a Dorian name, but places like Gortyn and Arcadia presumably owe their Peloponnesian names to Achaean settlers.[1] Even such an aggressively Dorian city as Lyttos bears a pre-Hellenic name meaning 'upland'.[2] River names we expect to include a large number of pre-Dorian and even pre-Hellenic names, just as the river names in England and France tend to be Celtic. It is surprising, however, that such an overwhelming proportion of the city names should be pre-Hellenic and it suggests that the classical population of Crete must have been characterized by a large percentage of Minoan blood. On a map of Hellenistic sites in Crete, I noted twenty-one that had modern Greek names (of which the ancient equivalents were unknown), eighteen that seemed to have pre-Hellenic names, three ancient Greek names, and two of Venetian origin. Many of the cities famous in classical times bear names that must date back to the Bronze Age if not earlier, cities such as Kydonia, Phalasarna, and Sybrita in the far west, Rethymnon and Lappa in the middle west, Knosos, Tylisos, Rhaukos, Phaistos, Pyranthos, etc., in the centre, Lyttos in the middle east, and Eteia and Praisos in the far east. During the very gradual process of the Hellenization of Crete, large numbers of the native

1. It has been suggested that Gortyn is a Pelasgian name.
2. The description by Polybius (Book IV, Chaps 53–5) of Lyttos as 'the most ancient city of Crete' might possibly imply that it was the earliest Dorian colony; the statement is certainly untrue in any other sense.

population were absorbed into the new states as slaves and dependants, but the more independent elements of the population retired to the hills, and we find settlements of Geometric dates, but still Sub-Minoan in character, occupying hilltop villages at Kavousi and Vrokastro in the east, at Karphi, a key site commanding the road from the coastal plain at Mallia to the upland plain of Lastithi, at Prinias, another key site commanding the most direct route between the north coastal plain and that of the Mesara, and another at Axos commanding another north-south road.

SUB-MINOAN CITIES OF REFUGE

Karphi

The village of Karphi ('the Nail') lies on the saddle just below the jutting peak from which the modern name is derived and which forms a landmark for sailors from Cape Stavros eastwards almost as far as Milatos. 'The Nail' itself was perhaps already a peak sanctuary in the Middle Minoan period, when it must have attracted worshippers from villages in the plain of Lasithi or in the valleys immediately to the north of it, but the pottery from that village site is chiefly in a late version of Pendlebury's 'Middle-East Style'.[1]

The foundation of the Sub-Minoan village on the saddle of this mountain is evidence of a gallant attempt by refugees of Minoan race, whose fathers had known better conditions, to construct something that might recall a small market town comparable to Gournia, but on a site that was exposed to bitter weather in winter and that had obviously been chosen for reasons of defence rather than of comfort. Nevertheless Karphi, like Gournia, also possessed its civic shrine, consisting of a large room entered from the east side, and two smaller rooms on the west side. Towards the north side of the large room there still stand the remains of a large altar, but, if a north wall to this room ever existed, it must have fallen down the precipice on to which the shrine abuts. The cult statues and objects in clay (Plate 21) are particularly interesting, and illustrate how the Minoan cult of the Household Goddess persisted in its native form long after the collapse of the political power of the Minoan state. One of the Karphi

1. M. Seiradhakis suggests that the patterns were influenced by Mycenaean textiles.

Fig. 65. Plan of Karphi

Scale of metres

0 10 20 30

T—L

figurines was taller than the others and had birds instead of Horns of Consecration on her diadem, so perhaps we ought to regard her as the goddess and the two smaller figurines as only attendants (whether human or semi-divine), like the clay votaress in the Shrine of the Double Axes, the faience votaresses of the Snake Goddess in the temple repositories, or the two maidens who stood on each side of the Bronze Apollo of Dreros. (See p. 344 and Plate 27.) The cult objects from this shrine also include a charioteer group, a curious tripod altar with three looped legs and three bulls' heads attached, and a tetragonal clay altar.[1] The period of occupation perhaps lasted from 1050 to 950 B.C.

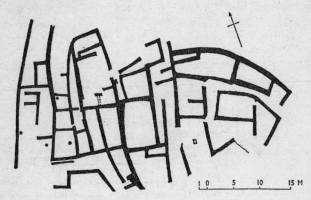

Fig. 66. Houses at Vrokastro

The path leading up from the plain of Lasithi to the village of Karphi served as a primitive 'Appian Way', or Street of Tombs, with small *tholos* tombs opening on to it. The chambers of these tombs were normally rectangular, but were covered by rude, circular vaults resting on rough squinches.

Vrokastro

A similar city of refuge was built at Vrokastro on a lofty hill overlooking the Merabello coast, an easily defensible site, but less uncomfortable than Karphi. The house-plans still ambled about in

1. M. P. Nilsson, *The Minoan-Mycenaean Religion*, 1950, Fig. 81.

the 'agglutinative' manner of Minoan towns, and the streets still had drains along one side, but the long *megaron*-like rooms may reflect Achaean influences. It is still very hard, however, to define where one house ends and another begins. Pendlebury suggested that the existing remains may have belonged to three houses, two of them entered from the south, and a third running east and west with no means of entrance visible.

Kavousi

At Vronda (or 'Thunder Hill') Kavousi, a peak sanctuary had existed in Middle Minoan days, as at Karphi, and the name of this site, coupled with that of Effendi Kavousi, the name of the great

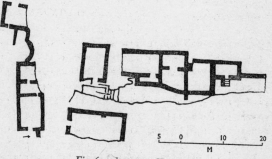

Fig. 67. Houses at Kavousi

mountain overlooking this area and conspicuous along the whole stretch of the Merabello coast, suggests that the deity of the peak sanctuary at Vronda was in all probability the Cretan Zeus, Velchanos.

Here also, on 'Thunder Hill', Minoan refugees gathered in the latest Minoan period and built a small city of refuge, of which Miss Boyd excavated the scanty remains, a forecourt and one or two other rooms. The rooms were constructed with shale slabs set in clay mortar, and were of better masonry than those of Vrokastro, where there was only dry stone walling, and not very good specimens of the method at that.

S. Alexiou has recently excavated a very interesting shrine of a goddess (very probably Eileithyia), on a site near Kavousi, called Pachlitzani Agriadha, founded apparently at the very end of the Late

Minoan III period but frequented by worshippers as late as the sixth century B.C. The little oblong building, with its ledge for the sacred objects, resembles the Late Minoan III household shrines as founded at Knosos, Mallia, Hagia Triada, and Gournia, but the figurines (all feminine) dedicated there include Sub-Minoan, Dedalic, and archaic examples, and one Dedalic plaque represents a naked goddess of the Qadesh type popular in Syria in the Late Bronze Age but rarely, if ever, represented in Minoan art.[1] A large cylindrical clay base with a cable pattern may have belonged to the cult statue of the shrine, possibly (Alexiou suggests) a figure like the one in the Ashmolean Museum said to have come from western Crete, and also paralleled by some cylindrical figurines from Praisos.

THE SUB-MINOAN PERIOD

Furumark dates the Sub-Minoan period from 1075 to 1025 B.C., but Brock dates the Sub-Minoan material from his tombs at Knosos between 1020 and 970 B.C. Sub-Minoan material, however, is rather plentiful in Crete, so that this period might well have lasted a hundred years.[2]

The pottery of the Early Iron Age displays no sharp break from the latest Minoan; Late Minoan III C fabrics glide imperceptibly into Sub-Minoan, and the latter into Protogeometric far more so than on the mainland, where the break between the Sub-Mycenaean and Protogeometric pottery is more defined, especially in Attica, where the repulse of the Dorian invaders who had overrun the Megaris and threatened Athens (a repulse traditionally associated with the self-sacrifice of the last King Kodros) allowed the development of a new Protogeometric style, which strongly affected many of its neighbours.

In Crete, however, the Sub-Minoan pottery was conservative, and the introduction of new shapes and ornaments correspondingly gradual. The Sub-Minoan pottery is perhaps best illustrated by the east

1. The so-called 'Ring of Minos' had a naked goddess, of course (Evans, *Palace of Minos*, IV, p. 957), but was that ring genuine? See Biesantz, op. cit. The naked females on a Middle Minoan vase from Mallia are genuine, but are they divine? See P. Demargne, *Explorations des Nécropoles*, 1945, Plate XXXVII, No. 1.

2. For evidence in favour of the earlier date see W. P. Albright in *The Aegean and the Near East*, 1956, p. 163.

Cretan tombs at Erganos, Vrokastro, and Milatos.[1] The pottery shapes included *larnakes*, *cratera* of a type very popular in Cyprus, stirrup jars, *kylikes* of champagne glass form (a shape that had died out elsewhere), cups with open trough spouts, small beaked jugs, and vase stands. The decoration includes degraded forms of the Minoan octopus.

THE EARLY PROTOGEOMETRIC PERIOD

The next fifty years (970–920 B.C.?) was marked by the appearance in the Knosian tombs of the Early Protogeometric pottery produced by the reaction on the Sub-Minoan pottery of Protogeometric pottery of an advanced character imported from Athens.[2] Thus Tomb 2 at Knosos comes early in the Knosian series,[3] but contained an Athenian *lekythos* of a form characteristic of the Later Protogeometric at Athens, while most of the ground was left in the natural colour of the clay, a trick inherited from the local Sub-Minoan tradition in the island. Some neck-handled and some belly-handled amphorae were probably actually imported from Athens, and certain ornaments such as cross-hatched and chequered panels on lozenges.

Nevertheless the Cretan tradition was so strong that the Early Protogeometric of Knosos, and still more that of Vrokastro, might almost be classed as a variety of Sub-Minoan. Cremation associated with iron weapons was now the rule, but inhumations still happened occasionally, and cremation was not unknown even in the Sub-Minoan period. The later burial in the Mouliana tomb may indeed have belonged to the Geometric period, as argued by Xanthoudides, and the Tylisos example is also open to question; but there can be no doubt at all about the Sub-Minoan date of the cremations in *pithoi* uncovered by van Effenterre at Olous.[4]

The instances of cremation at Vrokastro are on a different footing, because that site was a Sub-Minoan city of refuge occupied by people of Minoan race but probably lasting throughout the Protogeometric and into the earliest Geometric period.

---

1. Of these cemeteries Erganos is the earliest, since the published vases are Late Minoan III C in style.
2. (or 1020–970 B.C.?) V. Desborough, op. cit., pp. 247–9.
3. Brock, op cit., even calls it Sub-Minoan.
4. H. van Effenterre, 'La Nécropole d'Olonte', *Études crétoises*, 1948.

The Early Protogeometric pottery is well illustrated by tombs from Ayios Ioannis, Fortetsa, and the district round Knosos in general – chamber tombs like the Late Minoan types but usually with shorter *dromoi* or no *dromos* at all. Cremations were normal but inhumation also occurred. Many Sub-Minoan vase-shapes continued, such as the globular stirrup jar, the *amphoriskos*, the 'feeding bottle', the *crater*, and the three varieties of *pyxis*, but the 'bird vase' developed three legs, and the stirrup jars and deep bowls conical bases. The old Minoan and Mycenaean form of *crater* was replaced by a high, bell-shaped variety and neck-handled and belly-handled amphorae appear (following their Attic prototypes fairly closely).

Most vases had plain girding bands separating the shoulders from the belly and the belly from the foot. The main painted ornaments comprised simple linear patterns such as concentric circles on the shoulders of the amphorae, hatched triangles on those of the stirrup jars or small jugs, and wavy lines on those of the *amphoriskoi*.

At Vrokastro the Protogeometric period is best represented by the contents of Chamber Tomb I. Here, however (as might be expected in this Eteo-Cretan district), the influence of the Attic Protogeometric style is much weaker than at Knosos.

Only one vase, a neck-handled amphora, seems to be derived from an Attic vase form; the remainder are variations of Sub-Minoan or Sub-Mycenaean forms. The bronze tripod stand from Chamber Tomb I is of Cypriote type parallel to one from Tomb II at Fortetsa.

The Early Protogeometric period is well illustrated by Tomb 6 at Fortetsa and Tomb I at Ayios Ioannis. The latter, opened in 1939 and published 1960, contained the only recorded inhumation of this period, as well as at least one cremation in a cinerary jar with lid. Associated with the inhumation were a bronze belt and two iron spearheads. The other vases in this grave were five neck amphorae, one *amphoriskos*, four simple craters and one with pedestal base, four *oenochoae*, one jar, one *pyxis*, one stirrup cup, twenty-eight deep bowls, and nine or possibly ten cups. Three bronze rings and three clay beads might have belonged either to the inhumation (which was a man) or to the cremation.[1]

Tomb 6 at Fortetsa contained two imported vases, a footed bowl certainly imported from Attica, and an *oenochoe*, probably from the same source from which the Protogeometric style seems to have

1. J. Boardman, *B.S.A.*, 1960, p. 129 f.

expanded into other parts of Greece. The native tradition was represented by a splendid *crater* with panel designs consisting of two affronted goats like those of the Mouliana *crater* on one side, and of ships on the other.

The Middle Protogeometric period (920–870 B.C.) is illustrated by Tombs 3, 4, and 5 in the Fortetsa cemetery and by some cremations in the Khaniale Tekke tombs; Sub-Minoan shapes such as bell *cratera* and stirrup cups still persist. The necked *pithos* was also a common form. The ovoid cremation *pithoi*, rather clumsy in shape, had double-arc handles, sometimes alternating with a pair of vertical ones, and a very broad shoulder of geometric ornament. In this period there would appear to have been increased contacts with Cyprus, and Cyprian imports include a bronze tripod stand on which stood a bronze cauldron and two iron spears of Cypriote type, from Tomb 11. A few Cypriote vases appear and a large number (especially the duck-shaped *askoi*) appear to reflect Cypriote prototypes.

Tha Late Protogeometric period (870–850 B.C.) was short and ill-defined, but is perhaps best illustrated by Tomb 50 at Fortetsa. It is marked by the appearance of a new vase shape, the *hydria*, perhaps imported from the Cyclades, though it is derived from a Mycenaean prototype, and by the fact that the false spout of the stirrup cups is no longer closed but open.

THE TRANSITION TO THE GEOMETRIC CULTURE

The transitional 'Protogeometric B period' (850–800 B.C.) was contemporary with the reigns of Shalmaneser III and Shamshi Adad V in Assyria, and of Mesa, King of Moab, and with Athaliah's massacre of the prophets in Judah.

The 'Protogeometric B' pottery is marked by some new vase shapes and decorative motifs, but the fabric and technique remain the same, and many of the older vase forms continue, such as the bell *crater*, necked *pithos*, *kálathos*, bird vase, and straight-sided *pyxis*. To this period belongs a group in the Giamalakis collection including a unique clay shrine (Fig. 68). A shape new to Crete was the stemmed *crater*, which seems to have been imported from Early Geometric circles outside the island, probably from the Cyclades.[1] The new

1. R. W. Hutchinson and J. Boardman, 'The Khaniali Tekke Tombs', *Journal of the British School at Athens*, 1954, Plate XXV, No. 19.

decorative motifs include standing concentric semicircles, well known in Crete in the Early Minoan I period, but in this instance reminiscent of the Protogeometric pottery of Thessaly, the Northern Sporades, and Attica. With the pottery of the short Early Geometric period (820–800 B.C.) Cretan art resumes the even tenor of its way with the intrusive, oriental elements now fully absorbed and digested into the local style. A typical shape is a neck-handled amphora with rope handles from lip to shoulder (the shoulder often decorated with a horizontal s) and with a pear-shaped body adorned only with a few horizontal girding bands. To this period belongs the pottery from the 'Bone Enclosures' at Vrokastro with belly-handled amphorae, one of them equipped with a lid of the 'votive shield' type,[1] vases which Miss Hall called 'covered bowls' but which in Attica would have been termed *pyxides*, small jugs of the *lekythos*, or oil flask, type varying in size and shape but often recalling contemporary vases in Cyprus, and the solid (earlier) form of *kálathos*, a shape resembling a waste-paper basket and indeed obviously derived from a basket prototype. The open-work form of *kálathos*, which reveals its origin still more clearly, also appears in this period.

Fig. 68. Protogeometric
B shrine

The rather scanty jewellery from these tombs at Vrokastro included two pendants and some globular beads of rock crystal, small disc beads in faience, and Egyptian beads in blue glass.

The weapons included slashing iron swords with double-curved hilt and projecting tang for the pommel, spearheads with sockets folded in the old Minoan fashion but in iron, and knives with curved blades. To the same period may be attributed the contents of the *tholos* tomb at Rusty Ridge, near Kavousi, and the material acquired by Evans from Plai tou Kastrou.

1. Hutchinson and Boardman, op. cit., Plate XXIII.

THE MATURE GEOMETRIC CULTURE

The Mature Geometric period (800–770 B.C.) corresponds roughly with the reigns of Adad-nirari III in Assyria and of Joash in Israel. Egypt at this time was weak, and suffering from the oppression of various war-lords. First the Libyans set up a dynasty of kings, of whom the best-known was Sheshonk, and these were followed by an Ethiopian dynasty founded by Piankhi, who captured Memphis in 775 B.C.

To this period belong many vases from the Knosian Chamber Tombs, and probably also Miss Benton's Class 2 group of cast tripod

Fig. 69. Gold band from Khaniale Tekke

cauldrons.[1] We may also attribute to it the gold head-band (Figure 69) from the Khaniale Tekke treasure, which is clearly related to the embossed bands from Athens dated by Kunze 'very early in the eighth century', a dating confirmed by the recent discovery of an

1. S. Benton, 'The Evolution of the Tripod-Lebes', *Annual of the British School at Athens*, 1935.

embossed gold band inside a Late Geometric vase near Koropi in Attica.[1]

The pottery of the Mature Geometric period (800–770 B.C.) includes ovoid *pithoi*, often with conical lids with knob handles, and with four handles alternatively vertical and raking, dividing the main shoulder zone into panels of geometric ornaments, meanders, zigzag bands, etc. The lower part of the vase was simply adorned with broad bands of dark paint alternating with groups of thin girding lines, and sometimes the broad bands carried a line of concentric circles in matt white paint. Other common shapes were *hydriae*, slim amphorae, and a variety of small jugs from globular to spindle shapes, usually paralleled by contemporary shapes in Cyprus or in Corinth.

To the Geometric period in general I would assign the gradual desertion of the Sub-Minoan cities of refuge if (like Karphi and Vrokastro) they were too high and uncomfortable, or their gradual conversion into Greek city states if (like Lato, Prinias, and Axos) they were on more comfortable and accessible sites. Lato is the best illustration of the latter group since Prinias is too denuded, while at Axos the earlier buildings have been destroyed or covered by later ones.

Lato

By the eighth century, in all probability, Lato had not only established control over the little plain of Lakonia and the important east and north-west coast road, but had also probably planted a colony at Lato pros Kamara[2] (the present Ayios Nikolaos) which possessed a natural landlocked harbour.

The city of Lato proper, erected mainly on the saddle of a twin-peaked hill, certainly straddles the period from the Sub-Minoan to archaic Greek times, but the individual buildings are very hard to date accurately. This is the more unfortunate because the so-called

1. J. Cook, 'A Geometric Amphora and a Gold Band', *Journal of the British School at Athens*, 1951, p. 45; and, generally, W. Reichel, *Griechisches Goldrelief*, 1942; P. Jacobsthal, however, in *Greek Pins*, p. 18, dates my band from Khaniale Tekke to late eighth century.

2. Literally 'Lato towards the arch', presumably referring to a well-known bridge, since it is not likely that any vaulted building existed old enough to give a name to the port at so early a date.

agora, or 'market place', of Lato (Fig. 70) shows the town centre of a Greek city in its simplest and most primitive form. If you look forwards, its *prytaneion*, or 'presidency', may be regarded as the prototype of a French *hôtel-de-ville*, or of an English town hall, or, if you prefer to look backwards, as the descendant of a Minoan palace

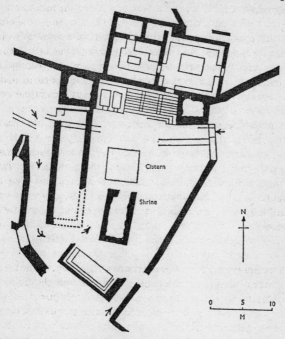

Fig. 70. Town centre, Lato

approached through its 'theatral area'. Immediately facing the steps of the last-named was a trapezoidal piazza with a cistern in the centre, and beyond that a small civic temple behind which was an *exhedra*, or shelter, open to the piazza along one of its long sides and perhaps serving, I suggest, as a dining-hall for the town councillors, like the *tholos*, the round shelter, at Athens. The municipal architect of Lato deserves to be complimented, first on his economic utilization of the very small space available, and secondly, on his ingenuity in using two towers of the inner town wall to provide an imposing entrance (almost in the manner of a Hittite *bit hilani*) for his *prytaneion*.

Dreros

A slightly similar civic centre exists at Dreros, near Neapolis, also placed on a saddle between two peaks, and containing a very early Temple of Apollo, a cistern, and a flight of steps and some rooms that may be regarded as the remnants of a *prytaneion*. The town centre as a whole is a less interesting than that of Lato, but the temple of Apollo deserves more attention. The temple consists of a single room orientated almost north-east to south-west. There is no obvious entrance; there might have been one at the north corner, which has been destroyed by a modern lime kiln, but so little remains of the north-east wall that the entrance might have been in the centre of it (Fig. 73).

In the centre of the temple lies a round base for a wooden column, and beyond it in the same line is a sunken hearth, of the type which the Greeks termed an *eschára*, in the form of a rectangular pit lined with stone slabs and filled with ashes. Beyond but more to one side lay a table of offerings. Against the western half of the south-west wall stood an altar of horns, reminding us of the far more famous horn altar at Delos around which Theseus and the Delian maidens were supposed to have danced the crane Dance (see p. 263) after his victorious return from Crete. In the west corner of the Dreros temple there was a ledge holding the bronze figures of Apollo and two attendant maidens (Plate 27 and Fig. 73). The temple itself does not seem to be older than the second quarter of the eighth century B.C., but it has a very odd, Sub-Minoan appearance with its central column, central hearth, table of offerings, and ledge at the inner end for the sacred images.

Prinias

A somewhat similar city existed on a hill overlooking and commanding what is at present the main north-south road linking Herakleion to the Mesara. The ancient name of this site is not known but it is now termed Prinias from the village immediately south of it. The ancient town was situated on a natural acropolis first occupied in Late Minoan III times, when it obviously formed a city of refuge, like Karphi or Vrokastro, for Minoan refugees forced up into the hills by the Greek invaders, but unlike those sites was not abandoned in the archaic Greek period.

The Italian Mission under Pernier excavated two temples here, of which the earlier and more important dated from about the middle of the seventh century B.C. It may be considered as a variety of the so-called *templum in antis*,[1] but, as at Dreros, there are several features that remind us not so much of an archaic Greek temple as of the little shrines of the Late Minoan III period, especially the ones at Hagia Triada and at Mallia. There was only one square pier between the *antae* of the porch (instead of the two columns normal in a *templum in antis*), and there were also apparently two wooden columns in line with this, in the middle of the *cella*, resting on low stone bases of the Minoan–Mycenaean type to support the cross-beams for a flat roof, and a central hearth between them. The central post of the entrance from the porch to the *cella* (which had an internal width of 5·94 m. against a length of only 9·75 m.) supported a stone transom with female figures carved in low relief on the soffit, and with an animal frieze on the front of the transom. Above the transom at each end were two seated female figures which helped to carry the true lintel. Fragments have also survived of low reliefs showing a procession of mounted spearmen, probably set up, not like an Ionic frieze between the architrave and the cornice, but as a parapet *sima* like the terracotta example with a procession of chariots from the temple of Dictaean Zeus at Palaikastro.[2]

THE LATE GEOMETRIC CULTURE

The Late Geometric period (770–735 B.C. according to Brock's dating) is chiefly represented by the contents of family chamber tombs excavated by the British School at Athens in the neighbourhood of Knosos and by some of the finds from Levi's excavations at Arkadhes.

The burials were normally cremations in ovoid *pithoi* with recti-

1. The term for the simplest form of Greek temple, entered by a porch with two columns between the *antae* or side-posts.
2. R. C. Bosanquet, 'Dicte and the Temples of Dictaean Zeus', *Annual of the British School at Athens*, 1943, p. 60, Plate 17.

linear geometric decoration in zones, and usually with conical lids adorned in the same manner. The smaller vases sometimes included small flasks decorated with concentric circles, either imported from Cyprus or more commonly emulations of such vases by the Cretan potters. Other imported vases include Late Geometric vases from Attica and the Cyclades, Protocorinthian *skyphoi*, and occasionally examples of *bucchero* looking rather like Lesbian *bucchero*. Almost identical limits are set by Miss Benton for her third class of cast bronze cauldrons with hollow rectangular or double T-shaped sections for their legs and with light flat handles (775–725 B.C.).[1] This is the period that witnessed the reign of Jeroboam II in Israel, and almost coincides with the reigns of Assurdan III, Assurnirari II, and Tiglath Pileser III in Assyria, and with the Bubastite dynasty's rule in Egypt.

To the second half of the eighth century B.C., perhaps, may be assigned an interesting series of small terracotta plaques found at Vavelloi, near Praisos, in the Eteo-Cretan country. These depict warriors like those of the bronze tripods, and, though they are inferior artistically, they may be used to supplement our idea of the art of this period because they are on a larger scale and preserve, in Mrs Dohan's words, 'the salient features of geometric art, a long neck devoid of modelling, a rope-like arm, a long sharp chin, an eye in the middle of the cheek, and a prominent crested helmet'. She proceeds to compare these figures with the bronze ship and figures from a tripod stand which is one of the dedications in the Idaean cave, and should belong to the end of the eighth century B.C.

THE CRETAN ORIENTALIZING CULTURE

The period from 735 to 680 B.C. is termed by Brock the early Orientalizing period. Tiglath Pileser III of Assyria (745–727 B.C.) had overrun Urartu and Syria and had carried off into captivity the two tribes of Israel and part of another one that lived east of the Jordan. Shalmaneser V (727–722 B.C.) had overrun another part of Palestine, though the actual capture of Samaria and the enslavement of its population was carried out after his death by his successor

1. S. Benton, 'The Evolution of the Tripod Lebes', *Annual of the British School at Athens*, 1935, p. 113.

Sargon II (722–705 B.C.). Sargon also captured Carchemish, the capital of the last surviving Neo-Hittite state of any importance, and Payne pointed out that, whereas the lions on Protocorinthian vases of the eighth century resemble those of Late Hittite sculpture, those on Corinthian vases of the seventh century resemble Assyrian forms. But culture is more spread by refugees than by conquering generals, and Sargon's conquests of Urartu and Damascus are reflected in the appearance of great bronze cauldrons with bull or griffin head handles of Vannic type, not only in Greece, but as far west as Etruria,[1] and of ivories of Syro-Phoenician type in the same countries.[2]

The early Orientalizing pottery of the graves round Knosos reflects these events, not by Assyrian vase shapes, but by the appearance of decorative motifs of oriental origin on native vase shapes. Some new shapes appear but they are borrowed from Cyprus or the Greek mainland not from Assyria, but the gay polychrome patterns including large cable patterns, the oriental tree of life, lotus garlands, and other stylized designs painted in the crusted technique in fugitive matt colours do remind us of the painted bricks of Assyria as found at Assur, and to a lesser degree at Nineveh. This polychrome work is confined to the neighbourhood of Knosos in Crete, though a few vases in a similar technique have been found near Athens. A favourite shape in this Knosian fabric was a *pithos* with cylindrical neck, ovoid body, and high inverted conical feet, derived, I suspect, from a shape popular in the Cyclades in the Early Bronze Age, revived in east Crete in the Middle Minoan III to Late Minoan I period, and again in the Cyclades and in Euboea in the Geometric styles of these districts. The lotus and bud garland, which recalls those of contemporary Rhodian vases, could have been borrowed from Assyria, since it appears sculptured in low relief on the floor slabs of Ashurbanipal's palace at Nineveh; but it appears in Assyria in this form only after Esarhaddon's conquest of Egypt, whereas it was an old Egyptian pattern, well known also in Syria, and had appeared among the ivories of Ahab's palace at Samaria.

1. K. R. Maxwell-Hyslop, 'Urartian Bronzes in Etruscan Tombs', *Iraq*, 1956, p. 150; P. Amandry, 'Chaudrons à Protomés de taureau en Orient et en Grèce', *The Aegean and the Near East, Studies presented to Hetty Goldman*, pp. 239–61.

2. R. D. Barnett, 'Early Greek and Oriental Ivories', *Journal of Hellenic Studies*, 1948.

The Dedications in the Idaean Cave

The mixture of oriental ideas was also reflected in a fine series of bronze shields with embossed and incised designs found by F. Halbherr and P. Orsi during their excavation of the Idaean Cave. More recently this material has been splendidly published by E. Kunze, who spread the dates of the shields over a hundred and fifty years, from the end of the ninth to the first half of the seventh century, and divided them into four groups without any very clear development from one to the other, though he noted the stylistic parallels between individual pieces and individual works of art outside Crete, such as the parallel between the earliest shields and the gold head-bands from the Dipylon cemetery at Athens. His dates have been criticized as too early by F. Matz and also by Miss Sylvia Benton, who has submitted a classification employing Kunze's numbers for the shields and relying for her chronology on synchronisms with the well-dated series of Protocorinthian and Corinthian vases.[1]

One Idaean shield belonged to the '*Herzsprung*' series (that derive their name from the type-site of the same name in North Germany). The characteristic of a '*Herzsprung*' shield is that its ornament of concentric bands of decoration is broken by indentations in the inner bands, sometimes even extending into the central boss of the shield. These indentations may be U-shaped or V-shaped in Western Europe, but only the latter kind have been found in Greece. Shields of this form were widely distributed in Europe during the eighth and seventh centuries B.C., and examples have been found in Ireland, Spain, Germany, Bohemia, Italy, and in the Aegean in the Idaean Cave, at Delphi, at the Samian Heraeum, and at Idalion in Cyprus. At least three of the Greek examples were found at Panhellenic sanctuaries, and the examples from other parts of Europe may well be related to the trade routes by which the Baltic amber was distributed. Cretan graves of this period do sometimes contain amber beads or jewels with amber inlay, though the amber in them seems to be less abundant than that of many Mycenaean graves in the Peloponnese. The Idaean shields, and the fragments of similar shields from Palaikastro, were not only decorated in an exotic manner, but seem too flimsy and too magnificent for ordinary warfare. They look like

1. S. Benton, 'The Date of the Cretan Shields', *Annual of the British School at Athens*. 1939, p. 52, and E. Kunze, *Kretische Bronzereliefs*, p. 1.

ceremonial shields, and, since the legendary Curetes were associated with both sanctuaries, it has been suggested that these shields were employed in a ritual dance or play celebrating the birth of the Cretan Zeus.

Oriental parallels are noted in an admirable article by H. Hencken who has remarked that the net-like treatment of the lion's mane on some Cretan shields, compared by Miss Benton to those of Early Corinthian lions, already occurred on the manes of Assyrian ivory lions apparently dating 'from the reign of Assur-nasir-pal II (884–859 B.C.)'[1] and that banded wigs like those of the sphinx on Shield 59 (one of Kunze's later group and dated about 650 by Miss Benton) are best paralleled by finds at Delphi in a hoard that can hardly be later than 700 B.C. Hencken also points out that the 'Hunt Shield' (of Kunze's earlier group and dated about 650 B.C. by Miss Benton) has oriental parallels in the ninth century rather than later (such as sculptures of Assur-nasir-pal II, Hittite reliefs from the Citadel Gate at Senjirli, and ivories from Ahab's palace at Samaria) though one feature in the design, the vulture on the back of the lion, recalls Assyrian examples of the eighth century (a relief from the reign of Tiglath-Pileser III (745–727 B.C.) and a bronze bowl from Nimrud from a palace restored by Sargon II (722–705 B.C.), with a Phoenician inscription on a doorway recording that the wing of the palace in which it was found contained plunder acquired during his campaign against Pisiris, King of Carchemish.

The round shields with concentric bands of ornament were only more splendid variations of the current war-shield which had replaced the indented shield typical of the Dipylon period, and of which we may see representations on the Hunt Shield from the Idaean Cave and on the bronze bands found in a tomb near Knosos, depicting a battle scene between bowmen in a chariot and foot soldiers.

The oriental influences discernible among the offerings in the Idaean Cave were not, however, confined to the bronzes (which were mainly a local Cretan product, despite their differences in style), but were also indicated by actual ivories imported from the Orient, including two single figures of naked goddesses of the Qadesh or

1. Here, however, Hencken was misled by Barnett's previous dating since later evidence suggests that most of the ivories were not earlier than Sargon II (714–700); compare R. D. Barnett, *The Nimrud Ivories*, pp. 133–5.

Astarte type native to Syria and Phoenicia, and a fragment of a group consisting originally of two figures back to back, supported by a column capital with a collar of leaves recalling the so-called Aeolic capital (of which the immediate prototypes were to be found in Syria and Palestine).[1]

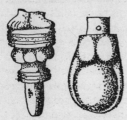

Fig. 71. Ivories from Idaean Cave

Nor were these ivory fragments the only imports from Syria and Phoenicia from the Idaean Cave. Two complete bronze bowls from that site and a fragmentary one from the Acropolis at Athens clearly resemble some of the bowls found in the north-west palace at Nimrud,[2] and appear to have been products of a Phoenician or south Syrian School of art very strongly influenced by Egyptian work, as is shown by the recurrence of such Egyptian works as the winged solar disk and the *uraeus* headdress of the sphinxes. Two other fragments of bowls from the Idaean Cave resembled an example from Idalion in Cyprus, and we may assume that some of these oriental influences were entering Crete by way of Cyprus and the Dodecanese.

The 'bronze gong' from the Idaean Cave, showing a god, attended by two wingless demons, wearing a curly Assyrian beard and brandishing two lions, may probably, as suggested by Herzfeld, have been imported from the neighbourhood of Lake Van.[3]

It appears, therefore, that the earliest bronzes from the Idaean Cave should be dated nearer to Miss Benton's 685 than to Kunze's 800, and perhaps ± 725 B.C. might be suggested as a possible date.[4] To

1. The oldest is an early tenth century example from Megiddo v; cf. W. F. Albright, *The Archaeology of Palestine*, 1949, p. 126.

2. Kunze, op. cit., p. 159, following H. Layard, *Nineveh and its Remains*, 1858, Plate 57.

3. See V. R. Maxwell-Hyslop, 'Urartian Bronzes in Etruscan Tombs', *Iraq*, 1956, p. 159; any Urartian bronzes should be dated not much before, and not much later than, 714 B.C., when Sargon II sacked Musasir the Urartian capital and when Urartian refugees must have been common all over the Levant.

4. This of course refers to the bronzes originally found, not to any found by Marinatos recently in his Mycenaean deposit.

Syro-Phoenician influence may be attributed some fragmentary figures in gold leaf which I found in the lower burnt stratum in the *dromos* of the destroyed *tholos* tomb containing the seventh-century treasure at Khaniale Tekke. The figures are in double gold leaf, which had presumably once covered a core of some less durable material such as wood.

The most complete figure is that of a man clad in a short tunic belted at the waist and carrying a ram on his shoulders. The upper half of a man or a woman (?) carrying a ram or lamb was found near, but this had been more damaged by the funeral fire. There were some other gold fragments in the same deposit that might have belonged to a larger figure. The oriental influence is very strong here, but I am convinced they are Cretan imitations of Phoenician work, not imports. They seem at least to be completely outside the currents of Dorian art, and may be products of that ill-defined school termed Eteo-Cretan by Langlotz and Matz, and more tentatively by Demargne.[1]

In the plastic arts, represented by sculpture, modelling, and carving in stone, clay, bronze, gold, and ivory, the Cretan school played a very important part in the eighth and early seventh centuries B.C., and its works are often characterized by the style which archaeologists have termed 'Dedalic', a word that is useful but rather ambiguous unless it is very carefully defined and employed. Greek folklore was hopelessly confused over the legendary craftsman Daedalus, who was said to have worked for King Minos before the days of the Trojan war, and a much later artist, the traditional founder of the Daedalid School, the man who, in the words of Diodorus, had been 'the first to give them [i.e. statues] open eyes and parted legs and outstretched arms, for before his time artists made statues with closed eyes and hands, hanging down and cleaving to the sides'.[2] Now if such an artist did really exist, and if Diodorus is not merely employing a legendary name to typify the work of a school, that artist must have lived in the eighth and not the fourteenth century B.C.

It is clear at least that when we encounter the word *Daedalidae*,

---

1. R. W. Hutchinson and J. Boardman, 'The Khaniale Tekke Tombs', *Annual of the British School at Athens*, 1954. P. Jacobstal, *Greek Pins*, p. 20, considers the more damaged figure to be a man, and that both are carrying calves; he considers that they come from the same workshop as the Idaean pendant.
2. *The Library of History*, Book IV, Chap. 76.

or 'sons of Daedalus', it has nothing to do with the legendary artist of the Bronze Age, but simply refers to this archaic school of Cretan artists, just as the term *Asclepiadae* does not mean the actual sons of Asclepius but simply the Coan school of doctors, and *Homeridae* not the sons of Homer but the school of epic bards and reciters. Archaeologists, however, have come to employ the term 'Dedalic' of the sculptural style characteristic of, though not confined to, Doric-speaking cities in the eighth and early seventh centuries B.C., and though 'Dedalic' in this sense does not coincide with the sense in which Pausanias might have understood it, it is nevertheless probable that most of the works, particularly the wooden statues which he

Fig. 72. Cretan imitation of Egyptian scarab, Khaniale Tekke

attributed to *Daedalidae* and to sculptors such as Dipoinis and Skylles, reputed as pupils or even sons of Daedalus, would be reckoned as 'Dedalic' in the modern sense also.

No major sculptures have survived in Crete from the Protogeometric and Geometric periods, and if such works ever existed they would have been made of wood. It is not likely that any great works of art have perished, since the bronze and clay figurines surviving from those periods, as illustrated by finds from the Psychro Cave, are chiefly but the degenerate offspring of the latest Minoan types, naturalistic in intention but feeble in execution.

The rise of the Proto-Dedalic style in Crete practically coincides with the reign of Esarhaddon in Assyria (681–669 B.C.), and with the destruction of the Phrygian power of Midas by the Cimmerians. In Egypt Psamtek had founded a new native dynasty in 661 and had enlisted Greek mercenaries in his service. This renewed contact between Greece and Egypt was reflected in a new influx into Crete of Egyptian scarabs and beads of faience, which appear at Knosos and elsewhere in tombs of the Late Orientalizing period (680–635 B.C.) and in some of the decorative motives that appear on the polychrome *pithoi* at Knosos. We also find imitations of scarabs with quasi-Egyptian designs, though whether any of these were made in Crete or whether they were all imported from Cyprus or Syria is more open to question. More important was the Egyptian influence on the rising school of sculpture. In Crete and other Doric-speaking districts, Egyptian influence is most obvious in the treatment of the hair which, on Dedalic statues, is often treated like a heavy Egyptian wig, and in the walking pose with the left foot forward. Egyptian influence was short-lived and is chiefly noticeable during the reign of Psamtek (661–609 B.C.), but it occurred at a very important period, when Greek sculpture was at a very impressionable stage of its development.

THE PROTO-DEDALIC STYLE IN SCULPTURE AND MODELLING

The forerunners of the new Doric style which we know by the name of 'Dedalic' are a small group of figurines appearing between 685 and 680 B.C. and lasting till 670 B.C. The style of this group has been termed by Jenkins Proto-Dedalic, and it already illustrates the dominant characteristics of the Dedalic style.

The head is regarded from a frontal point of view, almost as a mask, and has no proper profile view. Instead of the weak, round faces of the sub-Geometric heads, with their retiring foreheads, pointed retroussé noses, and a general lack of proportion between the features and the face, we now have a long, narrow, V-shaped face with a low but not retreating forehead, features roughly modelled but not out of proportion to the face, and a very pointed chin. The hair is generally treated like a perruque, suggesting Egyptian influence, but there are also examples of long braided locks.

Jenkins notes that the Cretan examples have a broader face and a more individual treatment of the eye, with strongly marked brows and two incised lines for the upper lids, distinguishing them from Proto-Dedalic heads from other parts of Greece. The new Dedalic style affected not only figurines of clay or bronze and jewellery, but also had a notable effect on a very ancient craft – the making of *pithoi* or large stone jars with moulded ornaments, a craft going back through the Minoan age into the Cretan Neolithic period. The *pithoi* of the Bronze Age or of the early Iron Age had for the most part been content with simple skeuomorphic patterns, such as imitations in relief of the rope slings with which such jars were moved.

The Dedalic artist (not only in Crete, but also in Boeotia, in the Peloponnese, and in the Cyclades) added friezes on the necks or shoulders of the *pithoi* with figures in relief – horses, warriors, sphinxes, lions, or chariots.[1]

Some of the Cretan relief *pithoi* are hard to date accurately but perhaps the one most likely to be contemporary with the Proto-Dedalic figures is a small group with figured decoration (modelled freehand and not in moulds); a fragment in this technique from the Psychro cave, depicting a leaping goat, is now in Oxford.

THE EARLY DEDALIC STYLE

The second, or early, Dedalic period (670–655 B.C.) was marked by the fact that the pointed chin was now rounded off; the face, though still long and narrow, was no longer V-shaped, but U-shaped.

Crete, or at least Dorian Crete as distinct from the Eteo-Cretan cities, seems to lag somewhat behind the other Dorian districts in artistic ability. There are plenty of Early Dedalic heads in the Herakleion Museum, and some in European or American museums from sites such as Vavelloi, but the quality of the work is very indifferent and sometimes individual features remind us of Sub-Geometric types.

The head is regularly too large for its body and the waist is about half-way down the figure (this applies not only to Cretan figures but also to Proto-Dedalic and Early Dedalic figurines in general). The hair is usually in a perruque. Both the figurines and the figures on the relief *pithoi* were cast in moulds.

1. Obviously cheap substitutes for bronze *pithoi*, such as the splendid example recently found at Vix in France.

One statuette in stone from Malles in eastern Crete seems to belong to this period. What remains of the head shows the long oval face and perruque hair, and the thin arms hanging from the shoulders may be paralleled by seated clay figures of Protocorinthian fabric. The Dedalic style reached its peak in the Middle Dedalic period (655–630 B.C.), which Jenkins divides into three stylistic phases.

THE MIDDLE DEDALIC STYLE, FIRST PHASE

In the first phase, though the faces of the heads are still oval with rounded chins, the increased breadth of the foreheads gives the general impression of a V-shaped countenance rather than the U-shape of Early Dedalic heads. The modelling is much better than before.

There is no Cretan free-standing statue of this period to set beside the Nikandra statue from Delos, but some stone reliefs and a number of clay statuettes illustrate the current fashion.

The most striking sculptures in stone are the procession of the horsemen and the goddesses from the soffit of the transom from Temple A at Prinias[1] (the two goddesses sitting above the transom are later, and must be due to a reconstruction of about 600 B.C.). To the same period should belong the middle of a relief of a running figure found at Knosos in the spring of A.D. 1936 in a mixed deposit, quite out of any sensible context, but obviously derived from a seventh-century work. The broken pottery heads of the period include an interesting example found at Knosos in the later strata above the Little Palace.

The finest bronze of this period (if it really is Cretan, as I think it is) is a bronze head from Olympia in the Karlsruhe collection – a very strong individual work, with its trapezoidal face, thin-lipped, faintly smiling mouth, and up-curving brows, but with the low flat cranium that is so characteristic of seventh-century heads in Crete; it is also one of the earliest, if not the earliest, example in Greece of hollow casting in bronze.

1. S. C. Casson, *The Technique of Early Greek Sculpture*, 1933, p. 66 and Fig. 22.

THE MIDDLE DEDALIC STYLE, SECOND PHASE

The second phase of the Middle Dedalic style (650–640 B.C.) is termed by Jenkins that of 'the Auxerre group', because its best and most characteristic work is the charming female statuette found at Auxerre in central France, now in the Louvre, and illustrated in almost every general book on Greek sculpture. The flat boardlike figure, with features and details cut out in the soft limestone by a knife, suggests the influence of woodcarving. Some archaic funeral monuments in the form of *stelai* from Prinias display an even simpler technique, since here all details are simply incised in the soft stone, giving an impression of low relief. These *stelai* are of some importance, since they are the earliest figured tombstones in Greece since Mycenaean times. The only complete *stele* surviving depicts a woman dressed in the Doric *peplos*, with a spindle in her hand, standing on a low base (suggesting that the dead woman is receiving the ritual of a consecrated heroine). The fragmentary *stelai* from the same district show either similar figures of women or else warriors dressed as heavy-armed hoplites, with large round shields and two spears. Sometimes the dead hero is approached by a much smaller figure, obviously representing a living member of his or her family. The clay figurines include a very interesting series excavated by the French at Anavlochos, a head from the Little Palace at Knosos, and another from Arkadhes.

Some moulds for clay plaques found in the Peloponnese at the Argive Heraeum and Perachora may have been Cretan work of this period.

To this period also may be assigned the splendid group of *sphyrélata* (or hammered) bronzes found in the little temple of Apollo at Dreros described on page 332 and regarded by Matz as Eteo-Cretan rather than Doric works of art.[1] There were indeed Eteo-Cretans at Dreros, as we know from a fragmentary inscription in their language found on that site, but Demargne is surely justified in claiming that these figures are closely related to the Middle Dedalic art of this period.

In the early seventh century, and indeed probably up to 650 B.C.,

1. Compare H. Megaw, 'Archaeology in Greece 1935–6,' *Journal of Hellenic Studies*, 1936, p. 152 and Fig. 11.

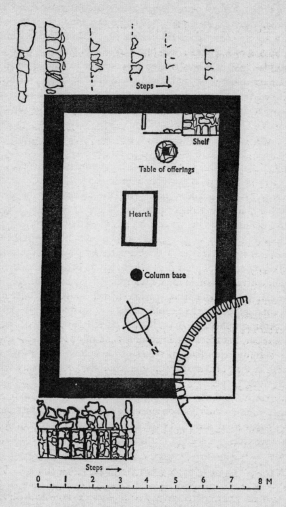

Steps →

Shelf

Table of offerings

Hearth

Column base

N

Steps →

0 1 2 3 4 5 6 7 8 M

Fig. 73. Temple of Apollo, Dreros

the *cire perdue* method of casting bronze was not practised in Greek lands and, while small statuettes could be cast solid, large statuettes or statues were executed by the *sphyrélaton*, or hammered, technique whereby a wooden statue was first carved and then covered with bronze plating which was riveted together, or in later times fixed with a hard solder (Plate 27). Gold could also be employed for the plates instead of bronze and was used for the colossal gold statue of Zeus dedicated at Olympia by Periander, the famous tyrant of Corinth.

THE MIDDLE DEDALIC STYLE, THIRD PHASE

The third phase of the Middle Dedalic Sculpture (640–630 B.C.) was christened by Jenkins 'the Mycenae group', from the fine Dedalic metope block found at Mycenae.[1] The faces on heads of this period are shorter and squarer than that of the 'Lady of Auxerre', and the cheeks are almost parallel. A fine bronze statuette of a youth found at Delphi is probably a Cretan work of this period. Among the clay heads of this period was one with very carefully painted facial details, modelled on a clay pilgrim flask which, up to 1939, was in Berlin.[2] The painted vases contemporary with these Dedalic heads are those of Brock's Late Orientalizing period, which he dates between 680 and 630 B.C. In the chamber tombs of the Knosos district polychrome ovoid *pithoi* continue. At Arkadhes the polychrome *pithoi* of Knosos did not occur, but there were occasional and more tentative attempts at polychromy reminding us rather of the colouring of east Greek vases rather than of Assyrian painting, combined occasionally with a motif or vase shape.

One curious motif, consisting of pot-hook spirals ending in panthers' heads, occurs both on a painted *pyxis* from Arkadhes and on a relief *pithos* from Kastelli Pedhiadhos, suggesting that their workshops were closely related (if not identical).

LATE ORIENTALIZING POTTERY

The painted vases contemporary with these Proto-Dedalic, Early Dedalic, and Late Dedalic heads is that of Brock's Late Orientalizing

1. A. J. B. Wace, *Mycenae*, 1949, Plate 107; Jenkins, loc. cit., Plate VI, No. 7.
2. Jenkins, op. cit., Plate VI, No. 6.

period, which he dates between 680 and 630 B.C. In the chamber tombs at Knosos the polychrome ovoid *pithoi* continue, and the smaller vases with decorations simply on the dark varnish, consisting of a fusion of geometric and oriental ornaments, is also paralleled on other sites (though polychrome vases are still confined to the district of Knosos).

Vases were also imported and imitated from Cyprus, Corinth, the Cyclades, and Athens. At Arkadhes, in the Pedhiadha, Levi excavated an interesting series of tombs of this period.[1] The vases here tended to be more rustic and provincial than those of Knosos, though Demargne's verdict that 'some of the products are often barbarous' seems unduly severe. I should prefer personally to say that the Arkadhes vases were the products of a very lively and original peasant art, often quite prolific in ideas and fancies, less sophisticated than those of Knosos but also more original.

The more common shapes include ovoid *pithoi*, *hydriae*, tall *pyxides*, jugs of various Cypriote shapes, and cups. A tankard from tomb R is an odd combination of a Sub-Minoan or Sub-Mycenaean shape, with an orientalizing decoration consisting of a large cable band. Some jugs have the plastic head of a horse or ass issuing from the shoulder. One vase in Oxford is shaped like two owls back to back (influenced by the owl-shaped vases in the white-shaved ware of Cyprus). Some jugs were influenced by examples from Rhodes or some other east Greek site.

Relief Pithoi

The Early and Late Orientalizing periods were marked by a fine series of *pithoi* with decoration in relief. Making store-jars with rope-work or medallions in relief was an old Minoan fashion which perhaps never entirely died out, but the relief *pithoi* of the eighth to sixth centuries B.C. were characterized by oriental motifs such as sphinxes, affronted lions, and cable patterns on the main zones of ornament on the neck and shoulders. Sometimes horses appear instead of lions, and a fine *pithos* from Prinias shows the *Pótnia Therón*, or Lady of the Beasts, flanked by two horses, though, as Dunbabin remarks, 'the attitude and proportions of these suggest that they might have begun

1. D. Levi, 'Excavations at Arkadhes', *Liverpool Annals*, 1905; one vase clearly imitates an Urartian bronze cauldron; compare R. D. Barnett, *The Aegean and the Near East*, Plate XX, No. 2.

life as lions, and the long muscular raised forelegs look like lion's legs'.

Thrapsanos, in the Pedhiadha, is the chief manufacturing centre for such large jars in modern times, and I suspect that the archaic centre was not very far from that village. Of the sites that have produced archaic relief *pithoi* or fragments of them, Afrati, Gonies, Astritsi, and Kastelli Pedhiadhos are all in the Pedhiadha area, while Knosos, Arkhanes, Prinias, Phaistos, and Embaros have easy access to it. A more eastern centre may have supplied Dreros, Anavlochos, Praisos, and Lithinais, but Plati could equally well have imported from the Pedhiadha. Dunbabin, however, has plausibly argued that the potters of the archaic *pithoi* may have worked in their own villages and travelled to work in other parts of the island in the summer, like the modern potters of Thrapsanos and Margaritais.

ENGRAVED SEAL-STONES

To the combined Minoan-Mycenaean traditions of the Eteo-Cretans and of the descendants of Mycenaean colonists we may perhaps attribute the persistence in Crete of the art of gem engraving. The art of writing may have died, or become very rare, before the end of the Bronze Age.[1] There was apparently no survival of the Bronze Age scripts such as occurred on Cyprus. The rare Eteo-Cretan inscriptions surviving from the classical period were all cut in Greek characters. Yet this very decay of literacy on the island may have helped to preserve the art of gem-cutting since seals always have an enhanced importance in an illiterate or semi-literate community. Unfortunately the Cretan seal-stones of the period between 1050 and 700 B.C. have not been adequately studied or published. In the nineteenth century A.D. most seals of this period, if not betraying obvious signs of connexion with Cyprus, Etruria, Phoenicia, Egypt, or Mesopotamia, were loosely grouped together as 'Melian' or 'Island' gems, very unsatisfactory titles, though many seals did indeed come from the islands and some even actually from Melos. These seals were regularly cut in soft stones, usually steatite. Many were poorly executed, but the best examples are of some merit and often remind us of

1. Compare M. Bowra, *Homer and his Forerunners* (Andrew Lang Lecture, 1955): 'There is no evidence that the Mycenaean script continued anywhere in Greece after *c.* 1200.'

Minoan or Mycenaean gems, either by the technique of their cutting with wheel and drill, or by the reproduction of old Aegean motifs, such as the *agrimi*, or the lion seizing a bull, or by the '*tête bèche*' arrangement of foreparts of animals. Watson has shown how the use of the drill in cutting such stones migrated from the Aegean to Mesopotamia and back again. Knowledge of the drill did not die out, but the degrees in which drill, saw, or graver were used varied with the fashions of individual schools. Sometimes Aegean and Hellenic elements are so blended that a seal is hard to date. Thus an engraved gem with two walking mules and a line of vertical chevrons was classified by Forsdyke as Late Minoan III B, but as Geometric by Casson, and the chevrons might belong to either period; Evans, however, assigned it to the Hellenic period, and I think correctly so, since the treatment of the mules resembles that on black-figured vases rather than that on Mycenaean *cratera*.

POST-DEDALIC ART

The last twenty years of the seventh century and the first twenty years of the sixth century B.C. were marked by sculptures, figurines, and relief *pithoi* transitional between the Dedalic art and the fully developed archaic style of the sixth century, and this transitional group has been christened Post-Dedalic. To this group we may plausibly assign the two seated goddesses perched above the transom of the door of Temple A at Prinias. These figures have been called 'Dedalic', but they are clearly later than the cavalry relief of the figures sculptured on the transom of the same temple, and more developed in style than the Auxerre goddess or the statue from Eleutherna; presumably the seated goddesses were executed in a later restoration of the temple.

To the same Post-Dedalic group belongs also a bronze figure of a *kriophóros*, or a man carrying a ram, dated 650 by Kunze and Neugebauer, but by Demargne more reasonably dated to 600 B.C., and till 1939 in the Museum in Berlin. The general conception of a *kriophóros*, however, had not altered so very much since the Late Minoan I period.

We cannot say very much about the pottery of the Post-Dedalic period in Crete because the rich cemeteries of the Knosos–Fortetsa area, which had provided such abundant material for the period between 950 and 630 B.C., quickly peter out. Was there another severe earthquake, or did Knosos suffer from a political disaster, or is the deficiency merely due to the fact that we have not yet discovered the cemeteries of the period after 630 B.C.? In other parts of the island the absence of cemeteries may be only apparent, but the immediate neighbourhood of Knosos has been so thoroughly tested by excavations and trial pits that it seems strange that so few tombs of the sixth and fifth centuries have been discovered. The district was not altogether deserted; sculptures, inscriptions, vases, and coins of this period do turn up, but no Greek buildings of any importance have been uncovered, though Roman buildings abound. A certain number of Attic black-figured and red-figured vases were imported, but the local potters seem to have produced nothing but domestic wares. The population must, I think, have declined in number, and a curious twilight descended on Crete which, in the classical period, seems to have acted mainly as a recruiting ground for bowmen and slingers for the richer cities of the mainland. The best Cretan artists emigrated, the sculptors Dipoinis and Skyllis to the Peloponnese, and the architects Chersiphron and Metagenes from Knosos to Ionia.

THE CRETAN TWILIGHT

A story in Book III of Herodotus's history provides a 'news flash' from Crete in the sixth century B.C. We hear how some Samian adventurers, who had failed to overthrow their local tyrant Polykrates, had seized the island of Siphnos and, when they had been evicted from that, had sailed to western Crete, expelled the Zakynthians who were occupying the site of Kydonia, and refounded that place as a Samian city. The Samians enjoyed their ill-gotten gains for five years, during which time they had founded a temple, later to become famous, in honour of the Minoan goddess Diktynna, but in the sixth year they were defeated by the Aeginetans, who captured the city and enslaved all its inhabitants, Samians and Cretans alike.

This is an isolated story, and an incomplete one too, but if these events were at all typical of what was happening in other parts of the island, we can perhaps understand the paucity of Cretan buildings and works of art attributable to the sixth and fifth centuries B.C.

Praisos, indeed, kept the Eteo-Cretan flag flying for a while and, in the time of which the historian Staphylos wrote, still controlled ports on both the north and the south sides of the island[1] and probably also the district round Eleia (Palaikastro) in the far east. But she gradually lost these outlying possessions to her Dorian enemies at Hierapytna and Itanos, and was finally completely destroyed by them about 144 B.C.

To the Eteo-Cretan twilight of the early sixth century we may perhaps attribute such works as the terracotta chariot *sima* from the Temple of Dictaean Zeus at Palaikastro and the curious fragment of a plate from Praisos with a splendid black-figure group of Herakles or some such hero grappling with a sea monster, or possibly Peleus wooing Thetis, on one side and a very dull horseman (surely by another painter) on the other.

Later still, probably about 560 B.C., is the fine clay head and shoulders of a clay statue from Praisos of a young god, perhaps Apollo, perhaps the young Cretan Velchanos, the latest surviving work of any importance from the Eteo-Cretan school of modelling, and here we may end our account of the prehistory of the island, for Dorian Crete in the classical period was a very different place, less cultured and less comfortable, a motherland of warriors, and sometimes of pirates, rather than of artists and architects.

1. Staphylos's own date has been set rather doubtfully about 300 B.C. I should prefer to date Staphylos much earlier, but since he was born at Naucratis he can hardly be earlier than the sixth century B.C.

BIBLIOGRAPHY
AND INDEX

BIBLIOGRAPHY

GENERAL

These references will not always be repeated after the individual chapters but most of them are relevant to all the chapters.

Aberg, N., *Die Bronzezeitliche und Früheisenzeitliche Chronologie*, III and IV, 1933.

Baikie, J. M., *Sea-Kings of Crete*, 1921.

Bossert, H. T., *The Art of Ancient Crete*, 1937.

Burrows, R. M., *Excavations in Crete*, 1908.

Childe, V. G., *The Dawn of European Archaeology*, 5th ed., 1950.

Cottrell, L., *The Bull of Minos*, 1956.

Demargne, P., *La Crète dédalique*, 1947.

Dussaud, R., *Les Civilisations préhelléniques dans le bassin de la Mer Égée*. 2nd ed., 1914.

Elliadi, M. N., *Crete Past and Present*, 1933.

Evans, A. J., *The Palace of Minos*, Vol. I, 1921–Vol. v, 1935.
   Scripta Minoa, I, 1909.

Evans, A. J., and Myres, J. L., *Scripta Minoa*, II, 1952.

Fimmen, D., and Reisinger, *Die Kretisch-Mykenische Kunst* (chiefly written by Fimmen in 1915), 1926.

Glotz, G., *La Civilisation minoenne*, 1921.

Hall, H. R., *Ancient History of the Near East*, 11th ed., 1942.
   The Civilization of Greece in the Bronze Age, 1928.

Hutchinson, R. W., 'Minoan Chronology Reviewed', *Antiquity*, 1954, p. 155.

Kantor, H. J., 'The Aegean and the Orient in the Second Millennium B.C.', *American Journal of Archaeology*, 1947.

Mackenzie, D., 'Cretan Palaces', *Annual of the British School at Athens*, 1904–8.

Matz, F., *Die Frühkretischen Siegel*, 1928.

Montelius, O., *La Grèce préclassique*, 1928.

Pendlebury, J. D. S., *The Archaeology of Crete*, 1939 (easily the best general account of the Minoan culture).

Schaeffer, C. F. A., *Stratigraphie comparée et chronologie de l'Asie orientale*, 1947.

Snijder, G. A., *Die Kretische Kunst*, 1936.

CHAPTER I: THE ISLAND OF CRETE

Allbaugh, L. G., *Crete (A Case Study of an Undeveloped Area)*, 1953.

Bate, Dorothea, *Geological Magazine*, May 1905, p. 196.

Chalikiopoulos, L., *Die Halbinsel Sitia*, 1903.

Elliadi, M. N., *Crete, Past and Present*, 1933.

Lehmann, H., *Geographische Zeitung*, 1939, p. 212.

Marinatos, S., 'The Volcanic Destruction of Minoan Crete', *Antiquity*, December 1939.

Pashley, R., *Travels in Crete*, 1837.

Pauly-Wissowa-Kroll, *Realenzyklopädie der klassischen Altertumswissenschaft*, article on Crete, 1922.

Pendlebury, J. D. S., *The Archaeology of Crete*, 1939 (especially for surface topography routes and distribution of sites).

Sharpe, R. F., *European Animals: Their Geological History and Geographical Distribution*, 1890.

Rawlin, V., *Description physique de l'île de Crète*, 1869.

Renz, C., 'Progress of the Geological Exploration', *A.J.S.*, 1947, p. 175.

Schaeffer, C. F. A., *Stratigraphie comparée et chronologie de l'Asie occidentale*, 1948.

Spratt, T. A. B., *Travels and Researches in Crete*, 1865.

Thomson, J. O., *History of Ancient Geography*, 1948.

Tournefort, J. P. de, *Voyage au Levant*, 1717.

Trevor Battye, A., *Camping in Crete*, 1913.

Vickery, K. F., 'Food in Early Greece', *Illinois Studies in the Social Sciences*, Vol. xx, No. 3, 1952 (an invaluable monograph).

For further works on the island, see also the bibliography given by Xan Fielding in *The Stronghold* (1953), a most readable account of the Sphakia district.

CHAPTER 2: THE STONE AGE

Evans, A. J., *The Palace of Minos*, I, 1921, p. 1–32.

Franchet, L., 'Rapport sur une mission', *Nouvelles archives des missions scientifiques*, 1911.

Furness, A., 'The Neolithic Pottery of Knosos', *Annual of the British School at Athens*, 1953.

Hutchinson, R. W., 'Cretan Neolithic Figurines', *Ipek*, 1938, p. 50.

Matz, F. (ed.), *Forschungen auf Kreta*, 1942, article by U. Jantzen.

Muller, V., *Frühe Plastik*, 1929, p. 1–6.

Pendlebury, J. D. S., *The Archaeology of Crete*, 1939, Chap. II.

Pernier, L., *Il Palazzo di Festos*, I, 1932, pp. 67, 105.

Schachermeyr, F., *Die Ältesten Kulturen Griechenlands*, 1955.

Weinberg, S., 'Neolithic Figurines and Aegean Inter-relations', *American Journal of Archaeology*, 1951, p. 121.

'The Relative Chronology of the Aegean', *Relative Chronologies in Old World Archaeology* (ed. R. W. Ehrich), 1954.

CHAPTER 3: THE CRETAN PEOPLES, LANGUAGES, AND SCRIPTS

Physical Characteristics of the Cretans

Angell, J. L., 'A Racial Analysis of the Ancient Greeks', *American Journal of Physical Anthropology*, 1944, pp. 329–76.

Buxton, L. H. D., 'The Inhabitants of the Eastern Mediterranean', *Biometrika*, 1913, p. 92.

Duckworth, W. L. H., 'Human Remains at Hagios Nikolaos', *Annual of the British School at Athens*, 1903.

    'Ossuaries at Roussolakkos', *British Association Reports*, 1903, 1910, 1912.

Evans, A. J., 'The Prehistoric Tombs of Knossos', *Archaeologia*, 1905.

    'The Tomb of the Double Axes', *Archaeologia*, 1911.

Hammond, N. G. L., 'Epirus and the Dorian Invasion', *Annual of the British School at Athens*, 1933, p. 131.

Hawes, C. H., 'Some Dorian Descendants', *Annual of the British School at Athens*, 1903, 1910.

Hawes, C. H., and Duckworth, W. L. H., *Proceedings of the British Academy*, 1908, 1909, 1910, 1912.

Koumaris, J., 'Notes anthropologiques sur quelques crânes', *Revue anthropologique*, 1934, p. 245.

Luschan, F. von, 'Beiträge zur Anthropologie von Kreta', *Zeitschrift für Ethnologie*, 1913, pp. 320–52.

Senyurek, M., 'A Short Review, etc.', Appendix I, *Early Anatolia*, by Seton Lloyd, 1956.

Sergi, A., *The Mediterranean Race*, 1901.

Xanthoudides, S., *Vaulted Tombs of the Mesara*, 1924.

Languages and Scripts

Beattie, A. J., 'Mr Ventris's Decipherment of the Minoan Linear B Script', *Journal of Hellenic Studies*, 1956, p. 1.

Bennett, E. L., *A Minoan Linear B Index*, 1952.

    'Fractional Quantities in Minoan Book-keeping', *American Journal of Archaeology*, 1950.

    The Pylos Tablets, 1951 and 1955.

    'The Mycenae Tablets', reprinted from *The Proceedings of the American Philosophical Society*, 1953.

Blegen, C., 'An inscribed tablet from Pylos', *Ephemeris Archaiologiki*, 1955.

Bosanquet, R. C., 'Inscriptions from Praesos', *Annual of the British School at Athens*, 1910, p. 258.

Caratelli, Pugliese G., 'Le Iscrizione Preellenici di Hagia Triada in Creta e della Grecia Peninsolaria', *Annuario*, 1945.

Chadwick, J., 'Greek Records in the Minoan Script', *Antiquity*, 1953. *The Decipherment of Linear B*, 1958 (Penguin Books, 1961).

Chapouthier, F., *Les Écritures minoennes au palais de Mallia*, 1930.

Conway, R. J., 'The Pre-Hellenic Inscriptions of Praesos', *Annual of the British School at Athens*, 1902, p. 125.

Cowley, A. E., 'A Note on Minoan Writing', *Essays in Aegean Archaeology*, 1927.

Daniel, J. F., 'Prolegomena to the Cypro-Minoan Script', *American Journal of Archaeology*, 1945.

Dow, S., 'Minoan Writing', *American Journal of Archaeology*, 1954.

Evans, A. J., *Cretan Pictographs and Pre-Phoenician Script*, 1895 (originally published in *Journal of Hellenic Studies*).

Evans, A. J., and Myres, J. L., *Scripta Minoa*, I–III, 1921.

Georgiev, V., *État actuel des inscriptions créto-mycéniennes*, 1954. *Lexique des inscriptions créto-mycéniennes*, 1955. (Both in Russian but with French summaries.)

Gordon, C. H., 'Notes on Minoan Linear A', *Antiquity*, September 1957, p. 124.

Grumach, E., etc. *Minoicae*. Essays dedicated to J. Sundwall, Berlin, 1958.

Hencken, H., *Indo-European Languages and Archaeology*, 1955.

Kober, A. J., 'The Minoan Scripts: Fact and Theory', *American Journal of Archaeology*, 1948.

Kretschmer, P. K., 'Die Ältesten Sprachschichten auf Kreta', *Glotta*, 1931.

Mann, S. E., 'Mycenaean and Indo-European', *Man*, February 1956. 'Documents in Mycenaean Greek', *Man*, November 1957

Meriggi, P., *Glossario miceneo* (in Italian), 1957. 'Relations entre le Minoen B, le Minoen A', *Études mycéniennes*, 1956.

Minos: A journal published by the University of Salamanca devoted to the study of Aegean Scripts with articles in English, French, German, and Spanish, 1951– .

Nuño, B. Gaya, *Lexicon Creticum* (in Spanish), 1953.

Palmer, L. R., *Achaeans and Indo-Europeans* (Andrew Lang lecture), 1955.

Pernier, L., 'Il disco di Festos', *Ausonia*, 1909.

Peruzzi, E., 'Bibliography of Linear A Script', *Minos*, 1957, p. 99.

Platon, N., Reviews in *Kretika Chronika* (in modern Greek), 1954.

Sundwall, J., 'Die Kretische Linearschrift', Jahrbuch des archäologischen Instituts, XXX. 'Der Ursprung des Kretischen Schrift', *Acta Academiae Abo*, 1920.

Treweek, A. P., 'Chain Reaction or House of Cards', *Institute of Classical Studies Bulletin*, 1957, p. 10.

Ventris, M. 'A Note on Decipherment Methods', *Antiquity*, 1953.

Ventris, M., and Chadwick, J., *Documents in Mycenaean Greek*, 1956. 'Evidence for Greek Dialect', *Journal of Hellenic Studies*, 1953.

Webster, T. B. L., 'Mycenaean Records, a Review', *Antiquity*, 1957.

CHAPTER 4: THE MINOAN MARINE, TRADE, AND COMMUNICATIONS

Barnett, R. D., 'Early Shipping in the Near East', *Antiquity*, 1958.

Casson, L., 'Fore and Aft Sails in the Ancient World', *Mariners' Mirror*, February 1956.

Childe, V. G., 'The First Waggons and Carts', *Proceedings of the Prehistoric Society*, 1951, p. 177.

Clark, G. D., 'Horses and Battle-axes', *Antiquity*, 1941, p. 56.

Clowes, G. S. L., *Sailing Ships*, Part I, reprinted 1951.

Cook, J. M., 'Pelino Omoioma Mykenaikon Phoreion', *Kretika Chronika* (in modern Greek), 1955, p. 152.

Evans, A. J., 'The Early Nilotic Libyan and Egyptian Relations with Minoan Crete', *Journal of the Royal Anthropological Institute*, 1927.

Faulkner, R. O., 'Egyptian Seagoing Ships', *Journal of Egyptian Archaeology*, 1941.

Furumark, A., 'The Settlement at Ialysus and Early Aegean History', *Opuscula Archaeologica*, 1950.

Hood, M. S. F., 'A Mycenaean Cavalryman', *Annual of the British School at Athens*, 1953, p 89, Figs. 47, 48.

Hyde, W. W., *Ancient Greek Mariners*, 1947 (with good bibliography).

Kantor, H., 'The Aegean and the Orient in the Second Millennium B.C.', *American Journal of Archaeology*, 1947, pp. 1–68.

Kirk, G., 'Ships on Geometric Vases', *Annual of the British School at Athens*, 1949, p. 23.

Lorimer, H. L., *Homer and the Monuments*, 1950, pp. 307–28.

Marinatos, S., 'La Marine créto-mycénienne' *Bull. Corr. Hell.*, 1933, p. 170 f. (still the best general account of this subject).

Ormerod, H. A., *Piracy in the Ancient World*, 1924.

Pendlebury, J. D. S., 'Egypt and the Aegean', *Studies Presented to David Moore Robinson*, Vol. I, 1951, p. 184.

Piggott, S., *Prehistoric India*, 1950, pp. 273–82.

Ridgeway, W., *The Origin and Influence of the Thoroughbred Horse*, 1905.

Rose, J. Holland, *The Mediterranean in the Ancient World*, 1924.

Starr, C. G., 'The Myth of the Minoan Thalassocracy', *Historia*, 1955, pp. 282–91.

Taylour, W., *Mycenaean Pottery in Italy*, 1958.

Vercoutter, J., *Essai sur les relations entre Égyptiens et Préhellènes*, 1954.

Wainwright, G. A., 'Asiatic Keftiu', *American Journal of Archaeology*, 1952, p. 196.

CHAPTER 5: MINOAN ART

Alexiou, S., 'Protominoikai Taphai', *Kretika Chronika*, 1951, p. 275.

    'Nea Stoicheia dhia ten Ysteran Aigaiaken Chronologian', *Kretika Chronika*, 1952, as summarized in *Antiquity*, 1953, p. 183.

    'The Boar's Tusk Helmet', *Antiquity*, 1954, p. 214.

BIBLIOGRAPHY

Banti, L., *Il Palazzo minoico di Festos*, Vol. ii, 1951.

    'Il Sentimento della natura nell'arte minoica e micenea', *Essays dedicated to A. Keramopoullos*, 1953.

    'Myth in Pre-Classical Art', *American Journal of Archaeology*, October 1954.

Bosanquet, R. C., and others, *Unpublished objects from Palaikastro*, 1923.

Bossert, H. T., *The Art of Ancient Crete*, 1937.

Chapouthier, F., and others, 'Fouilles de Mallia', *Études crétoises*, 1922.

Childe, V. G., *The Dawn of European Civilization*, 5th ed., 1950.

Childe, V. G., and others, *Essays in Aegean Archaeology Presented to Sir Arthur Evans*, 1927.

Dawkins, R. M., and Laistner, M. L. W., 'The Excavation at the Kamares Cave in Crete', *Annual of the British School at Athens*, 1913, p. 1.

Dunbabin, T. J., 'Antiquities of Amari', *Annual of the British School at Athens*, 1947, p. 184.

Evans, A. J., *The Palace of Minos*, 1921.

    'The Prehistoric Tombs of Knossos', *Archaeologia*, 1901.

    'The Tomb of the Double Axes, etc', *Archaeologia*, 1907.

Fimmen, D., *Die Kretisch-Mykenische Kultur*, 1924.

Forsdyke, E. J., *Minoan Art* (Hertz Lecture to the British Academy), 1929.

Frankfort, H., *Studies in Early Pottery of the Near East*, Part ii, 1927.

Hall, E. H., 'Excavations in Eastern Crete, Sphoungaras', *University of Pennsylvania Anthrop. Pub.*, 1910.

    The Decorative Art of Crete in the Bronze Age, 1907.

Hawes, C. H., *Crete, The Forerunner of Greece*, 1909.

Hawes, H. Boyd, and others, *Gournia, Vasiliki, and other Prehistoric Sites*, 1908.

Hazzidakis, J., *Tylissos à l'époque minoenne*, 1921.

    Les Villas minoennes de Tylissos, 1934.

Hutchinson, R. W., 'Prehistoric Town Planning in Crete', *The Town Planning Review*, October 1950.

    'Minoan Chronology Reviewed', *Antiquity*, 1953.

Heaton, N., 'On the Nature and Method, etc.', *Tiryns*, 1912, p. 211.

Hutchinson, R. W., Eccles, E., and Benton, S., 'Unpublished Objects at Palaikastro and Praesos', *Annual of the British School at Athens*, 1940.

Kantor, H., *The Aegean and the Orient in the Second Millennium B.C.*, 1947.

Karo, G., *Die Schachtgräber von Mykenae*, 1930–3.

Levi, D., Reports in *Illustrated London News*, 19 January 1954, 12 December 1953, 29 September and 6 October 1956.

Maraghiannis, G., and Karo, G., *Antiquités crétoises*, 1908–15.

Marinatos, S., 'Protominoikos Taphos . . . Krasi', *Archaiologikon Deltion*, 1932, p. 102.

    Crete and Mycenae, 1960

Matz, F., *Die Frühkretische Siegel*, 1928.

    'Torsion', *Abhandlungen der Akademie der Wissenschaften und der Literatur, Mainz*, 1951.

Pendlebury, J. D. S., *The Archaeology of Crete*, 1939.

    Guide to the Palace of Minos, 2nd ed., 1954.

Pendlebury, J. D. S., and others, 'Excavations in Lasithi', *Annual of the British School at Athens*, 1906.

'Guide to the Stratigraphic Museum', *Annual of the British School at Athens*, 1931.

Pernier, L., and Banti, L., *Il Palazzo di Festos*, 1935–51.

Seager, R. B., 'Vasiliki', *Transactions of Pennsylvania University*, 1907, p. 218.

'Excavations in the Island of Pseira', *Anthrop. Publications Pennsylvania University*, 1910.

Explorations in the Island of Mochlos, 1912.

Snijder, G. A., *Kretische Kunst*, 1936.

Taramelli, A., 'Ricerche archeologiche cretesi', *Mon. Ant.*,1899, pp. 289–446.

Vandier, J., 'À propos d'un dépôt de provenance asiatique trouvé à Tod', *Syria*, 1937, p. 174.

Wace, A. J. B., *A Cretan Statuette in the Fitzwilliam Museum*, 1927.

Xanthoudides, S., *Vaulted Tombs of the Mesara*, 1924.

Xenaki-Sakellariou, A., 'La Représentation du casque en dents de sanglier', *Bulletin de Correspondence Hellénique*, 1953, p. 46.

CHAPTER 6: THE EARLY MINOAN PERIOD

Aberg, N., *Bronzezeitliche und Früheisenzeitliche Chronologie*, IV, 1933.

Alexiou, S., 'Protominoikai Taphai para to Kanli Kastelli, Herakleion', *Kretika Chronika*, 1951, p. 275.

Bosanquet, R. C., *Unpublished Objects from Palaikastro*, 1923.

Ehrich, R. W., and others, *Relative Chronologies in Old World Archeology*, 1954.

Evans, A. J., *The Palace of Minos* (especially Vol. I), 1921.

Frankfort, H., *Studies in Early Pottery*, Part II, 1927.

Furness, A., 'Some Early Pottery of Samos, etc.', *Proceedings of the Prehistoric Society*, 1957, p. 173.

Hall, E. H., *Excavations in Eastern Crete, Sphoungaras*, 1910.

Hawes, H. Boyd, *Gournia*, 1908.

Hazzidakis, J., 'An Early Minoan Cave at Arkalokhori,' *Annual of the British School at Athens*, 1913, p. 35.

Hutchinson, R. W., 'Minoan Chronology Reviewed' (with bibliographical references), *Antiquity*, 1954, p. 155.

Marinatos, S., 'Protominoikos Tholotos Taphos para to Khorion Krasi Pedhiadhos', *Archaiologikon Deltion*, 1932, p. 112.

Matz, F., *Frühkretische Siegel*, 1928.

'Die Agais', *Handbuch der Archäologie*, 1950, p. 227.

'Torsion', *Abhandlungen der Akademie der Wissenschaften und der Literatur*, 1951, p. 9.

Mellaart, J., 'Preliminary Report ... Southern Turkey', *Anatolian Studies*, 1954, p. 75.

Pendlebury, J. D. S., *The Archaeology of Crete* (Chap. II B), 1939.

Pernier, L., and Banti, L., *Il Palazzo di Festos*, I, 1935; II, 1951.

BIBLIOGRAPHY

Schachermeyr, F., 'Vorbericht über eine Expedition nach Ostkreta', *Archaeologischer Anzeiger*, 1938, p. 465.

Seager, R. B., *Excavations on the Island of Pseira*, 1912.
> *Explorations in the Island of Mochlos*, 1912.
> 'The Cemetery of Pachyammos', *Anthro. Pub.*, 1916.
> 'Vasiliki', *Trans. Pennsylvania University*, 1907, p. 218; 1912, p. 118.

Xanthoudides, S., *Vaulted Tombs of the Mesara*, 1924.

CHAPTER 7: THE MIDDLE MINOAN PERIOD

Aberg, N., *Bronzezeitliche und Früheisenzeitliche Chronologie*, IV, 1933

Banti, L., 'Cronologia e Ceramica del Palazzo Minoico di Festos', *Annuario*, 1940.

Bosanquet, R. C., *Unpublished Objects From Palaikastro*, 1923.

Bossert, H., *The Art of Ancient Crete*, 1937.

Chapouthier, F., 'Fouilles de Mallia', *Études crétoises*, 1922.

Demargne, P., 'Crète et Orient au temps d'Hammourabi', *Revue Archéologique*, 1936.

Dussaud, R., 'Rapports entre la Crète ancienne et la Babylonie', *Iraq*, 1939, p. 53.

Evans, A. J., *The Palace of Minos* (especially Vol. I), 1921.

Forsdyke, E. J., *Minoan Art*, 1929.

Hall, E. H., *The Decorative Art of Crete in the Bronze Age*, 1907.

Hutchinson, R. W., 'Prehistoric Town Planning in Crete', *Town Planning Review*, October 1950.

Kantor, H. J., *The Aegean and The Orient in the Second Millennium B.C.*, 1947.

Levi, D., Reports in *Illustrated London News*, 19 January 1952, 12 December 1953, 30 September and 6 October 1955.

Mackenzie, D., 'Cretan Palaces', *Annual of the British School at Athens*, 1904–8.

Pendlebury, J. D. S., *Aegyptiaca*, 1932.
> *The Archaeology of Crete*, 1939.

Pernier, L., *Il Palazzo di Festos*, I, 1935.

Pernier, L., and Banti, L., *Il Palazzo di Festos*, II, 1951.

Petrie, F., *Buttons and Design Scarabs*, 1925.

Platon, N., 'To Ieron Maza', *Kretika Chronika*, 1951 (a comprehensive survey in modern Greek on the peak sanctuaries).

Sakellariou, A. Xenaki, 'Minoikes Sphagidhes, etc.', *Kretika Chronika*, 1949.

Santerre, H. G. de, 'Mallia, Aperçu historique', *Kretika Chronika*, 1949.

Seltman, C., 'A Minoan Bull's Head', *Studies Presented to D. M. Robinson*, 1951.

Smith, S., 'Middle Minoan I–II and Babylonian Chronology', *American Journal of Archaeology*, 1945, p. 1.

Vandier, J., 'À propos d'un dépôt de provenance asiatique trouvé à Tod', *Syria*, 1937, p. 174.

BIBLIOGRAPHY

CHAPTER 8: MINOAN RELIGION

Banti, L., 'Culti di Haghia Triada', *Annuario*, 1941–3, p. 9.
    'Myth in Preclassical Art', *American Journal of Archaeology*, 1942, p. 307.
Chittenden, J., 'The Master of Animals', *Hesperia*, 1947, p. 187.
Cook, A. B., *Zeus*, 1914–40.
Demargne, P., 'Culte funéraire, etc.', *Bulletin de Correspondence Hellénique*, 1932, p. 76.
Deonna, W. J., 'Tables antiques d'offrandes, etc.', *Bulletin de Correspondence Hellénique*, 1934, p. 1.
Evans, A. J., *The Palace of Minos*, 1921–36.
    'Mycenaean Tree and Pillar Cult', *Journal of Hellenic Studies*, 1901.
    The Earlier Religion of Greece in the Light of Cretan Discoveries (Frazer Lecture), 1931.
Frazer, J. G., *The Golden Bough* (abridged version), 1929.
Hesiod, *The Theogony*.
Mylonas, G. E., 'The Cult of the Dead in Helladic Times', *Studies presented to D. M. Robinson*, 1951.
Nilsson, M., *The Minoan Mycenaean Religion*, 1950 (the best general introduction on the subject).
Persson, A. W., *The Religion of Greece in Prehistoric Times* (Sather Lecture), 1942.
Picard, C., *Les Religions préhelléniques*, 1948 (with a very good bibliography and synthesis of the various authorities).
Platon, N., 'To Ieron Maza, etc.', *Kretika Chronika*, 1951, p. 96.
    'Nouvelle interprétation des idoles cloches, etc.', *Mélanges Charles Picard*, 1949, p. 833.
    'Ta Minoika Oikiaka Iera', *Kretika Chronika*, 1954, p. 428.
Rose, H. J., *Primitive Religion in Greece*, 1925.
Taramelli, A., 'The Prehistoric Grotto at Miamu', *American Journal of Archaeology*, 1897, p. 297.
Ventris, M., and Chadwick, J., *Documents in Mycenaean Greek*, 1956.
Xanthoudides, S., 'Cretan Kernoi', *Annual of the British School at Athens*, 1912.
    The Vaulted Tombs of the Mesara, 1924.

CHAPTER 9: THE SOCIAL AND ECONOMIC LIFE

Alexiou, S., 'The Boar's Tusk Helmet', *Antiquity*, 1954, p. 211.
Alvad, T., 'The Kafir Harp', *Man*, 1954.
Armstrong, E. A., 'The Crane Dance in East and West', *Antiquity*, 1943, p. 71.
Chadwick, H. M., *The Heroic Age*, 1912.
Curwen, E. C., 'The Significance of the Pentatonic Scale in Scottish Song', *Antiquity*, 1940.

Demargne, P., *La Crète dédalique*, 1947.

Evans, A. J., *The Palace of Minos*, 1921–36.

Forbes, R. J., *Metallurgy in Antiquity*, 1950.

Galpin, F. W., *The Music of the Sumerians*, 1932.

Glotz, G., *La Civilisation égéenne*, 1923.

Gordon, D. H., 'Swords, Rapiers and Horseriders', *Antiquity*, 1953, p. 66.

Hawes, H. Boyd, *Gournia*, 1908.

Hazzidakis, J., *Tylissos à l'époque minoenne*, 1921.

Hencken, H., 'Beitsch and Knossos', *Proceedings of the Prehistoric Society*, 1952, p. 96.

Lorimer, H. L., *Homer and the Monuments*, 1950.

Marinatos, S., 'Le Temple géométrique de Dréros', *Bulletin de Correspondence Hellénique*, 1936.

Myres, J. L., *Who were the Greeks?*, 1930.

    'Minoan Dress', *Man*, 1950, p. 1.

Nilsson, M. P., *Homer and Mycenae*, 1935.

    'Primitive Time Reckoning', *Acts–Soc. Litt. Human. Lund*, 1921.

Pendlebury, J. D. S., *The Archaeology of Crete*, 1939.

Ridgeway, W. G., *The Early Age of Greece* I, 1901; II, 1931.

Ridington, W. R., *The Minoan-Mycenaean Background of Greek Athletics*, 1935.

Swindler, M. H., *Cretan Elements in the Cult and Ritual of Apollo*, 1913.

Thomson, G., 'The Greek Calendar', *Journal of Hellenic Studies*, 1943, p. 52.

    'From Religion to Philosophy', *Journal of Hellenic Studies*, 1953, p. 77.

Vickery, K. F., 'Food in Early Greece', *Illinois Studies in the Social Sciences*, 1936, No. 3 (an excellent account).

Wace, A. J. B., *A Cretan Statuette in the Fitzwilliam Museum*, 1927.

Winnington Ingram, R. P., 'The Pentatonic Tuning of the Greek Lyre', *Classical Quarterly*, 1956.

Xanthoudides, S., *The Vaulted Tombs of the Mesara*, 1924.

CHAPTER 10: THE DECLINE OF KNOSOS

Alexiou, S., 'The Boar's Tusk Helmet', *Antiquity*, 1954, p. 183.

Biesantz, H., *Kretisch-Mykenische Siegelbilder*, 1954.

Blegen, C., *Prosymna, The Helladic Settlement Preceding the Argive Heraeum*, 1937.

Burn, A. R., *Minoans, Philistines and Greeks*, 1930.

Childe, V. G., 'The Final Bronze Age in the Near East', *Proceedings of the Prehistoric Society*, 1948.

Clarke, J. G. D., 'Horses and Battle-Axes', *Antiquity*, 1941, p. 50.

Demargne, P. and de Santerre, H. G., 'Fouilles exécutées à Mallia, 1921–48', *Études crétoises*, 1953.

Evans, A. J., *The Palace of Minos*, 1921–36.

    'The Prehistoric Tombs of Knosos', *Archaeologia*, 1905.

    'The Tomb of the Double-Axes', *Archaeologia*, 1913.

BIBLIOGRAPHY

Furumark, A., *The Mycenaean Pottery, Analysis and Classification*, 1941.
 The Chronology of Mycenaean Pottery, 1941.
 'The Settlement at Ialysos and Aegean History', *Opuscula Archaeologia*, 1950.

Hall, E. H., *The Decorative Art of Crete in the Bronze Age*, 1907.

Hazzidakis, J., *Tylissos a l'époque minoenne*, 1921.

Hawes, H. Boyd, *Excavations at Gournia*, 1908.

Hood, M. S. F., 'A Mycenaean Cavalryman' (with a useful bibliography on horses and chariots), *Annual of the British School at Athens*, 1948, p. 84.

Hood, M. S. F., and Jong, P. de, 'Late Minoan Warrior Tombs', *Annual of the British School at Athens*, 1952, p. 49.

Hutchinson, R. W., 'Prehistoric Town Planning in Crete', *Town Planning Review*, 1950, p. 261.

Kantor, H., *The Aegean and Orient in the Second Millennium B.C.*, 1947 (particularly valuable on the relations with Egypt).

Karo, G., *Die Schachtgräber von Mykenae*, 1930–3 (the final and comprehensive account of the Royal Shaft Graves opened by Schliemann and Stamatakis).

Muller, K., 'Die Funde aus den Kuppelgräbern von Kakovatos', *Athenische Mitteilungen*, 1909, pp. 269–305.

Pilecki, J., 'La disposition héraldique dans la civilization minoenne', (in Polish with French summary), *Swiatowit*, 1937, p. 15.

Rodenwaldt, G., *Der Fries des Megarons von Mykenai*, 1926.
 'Die Fresken des Palastes', *Tiryns*, 1912.

Santerre, H. G. de, and Treheux, G., 'Dépôt égéen et géométrique de l'Artémision à Délos', *Bulletin de Correspondence Hellénique*, 1948, p. 148.

Seager, R. B., *The Cemetery of Pachyammos*, 1916.

Stubbings, F. H., *Mycenaean Pottery from the Levant*, 1951.

Wace, A. J. B., *Mycenae, An Archaeological History and Guide*, 1949.
 'Chamber Tombs at Mycenae', *Archaeologia*, 1932.
 'The Date of the Treasury of Atreus', *Antiquity*, 1940, p. 233.

Weinberg, S., and others, *The Aegean and the Near East* (*Studies Presented to Hetty Goldman*), 1956.

CHAPTER II: THE DECADENCE OF MINOAN CRETE:
THE MYCENAEAN EMPIRE

Alexiou, S., 'Nea Stoicheia', *Kretika Chronika*, 1952 (English summary in *Antiquity*, 1954, p. 183).
 'The Boar's Tusk Helmet', *Antiquity*, 1954, p. 211.

Allen, T. W., *The Homeric Catalogue of Ships*, 1921.

Barnett, R. D., 'A Phoenician Inscription from Eastern Cilicia', *Iraq*, 1948, p. 56.
 The Nimrud Ivories, 1957.

Blegen, C., *Prosymna*, 1937.

Borda, M., *Arte Creteo-Miceneo del Museo Pigorini di Roma*, 1946.

Bosanquet, R. C., Dawkins, R. M., and others, 'Excavations at Palaikastro', *Annual of the British School at Athens*, 1901–5.

Burn, A. R., *Minoans, Philistines and Greeks*, 1930.

Burton Brown, T., *The Coming of Iron to Greece*, 1954.

Catling, H. W., 'Bronze cut-and-thrust swords in the East Mediterranean', *Proceedings of the Prehistoric Society*, 1956.

Childe, V. G., 'The Final Bronze Age in the Near East', *Proceedings of the Prehistoric Society*, 1948.

Evans, A. J., *The Palace of Minos* (especially II and IV), 1921–36.
    'The Prehistoric Tombs of Knosos', *Archaeologia*, 1905.
    'The Shaft Graves and Beehive Tombs', *Archaeologia*, 1929.
    'The Tomb of the Double Axes', *Archaeologia*, 1906.

Finley, M. I., *The World of Odysseus*, 1956.

Forsdyke, E. J., *Greece Before Homer*, 1956.
    British Museum Catalogue of Vases (Vol. I, part I), 1925.

Furumark, A., *The Mycenaean Pottery*, 1941.
    The Chronology of Mycenaean Pottery, 1941.

Hawes, H. Boyd, *Gournia*, 1908.

Heurtley, W. A., 'The Relationship between Philistine and Mycenaean Pottery', *Palestine Quarterly*, 1936.

Huxley, G. L., 'Mycenaean Decline and the Homeric Catalogue of Ships', *London University Bulletin*, 1956.

Kantor, H., *The Aegean and the Orient in the Second Millennium B.C.*, 1947.

Lorimer, H. L., *Homer and the Monuments*, 1950.

Loud, G., *The Megiddo Ivories*, 1932.

Marinatos, S., 'The Volcanic Destruction of Minoan Crete', *Antiquity*, 1939.

Mylonas, G. E., *Ancient Mycenae*, 1957.

Myres, J. L., *Who were the Greeks?*, 1930.

Santerre, H. G. de, 'Mallia, Aperçu historique', *Kretika Chronika*, 1949.

Seltman, C., 'A Minoan Bull's Head', *Studies Presented to D. M. Robinson*, 1951.

Smith, S., 'Middle Minoan I–II and Babylonian Chronology', *American Journal of Archaeology*, 1945, p. 1.

Wace, A. J. B., *Mycenae*, 1949.

Weinberg, S., and others, *The Aegean and the Near East*, 1956.

CHAPTER 12: THE DORIAN COLONIZATION, ORIENTAL INFLUENCES, AND THE GROWTH OF THE CITY STATES

Amandry, P., 'Chaudrons à Protomés de taureau, etc.', *The Aegean and the Near East*, 1956, p. 239.

Barnett, R. D., 'Early Greek and Oriental Ivories', *Journal of Hellenic Studies*, 1948.
    The Nimrud Ivories, 1957.

BIBLIOGRAPHY

Benton, S., 'The Date of the Cretan Shields', *Annual of the British School at Athens*, 1939, p. 52.

'The Dating of Helmets and Corselets in Early Greece', *Annual of the British School at Athens*, 1940, p. 75.

'Bronzes from Palaikastro and Praisos', *Annual of the British School at Athens*, 1940, p. 49.

Brock, J. K., *Fortetsa*, 1956 (the first comprehensive survey of Cretan pottery of the Early Iron Age).

Burn, A. R., *Minoans, Philistines and Greeks*, 1930.

The Age of Hesiod, 1936.

Conway, R. S., 'The Prehistoric Inscriptions of Praesos', *Annual of the British School at Athens*, 1902, p. 125.

Crowfoot, J. W., and G. M., *Early Ivories from Samaria*, 1935.

Demargne, P., *La Crète dédalique*, 1947 (the best general survey of this period).

Desborough, V., *Protogeometric Pottery*, 1952.

Dohan, E. H., 'Archaic Cretan Terracottas in America', *Metropolitan Museum Studies*, 1931, p. 127.

Dunbabin, T. J., Review of *La Crète dédalique*, *Gnomon*, 1947, No. 132, p. 19.

'Cretan Relief *Pithoi* in Giamalakis Collection', *Annual of the British School at Athens*, 1952.

The Western Greeks, 1944.

Effenterre, H. van, 'Reports on Excavations in Eastern Crete', *Bulletin de Correspondence Hellénique*, 1933, p. 293; 1938, p. 694.

Ferté, E. C. de la, *Les Bijoux antiques*, 1956.

Gray, D. H. P., 'Metal Working in Homer', *Journal of Hellenic Studies*, 1954.

Guarducci, M., *Inscriptiones Creticae*, 4 vols., 1935–50. (With commentaries in Latin, a regional survey of all classical inscriptions from Crete.)

Halbherr, F., 'Three Cretan Necropoleis', *American Journal of Archaeology*, 1901.

Hammond, N. G. L., 'Epirus and the Dorian Invasion', *Annual of the British School at Athens*, 1932, pp. 131–79.

Hartley, M., 'Early Greek Vases from Crete', *Annual of the British School at Athens*, 1930, p. 75.

Hencken, H. C., 'Herzsprung Shields and Greek Trade', *American Journal of Archaeology*, 1950, p. 205.

Hogarth, D. G., 'The Dictaean Cave', *Annual of the British School at Athens*, 1900, p. 70.

Hutchinson, R. W., etc., 'Unpublished Objects from Palaikastro and Praisos', *Annual of the British School at Athens*, 1940, p. 38.

Hutchinson, R. W., and Boardman, J., 'The Khaniale Tekke Tombs', *Journal of the British School at Athens*, 1954.

Jacobsthal, P., *Greek Pins and their Connexions with Europe and Asia*, 1956.

Jenkins, R. J. H., *Dedalica*, 1936.

Kirsten, E., *Das dorische Kreta*, 1942.

Kunze, E., *Kretische Bronzereliefs*, 1931.

Lamb, W., *Greek and Roman Bronzes*, 1929.

BIBLIOGRAPHY

Levi, D., 'Early Hellenic Pottery of Crete', *Hesperia*, 1945.
    'Excavations at Arkades', *Liverpool Annals*, 1925.
    'I Bronzi di Axos', *Annuario*, 1933, p. 33.
Lorimer, H. L., *Homer and the Monuments*, 1950 (especially Chapter v).
Mallowan, M. E. L., 'The Excavations at Nimrud (Kalhu) 1953', *Iraq*, 1954, Part I, p. 59.
Marinatos, S.,'Report on Dreros Temple', *Bulletin de Correspondence Hellénique*, 1936, p. 219.
Maxwell-Hyslop, K. R., 'Urartian Bronzes, etc.', *Iraq*, 1956, p. 150.
    'Notes on some Distinctive Types of Bronzes etc.' *Proceedings of the Prehistoric Society*, 1956, p. 102.
Ormerod, H. A., *Piracy in the Ancient World*, 1924.
Payne, H. G. G., 'Early Greek Vases from Knosos', *Annual of the British School at Athens*, 1929, p. 229.
Pendlebury, J. D. S., *The Archaeology of Crete*, 1939.
Pernier, L., 'New Elements for the Study of the Archaic Temple of Prinias', *American Journal of Archaeology*, 1939.
Svoronos, J., *Numismatique de la Crète ancienne*, 1890.
Wason, C. R., 'The Drill Style on Ancient Gems', *Liverpool Annals*, 1936, p. 51.
Weinberg, S. S., and others, *The Aegean and the Near East*, 1956.
Willetts, R. F., *Aristocratic Society in Ancient Crete*, 1954.
Williamson, G. C., *The Book of Amber*, 1932.

ADDENDA TO BIBLIOGRAPHY

Alexiou, S., 'Ἡ Μινωικὴ Θέα μεθ 'ὑψωμε΄νων Χειρῶν' *Κρητικὰ Χρονικά*, *Ἡράκλειον* 1958.
Andronikos, M., 'The Dorian Invasion and Archaeology', *Ελλςνικά*, 1959, p. 45.
Banti, L., Carratelli, G. P., and Levi, D., *Arte Minoica e Micenea*, Rome.
Boardman, J., *The Cretan Collection in Oxford*, Oxford, 1961.
Chadwick, J., *The Decipherment of Linear B.*, Cambridge, 1959.
Dakaris, S. I., Higgs, E. S., and Hey, R.W., 'The Climate, Environment and Industries of Stone Age Greece', Part I, *Proceedings of the Prehistory Society*, XXX, p. 90f., 1964.
Desborough, V. R. D'A., Hammond, N. G. L., Hayes, W. C., Matz, F. Rowton, M. B., and Stubbings, F. H., Chapters on Minoan Art, Chronology etc. in the *Cambridge Ancient History* I, Cambridge, 1962.
Gill, M. A. V., 'The Knossos Seals, Provenance and Identification', *British School Annual*, 1965, pp. 58–98.
Graham, J. W., *The Palaces of Crete*, Princeton, 1962.
Higgs, E., and Finzi, C. Vita, 'The Climate and Environment of Stone Age Greece', Part II, *Proceedings of the Prehistoric Society*, London, 1966.
Hood, M. G. F., 'Minoan Sites in the Far West', *British School Annual*, 1965, pp. 96–113.
Hood, M. G. F., and Boardman J., 'Early Iron Age Tombs at Knossos', *British School Annual*, 1956.

ADDENDA TO BIBLIOGRAPHY

Kenna, V. E. G., *Cretan Seals*, Oxford, 1960.

Matz, F., 'Gotteserscheinung und Kunstbild im Minoischen Kreta', *Abhandlungen des Wissenschaften and des Literatur*', Mainz, 1959.

Matz, F., 'Zur ägäischen Chronologie der frühen Bronzezeit', *Historia*, 1950.

Ninkovich, D. and Heeze, B. C., 'Santorini Tephra', *Colston Research Papers*, 1965, p. 413f.

Palmer, L., *Mycenaeans and Minoans*, Oxford, 1964.

Palmer, L., and Boardman, J., *On the Knossos Tablets*, 1963.

Platon, N. and Touloupa, E. G., 'Unique discoveries in Boeotian Thebes', *Illustrated London News*, 28 November 1964.

Platon, N., and Touloupa, E. G., 'Ivories and Linear B from Thebes', *Illustrated London News*, 5 December 1964.

Renfrew, C., Cann, J. R., and Dixon, J. E., 'Obsidian in the Aegean', *British School Annual*, 1965, p. 225f.

Renfrew, J., 'Carbonised Grains from Prehistoric Thessaly', Θεσσαλικά, 1966, p. 21.

Sackett, L. G., Popham, M. R., and Warren, A. M.,'Excavations at Palaikastro'. *British School Annual*, 1965, p. 245f.

Sakellarakis, J. A., 'Minoan cemeteries at Arkhanes, *Archaeology*, 1967, p. 276f.

Uckes, P. J., *Anthropomorphic Figurines*, London, 1965.

Willetts, R. F., *Ancient Crete*, Bristol, 1965.

Willetts, R. F., *The Law Code of Gortyn* (*Kadmos* Supplement I), Berlin, 1967.

INDEX

MORE ABOUT PENGUINS
AND PELICANS

If you have enjoyed reading this book you may wish to know that *Penguin Book News* appears every month. It is an attractively illustrated magazine containing a complete list of books published by Penguins and still in print, together with details of the month's new books. A specimen copy will be sent free on request.

Penguin Book News is obtainable from most bookshops; but you may prefer to become a regular subscriber at 3s for twelve issues. Just write to Dept. EP, Penguin Books Ltd., Harmondsworth, Middlesex, enclosing a cheque or postal order, and you will be put on the mailing list.

Some other books published by Penguins are described on the following pages.

Note: *Penguin Book News* is not
available in the U.S.A.

THE DEAD SEA SCROLLS IN ENGLISH

G. Vermes

A 551

Many books have been written about the Dead Sea Scrolls since their discovery in 1947, but until now the ordinary reader has had little opportunity to get to know the texts themselves, and so to make any personal judgement of their value or relevance. In this volume a clear, faithful translation of the non-biblical scrolls from the Qumran caves is accompanied by brief introductory comment on each, and by a general description of the beliefs, customs, organization, and history of the Community they derive from. The teaching of this sect of Jewish schismatics sheds the light of comparison and contrast on to that of their contemporaries, the Christian dissenters, and also on to the mother faith of both – Palestinian Judaism. This book reveals the Dead Sea Scrolls as fascinating documents that give us new insight into the history and philosophy of religion.

ARCHAIC EGYPT

W. B. Emery

Between 1936 and 1956 archaeological discoveries at Sakkara, the necropolis of ancient Memphis, have produced evidence which has caused historians to revise many of their previous conceptions of Egyptian civilization of the first two dynasties (3200-2780 B.C.). The origins of the Egypt of the Pharaohs still remain obscure, but the new material uncovered by the pick of the excavator shows that the people of the Nile Valley at that remote period enjoyed a far higher degree of culture than has hitherto been recognized. Architecture and the arts had reached a degree of excellence which in some ways was hardly surpassed when the full flower of Pharaonic civilization was in bloom.

The aim of this book is to put before the reader a general survey of what we now know, through these recent discoveries, of the cultural achievements of the great people who lived on the banks of the Nile nearly five thousand years ago. While in no sense a textbook this absorbing study will make an equal appeal to the student and to the layman.

THE IDEA OF PREHISTORY

Glyn Daniel

In this collection of published lectures, Dr Daniel describes prehistory as a study of 'the unwritten remains of the early past of man'. He studies the origins of the subject, going back to the seventeenth century and the current thunderbolt explanation of man's early flint tools (which one contemporary scientist thought to be 'generated in the sky by a fulgurous exhalation conglubed in a cloud by the circumposed humour'). The influence of the evolutionary thinking of the last century is studied, and there is a brilliant discussion of the rival theories of a cultural diffusion from one evolutionary source as against the idea of cultures evolving in parallel in different racial groups. Dr Daniel concludes that the real justification of prehistory lies in the pleasure of recovering the treasures of man's prehistoric past that have been dropped on the way and lost.

'Needless to say Dr Daniel's erudition is as immense as his turn of phrase is subtle' – *Discovery*.

'The lucid and logical presentation gives it a new force and vigour' – *Nature*.

Also available
The Megalith Builders of Western Europe

THE ARCHAEOLOGY OF PALESTINE

W. F. Albright

This book is written for the reader who wants an up-to-date, authoritative, and clearly written account of the subject. The author has been engaged in active excavation and research in this field since 1920, and he has utilized his command of it to write a survey which emphasizes the most important and most interesting phases of Palestinian archaeology. Besides summarizing the results of the archaeological work of the past twenty years, during which the subject has been revolutionized, he brings the reader up to date with references to the very latest finds. Here for the first time the latest discoveries in Sinai and the sensational finding of the Jerusalem Scroll of Isaiah are set in their proper historical perspective.

The book contains chapters which explain how the archaeologist carries on his excavations, how the subject developed from a treasure hunt into a science, how civilization unfolded from the Stone Age to the height of the Roman Empire. There is a chapter on the races and languages, scripts and literatures of ancient Palestine, as well as a chapter on the everyday life of the people. Two chapters summarize the bearing of these researches on the Old and New Testaments, including previously unpublished material. A final chapter on 'Ancient Palestine in World History' places the book in the full current of the philosophy of history, showing how profoundly archaeological research is influencing historical and religious thought.

ARCHAEOLOGY IN THE U.S.S.R.

A. L. Mongait

The Soviet Union is a country of many different languages and peoples. So a book dealing with its archaeology must range from Stone Age Russia to the Greek colonies on the Black Sea – from the Slavs of what is now European Russia to the desert forts of Central Asia, held by Arab, Turkic, and other rulers.

This book is also fascinating for two other reasons. In the first place Soviet archaeology is almost unknown in the West, and the reader will discover that Russian achievements here fully match those in better known fields such as space travel.

Secondly Dr Mongait is a Communist, and this will be a chance for many people to see the Marxist interpretation of history applied to archaeology. There are many illustrations in the book.

THE AZTECS OF MEXICO

George C. Vaillant

Dr George Vaillant was that rara avis, a great specialist who could make his speciality as interesting to the layman as it was to himself. For many years curator of Mexican archaeology at the American Museum of Natural History, and acknowledged an outstanding authority on the early civilizations of Mexico and Central America, in this book he wrote what is still the most important account of the birth and death of one of the world's great civilizations.

In the eleventh century the Aztecs arrived in Mexico from the north. Even today their speech is much like that spoken by the Indians of Oregon and Montana. In less than a hundred years, rising on the ruins of the older Mexican cultures, they developed an extraordinary indigenous civilization. Here is the strange story of the rise, and of the even swifter fall under the impact of Cortes and his followers. Dr Vaillant vividly re-creates the Aztec way of life. In one fascinating chapter he takes his reader to the great Aztec city, Tenochtitlan, now Mexico City, in the days of the height of the Aztec power, and wanders with him through the town. We learn not only the history of the Aztecs and how their society was organized, but how the children went to school, modes of dress, and many interesting aspects of an ancient daily life.

'One does not know which to admire most, the care with which the details are assembled or the imagination which has constructed cultural and political history out of them. No reader of *The Conquest of Mexico* should miss this book' – *Time and Tide*

THE ANCIENT CIVILIZATIONS OF PERU

J. Alden Mason

Our detailed knowledge of the people of pre-Columbian Peru has grown enormously since 1940. Many expeditions have made excavations and published their reports. Regions archaeologically unknown hitherto have yielded their secrets, and far more is known of all of them. Especially is this true of the cultures that preceded the Inca whom Pizarro found and conquered in one of the great adventures of history. Four thousand years before his day, radiocarbon analyses now permit us to state with confidence, simple fishermen-hunters on the coast were beginning the long climb towards the extraordinary blend of communism and monarchy that was the Inca empire. Our concepts of the latter and of its history also have been altered somewhat by recent studies. This book presents a summary of our present knowledge and point of view regarding the development and nature of these past civilizations and their fascinating and diversified country, with 64 pages of plates.

TWO IMPORTANT NEW PENGUIN
REFERENCE BOOKS
*

THE PENGUIN ENGLISH DICTIONARY

Containing more than 45,000 entries and specially prepared for Penguins by a team led by Professor G. N. Garmonsway of London University, this new dictionary places particular emphasis on current usage. Definitions, which include hundreds of post-war words and senses, are as direct and simple as possible, and a new and immediately understandable system is introduced as a guide to pronunciation. In all *The Penguin English Dictionary* makes an unrivalled catalogue of English words as used today in print and speech.

THE PENGUIN ENCYCLOPEDIA

This concise and authoritative new encyclopedia has been geared deliberately for use in the second half of the twentieth century. Articles by specialists, under more than 6,000 main headings, pay particular attention to the rapidly advancing areas of science and technology; but the arts and humanities have not been neglected. These simple, accurate and intelligent explanations are likely to prove equally handy for the schoolboy, the student and the family bookshelf. Specially commissioned for Penguins, this up-to-date work is remarkably comprehensive and fully cross-referenced. It will be followed by a gazetteer and a dictionary of biography.